MICHAEL
HUSSEY

**Underneath
the Southern Cross**

MICHAEL
HUSSEY

Underneath
the Southern Cross

hardie grant books
MELBOURNE · LONDON

This edition published in 2014

First publised in 2013
by Hardie Grant Books

Hardie Grant Books (Australia)
Ground Floor, Building 1
658 Church Street
Richmond, Victoria 3121
www.hardiegrant.com.au

Hardie Grant Books (UK)
Dudley House, North Suite
34–35 Southampton Street
London WC2E 7HF
www.hardiegrant.co.uk

Cataloguing-in-Publication data is available from the National Library of
Australia.

Underneath the Southern Cross
ISBN: 9781742708065

Publisher: Pam Brewster
Cover and text design: Luke Causby/Blue Cork
Typesetter: Kirby Jones
Statistics: Ross Dundas
Cover photographs: Getty Images
Colour reproduction: Splitting Image Colour Studio
Printed in Australia by Griffin Press

I dedicate this book to Amy, Jasmin, William, Molly and Oscar for inspiring me to be better every day.

CONTENTS

ACKNOWLEDGEMENTS

I would like to give thanks to my mum and dad, for their support and guidance over the course of my life so far. Thank you to Amy and her extended family for their love, support and help over my cricket career, which took me away from home for up to eleven months a year. Thank you to all of my teammates and coaches, with whom I have spent the best part of twenty years travelling the world, playing a game we all love very much. My best memories of playing cricket have been because of you. A big thanks to the fans; the support for the team and players is a huge source of inspiration and motivation to perform well for the team and the country. Thanks too to the WACA and Cricket Australia. Thank you to Neil Maxwell and Judie Anderson, who have been advisors, counsellors, confidants, but most of all good friends over the journey. Lastly, I would like to thank Malcolm Knox for helping me compile my story. Many hours on Skype while away on tour in India have produced a book that I am extremely proud of, and without your guidance it certainly would not have been possible.

FOREWORDS

By Allan Border

It was a throwaway line, and I only meant it tongue-in-cheek. But Michael Hussey's reaction says a lot about the type of cricketer he is.

I was coach of an Australia A tour to Scotland and Ireland in 1998. Michael was one of a group of outstanding young cricketers who couldn't break into a very strong Test XI. It's not too parochial to say that Australia A was just about the second-best team in the world.

We had a training session in Edinburgh, and the boys were resting after short hit-outs in the nets. I said something along the lines of, 'It's no good batting for fifteen minutes in the nets and thinking you can put it together for six hours in the middle. Practise as you want to play.' To be honest, I don't remember it very well, and am sure I didn't mean it literally, but there was one player who took my half-joking remark and ran with it.

Some time later, I heard that Michael Hussey had gone back home to Perth and followed my 'advice', batting for three two-hour net sessions in an exact replica of a full day's play, and telling people he was only doing what I'd told him!

Jokes aside, there is a serious lesson there, one of many that a young cricketer can learn from Michael. He was always wondering, 'What's going to make me a better player?' And once he found it, he would go to any lengths to achieve it.

There are many such lessons from Michael's extraordinary story. After waiting so long to become a Test cricketer in his thirties, he ended up being an outstanding international batsman not just in Test matches but also in one-day and Twenty20 cricket. In 2013, after retiring from the international scene, he was the top run-scorer in the Indian Premier League, which is amazing in itself. Any young cricketer who wants to find out what makes a great career, in all formats, would do well to read Michael's story.

When I first came across him, I was near the end of my playing career and he was at the beginning of his. Queensland was playing Western Australia at the Gabba in 1995–96. Michael, who was opening the batting, was very fidgety. He reminded me of Graeme Wood, the former West Australian Test opener. He never stopped moving: shuffling about, marking his crease, walking towards square leg. But although he was nervous, and didn't rate himself as highly as his peers, I was immediately impressed and thought his quality stood out. Oppositions see a different character from how the individual sees himself, and we had a healthy respect for Michael's batting. We could tell he was intense and passionate, well prepared and fit, and it all came through in his actions. I can't remember how many runs he scored in that first game, but there was something about him.

When I coached Australia A, he got involved in the team environment with typical enthusiasm. Sometimes a game of touch Australian rules was the only way to get the boys training in the cold weather in Scotland and Ireland. In games that quickly descended into tackle, Michael was in the thick of it, loving every minute. But he was still very modest and respectful. He says he was too shy to tell me that he had become a left-handed batsman because as a kid he'd decided to copy me. I guess we're both embarrassed by that sort of thing, but some years later, once he'd loosened up and grown more comfortable, Michael revealed the truth.

He had his ups and downs before realising his dreams. I was a national selector during that very rich period for Australian cricket, and Michael had to wait a long while. He was even sent back to club cricket after being dropped by Western Australia, so it was by no means an easy road. But he studied hard for his university degree in education, giving himself a fall-back position if cricket didn't work out. Marriage and fatherhood also helped make him a very well-rounded character by the time he became an international cricketer.

I am among the millions of Australians who took great pleasure from his success. The cricket public has an innate ability to recognise an Aussie battler doing his best, no rubbish, no pretentions. They see Michael as what he is, a good bloke who works hard, and they want him to do well. His popularity comes down to that whole package: he played well, he's very humble, he's intelligent in his dealings with the public, and he's always ready with an encouraging smile. That he spent all those years battling away to get to the top made it that much more rewarding when he did.

Off the field, Michael celebrates as joyously as anyone, has a great sense of humour and sense of fun, and is an all-round good bloke who has contributed to every team he has played in. Australian cricket really misses him. Let's hope that his experience can be utilised to the utmost. Michael is very much the prototype of the modern cricketer, adapting seamlessly between the three formats, while also playing the game for the right reasons.

Michael deserves strong recognition for the role he has played in Australian cricket over the years. He is a cricketer and a man for whom I have the greatest respect. These pages tell his extraordinary story.

By Adam Gilchrist

What was that saying? Something about good things coming to those who wait.

Well, wait Mike Hussey did. He waited for an opening in the team, a form slump from someone else, an injury perhaps, and eventually it came. With it came a mountain of first-class runs. As Mike himself would agree, so too any cricket follower, the end result was well and truly worth waiting for. He built a brilliant international cricket career based on good old-fashioned values, dedication, professionalism and respect.

Not many people like a nickname that others bestow upon them, and Huss was no different. Unfortunately for him, the moniker 'Mr Cricket' was just too perfect a fit for it to be shaken off. But whilst that nickname may lead to the correct assumption that Mike was meticulous in his preparation, training, research into the game and execution of match plans, there was so much more that made the name so appropriate.

Huss was amazingly committed to whatever team he was a member of, which resulted in friend and foe always regarding him highly. Various tales throughout this book show his desire to carry out the team requirements, often foregoing any personal accolades in the process. To receive the great honour of leading the Australian cricket team victory song wasn't so much an indication of Huss's vocal ability, but more an indication of the respect his teammates had for him and appreciation for the commitment he afforded them.

There can't have been too many more nervous players in the history of the game than Huss whilst waiting to bat. The legs would be constantly bouncing up and down, his body fidgeting, and he'd be jumping up into a full stretch of the legs, sides, arms and neck. But somehow he curtailed that nervousness as soon as the wicket fell that allowed him to enter the contest; he'd spring onto the field, flowing through the routines like clockwork and embracing the challenge that awaited him. More often than not, those on-field challenges were dealt with comfortably, entertaining those of us fortunate enough to be witnessing a skilled craftsman at work.

Like anyone in a profession that requires mountains of time away from family and friends, Mike also faced challenging times away from the hype, profile and glamour of game day. He and Amy have navigated their way through these times via a strong bond and understanding, with the result being a gorgeous young family who care not for Mr Cricket, but only for Dad.

Huss is a wonderful mate. He is intelligent, informative, entertaining, engaging and respectful, exactly the words I'm sure you as a reader will find ring true throughout this recollection of his experiences.

ONE

For as long as I played cricket, I was never sure, deep down, if I was good enough.

At every level of the game, any success I had was like a sugar hit. The satisfying sense that I'd proved myself only lasted as long as the next failure, when the old demons came creeping back in. I tried to keep this insecurity to myself, but it was a big burden to hide, and sometimes it just became all too much.

Kingsmead in Durban was a cricket ground haunted, for me, by an incident in the second Test against South Africa in March 2009. We had just lost a Test series at home for the first time since 1993 – to these same South Africans. The Proteas were the number-one team in the world, and played like it. We were trying to rebuild after the retirements of some of the best cricketers to ever play the game: Shane Warne, Glenn McGrath, Justin Langer, Damien Martyn, Adam Gilchrist and, at the end of that series in Australia, Matthew Hayden. You can't lose so many players of that quality and recover quickly.

But against all the odds, we were doing just that. We had gutsed out a face-saving win against South Africa in Sydney, and then, when the teams travelled to Johannesburg, we shocked them again. Mitchell Johnson, Marcus North, Ricky Ponting and Michael Clarke produced brilliant performances, and I led the team into the middle of the Wanderers ground to sing our victory song with three debutants: North, Ben Hilfenhaus and Phil Hughes. I wanted to make *Underneath the Southern Cross* a special experience for them in their first Test match, and to this day it's one of my favourite renditions, bringing three guys into the brotherhood, showing them how good it felt to win a Test match for Australia against the odds.

We rode that wave into Durban, and everyone was full of confidence. Everyone else, that is. In Johannesburg, I scored 4 and 0. After the game, I wandered around the team hotel looking for a shoulder to cry on. I said to Nathan Hauritz, 'I'm finding this game so hard, every innings is like a vigil.' I went to Michael Clarke's room and said, 'I'm really struggling. What can I do?' Pup said, 'Get your head down and work your backside off and it'll turn around.' That was what I'd been trying to do, and where had it got me?

On the first day in Durban, Ricky won the toss and we batted. Kingsmead is a tough place to play cricket. It's a long, rectangular, spartan kind of ground, and the heat and humidity are fierce. That day was 30-odd degrees and nearly 90 per cent humid. Plus, the pitch had a ridge in it and the ball was flying all over the place. Later in that match, Mitch Johnson would break Graeme Smith's hand and send Jacques Kallis to hospital for X-rays on his jaw. When you were as low on confidence as I was, you looked forward to batting on that wicket about as much as walking to the gallows.

But we – actually, the other Australian batsmen – had another incredible day. Hughesy blasted a maiden century, driving Steyn back over his head for six and carving all the bowlers far and wide. Simon Katich, the best man at my wedding six years earlier, was on his way to the sixth of his ten Test hundreds. But when

I went in at 2/208, just before tea, I had the weight of the world on my shoulders.

I'm not the only batsman to have struggled against South Africa, but they seemed to have a stranglehold on me. In Australia, I'd had the first really poor series in the four years I'd been playing Test cricket. I had found every possible way to get out, including, in the decisive Boxing Day Test in Melbourne, being given out caught off my helmet. To make matters worse, during the partnership between JP Duminy and Dale Steyn which swung the whole series, I had the most embarrassing moment of my career, fluffing a high overhead catch in front of about 80,000 people. My confidence was at an all-time low.

All South African wickets were hard to bat on. They weren't as true as Australian wickets, but were still quick, and there was always some movement for the fast bowlers. The bounce just wasn't even. And they had some very good bowlers. Morne Morkel was extremely awkward to face if you were a left-hander. He was tall, he was quick, he got bounce and cut and reverse-swing. I rated him one of the two or three best bowlers in the world. He'd been the one who hit me on the helmet in Melbourne.

In Durban, I was hanging on by a thread, and when I was on four, Morkel hit me plumb in front. The umpire, Asad Rauf, gave me out. I walked down the wicket and had a long think before referring it to the third umpire. The Decision Review System hadn't even been officially launched in Test cricket. Video referrals were still an experiment, but I decided to challenge the decision and the tape saved me, the replays showing that the ball had pitched outside leg stump.

While Kato went on serenely, I battled away against Morkel and Makhaya Ntini, who, although he was coming to the end of his career, got more difficult as he got older. With his tendency to deliver the ball from very wide on the crease, he had slid the ball across the left-handed batsmen, allowing me to let a lot of balls pass by. But late in his career, Ntini developed a ball that cut back in. He'd got me out several times that summer. Then Jacques Kallis came on – 300 Test wickets, enough said – and the left-arm spinner, Paul Harris. Many people thought Harris was pretty innocuous, but I found him tough work also. I would struggle to get the ball off the square against the pacemen, and then Harris would come on and I'd think, *You beauty, I can cash in.* Or at least I wanted to. The truth was, I couldn't score off him either. Tall and quickish, he bowled into the rough outside my off stump. Some spun and some didn't. I was too scared to leave the crease. When I wasn't batting well, which now seemed to be all the time, I found him really tough to handle. If I couldn't get him away, how was I ever supposed to score a run against the other blokes?

We lost two quick wickets after tea – it was Harris who got Michael Clarke – leaving me with Northy to try to hang around until stumps. In Durban, the light can be good all day but then it closes in quickly. Marcus and I were in survival mode. That suited me, because I was in survival mode anyway. I didn't mind if there was no expectation to score runs.

I'd limped along to 25 or 30 when they took the second new ball, which meant Dale Steyn was coming back on. I haven't said anything about my Dale Steyn problem, have I?

All the South African bowlers were a nightmare for me; their wickets were minefields, my confidence was shot, and if the entire catastrophe had a single cause, it was Steyn. He was without a doubt the most difficult, skilled fast bowler I faced. To start with, he was very quick, anything up to 155kmh and rarely below 140kmh. As his right arm came over, his wrist remained cocked back, only to whip forward in the last microsecond. This delayed release was very hard to pick up early in your innings, and his wrist position not only gave the ball an extra jolt of pace but released the seam perfectly for outswing, or inswing to a left-hander like me. On top of that, he was quietly, menacingly aggressive. He wanted to hit you and hurt you and get you out, preferably in that order. He didn't say much, but you felt that he just detested you and your Australian helmet.

Late in the day the floodlights came on, but all they were doing was making it technically bright enough to stay on. They didn't make batting any easier. I wished they didn't have lights. I could have got off the ground and savoured my precious 30 not out as if it was a hundred. But the umpires deemed the visibility good enough to prolong the agony for an extra half hour.

Like the best fast bowlers, Steyn preyed on weakness. And I was at a weak point. He'd got me out in the first innings of the first Test that summer, back in Perth, and regularly since. It had been his skied slog that I'd made a meal of on Boxing Day. With bat and ball, whenever he was anywhere near me, he was my nemesis. He knew it. So that afternoon he decided to crank it up and hit me with every single ball.

If that pitch wasn't unpredictable enough already, with Steyn bowling I just didn't have a clue. I played forward to one ball, and found myself fending it off my eyebrows. I wove out of the way of another, and wicketkeeper Mark Boucher, 25 yards behind me, had to leap overhead to stop it going for four byes. I parried another delivery away from my face, and the next leapt at me so fast I only escaped injury by wrenching my head away from it – not a good look.

Fortunately, that afternoon, Northy – in his second Test match! – took most of the strike, protecting me, and the umpires eventually showed pity, calling stumps after 89 overs.

I was trembling as I came into the dressing room, somehow 37 not out after about three hours of scratching away.

The first faces I saw were those of Brad Haddin and Andrew McDonald, the next two batsmen in. They were ashen. They both came up to me and said, 'Thanks, Huss, thank you so much.'

I was grumpily getting my pads off. 'What for?'

'Mate, you gutsed it out for us, we were absolutely petrified, we didn't want to go out there. That's the best Test cricket we've ever seen. You fought your way through it.'

I thought, *You've got to be kidding me.* I'd felt like a fourth-grade player out there, out of my depth. But the way they saw it, this was Test cricket at its best. Steyn was threatening to wreak absolute havoc and I was surviving for my country, shielding the lower order. I felt the complete opposite, like someone who had failed. Perception is an amazing thing.

Normally, getting through until stumps gives you time to regroup. Everything looks different the next morning. But when we got to Kingsmead for the second day, it was just as humid but wet and gloomy, ideal for fast bowling. After a half-hour delay to dry the outfield, we were on again, and Steyn seemed even angrier than the previous evening. He was bowling with, if possible, more pace and hostility.

For all the drama, I had only had to face nine balls from him on the first evening. The second morning, he had his fill. His first 21 balls of the day were all at me. I scored off three of them. Otherwise it was *Boof* in the chest ... *Crack* in the arm ... *Clang* off the helmet ...

I got off strike for a few balls, but then he bowled another two full overs at me. One hit a crack in the pitch and zapped me like an electric cattle-prod in the forearm. Then he got me on the arm again. In his first six overs of the morning, he bowled 31 balls at me – and I mean *at* me. He got me on the helmet again, and we snatched two leg byes. My head was still ringing the next ball, which was short again. I prepared to fend it off my chest, but it jumped off the ridge and skimmed the peak of my helmet. I got out of the way by millimetres.

Steyn stood there surveying his handiwork, almost like he was happier to have me dying slowly out there than he would have been to get me out.

I felt my blood bubbling up. The tingling started in my toes, worked its way up my legs and into my body, and eventually exploded out the top of my head. For the only time in my career, in countless matches over a quarter of a century, from Test cricket to one-day to Twenty20 all the way down to struggling away in fourth grade as a kid, I lost control on the field.

Like a child having a tantrum, I blew up, shouting and screaming at him.

During confrontations, Steyn gets a wry half-smile on his face. He looked at me and said quietly, 'Excuse me, what did you say?'

I kept carrying on, shouting.

The thin-lipped smile widened just a little, and he said, 'You're scared, aren't you?'

'Too right I am! Now get back and bowl!!'

I completely lost it. The South Africans were chuckling away behind me, and at the other end, Marcus North, who'd been my clubmate since teenage days at Wanneroo in Perth, was also laughing.

He called out, 'Yeah, you stay down that end, Huss, I'm happy down here.'

The next over, Morkel knocked out my off stump with a very good full-length ball. I'd made 50. It was my only decent contribution in the series, and we won the Test match, thanks to another Phil Hughes ton and some great bowling by Peter Siddle. We'd won the series, probably up with the best two or three team achievements in my time in the Australian team. But personally, I took some scars away. I have been back to Durban a quite a few times since, and every time I have thought of the eighteen bruises I got all over my body from Dale Steyn. For all of 2009, I carried an inferiority complex against the short ball, due to this working-over he had given me. I lost all confidence in that part of my game. When there's nowhere to hide, you feel like a dartboard. It's not a nice feeling.

I appreciated what Hadds and Ronnie said about how they were grateful to me for taking the brunt of the attack. It was fantastic Test cricket, I suppose, if you were watching it. But getting pummelled like that was tapping into my deepest insecurities. I might have been making a pretty important half-century for Australia in a Test match, but the voice in my head was saying, *This is such a struggle, I'm not sure I'm good enough for this.* It was the same voice that had said I wasn't good enough for Test cricket, for first-class cricket, even for A-grade cricket in Perth. It came from very deep in my psyche and way back in my past. And no matter what I did in the game, I never overcame the feeling that I wasn't one of the gifted few, but just an ordinary guy, one of the battlers. To get anywhere at all, and to win my victories – and ultimately making 50 in a Test match against Dale Steyn was a victory – I had to make the very most of whatever ability I had.

TWO

As a kid, I didn't realise how lucky I was. I imagined that most children had a life like mine: great parents, lots of love in the house, siblings to play with, a beach across the road, plenty of sunshine and as much sport as you could fit into the day.

Most of my early memories are around sport. My dad, Ted, loved his athletics and had been a good sprinter himself until he broke his ankle playing basketball the week before trialling for the Commonwealth Games. He and my mum, Helen, had met through track and field: he was a coach and she was a middle-distance runner when they first crossed paths. Dad worked for the post office, just like his father, though Ted senior was a telephone technician while Dad worked in the PR department. Mum's family came from Kalgoorlie, but had been living on the west side of Perth for some years before she met Dad. Both of them had fathers, uncles and grandfathers who had fought for Australia in the first and second World Wars, and they settled down in Mullaloo, a beachside suburb north of Perth, in the house they still live in today. I was born on 27 May 1975 at St Anne's Hospital in Mount Lawley, the same place where Dad was born.

Home was a modest three-bedroom brick-and-tile house which, when I was young, was part of a new, sparsely developed Perth suburb with lots of bush around us. We had a very safe and secure upbringing, and about the worst thing that happened was when, one day while showing Mum how fast I could run, I tore off straight into a chair and cut my head, leaving a permanent scar. I loved the feeling that we were in our own isolated little world. My brother David was born two years after me. Dad wrote a newspaper column on local athletics meets in Perth, and took Dave and me along to watch him coach the sprinters and middle-distance runners on Saturday mornings at the old Perry Lakes stadium. He'd shout instructions at them and I'd pretend to shoot them with my hockey stick as they ran around. Dave, who obviously wasn't as mature as I was, got into trouble for sitting in the long jump pit making sandcastles while they were trying to hold an event.

Dad was serious about running as a foundation for any sport, and by the age of four I'd been schooled in the basics of balance and efficiency. We lived right by Mullaloo beach, and I went with him to the sandhills where he took local runners for training on the soft, uneven ground, in the belief that this built up the ankles. Dad was a devotee of Percy Cerrutty, the legendary athletics coach and also a noted tough nut. On 'Hussey's Hill', as the big sand dune was known, Dad barked out instructions and took no nonsense as he pushed the runners along. Our carnivals were the highlight of Dad's year. He prepared us in getting our arms and knees up, and annoyingly made us pose for photos on the morning of the carnival for our school house faction with our blue-coloured sashes on. I loved the carnivals as much as Dad did.

Although athletics was his sport, Dad wasn't one to push us into it. He liked us to try different things and his maxim was, sport is there to be enjoyed, and if you're not enjoying it, try something else. So he also taught us how to kick an Aussie rules football with either foot, and I would later spend a lot of time kicking with my cousin, Brian Farrell, who was the same age as me, lived just up the road, and was a huge footy fan.

Dad didn't have a lot of interest in cricket, but Dave and I must have been watching it on TV at an early age, and we got Dad to help us set up a game. We didn't have bats or balls, so for a bat we'd swing an old stick, and for a ball Dad would lob little blue-metal rocks at us. When he realised we enjoyed it, we graduated to a tennis ball and a wooden bat he made. I didn't realise that he hated cricket, so it's a testimony to his principles that he encouraged us all the same.

Before long, we couldn't be stopped. Like kids all around Western Australia, we would watch a Test match until it finished at around 3pm our time, and then go outside to re-enact it. The house had a long driveway up one side that curled around the back in a big expanse of concrete slabs that formed our cricket pitch. Between the slabs were grooves we could aim at for some seam movement. We used a tennis ball, taping up one side with electrical tape to make it swing, and picked up whatever tips we could from other kids. On the right-hander's off side there wasn't a lot of space, and Dad, who held to the belief that if you hit the ball on the ground you couldn't get caught, made it a firm rule that if you hit it over the fence surrounding the yard you were out. So the main area for scoring runs was by hitting straight, within the vee, along the ground, a pretty good lesson for beginners.

I was a right-hander to start with, and still play golf right-handed, as well as writing and everything else. I only became a left-handed batsman to be like Allan Border. When I was about seven, I watched him make runs in a Boxing Day Test match in Melbourne. It might have been the famous 1982–83 Ashes Test, when he batted for ages with Jeff Thomson only to fall three runs short. I remember getting up to watch them on the last day, and being very grumpy when they lost. The only cure for that was to get outside and start playing, and in imitation of the Australian captain I gave left-handed batting a try. It felt all right with my strong hand on top, and I stuck with it.

We played these backyard battles as individuals, not as teams. I didn't force Dave to be England because he was the younger brother. When I bowled, I was usually Craig McDermott, and when I batted I was AB. But we would chop and change depending on who was doing well. I loved trying to bowl like Merv Hughes. In batting, I'd emulate Dean Jones one day, Geoff Marsh the next, then AB, depending on who was doing well at the time. Sometimes we chose to be the West Indies as opposition. I don't remember England being involved at all.

The old enemy, to be honest, was my brother. Dave and I were together day in, day out, sharing a bedroom for many years, and we were competitors more than best mates. Whatever we were doing, we were trying to beat each other. We had a Commodore 64 computer and played very hotly contested games. Otherwise it was sport. But we competed in pretty much everything we did. This, of course, resulted in our fair share of blues.

I blame Dave for most of these. Even when I got him out three times, he wouldn't go. He was smart, and used bribery quite a lot before he would agree to play. He knew how desperate I was to have someone to play against. It was 'I'm not playing unless I bat first', or 'I have to get three chances', or 'I have no automatic wickie'. It didn't matter what conditions he imposed, though; the matches invariably ended in fights. I'd be shouting at him and chasing him around the house wanting to beat him up until I could get him in a headlock or throttle him. Being the elder brother by two years, I didn't have the heart to hit him. But Dave, he'd let fly at me with a haymaker or two.

Mum did her best to control us, but she had her hands full. We had two sisters – Kate, four years younger than me, and Gemma, nine years younger – so Mum had enough to do without being the umpire between Dave and me. Soon enough, Dave and I had patched up our differences. If we didn't get a game of cricket or footy going, we'd go to the beach and skim rubber balls off the water to take 'classic catches', or throw high balls for each other. We'd finish off with a swim, and if it wasn't windy in the afternoon we'd go back for another. There were no rips, but big enough waves for kids to bodysurf, and rocky headlands to explore – the perfect back yard for Aussie boys.

At the end of the day, we came in for dinner, at which the family always sat down together. Our typical meals were basic – we were a meat and two veg family, without much straying. As children we didn't like to explore new foods, not even soups or cheeses. Breakfast was a cereal like All-Bran or Weet-Bix, and lunch, for me, hardly ever changed from a peanut butter sandwich and a piece of fruit. Where treats were concerned, a bowl or cone of ice-cream was our choice of dessert.

But Mum was quite strict, and was certainly the authority figure in the house, no question. It came out most of all at mealtimes. Table manners were important, as was eating all our food and never leaving a scrap. We had to eat everything even if we didn't like it. In her will to find ways to make us behave well at the table, she would try to speak our language. Once that had a funnier result than she intended. We were trying to eat peas, and Mum was showing us how to do it the genteel way, with our forks upside-down and pushing the peas onto them. We preferred to do it the uncouth kids' way, scooping the peas up. Trying to think of some way to impress on us how important this was, Mum said, 'Can you imagine sitting in front of Mervyn Hughes? Imagine how mortified you'd be if you ate like that in front of him!'

Having got to know Merv later in life, I think she could have chosen a better role model.

In general, though, Mum's standards were all about treating people with respect. She was very big on manners and speaking politely, with correct language. She picked up on any grammatical slips, but maybe more importantly, she was extremely harsh on us if we showed disrespect or were rude to anyone.

Nowadays Mum and Dad say I was too sneaky to get into much trouble, but I remember it differently. I particularly remember long car trips with all the kids in the back. We'd niggle and pinch and annoy each other. Mum and Dad would tell us to stop several times, and that is when we got into real trouble.

The longest driving trip we went on was to Eyre, many hours south-east of Perth. We'd pack a tent and drive to Esperance, on the coast, for the night, and then bump along the dirt tracks to Eyre, which had an old telephone exchange where Dad's father had worked. There was just one house in Eyre – and nothing else. We spent a week or two as a family, making our own fun. I remember a lot of board games and pick-up sticks, and a thong-throwing contest from the top of a sandhill. Sometimes the simple things are best, and I loved it. I had no stresses or worries in my life. We didn't have a lot but didn't want for anything. For me, it was a brilliant upbringing.

We were lucky enough to be able to get to know three of our four grandparents. Dad's father, Ted senior, came from Irish stock who had moved to Queensland in the 1880s. Dad's grandfather fought in World War I, and Ted senior went to New Guinea in World War II as a communications technician with the army. He'd passed away before I was born, but we saw Dad's mother, Kate, or Nana to us, every Sunday to take her to church. Afterwards, we went back to her place, where she always had lollies and biscuits or a can of Coke for us. She had a nice big back yard too. At Christmas and Easter she came to our place for a big lunch. We also spent time with her during the week sometimes, helping her with her shopping.

Mum's parents lived closer to us, so we often saw them during the week. Mum's father, Bern, was a World War II veteran who had fought in Crete and marched up into Germany before coming home and rising to a high position in the Department of Mines at Kalgoorlie. He was a hard kind of man, firm but ambitious for us to achieve our best. When we had a school report, he would want to sit down and see them. 'You've done very well,' he'd say, 'but there's room for improvement here, make sure you keep improving.' Mum's mother, Min, and also Nana to us, was very kind and loved all her grandkids; you could see where Mum got her standards.

Unlike a lot of sport-obsessed kids, I enjoyed school. I was a very early riser, up for anything and keen to get going. I went to Whitford Catholic Primary School at Craigie, where I concentrated my energies on athletics and school footy. At lunchtimes we played cricket – we didn't have a school team – and British Bulldog, even though the teachers had banned it.

Any sport was fair game. A bloke named Mike Wheeler, who lived nearby and had a milk run, had the idea of starting up a squash centre in Mullaloo. Being good neighbours, Mum and Dad thought we should support Mike and his new business. Dad was also keen to give me an alternative to football, as I was starting to get roughed up by bigger boys. I had always been small, but when I got to about ten or eleven years of age, and the other kids were starting to shoot up, I wasn't growing at all. Suddenly, I was looking tiny among them all on the footy field. I played as a rover and got flattened in many contests. My parents probably worried that I was going to break a leg or an arm. I actually enjoyed the footy. The training was fun, I played with my cousin Brian, and it was great being part of a team.

Dave and I headed to the squash centre on our pushbikes and soon became quite good at the sport, with Mike enthusiastically teaching us the fundamentals of watching and hitting the ball and moving into position. Before long, Dave and I were playing in competitions and moving up the state rankings. As with everything else, Dave had more natural talent than I had but I would make up for my deficiencies by working obsessively to improve myself.

Although I loved my squash, I still played footy and dabbled in a lot of other sports, including golf and tennis. But when I got to about sixteen, it was clear that they were going to have to give way. I had found my true love.

THREE

At primary school, I had two good friends. Brett Davis and I seemed to click from grade one, even though we must have made an odd couple, with him about two feet taller than me. He loved his Aussie rules and was soon doing very well at it. My other close mate, Brad Michaelson, wasn't very interested in sport, but his parents and mine socialised out of school and our friendship grew through those times.

It's ironic that Brad wasn't really into his sport, because he was the conduit through whom I discovered cricket.

Although I was deeply involved in cricket in the back yard and the school playground at lunchtimes, by the age of nine I had had no contact with any organised competition. Brad was playing for the Whitfords Junior Cricket Club, and for the second game of the season his family took me to watch him. I came home to Dad, all fired up, and said, 'I want to play cricket.' He told me I would have to wait until the next season. I was very unhappy. I was already hooked and was desperate to join the club. But it wasn't possible. I watched a few more of Brad's games that season, and another summer of watching on TV as well as playing with Dave in the back yard had me on an irreversible course by the time the next season started.

I remember turning up punctually at registration day and meeting my team. As a ten-year-old, I was enrolled in the under–12s. I felt excited, but nervous because I didn't know the guys, didn't know if I'd be any good, didn't know how the team worked.

Having watched those games the previous year, I knew the rule about how you earned the Whitfords baggy sky-blue cap, which to me was even more of a prize than the baggy green. You had to get 5 wickets or 50 runs in an innings. It was a big ask, but that only enhanced the value of the baggy blue.

In the first game, I actually made 50, only to be told that this had been a practice game and didn't count. Going into the first competition game, I was desperate to get this cap. We fielded first and a guy I went to school with named Michael Windle got 6 wickets for 4 runs. He was awarded his cap. The next week, I managed to get 50, and this time it was for real. The presentation of my baggy blue was – seriously – just about the proudest day of my life.

A taste for baggy caps, of whatever colour, wasn't the only habit I developed at Whitfords. Mum was very conscientious about sunscreen and stopping us getting burnt. Even when we went to school, we had to rub sunscreen into our faces. At cricket, she was resolute about the white zinc cream going on our noses and lips. It was non-negotiable. So I became a zinc cream wearer from a very early age!

Our coach was Bob Mitchell, and he was terrific. Seeing how small I was, he encouraged me to work on my defence and my technique. 'As you grow older,' he said, 'that defensive foundation will hold you in good stead against the better bowlers.' In hindsight, it proved to be great advice. There were other guys who could slog but soon perished, while I was able to hang in longer. I was given a couple of cricket skills books, showing how to play the cover drive or bowl the leg-spinner. I studied them religiously and practised them in the back yard. I knocked a ball in a sock hanging off the pergola for hours at a time. When I had to go to the mailbox, I played top-hand straight drives all the way down and all the way back. I developed what became a lifelong love of cricket technique, believing that success wasn't just about instinct or flair, but about the mechanics of playing the correct way.

My batting game was all about hanging in there. I couldn't hit the ball over the top or score quickly, getting my runs instead through flicks and deflections. I wished I could hit it harder, and was desperately envious of the bigger kids. I certainly never thought about going far in the game, because I assumed that you had to be a dominant batsman at this level to go on to the next. I was always in survival mode against big, quick bowlers. I'd say to my partner, 'Let's get through him and get our runs against the other guy.' I have a vivid memory of a bowler from Wanneroo called Sean Coffey, who actually swung the ball. He was better than anyone I'd ever seen, and got me out cheaply. But in general, even though I was small and not dominant, I could hang in there and be competitive.

What helped was my hunger to always be in the game. I hated sitting and watching, so I would try to keep my wicket to avoid that. Then, when we were in the field, I was dead keen to get the ball in my hand and bowl leg spin. Then I took up wicket keeping. Anything to be involved!

I was so enthusiastic in those first years, I didn't get teary too often about getting out (that came later). Nor was I very affected by nerves (that did too). I heard coaches and Dad say things like nerves were a good thing and you could use them to your advantage because they helped you concentrate and react quickly, but I didn't understand any of that yet. I had an uncomplicated, positive approach to the game. I didn't see myself as being that good at cricket, and I don't remember our teams winning premierships.

It was just the pure fun of it that drew me in and kept me there. Playing for fun tended to clear the mind, and I managed to score runs consistently. Even though it took me a while to get them, I was making enough runs to get picked in some representative teams.

But there were always hurdles. Our coach sent me to the Wanneroo District Cricket Club to try out for their under–15s even though I was still only thirteen. It was a winter trial, and there were only a couple of openings for kids in the younger age bracket. I was shattered when I didn't get picked. I cried all the way home. Dad said, 'Don't worry, they're all older than you, enjoy your year with your mates at Whitfords.' My disappointment only lasted a few days and I made the under–15s the next year, but it was a first taste of the bitterness of rejection. It showed me that I was beginning to take this game much more seriously.

At home, Dad had come up with a new idea. Because the four of us kids were going off and doing different things and Mum and Dad were so busy, we never had a lot of time together, aside from eating dinner. Dad came up with the suggestion that we hold regular family meetings. Being someone who worked for the government and wanting to do things the correct way, he insisted that we have a secretary and an agenda and someone leading the meeting. He genuinely wanted us to learn what meetings were like as a life skill.

Dave and I dreaded them. They were held every fortnight and were a bit serious in tone for us. They did have some useful outcomes. When Mum was pregnant for the fourth time, one agenda item was to choose names for boys and girls. We came up with Robert for a boy, but she had a girl, so Gemma it was.

It was at a family meeting that I could also make a big announcement. When I was sixteen, I was number three the state in squash for my age group and was also in junior cricket development squads at the WACA. At a meeting, I announced to the family that I was going to dedicate myself to cricket. I wanted to chase the dream of playing for Western Australia. I expected a good reaction, but everyone sat in stunned silence. I went to bed wondering what I'd done.

I still enjoyed school. At Prendiville Catholic College, Joondalup, where I'd been going since year eight, they had young, keen teachers – it was only three years old when I started. I liked maths and chemistry, and also physics, but though I tried very hard I wasn't naturally very good at it. But the main thing was, I enjoyed it and tried my best and didn't want to drop out. Sport as a professional career seemed way beyond my capabilities, and of course Mum and Dad would encourage me to finish school and go to university. So I didn't think that dropping squash to concentrate on cricket was such a radical move.

When I finally made the Wanneroo under–15s, I was extremely happy. The Wanneroo District Cricket Club was an interesting club. The newest in the WACA competition, the club was a northern outpost that had been developed over a long period to get to this point. Because it was isolated, it had a huge, strong catchment of juniors. It was only a matter of time before that strength filtered through to the senior club, which hadn't been successful yet. I came in during that transitional phase.

Wanneroo's home ground was Kingsway Reserve, a huge sporting complex of cricket ovals, netball courts, and fields for Aussie rules, soccer and rugby, all dumped in the middle of a big market-garden area. The club was criticised for the amount of flies and the smell of manure that strayed into the viewing area. It was better in the middle. Now it's a beautiful area and a great club, but back then it was just tin sheds and flies. The pitch had been so treacherous that guys had T-shirts saying, 'I batted on Kingsway Reserve and survived', but it had settled down by the time I came along.

While I was playing for the under–15s, after our games I tended the scoreboard for A-grade. I put my hand up for that job every single week. The payment was two free hot dogs and Cokes all day. Life couldn't get any better.

But there was a special reason to watch A-grade, and that was Damien Martyn. To put it simply, I was blown away by how he played. He was four years older than me, but might as well have been in a different universe. From the first ball, he would walk down the pitch and smack the opening bowler over his head or over cover, just teeing off, charging A-grade opening bowlers and smashing them into the trees. Later, I realised he didn't take grade cricket all that seriously, and he'd get out. He had his eyes set on higher honours, and was only two years away from representing Australia. But the one or two days of the season when he tore attacks apart were what stuck in the memory.

I came into contact with more of these gun players when I was picked in my first representative team, a city side playing in a statewide under–15 carnival in Bunbury, south of Perth. From that carnival they selected a group of players to try out for the West Australian under–17 team the following year. I was captain of one of the teams, opened the batting and bowled leggies. I only got one decent score in that carnival, but gradually worked my way into the state under-age teams.

Our reputation in the carnivals was as a pretty boring team, bowling to a plan wide of off stump, setting defensive fields, and making the batsmen get themselves out. We were disciplined and patient and a bit negative, but our strength was in our batting.

The two stand-out batsmen in my age group were Simon Katich, who looked a class above everyone else, and Robbie Baker, who would captain the Australian under–19 team and play Sheffield Shield for Western Australia. Robbie eventually got ill with a chronic fatigue–type syndrome which debilitated him and was a roadblock to his career. But back in the junior carnivals, he was the gun – a dominant, classical batsman who scored well off the front and back foot.

I was a little overawed going into those groups. A couple of them were sponsored. Kato got his gear at his club, Midland-Guildford, through the Slater-Gartrell sports store, which was connected with the famous bat makers Millichamp and Hall. When we got to carnivals and we saw sponsored guys from other states, it was a bit intimidating. The New South Wales boys were always very confident, their batsmen strutting around with blond tips, earrings and pristine sponsored gear. Meanwhile, I dreamt of getting Velcro pads – if I got them, I thought I would have made the big time. When I was younger, I even cut up pieces of Velcro and tried to stick them onto my pad buckles, but it didn't work.

That was typical of my experience in those rep carnivals: feeling out of my depth. The main reason for this, still, was my size. When we went to Canberra for the national under–17 championships, I became very self-conscious. When we had our shirts off in the changing rooms, everyone else was muscly with hair under their arms. I didn't have any of that and my voice hadn't broken so I was very shy and uncomfortable about showering at the end of the day. It was an apprehensive time of my life.

Being pre-pubescent set back my self-confidence off the field, but being so small had a major impact on it. When we played New South Wales, all of their bowlers looked like fully grown men. The truth was, I found every bowler hard. I didn't have 'scoring zones'. Being an opener, I was able to aim to drive through cover, which was always left open. Bowlers wanted to tempt me, and were happy for me to have a go with my cover-drive. So that was the origin of what eventually became probably my best-known shot: cover was the only gap in the field, and I had to be pretty good at the cover-drive to get away with it. Otherwise, I was never someone who played a lot of shots. Mostly, I was blocking the living daylights out of it. When the ball started swinging, I had a reasonable defence to keep the good ones out. Overall, my game was to bat for a long period, and try not to panic about not scoring fast enough. I pushed singles, defended solidly and tried to stay busy. I didn't know any other way. It was my physique, more than the conditions or the coaching or any other factor, that ultimately determined the type of batsman I became.

All those years of being outsized also conditioned my mentality. The stigma of being small and weak never left me. In my teens, if I was going to score a hundred, it would take me an entire day, whereas someone like Damien Martyn or Simon Katich would do it in not much more than an hour. It seemed so much easier for them! For me, the fielders seemed huge, covering every gap. Every bowler towered over me. I loved batting so I wanted to stay in the middle, and I applied the lessons I'd learnt about keeping the ball on the ground, never giving my wicket away, and never giving the opposition anything. But the truth in my mind was, I didn't know where I was going to get my next run from.

I dreamt of playing for Australia, but at that age never really believed it was going to happen. When I saw all those brilliant, fluent batsmen at national carnivals, I thought that I wasn't quite good enough. I could practise all the time and try my hardest, but deep down felt there were better players out there than me. I was never even one of the better players in any team I played in.

What changed? The shocking truth is that I don't think anything changed. I never cast off that stigma. I felt under pressure for my whole career, even when I got to play for Australia and started to do well. It didn't matter what happened; that childhood legacy never left me. People would eventually point out that I could score fast and hit sixes, but I didn't see that, and I still don't. I see myself as a nicker and nudger, someone who works the ball and runs hard between wickets, more of a defensive player. In spite of all the evidence, in my mind I am still the boy I was.

FOUR

By my late teens, pretty much every day in summer was filled with cricket. We didn't have family holidays, because Dave and I had matches to go to. He was coming up through the Wanneroo District system, just behind me, appearing to find it a lot easier with his superior natural talent.

There wasn't much outside cricket. Schoolwork began to stretch me in the last two years at Prendiville, probably because this period coincided with my increased attention on cricket. Even my leisure interests were narrowing. The posters on my wall were cricket only. I loved movies, but wasn't into music – I struggled to understand it. Mum tried to get us to do a musical instrument but I didn't last three weeks. I had to play the recorder at school and was hopeless. It was just cricket for me.

As with any cricket-mad kid, I never thought I was sacrificing anything. I didn't care if my schoolmates were going to the beach or the movies and I couldn't go because of a match. I didn't want to be anywhere but cricket. I never went out on a Friday night, or a Saturday if we were playing on Sunday. Guys from school would party on Friday nights, but I didn't socialise with them on those nights. They didn't mind, as they knew how dedicated I was to cricket.

My mates at the club were in the same boat. As a result, my friendships began to grow through the Wanneroo District club. Once I was eighteen, I went to pubs and nightclubs with my teammates. It was a great time in my life: training hard, playing on the weekend, then going to the pub together on Saturday night, and on Sunday morning going to the beach and telling each other stories about what we'd got up to the night before. That was my life and I wouldn't have had it any other way.

In the off-season, Dad devised a training program for Dave and me. He believed he could prepare us physically, and then turn us over to the coaches to work on our skills. I was trying to break into A-grade at Wanneroo, but was still not quite there. We started with two 4- or 5-kilometre beach runs a week. Then he had an 800-metre track marked in the sand hills, and the first week we had to do three circuits. Each week we added on another circuit, all the way up to ten. Dad timed everything, and we built up an incredible amount of fitness. The last part, leading into spring, was back on the grass ovals doing sprint work.

When I look back now, I think it was brilliant training. Dad had a lot of expertise in the area. I enjoyed the training, knowing I was doing it for a purpose. A couple of mates from the club came and did it with us; as always, Dad was keen to coach anyone who was willing to put in the work.

By the time summer came, I was physically ready. I'd done everything I could to make up for my small size. Now it was time to put the runs on the board. I was in 2nd grade now, and early in the season there was a day when the turf nets at Kingsway were wet and we had to train on some Astroturf wickets. They were shocking, with tree roots growing underneath the artificial grass and making it ridge up like corrugated iron, but more irregular. To make it an absolute horror-show, Peter Clough was bowling.

When I'd started at Wanneroo, as a kid in the 4th grade team, Cloughy was my captain. He was in the veteran class by then, but he had opened the bowling for Tasmania and Western Australia over a six-year period in the 1980s, taking 139 first-class wickets. Physically, he was an absolute man-mountain. I barely came up to his navel. He was very gentlemanly, never speaking ill of anyone, but when he had the ball in his hand he would steam in and terrorise poor 4th-grade batsmen.

This dark, damp, overcast day, he was coming in at me off his full run-up and the ball was flying everywhere off the tree roots. I was absolutely petrified, and don't think I hit a ball in the middle.

After I came out, the club coach, Ian Kevan, came up to me while I was unpadding. I got the shock of my life when he said that he and Damien Martyn wanted me in A-grade. I thought, *He can't have seen my net session!*

I'll never forget the boost in confidence I got from being spotted by Ian and Marto. They identified me before a lot of other people did. I was still very small, but they saw enough to want to develop me. I was in awe of Marto, and he didn't say much to me, but that didn't matter. You always feel you owe a debt to the people who give you your first big chance. I was very nervous in my first A-grade game against Claremont-Nedlands and as usual didn't know where I was going to score a run, but I hung in there well and scored 17 on debut. Although I was very disappointed to get out, I was ecstatic to get the opportunity to play in the top team at the Roos and gained a lot of motivation to train harder and improve my game.

Playing with Damien in A-grade was a double-edged sword, though, as far as my further ambitions were concerned. He was in the West Australian team, and was just breaking into the Australian team, in one-day cricket and then in Test cricket. That meant I was only one step from playing state cricket – and two steps from the very top! But on the other hand, I thought, if you wanted to play for Australia you had to be as good as Damien. That pretty much put an end to it for me, because I was never going to be in the same league as him. For me, it was enough to dream that I might, perhaps, if I was lucky, one day get a game for Western Australia. That would be out of this world. It was my goal. I felt miles away, but if I went well, that would be the next step.

It was a great time to be playing A-grade for Wanneroo. We were building a quality team that started to challenge for titles. Damien Martyn was the club's first Australian representative, but in our generation there were players bound for state cricket such as David Fitzgerald, Marcus North, Stephen Glew, Callum Thorp and Matt Mason, as well as Dave and me. We played all around Perth on generally fast and bouncy wickets against quality opposition from many other clubs. Midland-Guildford had state or national stars such as Jo Angel, Brendon Julian and Tom Moody, who were enormous men and very intimidating. In my first years, I was scared of them and they certainly got the better of me. Most clubs had at least one bowler in the state squad, and I would have to dig in and survive against the likes of Craig Coulson, Sean Cary and Mark Atkinson, and try to score my runs off the others. I had to learn to play off the back foot, pull and cut and duck and weave. I learnt how to leave the ball very well, on length as much as line, playing grade cricket in Perth. The Kingsway pitch did a fair bit in the morning, and my mission, as an opener, was to survive until lunch. With a couple of hours' sun on it, it would always flatten out in the afternoon. I looked ugly doing it, nicking and nudging and inside-edging and running quick leg-byes. But if I got through, I could reap the rewards later in the day.

Dave started playing A-grade a year or two after me. I felt he was a much more naturally talented player who could dominate bowling. He wasn't as consistent as I was, and when he wasn't going well, you wouldn't think he'd survive five balls. But generally, I felt that I had to work harder for my runs than Dave did. When he was on his game he was unstoppable, hitting attacks to all parts.

I still think he's a more dominant player than I am. He's always had the ability to take games away from the opposition and put his team in a position to win very quickly. With me, it takes a long time. We were totally different. I might have had a stronger mental side, but he was a lot better in natural hitting ability.

For all the time we'd spent together, however, we didn't talk about tactics or skills or how to help each other improve. It's a bit bizarre, but we were always competitors. I wasn't motivated by wanting to outdo him, but he quite often said, 'I don't care how many I get, as long as it's one more than Mike.' And that got my competitive juices going. We would be batting together in a tense situation for the Roos, and in chats between overs I would say something about what we needed to do to win the match. But if I was on 85 and Dave was on 81, I suspect he'd be thinking about how he could get to 100 before me. He was motivated by outdoing his older brother. We almost saw each other as rivals first, teammates second.

We had some very good partnerships at Wanneroo, but I'm amazed that we did. Before games, we would have a fight in the morning and I would refuse to drive him to the game. Then, after Mum or Dad gave him a lift, we would find ourselves batting together and putting on an amazing partnership. Somehow we found a way. When we eventually played one-day and Twenty20 cricket together for Australia, we had a few good partnerships but not as many as we'd have liked. I enjoyed batting with him, because he usually scored so fast and dominated the bowlers, it took the pressure off me. But – like the Chappells and the Waughs for instance – we didn't really click as partners in the middle, and didn't have as many big partnerships as we should have had.

There was a game for Wanneroo against Scarborough, the pretty boys of the Perth competition. They were a very successful team and club. We – everyone – *really* wanted to beat them. Their state players included Justin Langer, who was also in the Australian Test team by then. Justin was a different kind of player from Damien Martyn, not as dominant or beautiful to watch, but no less effective. As a fellow left-hander, I studied him closely, but compared with me he was very fluent, not just a nudger and nicker. I saw him as a much better player than I could ever dream to be, but not only that, he had a work ethic that was truly frightening. Even in A-grade games, if he got out cheaply he would have the pads off and the next thing you'd see from the field would be Justin running up and down stairs beside the ground to get fitter and stronger. I wondered, *Did you have to work that hard to make it?* I thought I worked hard on my game, but this guy pulverised himself, running laps, doing sit-ups. It was another means of intimidation, showing everybody that this was the work ethic you needed. Just as Marto dazzled the whole club scene with his strokeplay, JL did it with his steely-eyed commitment.

Anyway, that day when we were playing Scarborough, Dave and I had another blue in the morning and Dad had to take Dave to the ground. Even later in the day, by the time we were batting together, we weren't talking to each other at all between overs. The unspoken agreement was, *You stay down that end, I'll stay down this end.* It turned into quite a silly hitting competition. When one of us hit a four, the other had to hit a six. We raced each other to get to a hundred. We had no mind on the bigger picture, the game, but in spite of ourselves, we won. The song got sung very loud, as always when we beat Scarborough, but even then, I doubt Dave and I were in tune.

The biggest influence on me at Wanneroo was Ian Kevan, who spent countless hours with me. Club training was Tuesdays and Thursdays, and I spent at least three other sessions personally with him each week, on Monday, Wednesday and Friday, until I cut Fridays because they left me too tired for Saturday's game. In winter, Ian and I met three times a week in the club's indoor centre. He was amazing, and there's no way I would have got to where I did without him.

I had a strong desire to perfect this art of batting. The only way to do it was to hit thousands and thousands of balls. We did a lot of underarm drills – what were called 'Inver' drills, after the long-time West Australian captain and all-rounder John Inverarity, who devised them. The drills were about teaching you to get into good position to drive. Ian varied the line so I would have to play the ball in each direction, between cover and wide mid-on, getting into position so the bat's impact with the ball happened right under my chin. I was very hard on myself. Even if a ball was a couple of degrees out from where I intended to hit it, I got angry. I analysed every single ball that I hit. I enjoyed striving for the goal of playing perfect drives all the time. Ian's emphasis was more on getting technique perfect than on challenging me with great pace. Sometimes slower bowlers are hard to hit. So he worked on getting me into good position. After a couple of years we eventually did some bowling-machine work. I wouldn't use bowling machines as much after thirty years of age, but as a young player, getting that volume of balls and training your mind and body to get into certain positions, practising every shot thousands of times, is invaluable. You're not training with a bowler's load-up to time your movements, but you're training your body in how to automatically play the shots the right way. I think that volume is important when you're young.

Why was Ian giving me so much time? I didn't think I was a special player, though he might have seen it differently. I just thought this kind of coaching was part of his duties as club coach, to improve the team. I felt I had to work harder than everyone else, even at club level. But in later years, with a bit of distance between myself and those days, I am quite amazed at how responsive Ian was to my obsessiveness, and how much time he gave me, purely out of love of the game and the goodness of his heart.

FIVE

I might have been playing cricket with a full-time professional's mindset, but first-class cricket wasn't a viable career, financially. There were no state contracts, just match payments of a thousand dollars a game and only ten games a year. As a uni student that seemed like a lot of money, but it certainly was not enough to set me up for life. I wasn't thinking of it as a career. I was just dreaming of playing for Western Australia. If I made one dollar from it, that would be a bonus.

Which meant I needed a proper career. In years 11 and 12 at school, we had to choose five TEE (Tertiary Entrance Exam) subjects. I chose five of the harder subjects, not because I was any better than an average student, but because I figured that the hardest subjects were scaled up. Even if you only got 60 per cent in your exam, the difficulty of the subject might push your mark well up above that. So I did two higher-level maths subjects, physics, chemistry, geography and English, hoping I'd go half-decently and benefit from the scaling system. The hitch in my clever plan was that the subjects I'd chosen were so difficult, I had to work extra hard.

Mum and Dad were big on my having something to fall back on in case the cricket didn't work out. I wanted to go to the University of Western Australia to study science. I didn't know what I wanted to do, but a general science degree could open up a few avenues in science, and possibly teaching. (What I really wanted to do was play cricket, which wasn't offered as a course at university.) After science, I put down teaching as my number-two choice for all the wrong reasons – long holidays over the summer period, and finishing at three o'clock so I could go to training.

As it turned out, I didn't get the marks for science at UWA, so I went to Curtin University to study secondary teaching. I ended up taking just about a world-record length of time of eight years to graduate, but finish it I did. And, as I'll get to later, going to Curtin would turn out to be the best decision I ever made.

In the meantime, I could give whatever energy was left over from cricket to my studies. In years 11 and 12 I worked incredibly hard on my studies and found it very tough. At home, there were no pressures to move out or pay board. I did some indoor cricket umpiring to have some money coming in. But basically I could dedicate myself to improving my game and finishing my secondary education.

As an eighteen-year-old, I played three games for a Western Australia Colts XI that introduced me to some cricketers who would become career-long friends. Our number-three batsman, another left-hander, was Brad Hogg, who came from the country and played for Fremantle. Hoggy was one of life's enthusiasts. We trained together, doing one-on-one fielding drills and fitness work. I'd never known anyone fitter: we did a 10-kilometre run around the bridges over the Swan River, and I couldn't get within cooee of Hoggy. He batted more than he bowled in those days – in fact I recall him bowling fast-medium, not wrist-spin – and in my opinion he was a much better player than me. Soon he would be chosen in the West Australian Sheffield Shield team, and when it happened I was very excited for him. He was so genuine and simple, without any ulterior motives, and would have felt the same for me if I'd got in ahead of him. My next thought was, *Wow, maybe I could get a game for Western Australian because we're not that dissimilar.*

Another member of our Colts team was Stuart MacGill. He was loud and full of confidence. I don't know what he saw in me – maybe a foil for his brash side – but we really clicked from the word go. He was already a good enough leg-spin bowler to play first-class cricket, but he wasn't getting many opportunities, as the WACA pitch wasn't conducive to his art. I knew from experience how hard it was to bowl consistent, accurate leg spin. Not only could he do that, but he spun it a long way. In any other state, he would have been in the Shield team for sure. I had enormous respect for him.

Magilla was pretty boisterous on the field. He could abuse fielders when they misfielded off his bowling, and had a go at umpires when he felt their decisions weren't competent. Sometimes I worried if it was going to get him into trouble. I don't know why, but he wasn't that way with me. He never said a bad word to me personally. But that didn't stop us from remaining good friends throughout our careers. I think I only went out with him once or twice at night; our relationship was built more at the cricket rather than after dark.

I didn't do particularly well in those Colts games, but in the under–19s national carnival in Melbourne, Western Australia won the trophy and I had a good carnival, establishing a successful rapport with my opening partner Justin Cantrell. I managed to get a few wickets with my leggies as well. At the end of it, they were selecting an Australian under–19 team for an eight-week tour of India. I thought I was a chance, and when my name was called out I felt an overwhelming surge of pride. I couldn't believe I'd been picked as one of the best fourteen guys in my age group in Australia.

It was a tough tour in every way, but those of us who were on it still talk about what a great time we had. It was hard at the time but, looking back, I have to say it was one of the best tours I've been on.

Not that it started very well for me. Our first match was in a town called Secunderabad, close to Hyderabad in the southern central part of the country. Robbie Baker, our captain, won the toss and chose to bat. Before I knew it I was walking out with Justin Cantrell, holding a bat from Gray-Nicolls – my first sponsorship! I was extremely nervous, playing my first game for an Australian representative team, and to get it out of my system I asked Justin if I could take the first ball. The bowler, called Rana, jogged in, his arm whipped around, and before I could focus the ball had skidded straight through me. All the pride and nervousness evaporated and gave way to embarrassment. I walked off, bowled by the first ball of the tour, the first ball I faced with an Australian crest on my shirt. As someone who lacked self-confidence, I was crippled.

Luckily, I was picked for our second game, in the Chinnaswamy Stadium, the Test ground at Bangalore. I shook off my feelings of shame from the first match and scored 120 in the first innings and 71 not out in the second, which sealed my selection for the first youth Test, which to me was as important and prestigious as a full-blown Test match for Australia. In that century in Bangalore, I managed to hit my first six in *any* competition. I guess that showed two things: one, how weak I was as a hitter, and two, how firmly I stuck to the rule of keeping the ball on the ground. To have finally hit a six, though, I was chuffed, and had my photo taken with the bowler I'd hit it off: Rahul Sanghvi, a very good left-arm finger spinner who ended up playing internationals for India.

To this point, my existence had been sheltered. The whole world had revolved around our little community in northern Perth. I didn't read the newspapers or watch the news a lot, and on family holidays we didn't go far. Going to Canberra on that under–17s tour had been my first experience of the wider world. Canberra! I went to Melbourne for the under–19s carnival and to Adelaide and Sydney on the Colts trip.

So with that innocent background, I was a bit overwhelmed by India. The streets were loud with honking and shouting and whistling, the open sewers and rivers stank, and whenever we drove anywhere, there were a lot of beggars knocking on the window. I felt terrible and helpless to see such poverty. The volume of people on the road, walking, riding bikes, driving cars and trucks, the cows sharing the street, the absence of lights or road signals at night – it was certainly not something I was accustomed to, and drained me emotionally. At the end of each day I was exhausted from taking in so many sense impressions, and from so many mixed emotions about what I was seeing.

We didn't stay in the cleanest or most comfortable hotels, probably three-star at best, and in the first few days our number-one paceman from New South Wales, Brett Lee, got very sick. He couldn't break his habit of taking a big gulp of water while he showered, and he got so ill, for days it was coming out of both ends. We all fell sick at some stage of the tour. We hadn't been to the country before and the food wasn't always hygienically prepared. One night I ordered prawns off the room service menu, having stupidly forgotten the advice against ordering seafood. In a moment of weakness I ordered it, and was out of business for a week.

Shane Jurgensen, another fast bowler, hurt his back very early in the tour and had to be sent home. His replacement was Jason Gillespie, an interesting character from Adelaide with long black hair, one side of it interrupted by a shaved pattern of lightning bolts.

Dizzy had bowled me during a Western Australia Colts match against South Australia Second XI, but most of us regarded him as a decent medium-pacer, steady at best. He hadn't been chosen initially, but that didn't stop him from making some pretty bold declarations. We would be sitting eating and Dizzy would say,

'Within a year I'll be playing for South Australia in the Shield, and within two years I'll be playing for Australia.'

When we weren't hooting and laughing, we would say, 'Come on, Jase, you're an idiot, you can't say that. You're an average bowler.' Sure enough, within a year he was playing for South Australia and within two years he was playing for Australia: exactly the calls he'd made. And he turned into one of Australia's best ever new-ball bowlers. I think the reason for his rapid improvement was firstly that his pace increased out of sight, and secondly that he had phenomenal discipline, work ethic and self-belief. He came from a pretty tough upbringing. He'd had a partner from an early age, and they already had two children. He was trying to juggle training and cricket with a full-on family life, and having to endure such tough times would have stood him in good stead. Although he was very laidback, he was unshakably determined, and hell-bent on reaching the top. With all his responsibilities, he was a rounded kind of guy. It was an eye-opening experience for me, as a very young eighteen-year-old, to be mixing with people from such varied backgrounds.

Dizzy's maturity also, no doubt, helped him put up in good spirit with being the butt of jokes, because of his hair and his ambition and his various other quirks. In taking the mickey out of him and others, the man leading the charge was Andrew 'Roy' Symonds.

My first impression of Simmo was, to be brutally honest, that he was a very arrogant bloke. At the under–19 carnival in Melbourne there was a common room for all the players. Simmo would walk in and kick guys off the pool table. 'You're out of here, we're doing this.' The way he batted only reaffirmed this: he was so athletic and strong and brilliant, with a true arrogance about his demeanour towards bowlers, I hated the guy.

During that under–19s tour, I got to know him better, and will say that he is the funniest guy I've ever played with and one of the most gifted cricketers. One of the exciting things about Simmo was, he was so confident he would respond to the crowds. In the second youth Test, at Thiruvananthapuram, we were looking down the barrel after chasing balls all day hit wherever he wanted them by a young VVS Laxman. It felt like the ground was right out in the bush, with straw huts for dressing rooms, but there were, as always in India, hundreds of people watching. We were 3/65 on a pitch which, to this day, was the biggest turner I have ever played on. You had to land the ball on the edge of the pitch for it to have any chance of hitting the stumps. The spinners were Sanghvi and Hrishikesh Kanitkar, who also went on to play for India. It was almost turning backwards, it was going so far.

Coming from non-spinning Perth, it was a great education, both to play on it and to watch how Simmo dealt with it. I was up the other end scratching to survive. When he came in, he had two tactics, depending on the delivery. If it looked dangerous, he kicked it away. He knew it was turning so far, he didn't stand much risk of being out lbw. All other balls, he tried to slog out of the ground.

He began connecting with a few, and the crowd loved it. They began to chant. 'Sixer! Sixer!' Once that happened, Simmo decided he only needed one tactic. He started trying to hit *every* ball for six. He played a phenomenal innings. He wanted to please the few hundred who were there, and they fell in love with him. We put on 70 together, of which I scraped out about 20. We lost our last 6 wickets for 8 runs. In between, Simmo plundered 163 runs out of 210 scored while he was in.

Later in life, when we played for Australia together, my fondness for Simmo grew more. He was unbelievably competitive, always energetic and ready for action, and, once he'd decided you were part of his team, he would do anything for you. I quite often said to him over an emotional beer after a game, 'I wouldn't say this to more than a handful of people but I'd be happy to dive on a grenade for you, mate.' That's how much I loved him.

And he was quite hilarious, the things he came out with. Once we were in Perth walking down the Hay Street Mall and a lady was selling raffle tickets.

Simmo said, 'What's the first prize?'

She said, '$1000 cash.'

'Okay, I'll be in that.'

And he bought some tickets. As we walked away, he stopped. He went back to the lady and said, 'What date is it drawn?'

'On the thirty-first of the month.'

'Right,' Simmo said. 'Well, I'll be expecting a call on the thirty-second.'

He was a constant source of humour in every team he played with.

We had a pretty successful tour. A senior Australian team hadn't been to India in eight years, and youth tours were a way of paving the ground for a resumption of more regular cricket relations. I was the back-up leg-spinner, which I really enjoyed. I doubted my ability a bit, but worked very hard on my consistency, working with Brad Birrell, an off-spinner from South Australia, with the aim of bowling six balls in a row on the spot – like Stuart MacGill could. I still tended to bowl one or two loose balls an over, and there was nothing to keep you on your mettle like bowling to VVS Laxman on Indian wickets.

We drew the first Test and lost the second, and came to the third Test in Mumbai having to win to square the series. It was during the lead-up to that match that I'd eaten the prawns and got sick, but I was okay to play and we chased down a big target in the last innings. Robbie Baker and Simmo played brilliant innings, and Corey Richards and I made some runs as well, while Jerry Cassell scored runs and also took vital wickets. On the last day, we were under a lot of pressure to score the runs in time – 311 was the target, in four hours. We got there with 4 wickets down, and celebrated like we'd won the World Cup. Coming home, I reflected on India itself. The truth was, I had found it confronting off the field, though the cricket was always enjoyable. The foreignness of the country was a big culture shock for a boy from the beach in Perth. I hoped I would get back there one day. I could never have guessed how big a part of my life India would become, and how strongly my affection for the country and its people would grow.

SIX

Arriving home in early 1994, my motivation for cricket was at an all-time high. I'd played for an Australian team and was pushing to get into the West Australian squad. I had to negotiate university, but that felt like a mere detail.

During that year, I was called up into the West Australian senior squad. I looked at it as a time of gathering experience among the men, and had no expectation that I would play a game. It was intimidating enough joining a squad containing names such as Tom Moody, Damien Martyn, Brendon Julian, Geoff Marsh and Bruce Reid. These were my heroes. The only time I'd been on the same field as them was as one of the kids who came onto the WACA to play Kanga Cricket during the breaks in their games, and now here I was, hoping not to make a fool of myself as a member of their training squad.

I needn't have worried about whether they would see me as their equal. They quickly made it clear that there would be no illusions about thinking I was on the same level as them. It was a tough, old-school environment, and the senior players made sure you knew your place and did what they told you. If you dropped a catch at practice, you would cop a bit of stick. If you put one foot out of line, they were onto you. I'm not sure if the other states were like that, but to me it seemed particularly harsh, and after many sessions I would go home and sit on my bed and wonder what I was doing. Having played in nurturing team environments at Wanneroo and in the representative under-age teams, I was confused more than anything. Were they trying to help me, or cut me down and exclude me? If it was tough love, it was different from any kind of team psychology I'd experienced or even heard of. If it was the jealousy of senior men against up-and-comers, why would they bother? What threat was I to them?

Amid one rugged training session after the other, it helped to have one friendly face. The week before state practices had started, I went on a spinners' and wicketkeepers' camp at the Australian Cricket Academy in Adelaide, and among the keepers was Adam Gilchrist. Gilly was en route from Sydney to Perth, where he was moving to try to establish himself as a first-class gloveman. In his home state, his path had been blocked by Phil Emery, the New South Wales captain and a former Test wicketkeeper. Gilly and I roomed together in Adelaide, and he asked me a lot of questions about the people and politics in Perth. Of course, I knew nothing. Gilly was four years older than me and much more worldly. Every night, he went out for a few beers and I'd be tucked into bed early. The next morning he'd be going off at me for farting too loudly in my sleep.

When he came to Perth, I tried to help him settle in. We socialised away from the squad and had dinner or went out together. He was a very sympathetic person, and we were able to share our different troubles. For me, it was getting a hard time at the hands of the senior players, whereas for Gilly, it seemed like the whole of the state hated him. He was picked for the first Mercantile Mutual Cup one-day game, at the WACA against Victoria (who wore shorts), and I was really excited for him. He seemed really nervous and withdrawn.

I asked him what was the matter.

He said, 'I've just taken the place of a West Australian legend. They won't forgive me.' Tim Zoehrer, the long-term wicketkeeper, had been entrenched in the team alongside his clubmates Tom Moody, Jo Angel and Brendon Julian. The senior guys, to everyone's relief, had quickly warmed to Gilly, but he was worried about the general public, who felt that Tim had been pushed out by the administrators. In that one-day game, the locals abused Gilly and waved 'Bring Back Zoehrer' banners. I really felt for him, it was a tough initiation. But he performed so well and behaved so cheerfully, the public soon grew to like him as much as the players did. He went out into the community and the media and was always positive, energetic and enthusiastic. Soon they forgot about Tim Zoehrer and Gilly was the flavour of the team.

I didn't expect to play a game that season. The openers, Geoff Marsh and Mike Veletta, were internationals. Behind them were Mark Lavender and Rob Kelly. Western Australia were well stocked with top-order batsmen. But Swampy Marsh, after doing the whole pre-season, suddenly announced that he didn't have the desire to play anymore. I thought that was strange, considering all the hard work he'd put in. Then, in the opening first-class fixture of the season, against the touring English team, Veletta got injured. Still, I expected Rob Kelly to be put in with Lavender.

I went to the WACA to watch the last day of that match against England. I could see Rob talking angrily with the coach and selectors. Rob eventually walked over to me and said, 'I'm really angry I didn't get the chance, but it's not your fault, I'm angry with the selectors, not you. So good luck and do well.' That was a really nice thing to say. And that was how I learnt I'd been selected to play for Western Australia.

I was told to go to the cricket manager's office to get my baggy gold cap and jumpers and playing shirts. I walked back to my car. There was a parking ticket on my windscreen but I didn't care at all. I got in and started driving. As soon as I was on the road, I began screaming at the top of my voice. No words, just a primal scream of sheer excitement. I couldn't wait to get home to tell Mum, Dad and Dave. I was playing for Western Australia. This was everything I'd dared to hope for in cricket, and it was happening!

Once we were in Hobart, there was one person who was more amped up than me. My roommate was my old mate Brad Hogg, which was quite an experience. He woke up at four o'clock in the morning to bowl balls at the wall, put his pads and gloves and box and thigh pad on – with nothing else – and play shots in front of the mirror. Even by Hoggy's standards, this was extreme. I thought, *Gee, this Sheffield Shield must be serious stuff.* But then, Hoggy was a one-off.

Fortunately, for the state of my nerves, we lost the toss and bowled first at Bellerive. Unfortunately, for the sake of the team, Ricky Ponting batted for a day and a half. The temperature was four or five degrees Celsius and there was snow on Mount Wellington. None of that had any effect on the boy genius.

It was the first time I'd seen Ricky. We had been due to play him in the previous year's under–19 carnival, but he was suspended from our game for smashing down his stumps when he got out in an earlier game. Then, he hadn't come on the tour to India because he was called up to play Sheffield Shield.

I had no trouble, and plenty of time, to see why he had been promoted at his age. We had a very good attack, with Bruce Reid, Brendon Julian, Sean Cary, Tom Moody and the left-arm spinner Jamie Stewart. Ricky made it look easy, cutting and pulling and driving with absolute ease, and we never looked like getting him out.

By the end of it, when Tasmania declared on the second day and gave us a bat, I was too exhausted to be nervous. I'd never fielded for that long or chased so many balls.

I waddled out with Mark Lavender, my legs stiff. The new ball was taken by Chris Matthews, another in a long line of man-mountains I'd got used to trying to knock me over. Matthews was a burly and aggressive left-armer. Originally from Perth, he had played three Tests for Australia in the 1980s, with unfortunate results when he lost control of the ball. But even though he was coming to the end of his career, he had a superb first-class record, with nearly 400 wickets. The guys had warned me that he was going to sledge me, but said not to worry, his bark was worse than his bite.

When I was finally facing him, he didn't say much, which was a surprise. What was more challenging was that he tried everything: outswingers, inswingers, bouncers, slower balls, bowling wide on the crease and in close, a bit of everything in every over.

I got a straight drive away for my first runs, which I was overjoyed about. I thought, *I've made first-class runs! No-one can take that away from me!* But then, when I'd got to 16, I was out to David Millns, an English bowler. Chris Matthews was fielding at a fine short leg. I hit a pull shot quite well, but Matthews put out his hand and it just stuck.

It was only when I sat next to Tom Moody in the dressing room that it hit me that I was out. I was hiding my disappointment as Tom was padding up. Then he went out and scored 272. Damien Martyn made a hundred, Gilly, in his first Sheffield Shield game for the state, got a shocking decision to be given out for a duck, and we got the two points.

That was it for my season as a Sheffield Shield player, and for all I knew, that was my first-class career. My disappointment at only making 16 didn't last long. I was thrilled to have my baggy gold cap. That was my ambition, and I'd achieved it.

I was twelfth man for the next three games after Hobart. I took this job very seriously, and tried to run the drinks and gear to the players on the field and help out with all the odd jobs in the most professional way. Unfortunately, in the atmosphere of that team, my intensity set me up as a target.

During the match against Victoria at the WACA, Tom Moody was in the dressing room. Seeing me buzzing about, the diligent young twelfth man looking for work, he called me over.

'Huss, I've been struggling with a back injury. I've got these two pills I have to take.'

'No worries,' I said, ever eager. 'Do you want me to get you some water or Powerade to wash them down?'

'No,' he said, straight-faced. 'They're suppositories.'

I gave him a blank look. Sup-what? I didn't have the slightest idea what he was talking about.

'Suppositories,' he went on, patiently. 'It means you – *you* – need to stick them up my bum.'

'Er, I don't know,' I stammered. 'You're joking, right?'

At that moment – they must have had it all set up – Justin Langer, who was sitting on Tom's other side, joined in. 'Come on, Huss! You're the twelfth man! You have to help your teammate out!'

Then it was the turn of Daryl Foster, the coach. 'Huss, you heard him, you're the twelfth man! Do as you're told!'

Innocent and fearful as I was, I was easy prey for them. I still thought they were serious. Big Tom grabbed me by the wrist, said, 'Come on, let's go,' and started dragging me towards the toilets. Beside myself, I was about to start screaming when they all burst out laughing. They all enjoyed it. I was extremely relieved that I didn't have to go through with the deed. They were tough on the youngsters and I had to grow up quickly being around these guys. Thankfully my experience of joining the Australian team would be a lot smoother.

After playing out the season with Wanneroo and the West Australian Colts, I was invited at the start of 1995 to go to Adelaide for a year at the Academy. It meant deferring my uni course, which was no hardship. The bigger question was whether it would be good for my cricket.

That may seem a no-brainer, but in Perth the Academy had a bit of a stigma as a pretty boys' club. It was said that they all had it laid on a bit easy. I had a really good training program at home, with Ian, Dad and the WA squad, and had convinced myself that I couldn't get much more from going to the academy.

All this was before the offer came. When it did, I changed my mind! I jumped at the chance, and looked forward to what I hoped would be one of the best years of my life. With my ongoing battles against self-doubt, it was a fillip just to be invited, to think that the head coach, the legendary Rod Marsh, might even have heard of me. So I went to Adelaide full of excitement. Cricket, cricket, nothing but cricket. What could be better?

I headed across in April, and was assigned a part-time job to fit in around my training. It was a good part of the Academy's policy to keep the guys busy with work. I fell on my feet with the cushiest job imaginable. Other guys had to work for sponsor companies, or had jobs at the Adelaide Oval, but all I had to do was clean the gym and drive the team bus to drop everyone at their jobs. Each morning I dropped them off, went back and tidied up the gym, and then had a sleep, played table tennis or watched movies until the training session in the afternoon.

My roommate was Clinton Peake, a bit of a child prodigy who'd made a triple-century in an Australian under–19 game. I also got on well with Peter Roach, the Victorian wicketkeeper who had been on the tour to India with me. We loved watching our footy. I was also mates with Corey Richards, Matthew Mott and Clinton Perren, who all became good first-class cricketers. We had a friendly group, solid but not the most talented – which Rod made sure we knew.

It seemed that the main lesson Rod wanted to pound into us was that we were nowhere near as good as the guys who had been there the previous year. It's true that it was an extremely talented intake, including Brett Lee, Ian Harvey, Andrew Symonds and Ryan Campbell, all aggressive and confident players. Rod kept going on about how good they were, how much fun they were to watch, and how much better than us they were. Rod loved flair and aggression. I couldn't help suspecting that like he didn't like me or rate me because I could never be that kind of player. Years later, as a selector, he told me he respected the way I played, and I realised he did quite like me as a player. But at the time, I struggled with the usual feelings of inferiority.

My one compensation for my lack of natural talent, real or perceived, was my work ethic. Maybe I overcompensated. In the first couple of months at the Academy, I felt we weren't training as hard as I had at home. Each month we were scheduled to have one-on-one meetings with Rod. After two months, I swallowed down my fear of him and said, 'Rod, I'm sorry but I don't think we're working hard enough. I train harder at WA.'

That didn't go down well. For the next month he pulverised us. I wasn't exactly popular with the boys.

At our next one-on-one, he fixed me with those blank brown eyes and said, 'Okay Huss, do you think we're training hard enough now?'

'Yes, Rod,' I said. 'This is more like it.'

He sat back. I fancied I saw him masking a bit of shock. He clearly hadn't come across many kids who had a Ted Hussey training program behind them!

After that settling-in period, I've got to say that it really was a great year. I absolutely loved it. I was with my peers, and even if they weren't as good as the 1994 group they were considered the best players in the country. There was non-stop fitness, skills and specialist coaching. We also built a great team spirit by going out on weekends as a team.

I learnt a lot from individual visiting coaches. Richard Chee Quee from New South Wales, the associate coach, was a great guy and very informative on what it was really like to play first-class cricket. He kept stressing that we enjoy the experience, if it came, and not to put too much pressure on ourselves.

Cheeks had always been a very attacking batsman, which I didn't think I could be. But it was great to get the encouragement. Ian Chappell came in for Bouncers Week, when the quicks were given the freedom to try to hit us in the head every ball. Ian came in and talked about getting into position to hook and pull – he was never about evasion, but rather putting pressure on the bowler. Against the spinners, Ian had us practising getting down the wicket and hitting over the top. When we had so much time and freedom, this was the space to practise being positive without the risk of failure. I was keen to learn as much as I could about this aggressive style. When you did it successfully a few times, you had confidence you could take your game to a new level.

At the end of my year at the Academy, we had some games against state Second XIs and a tour to Pakistan. I liked Pakistan from the start. Compared with India, I found it cleaner and better organised. There wasn't that mass of humanity. The hotels and food were great, the pitches were beautiful for batting and the other teams played good, positive cricket. It probably also helped that I was nearly two years older than when I'd gone to India, and had been living away from home for several months.

We played six games against Pakistan A teams, all around the country, from Peshawar to Lahore and Rawalpindi. They were enterprising cricketers, with some fast bowlers including Shoaib Akhtar and Mohammad Zahid, and I recall their spinners being very hard to get away. The Salim Malik match-fixing scandal had broken earlier that year, but that seemed to be in a different world from what we were doing. I don't even remember anyone discussing it. We were just out to enjoy our cricket and the experience of being on tour.

I did like the food, but again made some kind of mistake –
I don't know what – and two minutes before I was to go out to bat
in one of the matches, I was violently ill. I managed to bat for the
first hour, but when the drinks came out and I was hurling up my
guts on the outfield. I couldn't drink. There was nothing else for
it, so I decided to be the kind of cricketer Rod Marsh and Richard
Chee Quee would like to see, and tried to hit every ball for six.
For some reason, when you're sick and you've given up, it seems
to come off. It was a first for me. I belted seven or eight sixes
and scored about 70. I felt terrible but had gained some respect
from the team, for still wanting to play and score runs in the state
I was in. And if I didn't surprise a few people with my big hitting,
I certainly surprised myself.

With that experience under our belt, we came back and toured
Australia to play the state Second XIs. Without a doubt the
highlight of the summer, and the capping of a great year at the
Academy, was a limited-overs match we played against the touring
West Indies team at North Dalton Park, Wollongong. It was the
first time I'd played a senior international team, and the first time
I'd been to Wollongong. Even though it was nearly Christmas it
was a wintry, windy day. We couldn't believe we were playing the
mighty West Indies, who we'd watched beat up on Australia all
through our childhoods. We *really* couldn't believe it when we
bowled them out for 92. I guess the West Indians weren't enjoying
the weather very much and were less than fully motivated. But we
were ecstatic as the wickets kept falling.

The only problem was, as an opening batsman, the nagging
question as it got closer to our turn. If the conditions were this
hard for international batsmen against young bowlers, how hard
were they going to be for young batsmen against international
bowlers?

When I walked out to open with Corey Richards, I was
absolutely petrified. The whole West Indian team looked at me like

they wanted to kill me. Their attack didn't have Curtly Ambrose and Courtney Walsh, but as far as I was concerned, Ian Bishop, Anderson Cummins and Ottis Gibson were terrifying enough. They all seemed very, very fast to me with Gibson the quickest. I somehow scratched out 23, Corey did much the same, and we got over the line. Rod allowed us to have a big celebration – a great way to finish off our time at the Academy. It was just lucky we weren't chasing 250.

My time in under-age cricket was coming to an end. When I think back to all the gifted players I knew, I ask myself why some talented youngsters come through and realise their potential, while others do not. Clinton Peake had much more natural talent than me. In that match against the West Indies, while I was in a life-and-death struggle, Clinton Perren came out and made it look like he had all the time in the world. He had a good first-class career, but as far as I was concerned, he was a better player than I was.

I didn't know the answer then, but I've got a better idea now that it's all behind me. The higher you go in cricket, the more important is what's going on between the ears. I think the essence of it is putting distractions aside to focus on the one important thing, which is that ball coming at you. The further up the ladder you go, the more intense the scrutiny, the more heavy the pressure, the more numerous the distractions. It's very difficult to shut them all out. If it was easy, a lot more people would be doing it very well. Even the best players in the world can struggle with dealing with those distractions.

Anyway, easier said than done. I probably knew this at the time. What I didn't know was *how* to do it, and how to develop an ironclad mental routine that worked for me. To get that seasoning, I had to go up a level and test myself against the men.

SEVEN

I was overjoyed when Ryan Campbell joined the state squad in 1995–96. Not only was he a terrific, attacking batsman, but he rocked up with the strut, the long hair and the earring, and all of a sudden the old boys had a new target. They laid into Cambo like you wouldn't believe, brutally cutting him down, letting him know he wasn't as good as he thought. After that, the attention went off me. Ryan and I stuck together against the older guys – it was kind of us-versus-them – and established a good friendship right from the start.

That season, I played right through Western Australia's Sheffield Shield campaign to the final. It was a great experience to be up against the stars of the sport, beginning with my first game, against a New South Wales team including Steve and Mark Waugh, Mark Taylor, Michael Slater, Michael Bevan, Greg Matthews and Glenn McGrath. I managed to score 42 and 81, which set me up well for the season. To be able to make runs against an attack of that quality, even on what was a flat batting track, gave me a lot of confidence and, I hoped, won my teammates' respect.

The Waugh brothers were renowned for a bit of chat on the field, but I don't think they could be too bothered with me. I remember Mark taking the mickey a little, but more because I was an irritation than a threat. His attitude to me was that I was a pest, a tick in the backside.

None of that was as weird as Greg Matthews, who often tried to get into the minds of young players. On the first morning, I was happy to have survived to lunch with Mark Lavender and was walking off, pretty chuffed. Then I heard this lewd murmuring behind me, 'Great arse, Huss. Jeez, I wouldn't mind seeing you in the showers, that's a great arse.'

I didn't need to turn around to see who it was. I started running off. *What the hell is this guy?* When I got into the dressing room, I told some of the older guys and they burst out laughing. Typical Mo, or so it seemed.

But it worked. Sure enough, in the first over after lunch I nicked McGrath and was walking off, still shaking my head in confusion. At the end of the day I showered pretty quickly, nervous that Matthews was going to come in and check me out.

Every state had its own unique personality that usually permeated right down through to junior cricket. From under–17 and under–19 carnivals, I was familiar with the New South Wales way. They were super-confident, strutting around with fancy gear and fancy hair, blond tips, jewellery. They were pretty chirpy on the field also, trying to give you a sense that you didn't belong on the same field as them. For a long while, I believed them! I struggled with that until a few years later when I understood I might be as good as these guys and they were putting it on as a front for insecurity. But it takes a while to learn that.

In our return game against the Blues that season, I copped one of the biggest sprays I've ever received on a cricket field. It was a day–night Sheffield Shield match, and their Test stars were out, and I thought I might have had an easier time. Two mates, Corey

Richards and Richard Chee Quee, were in their team. On the first day and night, I was at my annoying best, nicking it through slips and hanging around like a bad smell but doing a reasonable job because we were steadily losing wickets at the other end.

They were all having a go at me, even David Freedman, the left-arm Chinaman spinner. Freddy wasn't in the New South Wales mould at all. He was modest and polite to everyone. He bowled well to me, and I think my nicking and nudging even annoyed him. I thought, *I must be really hated on this cricket field if even Freddy Freedman is having a go at me.*

Among the bowlers was Neil Maxwell, a tall all-rounder who would also play for Victoria. Maxi was known to suffer from a bit of white-line fever, a genial bloke who was a great competitor on the field. He had finished another unlucky over at me and was walking towards gully. As he took his cap from the umpire, he was muttering about how I was a young upstart and had no shots. Could I hit the ball in front of the wicket? He didn't think so. Then he went on getting angrier and angrier.

I was getting ready to face the next over, but Maxi's spray was still going on from gully. I pulled back and asked the umpire to hold up the game. I turned towards gully.

'Mate, have you finished?'

That really set him off. 'No, I haven't finished!' The spray went on for another thirty seconds or so, until finally the game could start again. It was quite funny, looking back, but at the time I felt intimidated. I'd learnt from earlier games how to suppress those feelings, though, and answered with a few runs, eventually making 105.

(The postscript to that story is that Maxi is now my manager, friend and confidant. Like I say, he just suffered from white-line fever.)

I was getting used to being sledged. The aim was to belittle me, make me feel like I didn't belong.

That hundred against New South Wales wasn't my first for the state. In a match against the touring Pakistan team at the WACA before Christmas, I'd broken through.

It was a great day, and a very flat pitch. Waqar Younis opened the bowling, but he wasn't at full pace and he went off after a five-over spell. I actually nicked him early in my innings, but was given not out. Most of the bowling was done by their world-class spinners, Mushtaq Ahmed and Saqlain Mushtaq. Saqlain was renowned for having developed a mystery ball, a 'doosra', which looked like an off-spinner but turned away from the bat (or into the-left-hander, in my case). We'd never seen a doosra, and were talking a lot about whether it would spin, how to pick it and so on. Mushtaq, meanwhile, was renowned for his wrong'un. I was excited by the challenge of surviving against them. But to be honest, the odds were stacked in my favour. It was an ideal location for me to be taking on spin bowlers of that order, because there wasn't a lot of turn in the pitch and the margin for error for slow bowlers was small. If they were just too full, I could drive through the line, and if they dropped a little bit too short I could get back and cut or pull. I didn't see any doosras from Saqlain, and Mushtaq couldn't get much purchase either way. Hoggy and I had a good partnership and we both made hundreds. Hoggy was playing freely, blazing and really enjoying himself, and I was beginning to feel that I belonged at this level.

Mum and Dad were there, taking photos, which made them very proud, but it also led to an unforgettable confrontation with Justin Langer.

Because I didn't have many shots, I had to rotate the strike with quick singles. In the early stages of that innings, I kept pushing the ball into a gap and calling 'Yes!' Up the other end, Justin was repeatedly standing still and sending me back. I eventually went up to him and said, 'JL, I don't have many shots, so I need you to back up and help me get some singles.'

He told me to look after my own game and not to worry about what he was doing. But later, I was looking through the photos that Mum and Dad had taken. In one, I was setting off for a quick single and there was JL standing in his crease, more or less sitting on his bat handle.

Stupidly, I took the photo to him in the dressing room and said, 'JL, here, look, this is what I'm talking about, I really need you to be backing up more.'

That went down like a lead balloon. We're good friends now, and we got to enjoy batting and playing together over the years, but at the time he let me know pretty bluntly that as a junior player, to criticise his running between the wickets wasn't the right approach and I should have kept my mouth shut.

That first season set a pattern for me. The key was making a good start. I came into each season with so many doubts and fears, I needed to make just one good score early to push them to the back of my mind. Once I'd done that, I could feel I had my teammates' respect and could relax and play without the constant anxiety about being dropped.

The downside, in that season and in several that followed, was that I put so much nervous and physical energy into preparing for the early games and making sure I got a good start, I ended up tailing off late in the season. As each summer wore on, I simply grew fatigued. That first season, I'd spent a year at the Academy, toured Pakistan, gone around Australia with the Academy team, and played seven first-class games for Western Australia before Australia Day. It was hectic for a twenty-year-old, and in the last five weeks of the season I only made one decent score, 85 against Victoria, among a string of failures.

But we had developed a successful team and the selectors wanted to keep it stable. I was opening with Mark Lavender or Ryan Campbell, and in our group we had Justin Langer, Damien Martyn, Tom Moody, Rob Baker, Simon Katich, Adam Gilchrist,

Brad Hogg, Brendon Julian, Jo Angel, Sean Cary and Bruce Reid. We benefited greatly from having so many international-class players who weren't able to break into the Test team. Jokes aside, Tom was a very good leader who commanded respect. We were playing an attractive brand of cricket. To be playing for Western Australia, contributing to the team, was my dream come true. It also meant a great deal to the state, and the senior players, to be succeeding again after a couple of years of indifferent results. We were all fanatical about winning the Sheffield Shield.

The Shield final, against South Australia in Adelaide, was my first taste of five-day cricket and a great match to be part of. I only made 11 runs in more than an hour on the first morning. I had to survive the new ball from Jason Gillespie and Shane George, a frightening bowler. He was pretty quick, but what made him scary was that he was a bit wild on the field, with crazy eyes. He'd stand on the pitch after bowling and tell you he wanted to kill you, and spit somewhere in your direction. I was pretty scared of him. I thought that at any moment he might bowl a hand-to-header, a beamer – he'd be happier to hurt you than get you out. I did manage to survive that pair, but gave my wicket away to Greg Blewett's medium pacers.

When you're young, you often don't appreciate how special some things are, but I'll never forget Gilly's 189 off 187 balls on the second day. It was simply phenomenal. Tim May was bowling, a Test spinner on his home ground, and Gilly kept slog-sweeping him into the stands, against the spin. I think it was the innings that made the national selectors sit up and take notice of him for the first time, and it gave our whole team the confidence to dictate terms, and the body language of the Redbacks changed. They were under pressure and behind in the match from then on.

As we had come second on the regular season table, we not only had to play away from home but had to win the match to win the Shield. South Australia only needed a draw. When it came to the last day, we had to take eight wickets, but the pitch was well-worn and we were miles ahead on runs, so could set attacking fields.

The Redbacks dug in. Greg Blewett had batted for more than five hours, and James Brayshaw lasted a session, but we had them seven down before tea. Jamie Siddons was in, but surely he couldn't last long. He had damaged his hip so badly, he would need surgery. He could hardly walk, let alone bat.

But tea came and went, and as the next hour dragged on, we just couldn't remove him or Tim May. They didn't bother with runs and just applied themselves to blocking. Brendon Julian, Brad Hogg, now bowling his Chinaman, and Tom Moody were bowling really well for us. We were positive, knowing that just one mistake would do it. Gilly was effervescent, saying, 'Just one ball, keep going boys, the pressure's on them.'

With an hour to go, we broke through. BJ got one through May, who had scored 0 off 52 balls in more than an hour. Then, minutes later, Hoggy had Siddons caught close in. He had scored 4 runs off 134 balls in a tick under three hours – considering his condition, an amazing feat of application.

But we were through, with nearly an hour to bowl at Peter McIntyre and Shane George, both ordinary batsmen. We thought we had it in the bag.

Straight away, McIntyre pushed forward at Hoggy and punched the ball straight off his glove. Robbie Baker took the catch, diving halfway down the pitch, and we were celebrating. We'd won! Then we looked around. The batsmen weren't moving. The umpire, Darrell Hair, was shaking his head.

We were upset, but still had forty minutes to go. So then there were thirty-five minutes, and then thirty, and then twenty-five to go. We were still very positive, thinking, *Surely we'll get another chance.*

But as the minutes ticked away, the momentum changed. McIntyre and George were gaining confidence from every ball they survived. The scoreboard was showing how many balls to go. South Australians were pouring into the ground from the city. They went nuts after every ball. Then it came to the last over. Six, five, four, three, two, one ... And we couldn't get them. We walked off pretty dejected while the South Australians were celebrating like crazy. It was their first win for a long time.

I felt sorry for the boys, but, being young, thought, *There's always next year, we'll win it.* I said to one of the others, 'We'll get it next year, don't worry.' It would have been fantastic to have won, but at the start of my career, to have had the breakthrough season I'd had, I was just happy to be part of it.

EIGHT

After my year off at the Academy, I was back into my uni course at Curtin, trying to chip away at my subjects. It helped that they tolerated me doing a couple of units per semester and handing in assignments late. A lady who worked for the dean of education offered to type up my assignments for me because she was a cricket fan, but I couldn't accept her generous invitation.

In May I celebrated my twenty-first birthday by organising a big party for family, and cricket and school friends at Wanneroo District Cricket Club. It was a great night, though I had to do the traditional yard glass. Not being a very good drinker, I couldn't get it down in one go in front of everyone. Instead, embarrassingly, I took forty-five minutes, carrying it around and sipping on it. A lot of other people were having a go, and even some of the mums were showing me up.

Among my uni courses was one called Personal Health for Teachers, which seemed an easy way of picking up some credit points. Each week, a student had to give a tutorial on a topic assigned to them. In my first week, this attractive first-year girl was giving the tutorial, and her topic was premenstrual tension. She was very good-looking, but was making some kind of statement by wearing extremely ugly, baggy denim overalls.

Listening to her talk, I was shifting in my seat. A mature-age student and I were the only guys in the class, and I have to confess I knew absolutely nothing about PMT. Even though I had two sisters, they were much younger than me and I hadn't spent much time with girls.

Finally, she opened the floor to questions. I was keeping my mouth shut. She decided she wanted to ask the guys in the room a few questions. The mature-age guy spoke up about this and that, and then everyone looked at me.

'Er, yeah, I find it helps to steer clear, and, yeah, er, just give them some space ...'

It was transparent that I didn't have the slightest idea what I was talking about.

After the class, downstairs at the education library, I saw her and said, 'That was an interesting talk, I didn't know much about that stuff.'

She looked straight at me and said, 'Just another uneducated male, are you?'

Set back on my heels, I thought, *Yeah, obviously I am.*

I was pretty attracted to Amy from the start, even with the overalls. I was quite inexperienced with girls. My big crush in primary school had been my year three teacher, Miss Santorelli. Through high school, I'd had a couple of girlfriends and liked the idea, but because I was so undeveloped, the girls I really liked were going out with guys much older than me. The ones I'd have wanted to ask out would never take me seriously and I never got close. I never gave the girls I did go out with the time they deserved, because cricket and schoolwork were my priorities.

But I was pretty determined to get to know Amy. A bloke I was studying with, another mature-age student, was doing some work for the university. Too scared to ask Amy for her phone number, I asked him to get onto the uni database for me.

It was pretty much my first serious date. I booked a restaurant, dressed up in a beautiful white linen shirt and drove to her house at the other end of Perth, in the south, with flowers and chocolates. I guess I've never been accused, over anything in life, of not trying hard enough.

I knocked on the door. Amy had told me that she had an identical twin sister, Kate. Their whole lives, people were mixing them up with each other, always asking, 'Are you Amy or Kate?' It drove them crazy. So I was standing there, and the girl who opened the door was wearing tracksuit pants, clearly not going out.

'Hi,' I said. 'So you must be the other one?'

That's possibly the worst thing in the world to say to an identical twin, and I'd just said it. Kate walked off and said to Amy, 'Not a very good start.'

As we drove to the restaurant, Amy said, 'So what's your last name?'

I was nervous about this. I knew Amy wouldn't follow state cricket, but in my mind, it might look like big-noting if I said, 'I'm Mike Hussey.' Like, *Haven't you heard of me?* I didn't know if she'd heard of me or not. And did it look even more big-headed if I expected her to know my name? I'd just got myself into a complete twist over it, second-guessing every option in the hope of making a good impression, and ended up with the worst of all outcomes.

'I don't want to tell you.'

Oh, gee. I could sense Amy starting to panic. *Who's this strange guy driving me off without telling me his name?* She probably wanted me to turn around and take her home. I was trying to dig my way out of my mess, but only made it worse. Eventually she made me tell her. She hadn't heard of me, which was a relief. I don't know what I was on about.

We went to an Italian restaurant, and I ordered my favourite, spaghetti marinara. I ended up with red spots from the tomato sauce all over my beautiful white shirt, but all in all the date went well. We had a lot to talk about; it helped me relax that she had some interest in cricket, at least she didn't hate it, but she didn't want to talk about the game.

The more I got to know Amy, the more I respected who she was and where she came from, and the more we found we had in common. Her grandmother, who had been married to an English military man, had flown to Perth from the UK on the 10-pound scheme. Amy's dad was a knockabout guy, an accountant who played footy locally. He and Amy's mother got married and had children very young: four daughters, including the twins, within three years. Amy's parents worked incredibly hard so they could send the four girls to private schools and the girls grew up with great personalities and strong values.

Amy was three years younger than me, but I was taking so long to do my course, we ended up graduating with our Bachelor of Education degrees on the same day. Amy did it in four years, while I did it in eight. She went straight into a Catholic primary school in Middle Swan, and absolutely loved it. It was quite a tough school, a challenge for her, but she was a brilliant teacher and made good friends among her colleagues. It suited me that she was working hard while I was also occupied. From the start, because my cricket commitments were heavy and getting more so, our time together was limited, but because we didn't have a lot of it we made the most of what we had.

A couple of months after that first date, I was into a new season, facing Curtly Ambrose and Courtney Walsh on the WACA. I was going along fine, thinking they weren't as fast or hostile as their reputations, and then Walsh let one fly out of nowhere. It was short, and it hit me in the glove before I had time to move. I looked at him with fear in my eyes. He gave me a little nod to say, *I know you think you can handle me, young fella, but we're a lot quicker than this.* From that one ball, I realised how much more they had than they were letting on.

I made my one-day state debut against the West Indians, and played the whole domestic limited-overs season, a surprise considering the type of player I was. I opened the batting, and there was a lot of talk, after the Sri Lankans won the World Cup a few months earlier, about how the top order had to really go after the bowling in the first 15 overs while only two fielders were allowed outside the restrictive circle. I put a lot of pressure on myself to up the ante, and didn't really do enough to warrant being chosen.

In my first domestic one-day game, I had my first brush with Shane Warne. I remember the day clearly. We had dismissed them for 143, but Warnie was at the peak of his powers and took the ball when it was only a couple of overs old to try to change the course of the match. Our senior guys had been saying, 'He doesn't like batsmen using their feet to come down the wicket. He also doesn't like left-handers sweeping him and putting the pressure on him.' Later that day, I recall Gilly hitting him way over midwicket, using a strong wind blowing in that direction.

One of the first balls he bowled to me just floated up juicily out of his hand. Full of positive attitude, I thought, *Yep, that's going over mid-wicket.* I skipped down the track to get it on the full. But as I got close, it seemed to want to avoid me. I could hear it whirring in the air, buzzing like a blowfly with the amount of revs he'd put on it. The nearer I got, the faster it dipped down. Suddenly, after thinking I was going to tonk it on the full, it pitched before I could get to it and spun through the gate. Darren Berry stumped me gleefully. Warnie ran past me.

'Ha, ha, see ya, idiot.'

It was an eye-opener, that's for sure. He did me all ends up. I had no chance whatsoever.

We beat them that day, and generally had a good record against them, but the Victorians were unpleasant to play against. Teams like New South Wales and Queensland could be arrogant on the field, but nothing was personal and they left it all out there. The Victorians, in my view, sometimes went a bit too far, saying things below the belt. They crossed a line – what they said went beyond the tactic of intimidating a batsman. They were a team I didn't feel comfortable socialising with off the field. Dean Jones gave me a monumental spray in one of my first games, which I thought was unjustified given I was barely out of short pants, and Warnie and Darren Berry said some very hurtful things to Gilly, just because he'd been picked in the Australian one-day team ahead of Berry and was, that day, belting Warnie over his head.

Sledging was a big part of the Australian first-class game, and I had to learn to cope with it, but it came in all flavours. The Victorians' abuse had a mean, personal edge. With New South Wales, it varied from the casual contempt of a Mark Waugh to the humorous ranting of Neil Maxwell to the downright bizarreness of what came out of Greg Matthews's mouth. The South Australians had the confidence that came from being a very good team with Lehmann, Siddons, Nielson and Blewett all working well together, while James Brayshaw managed to lighten things up by being quick-witted and belittling you in quite a comical way. The Tasmanians didn't sledge so much. It didn't seem to be in the character of guys like Jamie Cox, Dene Hills and Michael Di Venuto to be aggressively nasty. Mark Ridgway was just funny more than intimidating, and little Mark Atkinson, behind the stumps, would chirp away, but you couldn't be scared of a four-foot-two wicketkeeper.

The Queenslanders, on the other hand ... Ah, the Queenslanders I had a lot of trouble with.

That season, we played in both the Shield and the one-day final against Queensland. Because New South Wales players monopolised so many positions in the Australian team, the Shield teams of the other states were very powerful. We had the same squad as the previous season, and finished on top of the Shield table with a record number of points. Queensland had batsmen such as Stuart Law, Matthew Hayden, Martin Love, Andrew Symonds and Jimmy Maher, and their bowlers included Michael Kasprowicz, Adam Dale, Andy Bichel and Scott Muller – all internationals at some stage.

In the final of the Mercantile Mutual Cup, I batted for 15 balls before being out for a duck. Brendan Creevey bowled the first over. There were about fourteen wides in that over, and one good ball, which I managed to get an edge to. My form was tapering off, as usual in the late part of the season, and to counter it I was training even harder, exhausting myself. I was hanging on by a thread.

We won the one-day cup, but in the Shield final, which we hosted, Ryan Campbell and I couldn't make any runs at the top of the order and put our team under pressure from the start. Adam Dale got me both innings. He terrorised the West Australian team for a number of years. He didn't bowl a loose ball. On the WACA, the ball just wouldn't go straight. He could make it do anything, in the air and off the pitch.

And behind my back, the Queenslanders were experts at making me feel I shouldn't be on the same cricket field as them. Matthew Hayden, at gully for my first game against them, really let me have it and I was taken aback by his hostility. I thought, *Gee, this guy really doesn't like me.* Then Stuie Law and Jimmy Maher chimed in, and Wade Seccombe, one of the nicest guys around, started sledging me too. Adam Dale was so skilful, every ball made me feel worthless. It was so hard to lay bat on ball, I got desperate trying to show them I could play.

Most annoying of all was Andrew Symonds out at point. Simmo had a lot to say. He just folded his arms and stood there ridiculing me. When I'd let balls go, he started counting my dot balls. 'Twenty-five ... Twenty-six ... Come on boys, let's go for thirty dot balls!'

So I'd get impatient and nick it to slips, and they'd all come in laughing their heads off. I hated playing those guys! Then when they batted, they were so big and strong, they could score at will, like batting was easy. They were the best team in the competition and completely outplayed us in that Shield final.

The infuriating thing was, they were great blokes off the field. They'd come in for a beer and were all such nice blokes. Simmo, of course, was a great mate of mine, and had a good laugh about getting under my skin. I sort of grinned and bore it. On the field they made you feel like they hated you, that you were a piece of crud. Off it, you couldn't imagine a friendlier bunch. I guess that was all part of the education of a first-class cricketer. But after losing our second final in a row, I was feeling a bit dirtier than the previous year in Adelaide. We all were. It was time to finish the job off.

NINE

In 1997, my horizons were still limited to my home state. I had performed quite well for WA and wondered if the national selectors had noticed me. Internally, I wasn't sure if I could play at the next level and was desperate to be part of a winning Sheffield Shield team. The Australian Test side had Mark Taylor and Michael Slater opening the batting, with players like Hayden, Langer, Blewett and Matthew Elliott either in the team or able to step up if an opening position fell vacant. National selection was an unlikely dream.

Intermediate goals were satisfying me. I scored three centuries for Western Australia that season, helping us top the table and make another final. We enjoyed the immense pleasure of beating Queensland in Brisbane, and would host Tasmania in the decider. Also, during that season I batted against South Africa at the WACA, the best bowlers I'd faced. They put their best team on the park and played hard. I performed all right, though I was petrified of Allan Donald. He hit Gilly before he had the chance to move, smashing his helmet and cutting his face. I found Shaun Pollock just as quick downbreeze. It was very hard work, and I felt like I batted quite well, though I took a long time to score my runs.

I was building my mental strength, helping my resilience against sledging and my ability to play long innings, with the help of the psychologist at the WACA, Sandy Gordon. He taught us about goal setting, concentration routines, visualisation and other mental skills. I wrote down lists and kept training diaries and gobbled it up. Sandy showed me how to switch off between balls, and how to employ a routine. After each ball, I would switch off until the bowler was at the top of his mark. Then my sequence of thoughts was: check my stance, relax my arms, clear the doubts, then focus on the ball. Some days, when it was working, I would go into this trance-like routine and suddenly I would have faced 150 balls. It became my trusted routine throughout my career, through thick and thin, the mental bedrock of my batting.

In the Shield final, the Tasmanians were understandably desperate to win for the first time. David Boon was the captain. When he won the toss, he said, 'We're gunna bat first.' He said it so adamantly, I thought, *Gee, he means business.*

But there was a bit of moisture in the pitch and it was overcast and rainy, and we bowled them out for 285. Luckily the batting conditions improved for our turn. The Tassies had a good attack, with Colin Miller enjoying a record summer with his seam and spin, taking 70 wickets. I made 44, Ryan Campbell and Tom Moody hit hundreds, but when the game was really in the balance, Brendon Julian came to the crease and put the thing beyond doubt. I'd never seen anything like it. He usually teased us with the bat, looking so good and throwing his wicket away, but this day, it all clicked for him. A decent crowd was in, making a lot of noise, and a party atmosphere developed as BJ smashed them with 124 off 105 balls. The pitch flattened out, and with a lead of nearly 300 runs we were never going to lose from there. Michael Di Venuto scored a remarkable 189, belting the ball so hard it was like he had three bats stuck together. But in the end, we only needed to chase 80-odd to win. I was with Tom Moody when he hit the winning runs. It was so exciting to finally get our hands on that Sheffield Shield. Gilly organised cigars and we had a great celebration. It had been six years since Western Australia had won the Shield. Some of the past players came in to share the moment, and I asked Graeme Wood, one of the Test batsmen I used to imitate in the back yard, 'How many Shields did you win?'

He said, 'Eight or nine.' He didn't know exactly! I couldn't believe he'd won so many Sheffield Shields he'd lost count. That blew me away, knowing how hard we'd worked to win just one.

Unfortunately, Sheffield Shields were about to become a rarity in the west. The next season, 1998–99, would be a last hurrah. We were up and down through the summer and our last match was at the MCG. We needed to draw to qualify for the final, which would be in Brisbane, and Victoria needed an outright win. So it was a full-on game, with Darren Berry running the show from behind the stumps. There was nothing between the teams after the first innings, and on the last day, Victoria declared, leaving themselves 100 overs to bowl us out and make the final. We just needed to survive the day.

By lunchtime we were in enormous trouble. Damien Fleming, David Saker and Paul Reiffel had ripped out me, Ryan Campbell, Damien Martyn, Tom Moody and Adam Gilchrist. Simon Katich and Robbie Baker were in, two young players against the snarling Victorians on their home patch. Kato and Bakes were copping a fair bit of stick and the Victorians were appealing for everything, putting pressure on the umpires. But Simon and Rob lasted together for nearly four hours, until well after tea, and we thought we could pull it off. But then they both got out, and it was down to BJ and the tail. In the last over, we looked safe. David Saker needed a hat-trick off the last three balls. On the first of those balls, he had our fast bowler Mark Atkinson caught behind. Jo Angel came out.

The Victorians knew he'd expect a yorker, so they got into a huddle and devised a plan. If Saker bowled a yorker, Jo would be ready for it and would jam down on it. So they decided Saker would run right through the crease, bowl a deliberate no-ball, pitch it short and aim at Joey's head. They figured that would shake him up and stop him from playing forward. Then, on the next legitimate ball, Saker would go for the yorker.

So Saker ran in, bowled a big no-ball, and Jo ducked the bouncer.

Then it all went wrong for them. Darryl Harper, the umpire, didn't call the no-ball. To this day, I am not sure if he missed it or not. The Victorians were in a state of disbelief.

But we were on our way to Brisbane for the final. You should have heard the yelling coming out of our viewing area. We were so excited, we probably went a little over the top in letting the Vics know about it.

We went up to Brisbane, and our bowlers did a super job, delivering us an innings win. Kato made a century while BJ, who was inspired in every final, delivered with bat and ball. He always seemed laconic and casual, but in those big matches he invariably put in a huge performance. A great athlete, he did everything easily, whether it was throwing or kicking a football or all the cricket skills. It made you feel taller yourself when you had big guys like him and Tom Moody taking the lead in the finals. Gilly, Marto and JL were on the cusp of long careers with the Test team, while Tom, BJ and Joey Angel played a couple more seasons. When they retired, a team that had been settled for about five years was broken up. Unfortunately, to this day Western Australia haven't won another Sheffield Shield.

For me, yet again my season was tailing off. I scored 17 and 9 in that match in Melbourne, and only 4 in the final. I'd made a big hundred against Tasmania only three matches earlier, but a question was bubbling up in my mind about the type of player I was. Mark Taylor retired from Test cricket at the end of that season, and his place was taken by Matthew Elliott, the player of the year in Sheffield Shield. Michael Slater was hitting barnstorming Test centuries, and Elliott was a free-flowing, classy left-hander. Not only did I think he was better than me, but Justin Langer and Matthew Hayden were also my superiors, and they couldn't even get in. Now that Tubby had retired, it seemed that the next generation of Test players were more aggressive, looking at dominating the bowling and scoring more freely. JL was in the process of reinventing himself from a defensive kind of opener into a bit of a dasher at number three. He'd clearly seen that that was the way back into the Test team. If I wanted to stand a chance, did I have to do the same?

Going to Britain for the first time in 1998 was a tremendous experience, but it didn't exactly clarify matters for me. I'd spent a long winter in the UK – another reason for my tiredness at the end of the 1998–99 domestic season.

It started when I decided I'd like to play league cricket in England. Just about every leading Australian player did it at some stage in his life, and for me the time was right. I left my run too late to find a club, but there was still an option to play in Scotland. It wasn't what I'd planned, but I thought I'd do it anyway.

My club was Ferguslie, near the town of Paisley outside of Glasgow. I had a one-bedroom flat within walking distance of the ground, and the club looked after me really well, giving me a Rover Metro (albeit with a leaking so-called 'sunroof') and not asking too much of me, just to do some occasional school clinics, go to training, and play on weekends. The rest of my time was my own.

What they couldn't organise was the weather. It rained a lot and we missed half our matches. My teammates did their best to lead me astray, and we went out as a group for drinks at the cricket club or in Paisley or Glasgow. Fortunately Amy came over for her first overseas trip. As she was only nineteen years old, it was a huge leap of faith for her to come to Scotland. We went on day trips all over the country and indulged my love of castles, and had a great spell consolidating our relationship and confirming that we were in love.

When Ferguslie got onto the field, I struggled with the gluggy wickets and the expectation of scoring runs as the resident overseas professional, and didn't do too well. By August, an Australia A team was coming over, coached by Allan Border, and I would be in it. The funny part was, one of the early games would be a one-dayer against Scotland in Glasgow. The pitch, at the Hamilton Road ground, was much better than the seaming decks I'd been struggling on for Ferguslie, and I managed to score 136 not out. A few of my clubmates were there, yelling good-humoured abuse at me.

'You've never done this for Ferguslie!'

It was all very embarrassing.

We had a fantastic team. With people like Hayden, Symonds, Julian, Miller, Gillespie and Martyn on board, we were going to have a successful time on and off the field. A few of the games were rained out, so we needed to make our own fun. Ironically, as soon as we got to Dublin, the sun broke out brilliantly but the ground we were playing on had the pitch set up facing east-west, and the umpire couldn't see. We didn't play the second half of the day because there was too much sun. That could only happen in Ireland. My main recollection of the match is not so much the hundred I scored as the fact that Steve Waugh, who was guesting for Ireland, decided to bowl six bouncers in an over to Ryan Campbell, and Cambo hit him for four fours. I didn't know if Steve was doing it because he didn't like him, or had a plan. It turned out not to be the right place to bowl.

I'd had a lot of laughs with Ferguslie, and my year ended on a suitably comical note. I told them I wouldn't be coming back, and they said they really wanted a fast bowler. On my recommendation they signed up Mark Atkinson, the big-bowling all-rounder from WA.

At the start of the next season, a Ferguslie club official turned up to meet Mark Atkinson at Glasgow airport. Out strolled not the towering fast bowler they were expecting, but the four-foot-two Tasmanian wicketkeeper, with all his cricket gear. They'd got the wrong Mark Atkinson! He ended up staying for the year, played well, scored more runs than I had, and even did a fair bit of bowling.

It had been very encouraging for me to get picked in the Australia A team, but I still thought I was one of the last names chosen. I was behind a long list of players, to whom I could now add Di Venuto and Hills. What did I need to do to jump the queue? I approached Allan Border, who of course was my childhood idol and the inspiration for me to bat left-handed – not that I told him any of that. He was a great guy to talk to about cricket, and very unassuming for such a great of the game, but he sowed the seed for a really embarrassing moment.

We were training in Edinburgh. The bowlers were resting after ten or fifteen balls and the batsmen were batting for short sessions, to be fresh for the match the following day. AB, being very old school, looked on disapprovingly.

'What are you guys doing? How do you expect to bowl fifteen overs tomorrow when you only bowl fifteen balls in the nets? And you batsmen, how do you expect to bat all day when you're only batting for ten or fifteen minutes? You have to learn to bat all day.'

I began to think about this. When I went back to Australia, during the early part of the season my club team had a bye, which I wasn't happy about of course. I got hold of Ian Kevan and said, 'Right, Allan Border told me you've got to learn how to bat six hours. I want to bat all day.'

We started at eleven o'clock, doing drills and bowling machine work. We stopped at one o'clock for a forty-minute lunch break.

Then I batted from 1.40pm to 3.40pm, more drills and throws and the machine. Then we had a tea break, and finally I batted for another two hours until the end of the day.

I was absolutely exhausted. Against a bowling machine you don't have time between balls – it's ball after ball after ball. But those were Allan Border's words, and I took him literally. It all started from that training session in Scotland.

Over the next couple of years, though, I ran out of patience, and suffered my first big career crisis.

TEN

The first cracks showed in one-day cricket. I was growing increasingly frustrated with my inability to bat like Sanath Jayasuriya or Adam Gilchrist at the top of the order. The team probably wanted an opener in the Geoff Marsh mould, who could bat through the 50 overs and be a steady pillar around whom the strokeplayers built a total. But in my view, that era had passed, and if I wanted to get ahead in the game I had to be more attacking. Of course, the harder I tried, the worse I went.

The selectors finally dropped me in November 1999 for a one-day match in Brisbane. But I soon got a lucky reprieve. The next one-dayer followed a Shield match in Melbourne, in which I scored a stodgy half-century. Simon Katich was sick and Damien Martyn hurt his back, so I was called in as a late replacement, not as an opener, but slotted into the middle order at number five.

As it turned out, we lost early wickets and I was batting in the 14th over. Considering myself lucky to get a game, I played more freely. It helped that I had as my partner Brad Hogg, with whom I'd shared many good partnerships. Sure enough, I managed to get a hundred, bringing up the milestone on the last ball of our innings. We got a reasonable score and won the match. Nobody had thought of me as a middle-order batsman, playing that Michael Bevan role of hustling between wickets, working the ball, and finishing the innings off. (Incidentally, I also captured three wickets in that match, which I'm very proud of. I'd say I was bowling express pace, but most others would call it slow-medium.)

My one-day game was transformed by that innings, which set me on the path that would culminate with national selection. But that was still six years away; and at any rate, changing roles within the one-day team didn't solve my bigger quandary, which was how to propel myself up the list of openers-in-waiting in five-day cricket.

In 2000–01, I committed myself to changing my game. I tried to play more shots and score more freely. I trained harder than ever off the field, doing a lot of fitness and strength work, but no matter how much I did I pushed myself to do more. I thought that if all else failed, I could *will* myself to succeed.

All it did was place undue pressure on me, and the work, combined with the impatience to score runs more freely, had a detrimental effect on my game. I had by far my worst season with Western Australia, scoring only one century, which came in the last game, and barely averaging 30. Matty Hayden had stepped up into the Australian team – after being in and out of it for seven years – and this time he was there for good, having transformed himself into a standover man, bullying bowlers out of the game.

Unwittingly, though, he did me a favour that would ultimately turn me around.

The previous season, Hayden had been the overseas player for Northamptonshire in the English county championship. Now that he was playing regularly for Australia, Northants needed a replacement. Their coach, Bob Carter, was in Adelaide for the Test match in 2001–02, and my name was put forward by Haydos and also Justin Langer.

A short time later, I was sitting at home and out of the blue got a phone call from Dean Jones. I didn't know Deano personally. The only words he'd ever spoken to me were a huge spray in a Shield match.

'I've heard you want to go and play county cricket,' he said. 'Is it true?'

I said, 'Yeah, I'd love to.'

Deano said he would arrange for a player agent called David Manasseh to phone me that night. Twenty minutes later, David called and said he'd arrange everything for me. 'What do you want?' he said.

I said, 'I'll come for free! I just want to play.'

'No, no. You've got to ask for more than that.'

Hesitantly, I thought for a bit and said, 'Well, I wouldn't mind somewhere I can comfortably stay with my girlfriend.'

David wasn't satisfied with that. He said he'd get me a retainer, two cars, business-class tickets and a whole lot more.

I squeaked, 'Are you serious? Don't jeopardise it by asking for too much!'

'Don't worry, I deal with the counties all the time, it's fine.'

I put down the phone and thought I'd just stuffed up my chance of playing county cricket. But to his credit David was brilliant, brokering the deal, and getting us everything we needed.

When I got to Northampton, I didn't know a soul. The town was in transition from its heritage as an industrial, textiles and bootmaking centre – Doc Martens started there – to a commuter-belt satellite of London. Some factories were still going, but there were a lot of city people living in the area. Their most successful sport was rugby, in which Northampton had won European Cups. The Cobblers, the soccer team, were lower league. And the cricket club had been through a good previous decade, Curtly Ambrose and Anil Kumble having played there, and had earned respect among the bigger counties.

About the club, pretty much all I knew was that Matty Hayden had done extremely well the previous year, which they wasted no time telling me about. I was ushered into a meet-and-greet with the coach, players and officials. It seemed as though everyone was saying, 'Oh, Matthew Hayden this, Matthew Hayden that, you've got big shoes to fill.' I thought, *Oh no*.

Sure enough, I struggled with that expectation and pressure early in the season. I thought I had to take responsibility for scoring all the runs, and battled on the English pitches. I wasn't the first Australian to battle on springtime pitches in England, but, coming on top of my poor season at home and memories of how badly I'd done for Ferguslie, I was being circled by the demons. In my first three first-class innings, I scored 18, 21 and 3. I made 5 in the first one-day match, and after trudging off, out for 4, in another one-dayer at Bristol in early May, I plonked myself down next to Bob.

'Mate, I'm really sorry. You must think I'm the worst overseas player ever. I'm trying my best, I don't know what's wrong, but it's just not happening.'

Bob said, 'Huss. The next game is against Warwickshire. I just want you to go out there and look to hit the ball. Don't worry about getting out. Just relax and play your game. Forget the consequences.'

I sat there grumpily. Meanwhile Bob went off and found Amy in the stands. It was freezing cold, and he got her a beanie and some gloves and sat with her for a while. Bob was interested in making sure your life was settled off the field. We were having problems with our accommodation but hadn't said anything because we were so grateful to be there. When Bob asked her if she was okay, Amy burst into tears and poured it all out.

'We haven't got any cutlery, our vacuum doesn't work, the house is falling down.' And there was a whole lot more.

Bob went and got it all sorted out. I don't know if it was that or the talk he'd given me, but he had brought about a turning point in my county career. In the next one-day match I made 93, and my next six county scores in the following fortnight were 75, 67, 22, 17, 70 and 82. I felt I'd proven to Bob and my teammates that I wasn't a dud. We were more comfortable at home, and I relaxed and started to amass some good scores.

It wasn't until the end of June that I scored my first first-class hundred for Northants, but it just clicked from there. We were playing in the First Division, which was quite a coup for Northants, as they weren't one of the powerhouse counties such as the London clubs, Middlesex and Surrey, or those from the north like Nottinghamshire, Lancashire and Yorkshire. Nor did we have any Test players. But we played well as a team, and had some great personalities.

Graeme Swann, who was still some years from his Test debut, kept everyone amused and was one of those cricketers who had so much talent he didn't have to try very hard or listen to anyone else. He frustrated me at times because I thought he could be anything. His brother Alec was also very funny, a dour opening batsman who hated fielding; in fact Alec hated everything except batting. 'The only perfect training session for me,' he drawled, 'is where I have my pads on for three hours.' So I organised a training session just like that, and he was happy. He entertained the rest of us with the abuse he heaped onto himself whenever he got out. Honestly, his self-hating tirades were so funny, I'd sneak back into the dressing room to listen to them.

It was in England that some people started calling me 'Mr Cricket'. I had a reputation as someone who was always hitting balls in the nets or developing a new shot, or doing weights and fitness work or new mental skills. Anything I could do to get better, I was all over it. I trained three, four, or five times a day all up. People probably thought I was trying to do too much. Alec Swann, among others, claimed credit for starting the nickname, but as far as I know, the player who coined it was Andrew Flintoff, the Lancashire and England all-rounder. As they say, success (and a successful nickname) has a thousand parents!

Mal Loye was my opening partner, and a real mainstay of Northants cricket. He had played for North Perth, so we had that link. He ate, breathed and slept batting, and continually tinkered with his technique. He didn't play more than a handful of one-day internationals for England, but gee he was talented. One day we were playing Lancashire, who had Muttiah Muralitharan as their overseas professional, on a turning Northampton pitch. Ten minutes before lunch, Mal and I agreed, 'Let's just survive Murali till lunch.'

I walked up to the non-striker's end, hoping Mal would block Murali out so I wouldn't have to face him. Next ball, Mal came steaming halfway down the pitch and smashed the ball into the members' pavilion. *Okay*, I thought, *I guess that kept Murali out.* Then Mal he hit three more sixes – he absolutely destroyed the greatest off-spinner in the history of cricket when we were trying to survive until lunch.

We had a good group of solid English pros, including the all-rounder Tony Penberthy, a great competitor who absolutely loved his cricket, Darren Cousins, who whinged a bit but then forgot it all and gave his heart and soul to the team once he crossed the white line, and Jason Brown, a beautiful off-spinner who was actually our number-one choice ahead of Swanny. In the background was a young Indian slow left-armer called Monty Panesar. Monty just wanted to bowl, all day, every day. That suited me fine, because I wanted to bat all day, every day. The boys gave us stick, calling us 'the perfect couple'. After training, Monty and I would go off to do one-on-one sessions for a couple of hours. Nick Cook, the assistant coach, often had to come over to tear Monty out of the nets, to stop him wearing himself out by bowling fifty overs to me all afternoon. As far as I was concerned, Monty was the best cricket playmate I'd had since my brother, and unlike Dave,

Monty wouldn't chase me around the yard trying to belt me if I didn't give him a bat.

The team was led by David Ripley, the wicketkeeper, a conservative guy in his last season. I really liked Rips. We joked a bit about his very serious team talks about keeping up over-rates so as to avoid fines, but he had an old-school mentality and really cared for the players and the club.

I heard people voicing that long-held Australian belief that playing professional, low-intensity cricket dulled your game. But Matty Hayden and other Australians had been improved by it, and I had a healthy respect for English players. The competition was sound and strong. I loved the idea that you could play six days a week in different conditions, first-class and one-day cricket, against varying opposition, travelling from match to match with a great bunch of blokes. I only saw positives. I loved Bob Carter and he was very generous with the time he gave me. My game was getting better. So my experiences were only positive.

Because the perception was that county cricket was inferior, you had to score triple-hundreds to attract attention from Australia. In 2001, Steve Waugh was leading the Test team on a victorious Ashes tour, so perhaps people were showing a bit more interest than usual in the county scene. Against Essex in late July, it all came together for me and I made 329 not out. My appetite for runs by then was insatiable. Bizarrely, during my net session in the morning before the match I got out at least eight times, which didn't fill me with much confidence. It's amazing how the game works sometimes. Our home pitch was good, and if you were switched on and hungry, you could fill your boots. When I got in, I tried to go as big as I possibly could. I didn't throw it away. The grounds were getting so hard underfoot that my usual fear of being stranded at the wicket, unable to get the ball through the infield, went away. Even if I blocked it, if it went into a gap it ran off for four.

A couple of days later, Amy and I were driving to a game and my phone rang. It was Steve Waugh, calling to congratulate me on the 300. I nearly drove off the motorway. I pulled over and chatted to him for five minutes. He said, 'Keep trying to improve yourself, you're doing a good job.' When I hung up, Amy asked who it was. She couldn't believe it when I told her it was the Australian captain. To me, not that I was playing county cricket for Australian eyes, it was an added benefit to feel that someone of Steve's stature was taking note.

ELEVEN

After such a strong season with Northants, I couldn't really kick on when I came home. In another moderate summer for me and the Warriors, I only made one century and averaged 35. Late in the season, I was caught up in a minor controversy over a promotional gimmick in the domestic one-day cup. The sponsors set up 'targets' around the ground, and you could win a jackpot if you hit them. Sure enough, I got a ball in my leg-side hitting zone and managed to strike the sign.

The controversy arose over what to do with the money. There were no set protocols, so I called the Australian Cricketers' Association to ask what other players had done in the same situation. Steve Waugh and Shane Lee, playing for New South Wales, had hit the sign, and had taken a lion's share of the money before splitting the rest with their teammates. I decided to follow their lead. Some of my teammates complained that I hadn't split the whole lot evenly. When their opinions became public, it caused me some angst, and in hindsight I wish I had done an even split with the whole team and got it over with.

I did well enough in my new middle-order role in the one-day team to get a couple of games with Australia A, but I only had to look around the dressing room to see the calibre of players who couldn't crack the Australian team, be it in limited-overs or Test cricket. It was a tough club to get into, and for me it had just grown tougher, with Justin Langer's final ascent to the opener's position, which he would occupy alongside Matthew Hayden for the foreseeable future. The pressure was growing. I was twenty-six now, and just getting the first inklings of that worrying sense that my best years were slipping away.

What do you do in that situation? Get married! I'd been certain I wanted to spend my life with Amy almost from the day we'd met, and we set the date at 6 April 2002, after the Australian season and before I was to leave for another stint at Northampton.

The night before the wedding, we had a rehearsal. Simon Katich was my best man, and Robbie Baker and my brother were the groomsmen. I was ready and excited when the big day came around.

We were married at Christ Church School chapel in Perth, a beautiful setting overlooking the river. As soon as I saw Amy walking down the aisle I began to get emotional and had terrible problems getting my vows out. I couldn't even stammer through my own name without bursting into tears. I'd look at Amy, who was beautiful beyond words, and break down again.

I pulled it together after the ceremony. We had some photos taken and then enjoyed a great night with our friends and family at the South of Perth Yacht Club. Dad, Kato and I made speeches, which we tried to keep short. In our family we didn't show our emotions easily. My breakdown during the wedding had caught my parents by surprise, and Dad speculated about where I'd got that gene. He traced it back to a third-generation auntie!

For our honeymoon, we went to Maui for five or six days. We had a relaxing time, and arrived at Northampton as a newly married couple.

We were shown to our new house, a two-storey place in a different part of town from where we'd lived in 2001. Amy's older sister soon came to visit us, and on her first night, jetlagged, Trudy went downstairs and realised we'd been burgled. She raced upstairs and woke us. The whole house had been cleared out. The windows and doors were held open with knives. They'd filled our cars and taken off with them too. They'd gone through our wedding photos and scattered them all over the table, which was somehow the creepiest part of it all. Amy was so scared to be left in the house alone, she said she wanted to go home to Australia.

Eventually we moved back to where we'd been the previous year, inside a golf complex. We felt safer and more comfortable there, and it turned into another enjoyable year for us off the field.

At the cricket club, things were more complicated. Although I'd scored some runs, the team had finished in the bottom three in the first division and were now straight back down to division two. David Ripley retired, and I was put in as replacement captain. I didn't think I was ready for it, having been at the club for only one year and not having had much captaincy experience. But Bob was adamant that I take the leadership to help raise standards.

We had a poor year. My captaincy inexperience told, as I wanted to be mates with the guys more than taking a disciplinarian's role. My on-field tactics often didn't work, and rather than stick with them I wanted to listen to everyone and take in all ideas. In addition, we had a major off-field incident that divided the team, where one of my teammates had an affair with another's fiancee. When it came to light, as these things inevitably do, it had a huge effect on the team. We would be playing a game somewhere, the team would meet for a drink before dinner, and one or two players would be at one end of the bar while everyone else was at the other end. I tried to pull everyone together, and one of the boys said, 'What if it was Amy?' Fair point.

We knew what we had to do. The player who was doing the wrong thing, who was a key batsman for the team, was moved to the second XI and the following year had to move to another club. The 2002 year, when they were both still there, was a challenging season and I learned a lot about leadership, both on and off the field.

Northants finished seventh in the nine-team First Division. At that time the bottom three teams in the First Division were relegated to the Second Division and the top three in the Second Division were promoted. So we were heading back down after just one season in the top flight. A difference between divisions one and two in county cricket was the quality of the pitches. In the First Division, where the aim is to stay up, clubs prepare good pitches to get their batting bonus points and not lose matches. A good draw can keep you above water. If you lose games, on bad pitches, you're staring at relegation. In the Second Division, on the other hand, it's about winning games. We had spinners so we'd prepare fairly substandard spinning wickets, to win games and get promoted. But that made it very much harder for batting when you were in the Second Division than in the first. I'd gone well, boosting my average into the 70s with an unbeaten 310 in my last county game of the season, against Gloucestershire in Bristol.

Once I left, for an Australia A tour to South Africa, Matthew Inness, a left-arm fast bowler from Victoria, replaced me and did a good job. I hoped we could pick ourselves up again for the 2003 season, but was knocked about by an episode at the end of 2002.

There were plenty of reasons for our ordinary showing, but the club decided to make a scapegoat of Bob Carter. They knew I had a good relationship with Bob, so, rather than consult with the captain, they talked to some disgruntled players who had an axe to grind with Bob. I was completely blindsided. When management called me to a meeting and said they were sacking Bob, I was irate. I tried to get them to change their minds, but had no effect. I was very disappointed with the club, sacking a man who had had so much positive impact on many players, not just me.

Bob and I continued to stay in touch, as we do to this day. He was married to a New Zealander, and he moved there. He is now part of the national coaching set-up. He was sad about his removal from Northants, and saw New Zealand as a fresh start, a good place to bring up his children.

All this stress was not a great preparation for the Australian season. Since 2000, in contrast to my good results in England, my home performances had been slumping. I still thought the national selectors wanted me to be a more aggressive opener, and as a result I performed very inconsistently.

My horizons had changed. Just playing for Western Australia was no longer my dream. I started measuring up against Australian players and candidates. I'd received my first Cricket Australia contract around 2000 and thought the selectors must be thinking of me for the future. As it turned out, I'd lost my contract, got it back, and lost it again. It reflected an inconsistent time of being on the fringe and just off it.

One of the memorable moments of that summer was playing New South Wales at Newcastle. I'd seen Michael Clarke play in a one-day match at Coffs Harbour, where we'd bowled New South Wales out cheaply, but here in Newcastle he was so confident, so positive, charging down to the spinners, I thought he looked a bit cocky – but maybe that was my age and insecurity speaking. I was becoming a senior player, therefore wary of kids coming through. He batted well in the Shield game, looking the part alongside the Waughs and other big guns. We did drop a sitter off him, and some of our senior guys got into him because he was so brash with the bleached hair and the earring, a prime target for our bowlers. But he gave as good as he got.

Within the West Australian team, which was struggling for success, my role was more fluid than I would have liked. When

Justin Langer, the nominal captain, was playing Test cricket, I was opening the batting with Chris Rogers and captaining the side. But when Justin came back after the New Year, not being in the national one-day side, he took over the captaincy and the opening position, they shifted me down to number four, I assumed because they felt I'd shown my adaptability in the one-day format. To me, this was only more confusing, as I saw myself as an opener. My results reflected this state of mind, and I had easily my worst-yet summer. In first-class cricket my scores were 0, 14, 48, 9, 56, 33, 0, 62, 90, 19, 5 not out, and, in a game we lost to New South Wales in Perth, 14 and 12.

We were having a sad beer in the dressing room after that match when Ryan Campbell came in and belted his locker with his bat. He said he'd been dropped. I'd had my phone switched off, and when I switched it on again I saw that I had a voicemail message.

When I listened to it, my heart sank. It was Wayne Hill, one of the selectors, asking me to call him back.

He delivered the bad news: I wasn't going with the boys to Melbourne for the last Shield game of the season. I went home and sat out the back of the house, stunned and quiet and disappointed. I hadn't been dropped from any first-class team before. There were teams I hadn't made, but no, I'd never been left out of a team I was in. I was devastated, of course, and when I look at my scores, it confirms my belief at the time that I still deserved my spot. But I guess it came on the back of average performances in the two previous seasons. They weren't picking me on my Northants form, and nor should they. I still wrestled with the sense of injustice, but when it sank in, I was just sad. Not only was I out of the state team, but my dream of one day playing for Australia was gone.

Everything was eating away at me. One of the things that disappointed me most about being dropped was that I loved going to the MCG to battle Victoria, a team I loved to hate. Throughout my career, I treated every single game with the utmost importance.

There was no such thing as a dead rubber. They're all so precious to me personally. So even though Western Australia were out of the running for the Shield and the selectors might have been looking to blood new players, I felt as wounded as if I had been dropped for a final.

We had a team dinner that night. I really didn't want to go, but you've got to show good character when things aren't going well, and I put on the happiest face I could. It was miserable. Looking back, I don't think I was prepared to handle grief. The worst thing that had happened to me was my nanna passing away when I was a kid. But she had been very old. The truth was that I'd been sheltered. No divorces, no tragedies, no big illnesses or injuries. Dad's bad ankle had stopped him from trialling for the Commonwealth Games – that was about the worst of it. So being dropped from the state team, which I suppose is not a big deal at all in the scheme of things, hit me like a shattering blow because I hadn't been toughened by the scars that bad news can leave. I supposed that I had to look at it this way: only through overcoming it, and fighting my way back, could I become a better cricketer and a better person.

TWELVE

I had to start somewhere, and the national selectors gave me an unexpected opportunity by choosing me, five weeks after I'd been dropped by my state, to play for Australia A in a series against South Africa A. This was confusing – how could I be good enough to play for Australia A but not for WA? – but I seized the chance, and hit an 80 and a 140. For once, I was finishing off a home summer positively.

So I went back to Northampton with mixed feelings, happy that I had scored a few runs against an excellent South Africa A team but still very hurt by being dropped by Western Australia. Kepler Wessels, the former Australian and South African Test opener, had been appointed coach in place of Bob Carter, and by the time I arrived he already had the players a bit scared, with his reputation as a disciplinarian. They were training hard and on their best behaviour, which made it smoother for me as captain.

The previous months' events hadn't turned me off captaincy – quite the opposite. After the domestic ructions, poor results and Bob's sacking in 2002, and then the trauma of being dropped by Western Australia, I had a harder edge. I was, paradoxically, a lot more confident in my judgment. I had enormous respect for his playing record, to have scored thousands of Test runs for two countries with a very odd technique. He'd represented South Africa in two sports – lawn bowls and cricket – and was only just short of representing them in archery as well. Every morning at Northants, he was firing arrows at a target across the oval. He still did boxing and martial arts and looked very fit, which all added to the intimidatory aura.

You couldn't help respecting and even fearing him. At Graeme Swann's first meeting with him, Kepler said, 'I hear you're pretty good at impressions.'

Swanny said, 'Yeah, I am. Do you want me to do one of you?'

'You do one of me,' Kepler said, 'and I'll punch your f---ing head in.' And he walked off.

Swanny would do impressions of Kepler in the changing room, very funny and good ones, but only when Kepler wasn't around.

Initially I was too intimidated to speak my mind but thankfully our assistant coach, the former England spinner Nick Cook, wasn't so easily overawed. He didn't care about telling Kepler what he thought. Kepler was an emotional guy. If we lost a game, he'd be exploding. 'This guy's rubbish, get rid of him and him and him.' He would want eight changes to the team. Then Nick would say, 'Come on Kepler, that's rubbish, we don't need to change the whole team, here's what we should do.' I would generally come in after Nick, saying, 'Yeah, it's only one loss, keep the faith.' Kepler would eventually calm down and come around. Then we would win the next game and everything would be fine again.

Once Kepler calmed down, he was brilliant. He had a great understanding of technique, and a fantastic feel for the mental side of the game. I learnt a lot, good and bad, from him, including better ways to communicate with people. Kepler struggled to communicate his message without that harsh tone. He was very emotional, and his first response to a crisis was to switch on the abuse. Once, we lost a game to Glamorgan after Michael Kasprowicz took some wickets. I was struggling a bit with my game. In the dressing room later, Kepler said to me, 'We need to have a chat.'

I said, 'It's okay, let's give the boys some time to settle down a bit, we've got a session tomorrow, let's analyse the thing and discuss it when everyone's got over this.'

'No,' he said. 'We need to chat.'

He took me into his office and tore strips off me. 'Your batting's a disgrace! How do you expect to score runs batting like this? Your technique is rubbish.'

I was standing there copping this tirade. Eventually I said, 'Yeah, you're right. What do I need to do to sort it out? Let's go and work on it.'

He took a step back and said, 'Oh. Okay.' All the rage had disappeared. He listed a few things we should do about my stance and my positioning, and finally said, 'Let's work on it at training tomorrow.' The storm had blown over.

In my opinion there's a shelf-life for that form of leadership. It lost its punch as the season went on. The players lost their fear because they knew the bark was worse than the bite. As the season went on I gained more confidence, as a player and as a captain and dealing with different people and tough situations.

The thing about Kepler was, he saw batting as a permanent struggle, fighting for every single run, hanging in there, surviving and scrapping. That was the way he portrayed his career, and I could empathise with that. Self-doubt didn't put me in such a siege mentality, but I was coming from a similar place. So there was always something to learn from Kepler. He taught me a lot about the art of wearing bowlers down, and the mental side of the game.

After the burglary, we'd settled down and married life was suiting us well. One of the great things about living in England was that Amy and I could take breaks away. Every year there would be one week to ten-day break, and we always tried to travel somewhere new: Rome one year, probably my favourite place, then Paris and the Champagne district, once to Majorca, and another time to Porto in Portugal, which we visited out of a 'lucky dip' sense of pure adventure. Another time we went to the Isle of Man, where Amy's grandmother had been born. And to cap it off, during that 2003 trip we found out that Amy was pregnant.

Under Kepler, we ended up having the best of my three seasons at Northants. I wasn't batting well until just after the Kepler spray and some minor adjustments to my technique, when I scored 264 against Gloucestershire, which really sent me on my way. I also made my third triple century, a 331 not out against Somerset, and we finished second in the division to win promotion back to the top level. We benefited from having a new South African import, the burly right-armer Andre Nel. Big Nelly was a champion to play with. On the field he carried on a lot, sledging and swearing and screaming, prompting umpires to step in and calm him down, but he put in 100 per cent day in, day out. We relied a lot on our spinners to take wickets but Nelly pounded away at the other end, giving the batsmen nothing, no matter whether he was bowling his first over or his fifty-first. He wasn't your conventional seamer, with big legs, and a bustling action letting go from wide on the crease. What made him really tough was that even when he was wide on the crease he could take the ball away from the right-hander. Then there was his aggression, craving a contest, wanting to get into arguments with the batsmen.

He got pretty wild celebrating in the dressing room, and off the park, I didn't want to know what he was up to. He'd often come to the cricket with bloodshot eyes and smelling a bit funny, but you could never question his effort and performance on the field, and that's all I cared about.

I enjoyed the responsibility of captaincy at Northants, and after the dust had settled over Bob's sacking, I felt that I did a reasonable job. During the season, I was planning to come back for a fourth year in 2004. But as the county season drew to a close I was starting feel as though I needed a break. I was exhausted. I had played cricket all year round for three years straight with the Australian summer followed by county cricket, and the thought of a winter off to have a break from playing and do some pre-season physical work seemed more appealing. So I decided not to re-sign with Northants.

It started with a very unfortunate incident that left me confused and upset.

For the past two Australian summers, I had been taking some supplementary coaching from Neil 'Noddy' Holder. We got on quite well and I liked his methods. We had a great couple of years together, and I thought he was an excellent coach. He wanted to set up a business with Matthew Nicholson, my Warriors teammate, to bring out English county players and train them in the Australian summer, set them up with a Perth club and give them a full grounding in our style of cricket.

During that period, the English former player and coach Paul Terry already had a similar program up and running. Unbeknown to me, Paul brokered a deal with Northants to send some young players to Perth. When these guys eventually told me, I said they'd like the program, Paul was good, and they'd have a good time in Perth. I also suggested they contact Noddy Holder, recommending him as a good coach. I didn't think any more of it.

Soon after I got home, I was having a session with Noddy when I mentioned these guys coming over and asking if he'd mind if they came and had a hit with him. He said nothing. Instead he stormed out of the nets, got into his car and drove off. I stood there in shock. Had I said something wrong? I tried ringing him. He didn't answer. I tried to find him at the Scarborough cricket club. I felt terrible, but also bewildered. Finally I went to his house and knocked at his door, and he came out. We went into his backyard and I said, 'I don't know what I've done wrong. What did I say?'

Noddy said, 'I'm really disappointed in you. You had the chance to endorse my program and my business, and you obviously don't rate me as a bloke or a coach because you didn't endorse me, you endorsed Paul Terry instead.'

I explained that I hadn't known anything about it. Paul Terry had come to Northants and brokered the deal without my knowledge. It was weeks before I first heard about it, when the guys came and told me they were going.

Noddy didn't accept that, and our relationship ended there. He wouldn't coach me anymore. I tried to explain it, but nothing I said was going in.

The rupture hit me quite hard. I've always hated confrontation, and had hardly ever had any kind of falling-out with anyone. Noddy obviously told Matt Nicholson his side of the story, and that soured our relationship too. Our net sessions became heated as Nicko tried to hit me on the head every ball. One session, after about six bouncers in a row, I said, 'Have you got a problem with me?'

He said, 'You know what the f---ing problem is,' and turned around and went back to try to knock my head off again.

The whole episode affected me badly. What hurt me the most was that I knew I'd done nothing wrong, but these guys wouldn't believe me. I'd have been happy to accept responsibility, but the worst of it was that they wouldn't take my word.

I'd had my best season with Northants, averaging 89, and had done enough since I'd been dropped to fight my way back into the West Australian team. Mental strength was the key. In my personal trough, I'd been playing against Queensland, who had me on toast mentally. After getting out, I sat in the dressing room for ages, upset at myself for letting them get to me again. I was wondering how I could harden myself to sledging, and started writing to one of the toughest players in the world: Steve Waugh.

I wrote about how Queensland had cut down my scoring options, by bowling tight and blocking my favourite areas, and then tightened the noose by chirping non-stop. 'I really wanted to do well and I wanted to be tough and enjoy the challenge,' I wrote, 'but deep down I had this fear of failure or doubt in my mind. How can I approach similar situations? What can I do to prepare myself and believe that I can do it and become a more mentally tough player?'

They say that the journey is more important than the destination, and in this case the journey – the process of sitting down and opening up my thoughts to the Australian captain – actually did the trick. I ended up not sending the letter. But by penning all the things that were affecting me, I was devising plans to cope with them. Deal with your own game, bat for time, wear them down and you'll come out on top. I was answering the questions as I was writing them.

My 2003–04 summer was solid rather than spectacular, but I felt I was rebuilding myself as a harder-edged player. Unlike the previous two seasons, I was playing as Mike Hussey, not a wannabe Matthew Hayden. As always seems to be the case, when I stopped trying so hard to attract the selectors' eyes, they started looking at me more closely, and towards the end of the summer I received an unexpected reward.

The Australian team were coming to the end of a very competitive Test and one-day summer hosting India. Their schedule had them coming over to Perth on 1 February 2004 for one game. In a match in Melbourne, Michael Bevan hurt himself, and the selectors chose me to replace him.

I was over the moon, of course, even if it was completely against type that I would play for Australia as a one-day cricketer. I was such a grinding batsman, I saw four- or five-day cricket as my natural element. But in the Western Australian team, I'd carved out a Bevan-style niche in the middle order. I owe a lot to Bevo, because he more or less invented that template, and I modelled my one-day game on his.

In the two or three nights leading up to the game, I didn't sleep more than a few hours. Amy was now near full term with the pregnancy, and I can't have been easy to live with. I played my innings – an unbeaten century for Australia – dozens of times in my head. I was beside myself, as I guess every player is when he gets the call-up.

Fortunately, the Australian one-day dressing room was filled with a lot of guys I knew well. Gilly was captain, and in Andrew Symonds, Simon Katich, Jason Gillespie, Brett Lee and Damien Martyn, I could look around and see a lot of familiar and friendly faces. It relaxed me to be among what I considered friends, guys I knew from junior cricket or Australia A games.

Out on the ground, David Boon presented me with my cap. He'd been one of my heroes as a kid, and I'd had the privilege of playing against him in my early Sheffield Shield career. The presentation was simple. He said, 'You deserve to play for Australia, you've earned your chance, good luck and give it your best shot. You join a select group, you're number 150, congratulations.'

I was hoping we wouldn't bat first on what looked like a lively pitch, and my prayers were answered when Sourav Ganguly won the toss. The crowd was brilliant. Even in the warm-up lap people were cheering for me. Perth people are very parochial, and I was chuffed. Brett Lee rifled out their top order, but their tail-enders were fighting back when Gilly had a bizarre idea. I had caught Rahul Dravid in the gully, which settled me down, and then, I don't know why, but Gilly had a feeling that on debut I might be the guy – *with the ball.* I couldn't believe he wanted me to bowl my modest medium-pacers, and was more nervous than if I'd been batting. As I ran in, my hands were so sweaty I thought, *I don't know if I'm going to be able to hang onto the ball, let alone get it somewhere on the pitch.*

In the end, nothing terrible happened during my three overs, and we got India out for 203. I was listed to bat at number seven, so I was hoping the boys would do the job and I wouldn't be required. But the Indian bowlers were getting a fair bit of help from the pitch too, and Matthew Hayden, Michael Clarke and Damien Martyn were soon out. I was petrified, to be honest. I could see myself coming in under enormous pressure, needing to get Australia home. But thankfully, Gilly and Andrew Symonds belted the Indians to all quarters and the scoring rate went through the roof, which helped me relax. We had the game in our grasp.

Then, with about 40 runs required, suddenly they both got out. Kato was in ahead of me – a good place to have your best man by your side. I certainly felt the pressure. We could easily fall in a heap and embarrass ourselves. As I walked out, I couldn't hear very much. Later that night, Amy said, 'How loud was that roar when you went out to bat! It's the loudest roar I've heard in my life!' But I couldn't hear anything.

I don't remember my first runs. My first four was a nick past slip. Over the next half-hour, Kato batted really well and I knocked it around for 17, and we won without losing another wicket. As we walked off, I said to Simon, 'Isn't this amazing, playing for Australia? We've come a long way from being kids in Wanneroo-versus-Midland-Guildford matches.'

There were no celebrations that night, as the boys would have to get an early flight back east for the one-day finals the next morning, which I wasn't going to be part of as Michael Bevan would be available. I went out for dinner with Amy in Subiaco. I was pumped to have played for Australia, and to have been in the middle when we won the match, but it turned out to be one of the worst restaurant experiences ever. We ordered early, and after an hour it hadn't come. I'm not one to complain, but Amy, 38 weeks pregnant, was flagging, so I said to the waiter, 'Excuse me. Any chance of our meal coming?'

He said, 'You want your dessert?'

I said, 'We haven't had our mains.'

The waiter went white, ran to the kitchen, and said he'd forgotten our order. When the dinners came, we wolfed them down and got out as quickly as we could. So much for the special celebrity treatment as an Australian player!

Amy was going to be induced, so we were able to pick out the date. We chose 9 February – wedged between my trips to Hobart and to Brisbane for the next two Shield matches.

The big day arrived and we were in the hospital, with things progressing very slowly. I said, 'I might whip out for some lunch and come back in a while.' I was pretty relaxed, thinking we had plenty of time. I was standing in line at a Subway store, and my phone rang.

'You'd better get back here,' Amy said. '– It's happening now!'

I tore back in my car, the one time you're allowed to go 100kmh in a 60kmh zone. When I got there, Amy was doubled over in pain, pushing. Suddenly the baby's heart rate dropped dramatically. The nurses seemed panicky and said they needed to get the baby out, and then rushed Amy off for an emergency Caesarean. I stood in a helpless daze as injections were going in, beds were being moved, and Amy was panicking too. But the Caesarean went quickly and we had a beautiful baby girl, who we named Jasmin. Poor Amy had been through two births in one, more or less: the whole labour up to the end, and then the Caesarean.

With a full slate of Shield and domestic one-day matches coming up interstate, I missed most of Jasmin's first three weeks. But cricket was our livelihood, and Amy was totally supportive. Amy's always said, just as playing cricket for Australia is my dream, being a mother is her dream. She loves babies and was right in her element, and let me go away with full confidence in each other. Although, to be honest, I was hanging out for the end of the season and time at home, and my form tapered off. It had been an exhausting few months, and for once in my life, I was desperate to get away from cricket.

THIRTEEN

By the time Jasmin was born, I had played three straight years of twelve-month cricket. My plan had been to go back to Northants for another year, but the cumulative toll of professional cricket, and becoming a father, changed my view. I took some time off and really enjoyed being at home with Amy and Jasmin. I didn't pick up a bat for months but got stuck into the physical work with the Warriors, which was great.

During that time, Gloucestershire got in touch to ask if I would join them for the second half of their season. I saw it as a chance to get some cricket under my belt leading into the Australian summer, and Amy was happy to come over again. We set up in Bristol, but it was a challenge because our apartment wasn't great and Jasmin was waking up through the night. When games were on, though, Amy quickly got up for Jasmin, making sure I didn't wake up and got plenty of rest for the match. We were both pretty tired a lot of the time. It was a good experience for me having to change my routines and get used to not sleeping all night, a taste of things to come if we were going to have more children, as we hoped.

I was only there for seven first-class and nine one-day matches, and didn't set the world on fire. But the highlight was playing in the final of the Cheltenham & Gloucester Trophy, a one-day competition, at Lord's. I'd played at Lord's several times for Northants, but never before a packed house in a final. The atmosphere was like an international game, with people flowing in from the neighbouring counties cheer on their team. We restricted Worcestershire to 236, and chased it down pretty easily. I only made 20 but to be part of a trophy win on a day like that was a highlight of my five seasons in county cricket.

Coming home, my pre-season preparation was perfect. Off the field, I was the happiest and most settled I'd ever felt. We were comfortable and content as a family, living in a beautiful house we'd renovated. I had worked out that I was going to play my way, not try to be like Hayden or Gilchrist or Ponting, and I was determined to bring home the determination to convert good starts into not just hundreds but double and triple centuries. Justin Langer told me that selectors take notice when you make massive hundreds. In the first game, I managed to do just that, scoring 210 against Tasmania at the WACA. It helped my confidence for the whole season, having started that way.

The other guy to score three figures in that innings was Shaun Marsh, the elder son of Geoff. Shaun had been around the Australian team as a kid, when Swampy was coach, and had been batting in the WACA nets with the state squad since he was sixteen. I remembered how rushed and uncomfortable I had felt at that age facing grown men on quick wickets, but Shaun had something extra. He wasn't just surviving, but was playing good shots. He was a natural, and looked like he would be playing for Western Australia and possibly Australia for a good ten or fifteen years.

Gilly, who was state captain, was mostly away playing for Australia so I led the Warriors in his absence. I enjoyed the experience and we were playing a good brand of cricket. Most of all, I was hell-bent on making more big scores. In a tour match against the Pakistanis, I got to 124 against a strong attack including Shoaib Akhtar, Mohammad Sami and Danish Kaneria, and then, when I was set up for a big one, in what I thought was a more prominent match against international bowlers, I threw it away. I was the most irate I'd ever been after getting out, and was throwing gear in the dressing room and screaming at myself. One of the young blokes said, 'Why are you so mad? You've just made a hundred against Pakistan.' I calmed down, but felt I'd missed an opportunity.

Two games later, the chance arose against Victoria at the WACA. Shane Warne had retired from one-day cricket, so he was playing a rare Shield game. He had got me out quite a few times, and I wanted to prove I could convert a start into a big score against the best bowlers. I wanted to prove to him, personally, that I could play. I felt that if Warnie was talking about me positively around the place, that couldn't do any harm. The Australian players obviously talked a lot about who was doing well in state cricket, and the selectors might ask Warnie how I'd batted against him. It felt like an important chance.

I had a specific plan. It was well known that he didn't like left-handers sweeping him. I'd been stumped off him a few times, so, rather than charging down the wicket when he tossed it up into the breeze, I stayed back and swept. He tried all his tricks: sledging, going around the wicket, over the wicket, wrong 'uns, flippers and more, and I felt I was reading him pretty well. I eventually got 223 not out, an enormous boost to my self-belief to make such a score against one of the greatest bowlers of all time.

We only just missed the final, and I had my best Shield season for several years. I felt that my game was on track. I was taken on a tour to New Zealand for a one-day international tournament, and was beginning to feel comfortable in the Australian dressing room, for one-day cricket at least. Mates such as Andrew Symonds and Simon

Katich were there, and the idea of Ricky Ponting being the captain was less intimidating, for me at least, than a much older guy such as Steve Waugh. I was still outside the periphery for Test selection, though. When they picked the touring squad to go to England to defend the Ashes, the Hayden–Langer combination was rock-solid at the top, and there was no space for me as an extra batsman. Although there were several people saying I deserved a chance, I was a little disappointed. To be on a touring Ashes squad was a lifelong dream, and the next one, of course, was four years away.

We were going to be over in England anyway, for the one-day internationals before the Ashes tour proper, and for a season with Durham.

During my two months at Gloucestershire, I'd taken a call from David Harker, the chief executive of Durham. They were the newest club, struggling for results in the Second Division, and he wanted me to come up and captain the club. They offered to fly Amy and me up for the day, and showed us around the club, a brilliant set-up with impressive facilities. They really wanted to go places. But did I have the energy to put into a struggling team?

Gloucestershire had been indicating that they might want to re-sign me. I confided in Phil Weston, my opening partner. He said, 'No, I definitely wouldn't go to Durham, they're really struggling.' But the more I thought about it, the more I was excited by the challenge. When I was Northants' captain, the cricket committee would ask me what I needed to improve, and I'd ask for this, that and the other. Financially, it was always tight at the club and the club often couldn't afford ideas that I wanted to implement or bring in players I was keen to sign. At Durham, by contrast, the club said, 'Whatever you need, we'll get. No expense spared. We really want to go places.'

So I went against Phil's advice and signed as captain of Durham. Three present or future England internationals, Steve Harmison,

Liam Plunkett and Paul Collingwood, were already playing there. Early in 2005 they had a preseason tour to Dubai, which I flew over for, to meet the team and support staff and see how it ran. When I saw them in practice games, I got excited about the young players they had, including the right-arm seamer Graham Onions, and their Kolpak import, South Africa's Dale Benkenstein, a good solid professional and a great person.

When the county season started, we got off to a great start and things really clicked into place, which gave everyone at the club a lot of confidence and enjoyment. I scored freely away from home, making a double hundred on debut at Leicestershire and another hundred at Old Trafford against Lancashire, but struggled at home on what was still a new pitch settling down. It was very tough for batting as the ball seamed around, and most of our home games were over inside three days. Harmison was beloved in the northeast, Plunkett and Onions were very good on pitches conducive to seam bowling, and Mark Davies terrorised batsmen with his swing and cut. We steamrolled opponents. Collingwood was desperate to get into the England team, so we had him available and he was scoring big runs on that difficult pitch. Off the field, the club looked after our family very well and were always asking what more they could do for us. As players, we celebrated each other's success. I brought in a team rule that if someone scored a century or took five wickets in an innings, we would all go to the bar at the clubhouse and have one drink to toast him. It didn't have to be more than one drink, and a guy could have a soft drink if he liked; it was all about bringing new guys together and building team spirit. People thrived in that environment.

I had two months with Durham getting used to the conditions before I joined the Australian squad for two one-day international series, first a triangular tournament with England and Bangladesh and then a three-match contest with England. There was plenty of time for the two teams to sort each other out before the Ashes.

First was a Twenty20 game at the Rose Bowl in Southampton. As Australians, we were still struggling to take this format seriously. In our first Twenty20 international, a few months earlier in New Zealand, the Kiwis had grown 1970s-style facial hair and worn retro brown shirts, and everyone had gone by their nicknames on their backs. It was a less-than-serious, party-atmosphere game. But at the Rose Bowl, England came so hard, it was as if they wanted to kill us, to put down a marker to show it was going to be a tough summer ahead. They played like it was the first match of an Ashes series. Being bowled out for 79 and losing by 100 runs knocked the guys' confidence a bit. We were well off the pace.

Then we went to Cardiff and things got drastically worse. Andrew Symonds was suspended for being out late the night before the game against Bangladesh, which we ended up losing. Then Kevin Pietersen, the brash young South African starting a career for England, hammered us the next day at Bristol. It was an ordinary start. But the controversy and crisis galvanised the team. The senior players knew what they were doing, and lifted their work rate, pulling everyone together. Simmo, who was hurting badly, came back into the team and ended up being man of the tri-series.

That triangular event boiled down to a final between us and England at Lord's. We saw that as the moment where we could establish a psychological edge for the Ashes. It was one of those days at Lord's where the clouds were so low you felt you could touch them. The ball moved around a lot, and we got ourselves into trouble, which you almost expect in those conditions. I was lucky enough to be batting well down the order, and nudged my way to 62 not out, getting us to a below-par score of 196, which still might be enough if we could take early wickets under a still-heavy sky. We did that, and had them 5/33, but Collingwood and Geraint Jones fought back much as we had when the shine went off the ball. They were targeting Hoggy, hitting him to the short boundary. It was very tight coming into the last ten overs, and then I got the look I most dreaded. Ricky was indicating that he wanted me to bowl. I thought, *You've got to be kidding!* But he was serious.

I said to Gilly, 'What should I bowl?'

'Yorkers every ball,' he said, no doubt thinking he was being helpful.

Anyway, that's what I tried. I would come to the end of an over and assume Ricky had seen enough. Every time the over at the other end came to a close, I turned my face to the crowd so Ricky might not be able to get my attention. But he kept calling me. In spite of my lack of practice, confidence and competence, it came out okay. I was landing the yorkers and not going for too many runs. We ran out Collingwood, Hoggy got Geraint Jones, and I managed to jag a wicket myself, bowling Simon Jones. I was pumped at getting a wicket at Lord's, almost as much as I had been in making a half-century.

The match ended in a dramatic tie. I didn't know how to take it. We had done well after being 5/93 in the morning, but then we'd expected to win when we had them 5/33 in the afternoon. Sitting next to Ricky in the dressing room, I had no doubt how he felt. He was throwing his shoes around and carrying on. He saw it as a big loss of a chance to gain a psychological edge.

We did win the three-match series with England, though, after Ricky and Gilly scored hundreds in the decisive games. Then Simmo, Hoggy, Shane Watson and I, the one-day players who weren't in the Ashes squad, had to leave. It was odd to be part of the build-up and then having to go, and I left with mixed feelings. Obviously I would have loved to be part of the Ashes series. But I knew in advance where I stood, and felt happy with my own performances. I felt I'd cemented my place in the one-day team. And I had a passion for helping Durham have a successful season. Still, I was a little disappointed to leave the Australian team when I was playing with a lot of confidence.

I had a hugely enjoyable and successful season with Durham. We had some groundbreaking moments, one was beating a Lancashire team including Andrew Flintoff, James Anderson and Muttiah Muralitharan, at Old Trafford for the first time. We also beat Leicestershire for the first time ever away from home, and gained promotion from Division Two. I loved every minute of it – except when I was getting sledged over the Ashes results. Of course, I invited it, by making merry after Australia won the first Test, but ended up copping the brunt of it when England fought back and won the Ashes after sixteen years.

There was some speculation about me being drafted into the Test team. The middle order was battling for runs, as was Matty Hayden at the top. No part of me, not even a tiny demon at the back of my mind, was cheering the Australians to fail. Hayden and Langer were unquestionably the best openers available. The guys down the order were the best players and should all be in the team. When some of them were battling, I just thought, *If they're battling, there's no reason I wouldn't be battling as well.* I wanted Australia to win and I wanted the selectors to show faith in the guys they'd picked.

By the fifth Test, Australia could still retain the Ashes by winning. There was enormous pressure on Matty Hayden and some agitation for me. I was thinking, *No, I'm not the great white hope, I'm not Australia's saviour, I'm just doing my best for Durham, I can't win the Ashes.* Actually, I was praying the selectors wouldn't pick me. It felt like too much pressure. Happily, they stuck with Haydos and he made a hundred – as did JL – although it was not enough to save the Ashes.

While that Test was still on, I flew to Pakistan for a short Australia A tour. It was good to be out of the country when England received the urn. I would have never have lived it down from the Durham boys.

I had turned thirty during that English season and couldn't dodge the suspicion that now that Hayden and Langer had re-established themselves my time had gone. The New South Wales left-handed opener Phil Jaques went on that tour of Pakistan, and made good runs. Phil was an absolute run machine in first-class cricket. I felt that, when the time came to bring new blood into the Australian team, I might be overtaken by a younger generation.

Pakistan was enjoyable, but their team was slightly better than ours. We competed well and won the odd match. I was in an introspective mood. Staying in the Lahore Inter-Continental, I was rooming with Stuart Clark. One night, we were lying on our beds watching TV. We were the same age, and while it was great to be touring for Australia A, it wasn't Test cricket. Stuart asked if I thought I'd ever get to play for Australia. I said, 'I'd love to, mate, but my time might have passed.' We both went to sleep with those mixed feelings.

The cricket was very high quality and drove home how much harder the next level would be, if I was ever lucky enough to make it. The bowlers were quick and good. I made a hundred in a first-class match against Pakistan A at Rawalpindi, but must have played and missed 150 times. Their bowlers were faster and better, and the cricket was more intense, than anything I'd encountered. If Test cricket was another level up, I wasn't sure if I was good enough.

While we were in Lahore, we were caught up in controversy. We had a team dinner in Old Lahore, in a local restaurant beside a big mosque. The next day, we learnt that a bomb had gone off overnight very close to where we'd eaten. Some of the boys felt endangered. It wasn't a big bomb and it wasn't targeting us, but the team was split between those who wanted to go home and those who wanted to play on. Brad Haddin was captain and I was deputy, and he was going to head home anyway with an injured finger, so I had to help handle the question of whether to stay or leave. I met with the coach, Tim Nielsen, and the manager, who said that under no circumstances were we going home. It wouldn't be good for Pakistan–Australia relations. I was fine with that personally, but communicated to them that some of the guys were not at all keen to stay. Shane Watson was notably nervous about the bombing, and others had been away from home for a long time after a winter in England. I said to the concerned players, 'If you go home, it's got to be for the right reasons, not because you don't like Pakistan and are tired or homesick. But if you're genuinely insecure and scared, you can go home.'

After we requested and received assurances that our security would be stepped up, the team met as a group and agreed to stay on. It was good that we stayed. I think our cricket benefited from it. And as a captain, even if I was only a stand-in, I learnt a lot about the diplomacy needed in balancing out the wishes of every member of the team against the bigger picture of international cricket.

FOURTEEN

Australia's first international engagement after the Ashes was to host an ICC World XI in a one-day and Test series. It was great to be back in Australia. I felt I'd cemented my place in the one-day team. We had a big team meeting at Crown, where we were staying, led by Ricky, who inspired all of us. He was hurting big time. He said, 'We've lost to England. What do we need to do to get better?' His resolution was to try to get a little bit better each day, in every little thing, and maintain that intensity. I was ready to run through a brick wall for him. We trained extremely well. The Australian team wasn't used to losing.

I was conscious that I was under scrutiny as a possible Test player. At thirty, I felt that I was down to my last chance. The other guy who was brought into the one-day team as a possible Test candidate was Shane Watson. With Watto, it took me some time to get to know the real bloke. My initial thoughts were uncertain. But they were only based on superficial impressions. It took time to get to know the real guy, and I found him to be a brilliant bloke with a very good sense of humour, passionate and thoughtful about his cricket. He loved his music and wine and the finer things in life, which put him outside the usual pigeon-holing. Over time, the more I got to know him, the better I got on with him.

The limited-overs games were the first to be played under the closed roof of the Telstra Dome in Melbourne. We won the first two, and in the third match I came in with some time up our sleeve. I was facing Murali, which was a bit scary. I'd done okay against him in county cricket, taking my time, warding him off, but before long I was having to score runs off him. I could pick which way the ball was spinning about 80 per cent of the time, and there were some balls I was missing by 6 inches. *Far out,* I thought, *I'm sure I saw the ball spinning that way!* Luckily I got through it and had a good partnership with Watto.

Makhaya Ntini came on towards the end of the innings, bowling around the wicket. He put one right in the slot, and I don't think I've hit a ball better in my life. It made a beautiful noise, right out of the meat of the bat. I thought, *That's six.* I looked up and lost it in the lights. Then the ball dropped down – on the field. Their players were laughing, and the umpire was signalling dead ball. I couldn't believe it. I'd got it right out of the middle, it was definitely going for six, and they were giving me no runs for it. I ranted and raved to Watto, and he was laughing his head off. We won the game comfortably, but I wasn't happy about that ruling!

I loved playing against the World XI, even though they evidently saw the series as a bit of a holiday. I thought all my Christmases had come at once, seeing all the best players in the world up close. Chris Gayle is a huge man, and Kumar Sangakkara batted well. To be on the same field as Jacques Kallis, Brian Lara, Murali, all the great players, gave me a big buzz, and I felt good to be able to cut it with them. We were playing so confidently and with such determination as a group, after Ricky's inspiring speech at Crown, that no team, not even a World XI, could have come close to us in that series.

But I did not consider myself a part of the Test picture for the upcoming series against the West Indies. I felt the pressure was off me and I wasn't on trial every innings. Hayden and Langer were ensconced. If my destiny was to be an Australian one-day cricketer, and not a Test player, I felt that I would be happy.

On 29 October, that all changed. We were playing a domestic one-dayer against Victoria at the Junction Oval in St Kilda, and Gerard Denton got one to jump at Justin Langer. It hit him in the ribs and he had to retire hurt, which was unusual for JL, but he said he would be fine and I didn't think about it anymore.

Justin went up to Brisbane to prepare for the first Test, while I returned to Perth with the Warriors. JL was a tough nut. Even a broken rib, let alone a mere bruise, wouldn't stop him playing.

The next day, Amy and I took Jasmin for a long walk on the beach. When we'd got back to the car and were driving home, my phone rang. Trevor Hohns, the national chairman of selectors, was on the other end.

'Huss, how quickly can you get to the airport? We need you in Brisbane on standby for Justin.'

I nearly drove off the road.

'I can be there as quickly as possible,' I said. I raced home, packed and went to the airport, where camera crews converged on me. I felt like a bit of a rock star until, when I lifted my suitcase onto the conveyor belt at check-in, my zip broke and my clothes went all over the place, in front of the world.

On the plane, I was sitting next to a guy who asked what I was doing. I said, proudly, 'I'm joining the Australian cricket team.' He must have had twelve or fifteen scotch and Cokes on the flight, and by the time I was in Brisbane some of the fumes were sticking to my shirt and I smelt like a distillery.

When I got to the team's hotel, they were having a team dinner. As I walked in, they were very warm, shaking my hand and making me feel welcome. It was different from joining the one-day team: here were all the legends, Warne, McGrath, Ponting, Gilchrist, Hayden, guys I knew individually but had never been with before as a collective. I spoke with JL, who was drugged up on painkillers.

'How are you going, mate?'

He said, 'Huss, it's a waste of time you being here, I'm 100 per cent fine to play.'

He was determined, of course, but it was obvious that he was feeling the effects of the painkillers. I saw the physiotherapist, Errol Alcott, and discreetly asked him how Justin was really going.

'He's really struggling, Huss. I'd be ready to play if I were you.'

The next day at training at the Gabba, we started with some fielding. I was watching Justin like a hawk. He didn't do a lot, but didn't show too much discomfort. I was here now, fired up to play.

We went to the nets, where again I was trying not to be too obvious in the way I was watching him. He batted beautifully, playing all his shots, timing the ball well. My heart sank. So near, yet so far. He smashed all the bowlers everywhere. He'd be fine. That was that, then.

As his session finished, I was next in. We crossed as Justin came out.

'Huss, I just want to let you know, I'm out, mate. Good luck, you're in.'

I went to the crease and thought, *Holy cow, I didn't expect that*. My mind was all over the place. The first five balls, I think I got out four times.

I stepped aside and thought, *You're playing in a Test match – switch on!*

I was told officially after the session that I would be making my Test debut, and from there the circus started. I had to do media interviews all afternoon, and was organising family and friends to fly up. I'd promised Ian Kevan when I was eighteen that if I played a Test match for Australia I wanted him to be there. There was

Mum and Dad and Amy, my uncle Brian Rogers and some cousins. I thought, *I should really be concentrating on my first Test.*

We had another day's practice before the Test match, and I put all the other stuff aside and had a good hit in the nets. I felt calm and happy and ready to go, but sleeping was a problem. Sleep was a big part of my preparation. Normally, if I hadn't slept well, I didn't function. If I got a good eight or nine hours, on the other hand, my mind and body worked well and I batted better. I wouldn't compromise on that full night's sleep. As I lay in bed, my mind was very active thinking about the game, and I needed some help getting off to sleep. I had to take a sleeping tablet to get off, something I'd done since starting my one-day international career. I woke up in the middle of the night and had to take another. Two sleeping tablets the night before my Test debut was not ideal, but I just had to get some rest.

Waking up, I felt pretty relaxed and excited about the day. I got to the ground feeling happy. During our warm-ups, Bill Brown presented me with my cap. It was a real honour getting it from the oldest living Australian Test player, a member of the 1948 Invincibles. Bill didn't say a lot, just, 'Good luck, you deserve your chance, I hope you play very well.' I wanted to rip the Baggy Green out of his hands and get it on my head.

I warmed up well. Ricky went out and, to my consternation, won the toss and decided to bat. That's when things started flipping around inside me. *I'm going to be facing my first ball in Test cricket in half an hour.*

We went into the dressing room, and I went to the toilet for about the twentieth time that morning. Warnie was in there, in nothing but his underpants, smoking a cigarette. He could tell I was extremely nervous. Warnie was one guy I'd had some fierce battles with in Shield cricket, and even though I'd made that double-century in Perth I wasn't sure if he rated me. I was pretty much in awe of him. I wanted to impress him and be liked by him, but he hadn't given much away about whether he thought I was up to this level. Now, he pulled me aside and said, 'Huss, you're good enough to be here, you don't have to prove anything to any of us. Just go and play your way and you can't fail, mate.'

It made an enormous impression on me, getting that endorsement from one of the greatest bowlers to play the game. When you get a vote of confidence from someone of his stature, you feel like you have the respect of all your teammates. For anyone coming into the Australian Test cricket team, it's a test of your nerve as much as anything else. Do you belong? I made a pact with myself at that moment, if I stayed in the team, to try to make any new player feel the way Warnie had made me feel: protected by the team. I wanted to pass that feeling on to others.

I padded up and went out for the national anthem. The crowd really belted it out, but I had the sense of a disaster enveloping me. I lost feeling in my legs and my heart was pounding. I thought, *I've got to pull it together or else I'll be in real trouble. I'm batting in five minutes.*

I hadn't studied the West Indian bowlers much. I'd had a quick chat with some of the guys, who noted that Jermaine Lawson and Fidel Edwards were quite quick. I hadn't watched a lot of footage of them or done much homework. I was worried about Corey Collymore's accuracy and ability to move the ball, but to be frank I was just pumped to be out there, and there was only enough room in my head for coping with my own game.

Walking out with Matthew Hayden, I wasn't conscious of much except the complete loss of feeling in my legs. Haydos, taking pity on me, said he would take the first ball. I said, 'Yes, thank you.' Off the third ball he got a single, and I was facing Fidel Edwards. It's amazing how the mind wanders. He was at the top of his mark and I was thinking, *I can't believe I'm at the Gabba about to face my first ball in Test cricket.* I forced myself into my routine: *Stance, relax the arms, clear the negative thoughts out of your mind, watch the ball.* And then, another part of my brain wandered back through the years to back yard games with Dave, how I'd dreamt of playing for Australia. Then the other side screamed: *Huss, concentrate, watch the ball!* Then I thought about all the trials I'd been through with Western Australia, being in and out of the team … And a voice in my head belted out: *Concentrate! He's about to bowl!*

All this while I was waiting for the first ball. As Edwards was about to get to the crease, I was welling up with tears. I thought, *You can't cry before your first ball in Test cricket. CONCENTRATE!!!*

He bowled a bouncer. It was a quick one, whistling past my eyes, but I thought, *I'm lucky he didn't bowl on the stumps, because I didn't see it.* My mind was all over the place. I doubt I'd have been able to move. The West Indian boys were saying things like, 'Welcome to Test cricket, man!'

I was still blinking away the tears. It was like my life had flashed before my eyes, a near-death experience. For the next few balls I faced from Edwards and the other new-ball bowler, Daren Powell, I was all over the place. My bat felt like a toothpick.

In the fifth over, the thirteenth ball I faced, I pushed one past short leg and called: 'No!' But then it got away from the fielder and I screamed, 'YES!' Haydos stuttered, but we got through for the single.

I was exultant. I had a run! No matter how much money you've got in the world, you can't buy a run in Test cricket. It was overwhelming. I felt like a king.

Haydos played out the last three balls in that over, and then I was facing Daren Powell again. He bowled a short one and I went for a pull shot, but top-edged it straight up in the air. It was hard walking off. My family, relatives and friends were sitting right above the tunnel. I had my head down, but peeked up and saw them sitting there. The disappointment was written on their faces. I felt like I'd really let them down. I'd played a terrible shot. They'd made the effort to come here and watch me, and this was all I'd been able to give them.

About half an hour after I got out, however, I was settling down, thinking over what an amazing experience it was, something so many people would love but don't experience. The other guys were batting well, and by lunchtime I was pretty happy again. Ricky scored a century in the afternoon, and I thought, *I've made a run in Test cricket, I've got a baggy green cap. Hey, it's not the end of the world.*

I didn't take notice of any commentary on my performance or the fact that hundreds of thousands were watching. I felt I was representing those people, more than being the object of their criticism or praise. I wanted to do well for them as their representative.

When I got to the hotel that night, Mum, Dad and Amy were waiting. When I saw their excitement, that made me feel that I'd succeeded. Dad was desperate to look at my Baggy Green cap. I don't think he could believe he was touching one, and he didn't want to let go of it.

We were in the field by the second afternoon, with 435 on the board. It felt good to be fielding, much more relaxed than batting and having the whole spotlight on me. McGrath, Lee, Nathan Bracken and Warne had the West Indies under pressure, so it was fun to be out there. We got Lara for 30, the big wicket, and were on top from there. When we were circling the batsmen, I was thinking, *How good is this?* I misfielded a drive and it went away for three runs, which was embarrassing, but otherwise I was very happy.

But then, on the third morning, as the last wickets fell I started getting nervous about going out and batting again. Haydos and I were facing up before lunch for just one over, a really difficult assignment. This time I took the first ball, from Edwards. I got his second ball through covers for three and hit another in the middle, which took the edge off my nerves. After lunch, I worked my way quite nicely to 29 until they brought Chris Gayle on to bowl his part-time off-spinners. He dropped one short, and I pulled it hard, above midwicket's head, but Collymore put his hands up and snatched it. I'd batted quite well, but was very disappointed not to kick on after a good start.

Scores of 1 and 29 weren't the greatest start to my Test career, but I was on a high. Ricky made another hundred, we went back out and Nathan Bracken bowled brilliantly to seal a pretty comfortable win. Having a cold beer with the boys, I was over the moon to have played in a Test match and been in a winning team. But inside, a burning feeling was starting to niggle away. Now that I was here, I wanted to prove to myself and the world that I could perform at this level. But would I get the chance? We all expected JL to be back for the next Test match. A voice in my head was asking if this was to be my only opportunity. *Shivers, I might not get this chance again.*

There was this terrible swirl of positive and negative voices. I might be another of those one-Test guys. Nobody could take that away from me. I could be proud of it, even if it was my only chance. But I would be disappointed too.

Making it harder was knowing my destiny was in Justin's hands. Knowing him, he would fight through any pain to be right for the second Test in Hobart. We went home for a few days, and I was at the WACA for training. JL came up to me and said he wouldn't be at Hobart either. I felt for him but I also thought, *You beauty, at least I won't be a one-Test wonder.*

The Warriors flew to Adelaide and won a domestic one-dayer easily – and then I went on to Hobart with Gilly to prepare for the Test. Arriving a day before the rest of the Test team, we settled in, went for a nice long walk, had a laugh and a chat. The whole preparation was completely different from Brisbane. Hobart's smaller and more relaxed, and I didn't have the wall-to-wall media scrutiny or the fuss of organising flights. I felt infinitely calmer. In the nets, without the intensity of Brisbane, I felt my emotions were in check and I was batting quite well.

Things didn't go completely to plan, though. The last training session was optional. I decided to go down to Bellerive, have a quick hit and get my gear all ready. Afterwards, I told the manager, Steve 'Brute' Bernard, that I would walk back to the hotel myself. In my general daze, I hadn't realised how far Bellerive was from the city. I thought it would be a half-hour walk. From the first few minutes, as I looked down the Derwent, I could see it was going to be a lot longer than that. I took a short cut, and got lost. Two and a half hours later, I staggered into the hotel, exhausted, wondering if I'd gone crazy. I relaxed throughout the afternoon, though, and had a good night's sleep.

In the team minivan the next morning, the song that was playing was 'I've Had a Bad Day'. Coincidentally, the last time I'd heard that was the day we got hammered by Victoria at the Junction Oval and JL had broken his rib. Gilly joked, 'That's not a good sign.' I said, 'Gilly, don't remind me of that day.'

On a beautiful batting pitch, we lost the toss but bowled the West Indies out for 149. Haydos and I had to bat through the last session, and I got off to a streaky start, until Powell, trying to get me out the same way as in the first innings in Brisbane, bounced me. I pulled it for four and thought, *That's the best shot I've played in Test cricket. I can do it at this level.* It's amazing how one shot can loosen everything up. Throughout my career, I played innings when my confidence went from zero to full-throttle just from one or two shots. After middling that one, I felt like a different person. I was 26 not out at stumps and was happy to have got the team, along with Haydos, to the end of the day without losing a wicket, but I knew I had a big chance here.

The next morning was one of those sessions when everything fell into place. I played shots all around the ground and even outscored Haydos, which I couldn't believe. We rattled along and in the 50th over my hundred came off a clip off the pad off Fidel Edwards. I ran down the wicket punching the air and yelling and screaming. I gave Haydos an enormous hug and carried on for another five minutes or so. I was going so crazy, he couldn't stop laughing. I'd had that sinking feeling in Brisbane about not proving myself at this level – and now I'd done it.

Matty also made a hundred, and almost as exciting to me was being able to hit the winning run in the second innings. It's true that our opponents weren't the feared West Indies of the past. Their attack was workmanlike but not intimidating. They gave you balls to hit boundaries off, and if you stayed patient you'd get a four-ball every over or two. It took the pressure off someone like me, who usually struggled to turn the strike over. But it really wouldn't have mattered to me who we were playing. Two weeks earlier, I'd been celebrating one Test run. Now, beyond belief, I had a hundred.

At the end of the Hobart Test, we knew Justin Langer was coming back in. I thought I would be the one to make way, but the selectors dropped Michael Clarke for the first time in his career. As the celebrations started, I saw Michael get pulled aside and given the bad news. That made for a very awkward dressing room. He was devastated, and I was ecstatic while not wanting to show that too much to my teammate. This is always the way in cricket: balancing individual with team results, when they go in opposite directions, can be a delicate thing. I felt sorry for Michael, as I had for Damien Martyn and Simon Katich, who had paid the price for the Ashes loss. The selectors had now cleaned out the whole middle order, replacing Michael, Damien and Simon with me, Brad Hodge and Andrew Symonds.

All of a sudden, I was batting number five. I'd done the middle-order job in one-day internationals, but still saw myself very much as an opener. But I was so excited to have kept my place after Justin's return, I didn't care where I batted.

We already had the series won at 2–0 before the third Test in Adelaide. The guy we had really been worried about all series was Brian Lara. We managed to get him out without much damage in Brisbane and Hobart, but in Adelaide the West Indies batted first and Lara made 226, passing Allan Border's Test match run record. He batted out of this world, like the genius he was. He played everyone with ease: McGrath, Lee, Warne and MacGill. But the other West Indians didn't contribute a lot; we restricted them to 405 and on a typically beautiful Adelaide strip we felt confident. I sat beside Andrew Symonds, very relaxed listening to his usual hilarious nonsense, while our top order dug in. Justin Langer got to 99, a gutsy comeback innings, and with a couple of overs left in the day we were two wickets down and the boys were asking if I wanted a night watchman. I said, 'No, no, the pitch is good, if someone gets out now it's only one over.' I wanted to show I could take the responsibility. Sure enough, Justin gloved a hook down the leg side and I had to go out there to face Fidel Edwards.

That last over, I did not see a ball. I played and missed and nearly nicked a couple. Another few whizzed by my eyes. I felt rather than saw them, and don't know how I survived. I felt like Glenn McGrath with the bat in my hand, and maybe that's unfair to Pigeon. I resolved that if I was ever offered a night watchman again, I would take it.

But the next morning, as so often, was a different game. I saw the ball clearly and felt great (all the more reason to get a night watchman, unless he's the type who's going to spoil it for you and bat all day). Soon, though, we were in trouble. Dwayne Bravo, who I found very difficult, was reverse-swinging the ball and the scoring slowed down. We suddenly lost five wickets, and were 8/295, well behind in the match, when Stuart MacGill came out.

I went over to him and asked how he wanted to play it. Magilla was adamant. 'I do not want to face a single ball. I want you to face the first four balls each over, smack a four or six, and then get a single.'

I said, 'Okay, mate, I'll do my best!'

I blocked a few balls and the crowd started booing, because the field had been pushed back and we weren't running. Magilla said, 'It's okay, you stay down there. I don't want to face.'

Lara would bring the field back in after the fourth ball to try and keep me on strike and bowl to Magilla the following over. So I had a slog at the fifth ball and snuck a cheeky single off the sixth. This went on for ten, twenty or thirty minutes and the momentum swung. The West Indians weren't sure what to do. They brought the field in, and I hit fours. They left it out and I wouldn't run. My theory was to show faith in the lower-order batsman. Magilla didn't want that, but sometimes he did have to face a couple of balls an over, and he gained confidence. The West Indies grew extremely frustrated. I began to enjoy it more than just about any partnership I had ever been in, playing cat-and-mouse and coming out on top.

When Magilla got out, I was in the 90s. Glenn McGrath came in, and we put on another 40, using the same tactic. It's such an enjoyable time to bat in Test cricket, because fear goes out the window. You're just getting bonus runs for the team. If you get out, it doesn't matter, you're doing the right thing by the team. You're a hero if you score runs, and nothing's at stake if you get out. And you're driving your opponent insane – just like in the back yard! To get another Test hundred, at my favourite place to play cricket, was a wonderful feeling, and we edged in front of the West Indies' score.

By the fourth innings, we were chasing 182 to win. It wasn't easy. In the dressing room, the boys were nervous. Adelaide can be very tricky when it breaks up on the last day; the ball was reversing and there was a lot of spin. Luckily, the West Indies had only chosen Ramnaresh Sarwan and Chris Gayle as part-time spinners. We lost a wicket early and then a couple more before Haydos decided to take a few risks and smacked a couple. I chipped it around at the other end and we got away with a third win in three starts.

We snuck off for a one-day tour in New Zealand, which we won 5–0 and then came back to host South Africa for a three-Test series. The first Test was in Perth: my first home Test match, against tougher opposition than the West Indies.

We were really up for the challenge as a team, but on our first day we were bowled out, on a toughish pitch, for 258. I was one of several batsmen to make a start, before I was caught playing a terrible pull shot off Ntini. At the end of the day Ricky said, 'That's the worst day of Test cricket we've had for a long time. These guys aren't going to let us off – we have to improve.'

Improve we did, getting them out for 296 before posting 8/528 in our second dig. The highlight was Brad Hodge's fantastic unbeaten 203, against Pollock, Ntini, Nel and Charl Langeveldt. After he'd made mountains of runs for Victoria and waited for his Test chance, Hodgy's career looked like it was about to take off. But over the next few years, even though he generally did well – I remember a brilliant one-day 90 at Eden Park and a very good half-century in the West Indies at Jamaica in a Test – he was in and out of the team. Whenever someone else was coming back in, he seemed to be the one who missed out.

I'd known Brad since playing against him in an under–19s carnival in Melbourne. He was in the Robbie Baker class as a batsman, the best in our age group. He was also bowling off spin. I skipped down the wicket once and hit him through covers, and he said something like, 'If you do that again I'll break your legs.' So I was pretty intimidated by Brad from the start. He wanted to kill me just for hitting one through the covers. I thought, *That's a bit harsh!*

He played for Victoria at a very young age and was totally dominant in the junior carnivals. When we played together in

Australia A teams, I got on well with him. If we were on a long tour, people inevitably got a bit bored and down, and Hodgy could complain a bit. I remember a Test in Antigua, when he was twelfth man and I was next in to bat. Brad was talking about the bowler: 'This guy's a pie thrower. You can't get out to him. If I was batting on this, I'd be 150 not out.' Now, when you're worried about getting out first ball, it's not the type of thing you want to hear!

After his great innings in Perth, we declared with a day and a half to bowl South Africa out. But the pitch had flattened right out and Jacques Rudolph wouldn't let us find a way through, even with Warnie bowling like a Trojan. We'd got into winning ways, so that draw felt like a loss. It was my first Test that we hadn't won. I felt a bit flat. Conversely, the South Africans were very happy. Sometimes when you hang on for dear life and get through for a draw, it feels like a win. You've got away with one. You also think you've got a lot of improving to do, which is good for you, whereas the team that has dominated starts thinking that all they need to do is maintain that level. This same situation would affect us adversely in England three years later, and against South Africa in my last season.

We had a couple of days off and then Christmas in Melbourne to revive ourselves after the disappointment of Perth.

My first Boxing Day Test was another amazing experience. My preparation is important to me, but everything went wrong in the lead-up. Amy, who was pregnant with our second child, started having complications and we had to race to the Women's Hospital the day before Christmas Eve. I was shocked and scared. They got her into a hospital bed and said she had to stay there. I asked her, 'What do you want to do?' She said she had no choice: she had to do what they told her.

I remember trying to catch a taxi with Jasmin on the street outside the Royal Melbourne Women's Hospital at 2 am. The

Gilchrist family were a great help while Amy was in hospital, looking after Jasmin while I was at training the next day. When Amy came out on Christmas Eve, the doctors had given her strict orders of complete bed rest. She was scared and I was worried, but at the same time trying to train and get ready for the Test. For Christmas Day, we stayed in the room together rather than go to the big team function at Crown, and on Boxing Day her dad would come over and escort her back to Perth. At least I didn't get nervous for the Test match: I had more important matters on my mind.

The other big distraction from the Test was that Kerry Packer passed away. I was on the executive of the Australian Players' Association, and we were always very thankful to Packer, who had changed the game for us through World Series Cricket and the financial security it brought cricketers. I couldn't believe he'd passed away. We had a minute's silence and wore black armbands on match day.

For some reason, the pitch had been watered for too long before they'd put the covers on the night before the Test, so it was very wet on the first morning and they delayed the start by half an hour. Since the infamous Test at Edgbaston in 2005, when Australia had lost after sending England in, Ricky was determined always to bat first, and so when he won the toss, he decided to bat on a pitch the consistency of plasticine.

When I went out to bat at 3/176, I thought about Kerry Packer a lot, about what he'd done for the players, and set myself to honour him with a Boxing Day century.

The other big fella I had to thank was Glenn McGrath. After Ricky made another century, Big Nelly sparked a major collapse and we were 9/248 when Pigeon came out to join me. I was only 27 at the time. I was dropped by Jacques Kallis going for a cut shot, and then it was cat-and-mouse again, just like in Adelaide. I chipped singles, Graeme Smith brought the South African fielders in, and then I hit the ball between or over them for four. Glenn showed great courage to hang in there for two hours. The South Africans were getting very grumpy, particularly when I lobbed a few shots just between the fielders.

Playing a Test in Melbourne brought back many memories. When I used to run up sandhills with Dad, I'd think, *This is for a hundred on Boxing Day.* I loved watching that Test on TV at Christmas time. It got me out into the back yard to play with Dave, and later, the hope of one day playing on Boxing Day motivated me through my toughest times and toughest training sessions.

And now, in the middle of the MCG in the biggest Test match I could dream of, I was charging down the pitch uncaringly, wanting to slog the bowlers into Bay 13! Could life get any better? There was no pressure on me at all. I'll never forget that day.

Pigeon was pretty relaxed, and made some funny comments. After half an hour, he went for a massive cover-drive on the up. I came down and gave him a spray. 'No, Pigeon, you're not to play big shots! Just survive!'

He gave me a puzzled look. 'How am I supposed to score any runs?'

I had to stay on his hammer. I said, 'Leave the run-scoring to me!' I went back to the other end and thought, *I can't believe I've spoken to Glenn McGrath like that. It should be the other way around!*

He was always amusing. When I was finally bowled for 122, after a 107-run partnership (McGrath 11 not out), and we were walking off, Pigeon was saying, 'I can't believe how tired I am. I'm exhausted from all that concentrating. I don't think I'll be able to bowl.' I was in hysterics: this guy can bowl 35 overs without getting a sweat on, and here he was exhausted by a couple of hours' batting, which he'd probably never done before.

That partnership had let the air out of the South Africans. The momentum of the game had changed, and even though we'd only made 355 we held the whip hand in the match from then on. The bowlers then just ground them down with relentless pressure. Andrew Symonds got a couple of lbws in the first innings and Brett Lee bowled really fast. When I was fielding at short leg, Brett bowled a bouncer that whistled past Jacques Kallis's head. I could see the shock in his eyes. The next ball was a searing yorker that cleaned up the stumps. It was quite an experience to see, up close, this great batsman rattled by Brett's pace, accuracy and aggression. Warnie was also at his best, and in the end we won comfortably.

A few days later, the Sydney Test match was Ricky's 100th Test. He was in absolute supreme form in my first few years in the Australian team, and it was a real education for me to watch him. Ricky approached his net sessions like they were a Test match. He wanted the bowlers to be steaming in, and he'd be looking to dominate them. He brought total intensity to practice. When we did fielding drills, he would never drop a ball, and his throws hit the stumps more than anyone else's. He wanted to be the best at everything, and got dirty at himself if he missed a single throw. I've never known a more competitive bloke. Even friendly games of cards or mucking around, he'd be trying to crush you.

As a captain, what was so good about him was he had so much belief and backing from the players, and it was mutual. If you were struggling, he'd come up and tell you he had total trust in you, and a good score was around the corner. Once we were on the field, he wanted to win so badly he would try everything, even when the game was fading away. He was geeing the boys up – 'Just one wicket here and we're through!' – and getting into the opposition, leading every charge.

In Sydney, where he was indomitable year after year, he scored a hundred in each innings. To this day I've never seen anyone bat as well as he did in that match. I've seen Sachin Tendulkar on days when his bat seems to be the width of a king-size bed. I've seen Lara and Kallis at their best. But from ball one in Sydney, against very good bowlers, Ricky was just belting everything out of the middle of the bat.

I honestly thought he was playing a different game. The way he could come out and smash his first ball over square leg, taking on the best bowlers in the world with supreme confidence, it helped everyone else to relax and think, *It can't be too bad out there.* It was infectious. Whereas if your number three is playing and missing and nicking through slips and getting hit on the body, you're thinking, *Gee, it must be tough.* But Ricky made batting look easy, the best gift a number three can ever give to his middle order.

He and I put on 130 in the first innings, and I played the 'McGrath role', scoring 45. Batting with Ricky felt like I had the best seat in the house. I got to stand at the other end and chat with him between overs, and then to hear the grunts and groans of the bowlers, their screams of frustration that they had to keep getting smashed by him. His straight drives were the best – all you had to do at the non-striker's end was get out of the way and listen to the ball whistle past.

It was also beneficial to bat with him because when he got off strike, the South Africans automatically lost focus. So I began getting loose balls from tired, frustrated bowlers. I was proud to be on the ground with him. As a cricket fan as well as a player, I'd been privileged to be on the ground when Lara passed Allan Border's record, and two years later would feel the same way to be on the field at Mohali when Sachin passed Lara's record. I felt honoured to be on the field with those great players and to be a part of history.

South Africa were desperate to level the series with a win, and in the fourth innings set us nearly 300 to win, but Ricky simply went out and blazed. It looked like a comfortable 8-wicket win, but wouldn't have been anything like that without his batting.

FIFTEEN

It was the end of my tenth summer in first-class cricket, but what a change. After so many years of struggle, I was a Test player, and in my six matches for Australia just about everything seemed to have gone my way. We had won two series, and I'd already scored three hundreds.

In the home one-day series, we beat Sri Lanka in the finals and I was having unexpected success in the lower middle-order 'Bevan' role, needing to accelerate from ball one. Considering the way I saw myself as a batsman, it was bizarre to be scoring quickly. In a funny way, at the end of a one-day innings I thought the pressure was off me. Obviously the plan is, simply, to get as many runs as you can as quickly as you can. I could feel like a hero if it came off, and no great loss if I got out. It was a position where you had to think about the team's position more than your own. I enjoyed the challenge of working out what to do in each situation. I had a couple of areas, over cover or midwicket, where I thought I could hit a boundary – every left-hander needs a good cow-corner slog – and if it was anywhere else I'd just try to get bat on ball and run hard between wickets. Bowlers hadn't mastered

ABOVE: Receiving my Baggy Blue cap for scoring 50 for Whitfords Junior Cricket Club when I was ten.
LEFT: Proudly showing off my cricket and squash trophies.

ABOVE: Playing the semi-final for Western Australia Under-17s against Tasmania in Canberra. We won this game but lost the final to New South Wales. BELOW: The Western Australia Under-17 team. Manager of the tour, Ian Kevan, is third from left. I am fifth from left and the smallest in the team.

ABOVE: Celebrating a Pura Cup win against Victoria at the MCG. I am at the back in the middle with the zinc cream on my nose. BELOW: Western Australia's Super 8 team at a pre-season competition in Queensland. Western Australia was the eventual winner.

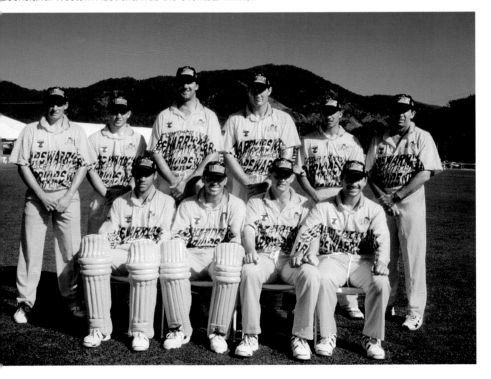

ABOVE: Playing for Northan▓
in 2001 and leaving the fiel◀
with Adrian Rollins, a huge
West Indian opening batsm█
who made me look like a te
year-old.

LEFT: Batting for Australia A
with India's wicketkeeper
Deep Dasgupta behind me
during a three-day match
in Hobart, on 19 December
2003. (Photo by William West/AF▓
Getty Images)

RIGHT: Batting for Durham during the first day of the Frizzell County Championship game between Somerset and Durham in Taunton, England, on 26 July 2005. (Photo by Stu Forster/Getty Images)

BELOW: Leaping into the arms of teammate Brett Lee after Australia defeated the International Cricket Council (ICC) World XI team, giving an unbeatable 2–0 lead in the three-match series on 7 October 2005. (Photo by William West/AFP/Getty Images)

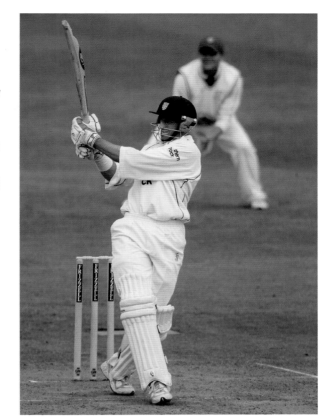

ABOVE: Congratulations from Brett Lee and Adam Gilchrist during training at the Gabba in Brisbane on 1 November 2005, after Justin Langer was injured. (Photo by Hamish Blair/Getty Images)
BELOW: Being presented with my Baggy Green cap by Bill Brown, Australia's oldest living Test cricketer, before day one of the first Test between Australia and the West Indies in Brisbane.

ABOVE: Sweeping a ball away on the way to a century against South Africa in the second Test match against South Africa at the Melbourne Cricket Ground on 27 December 2005. With tailender Glenn McGrath we put on 107 runs for the last wicket. (Photo by William West/AFP/Getty Images) BELOW: Captain Adam Gilchrist and me, as vice-captain, talk tactics during the VB Series between Australia and Sri Lanka played at the WACA in Perth on 29 January 2006. (Photo by Hamish Blair/Getty Images)

LEFT: Receiving the One-day International Player of the Year trophy at the Allan Border Medal dinner on 6 February 2006. (Photo ▮ Kristian Dowling/Getty Images)

BELOW: With Adam Gilchrist and Brad Hogg showing off our World Cup 2007 winning medals and rings on arrival back home.

death bowling yet, and I think batsmen were ahead of them. So I became the aggressive batsman I'd wanted to be, without trying. I didn't change my game to be a more attacking player. It just happened. That's how well things were going for me.

Then the summer ended with the best news of all, the birth of William on 23 February 2006, after a successful home one-day series and the team's departure for a three-Test tour to South Africa.

I stayed at home for the birth, which went smoothly. We organised an induce date again, and the process was like checking in to a hotel. William popped out healthy and happy, the biggest of our babies, eight pounds one. He did have one night in the neo-natal ward as precaution but generally speaking, he was in good shape.

But after one night in hospital, I was off to South Africa the next morning. I felt torn, wanting to be at home to soak it up and support Amy, but also desperate to get into my first overseas Test tour. Amy had been through a lot and could have done with someone to support her and share the joy for more than just one night, so it was really difficult to rush off. At least I was there for the birth. I've spoken to cricketers who haven't met their child for the first three or four months. It's time you can never get back.

At least I was rushing off to do something I loved. We had a T20 and five one-dayers to kick the tour off. Being late joining the squad, and having seen my son born, I was unusually pumped up for the first one-day game at Centurion. I was batting with Michael Clarke, and we needed a partnership. During a drinks break I was carrying on. 'Come on, Pup! Remember what's on your head! Don't give these blokes anything!'

To one side, Mark Boucher was chuckling away, and said to Pup, 'I'm glad I'm not playing with him, he's way too intense!' All of a sudden I got paranoid. *Everyone's going to think I'm the most intense person going around.*

The last game of a tight series was in Johannesburg. They'd smashed us at Centurion and Cape Town, and we had our backs to the wall before fighting back for a gritty win at Port Elizabeth and then a miraculous victory, nine wickets down, at Durban, with Stuart Clark and Mick Lewis bringing it home.

All through the summer beforehand, Australia's coach, John Buchanan, had kept on saying, 'With the talent in this team, you guys can make 400 in a one-dayer.' We didn't believe him. No chance. He said, 'What if one day you just let go of that belief? Maybe that's the only thing that's holding you back.'

The Wanderers pitch looked amazing, without a crack. The bounce was very even, and there was no swing. The outfield was like glass. When you know that, all you have to do is time the ball, not force it, so you get into better position. At altitude, the ball was flying further through the air. Every factor seemed to be working the batsmen's way. It was a great seeing day, very clear and sunny: in short, in every way a perfect day for batting.

Ricky, moreover, was playing at his all-time peak, and we approached the last 35 overs as if they were the last 10. I was promoted to number four, so we had a left-hander in, as there was a short boundary on one side. I said to Ricky, 'I'm going to have a go at everything.' He said, 'If you see it, back yourself.' We still had Damien Martyn and Andrew Symonds in the sheds, so with nothing to lose, I took them on, and ended up with 81 off 51 balls. My effort was about half of Ricky's: he got 164 off 105 balls, one of the best one-day innings anyone has ever seen.

I got out with a few overs to go and sat in the viewing area. When we got to 400, we were yelling and screaming with excitement. Buchanan had this knowing grin on his face. We totalled 4/434, a world record by almost 100 runs. Incredible! We were so elated after the beltings we'd taken early in the series and the fightback to get to parity, and now we were going to win!

At the change of innings, just before we went out, Ricky pulled us in and said, 'Take the score completely out of it. Let's pretend we're defending 200. Don't think you'll coast through.'

Nathan Bracken got a wicket in the second over, which brought Herschelle Gibbs in. We were staying in the same hotel as the South Africans, and the night before, we'd gone out for dinner at 6.30pm. Herschelle was at the bar when we left, seemingly sloshed already, with a glass of wine in his hand. When we came back at about 9.30pm, he was still there. Just before I went to bed an hour later I looked over the railing outside my hotel room and there he was, still in that spot. At least he was a free wicket.

Well, we weren't able to defend 200. In fact, South Africa got to 200 in about the 24th over with two wickets down. Herschelle played without any fear. He played like they said Doug Walters used to do when he was hung over. Herschelle and Graeme Smith managed to find a four or six every over, and the rate was eight, nine, ten runs an over. We couldn't stem the flow. The scary thing was, the comparisons kept going up on the board, and they were always 15 or 20 runs ahead of us. Batting without any hope of winning was such a dangerous thing. They had complete freedom. I thought, *Far out, they're going to win easily.*

Then, with about 100 needed off the last 13 overs, they seemed to start to think too much. They obviously saw that they were a chance to win, and the fear shifted back onto them. We got right back into the game, mainly thanks to Nathan Bracken, who took five wickets. He was the best one-day bowler in the world at the time. He could swing the new ball and get the early wicket, and then, in the middle section, he came on and bowled what were almost left-arm spinners. Finally, he was one of the best death bowlers, knowing exactly where he was landing the ball. And he was a good thinker under pressure. He took five wickets and may have been man of the match but for Herschelle, whose 175 off 111 balls outdid everybody.

When it all hung in the balance, Boucher came in and finished us off. In the dressing room, the South Africans were going off their heads. In our room, where we could hear all the shouting and yahooing, everyone was reacting differently. I was just empty. I couldn't believe it. Ricky was kicking chairs and throwing shoes. Buchanan was philosophical, saying, 'Amazing, that, wasn't it?' Gilly was stunned. Poor Mick Lewis, whose figures were 0/113, was devastated. We were all going over and saying, 'Bad luck mate, we'll have a beer and forget it.' But I think it affected him for a long time.

The selectors made some changes for the Test series, which was starting at Newlands in Cape Town a few days after that unbelievable one-dayer. It was hard for everyone to come down to earth. McGrath was injured, and to my great delight Stuart Clark had been brought into the team to play a similar constrictive role. We often spoke about that night in Pakistan when we'd wondered if we would get a chance. He was a fantastic bowler and it would have been a travesty if he hadn't played Test cricket. He was a very nice guy, intelligent, and like me, had had to wait a long time for his chance.

In the batting order, the selectors seemed to be acknowledging that they'd made a mistake in dropping Damien Martyn after the 2005 Ashes. He had been extremely unlucky in that series, receiving three lbw decisions that were clearly not out. It would have been hard to take, being scapegoated for the loss. For all his flamboyance, he would have taken that to heart. But he was the complete player. He played spin and reverse swing very well, and was one of the best timers you can imagine. Teammates still talk of him as one of the best players they ever saw. The history books may not indicate that, but his peers rate him in that league. Unfortunately for Brad Hodge, he was the one to make way.

Newlands is a beautiful ground, with Table Mountain in the backdrop, but it's definitely not one of my favourites. Whenever I batted there, the ball nipped around and eluded me. I heard stories of it being a great batting pitch, but I never saw it. It was quite wet on the first day and the bowlers took divots out of the pitch, which, as they dried, caused the ball to dart all over the place. Haydos, Ricky and Simmo were the only players to make half-centuries, and the man-of-the-match was Stuey Clark, who cleaned them up in both innings. We only had to chase 95, and I was with Marto. My shot to score the winning runs was typical for me in Cape Town: a sweep that ballooned off my glove and went over leg slip. Winning that match, my first away Test win, in three days was great, but batting was hard work.

Although I was missing Amy, Jasmin and Will, I loved the touring life. I got on well with nearly all of the guys, and didn't belong to any particular clique. After training or play, someone would say, 'What's everyone doing for dinner?' I'd go with whichever group was eating the type of food I felt like. So I ended up spending time with almost everybody. If I had close mates, there was Simmo, and I stuck close to Gilly and Magilla, having known them for so long. I got on well with Ricky, though he was very busy. The newer guys also tended to stick together, and I still considered myself one of them, so I hung out a lot with Stuart Clark and, during the one-dayers, Simon Katich and Shane Watson. I'm not really a strategic person when it comes to friendships, so I guess I went whichever way the wind was blowing.

The one off-field matter I'd struggled with since the start of my international career was stopping my mind from racing as I tried to get my non-negotiable eight hours of nightly sleep. I was discovering that the biggest mental hazard in Test cricket is that it leaves you with too much time to think. When you're waiting to bat, there's too much time to wonder what can go wrong. When you're out cheaply, there's too much time to relive it all and worry about what the selectors are going to do. When you're in the field, there's too much time to stress about your next innings and the stage of the game. And when you're back at the hotel trying to get to sleep, you're still playing out every scenario in your mind, a knock-on effect of all the doubts and clouds that have built up through the day.

Sleeping was a something I found increasingly difficult. If I'd had a very good sleep, my thinking was straight, I could see the ball more clearly, and I could generally operate a lot better. When I hadn't slept well or had a low number of hours, my mind was muddled, I wasn't seeing the ball as sharply, and I felt stressed and tense.

I saw sleep as a controllable factor in my performance. I wouldn't compromise on my sleep by staying out late, and I was now controlling it further by taking pills that were prescribed by the doctors at Cricket Australia. I wasn't worried about the risks. I struggled with getting off to sleep so I took one.

There were other strategies. I began using meditation, relaxation and breathing techniques, but I certainly found that sleeping tablets were the most effective. I was pretty open in talking about it with teammates. Some of the boys joked that I couldn't live without them. Other guys used them and thought they worked well. I didn't care what other people thought. I knew they were good for me. I didn't have a problem with them, which I knew because every time I went home, for however long, I never used them. I knew I didn't have a dependency.

The second Test in Durban was Warnie's hundredth, and Ricky was at the peak of his powers, making a hundred in each innings. I got 75 in the first innings but it was a real battle. My first twenty were very hard work, and then I was batting with the tail, which freed me up a bit, but I was streaky and a bit lucky, slogging a few at the end. I found Durban hard, and two years later it would leave me with some bruises I will never forget, courtesy of Dale Steyn. But to be honest, I found the whole of South Africa hard to bat.

In South Africa's second innings, Warnie wheeled away forever. He didn't have a great match in Cape Town and he was really pumped for Durban. Even at training he was working a lot harder. He ground away, hardly bowling a loose ball on a good batting wicket, and bowled us to victory. Towards the end it was getting really tight for time, South Africa looking like they might survive for the draw, and he bowled a wrong 'un that struck Ntini. It might have been going over the top of the stumps, but the umpire gave Makhaya out and we had a great celebration – we'd just beaten the team we considered our main challengers 2–0 and 2–0. It was a phenomenal feeling.

The Test pitch at the Wanderers was nothing like what we'd played on in the one-dayer. You needed a lot of luck to survive on a pitch that was both cracked and green. Ashwell Prince got 93 for them in dicey conditions. I thought it was going to be a nightmare chasing South Africa's 303. Then, on the first ball of our innings, Justin Langer, playing his hundredth Test, turned his head and – *Whack*, it hit him flush in the head and bounced all the way back to the bowler, Ntini.

We were effectively 3/68 when I came in, but the pitch had settled down a bit, and I had good partnerships with Warnie and Brett Lee. If you could survive the first thirty-five or forty minutes, it was okay for batting. I felt pretty chuffed to make 73, because it was so difficult, but we conceded a lead, and after South Africa's second innings we needed almost 300 to win.

Suddenly, with Justin having been in hospital with concussion, I was a Test opener again, in less than ideal circumstances. Haydos and Ricky had rare failures, and we still needed 260 when Marto joined me. I was extremely lucky, playing and missing repeatedly. Even Marto played and missed a lot and we both nicked a few. But we kept saying to each other, 'Play every ball on its merits. If we get a jaffa and get knocked over or get beaten, that's the way it is, so be it. Don't worry about anything else.'

We looked ugly, but we got the job done until I was out for 89 and we still needed nearly 100 to win. Simmo slogged a few and tried to get it over with, but he, Gilly, Warnie and Marto all got out in a rush and the final twist was that Brett Lee and Michael Kasprowicz, who had fallen agonisingly short at Edgbaston in 2005, were left with 20 to get. They edged and swished and inched closer.

Meanwhile, there was great drama going on in the dressing room. Ricky walked in from the viewing area and saw Justin padded up to go in at number eleven.

Ricky said, 'No JL, it's only a game of cricket, don't go out there.'

Justin glared at him. 'No, mate, it's not just a game of cricket, it's a Test match for Australia.' And it was also his hundredth.

'No, you're not,' Ricky said. 'I'm the captain.'

Justin looked him squarely in the eye and said, 'If you don't let me go out there, our friendship is over.'

I don't know how seriously Ricky took that, but he was saying, 'You've got a wife, you've got children, if you get another one in the head you might die.' He went off and arranged for big Steve Bernard to stand at the race and hold both sides, to block Justin from going out. Justin, predictably, was having none of it, so that it was a Mexican stand-off of sorts.

Thankfully nothing came of it, because Brett belted one over point and we'd won the series 3–0. During the celebrations, I think Marto, who had virtually won the match with his 101, was the proudest he'd been in his whole career. He'd really set out to prove a point since his reinstatement. Some of the guys said later that he should have retired on that day.

SIXTEEN

aving played tough cricket for nine Tests and more than twenty one-dayers since November, we were all exhausted and looking forward to going home. But no – we had to get on a plane the next day and head to Bangladesh!

I know I'd had to wait a long time to play for Australia, and I wasn't complaining, but still, it was a tough ask. Amy was juggling a toddler and a new baby, who I'd only seen for one day. The team was coming down from Johannesburg and the emotions of that win, and when we arrived in Fatullah we only had time for one training session, as the Test was starting the next morning. The Bangladeshis weren't very high in the world cricket rankings, so it was natural for the motivation of the guys to come down a notch.

We got off to a horrendous start. Bangladesh were 1/144 at lunch on the first day, with the left-hander Shahriar Nafees belting us everywhere. It didn't get much better for a couple of days, as we collapsed to 6/93 in reply to their 427. It took some pretty special individual performances to pull us out of the mire. Gilly made a great 144 in the first innings and rated it one of his best innings. He played differently from the usual Gilly. He was patient and responsible, still playing some big shots but constructing it as a batsman setting himself for a long innings. When all the others were out, he realised it had to be him. I wouldn't have said it was his best innings, but it was one of the most crucial. Then Warnie, who had struggled on the first day, bowled superbly in Bangladesh's second dig, and Ricky's determination, his single-mindedness in not letting them get him out, got us through in the end. Even the way he defended the ball, he was sniffing it off the pitch, watching it so closely, such concentration and energy. His unbeaten 118 was inspirational.

Gilly spoke before leading the song, which he was doing in JL's absence. He said, 'I know we're playing Bangladesh, but that's one of the best wins I've had in my career, to pull ourselves out of that, we should be proud of ourselves.' It was a really good speech.

Coming so close to losing was a big wake-up call. Our preparation had been inadequate and didn't pay the proper respect to a Test match. You can't drop your guard against a sub-continental team in their home conditions. They're very difficult when they get in front, and we'd let Bangladesh dictate to us.

However, it was hard to get over the feeling that we were being flogged by the scheduling, being sent here by a program that itself didn't properly respect Test cricket. If they wanted to pay Bangladesh the compliment of having a Test series there, the administrators shouldn't have programmed it on the back of a six-Test series with South Africa and a big home summer. The result was pretty low morale off the field. Some of the guys were complaining a lot and certainly didn't want to be there. Several guys were injured, including Marto. The strength in the team was that guys like Ricky and Gilly, the leaders, looked for the positives when things weren't going our way. That rubbed off on the others. I was pretty exhausted, having gone through my first full stint in international cricket and being away from home for a long time, but Ricky and Gilly were adamant about fighting our way through these Test matches and three one-dayers, and then there was light at the end of the tunnel.

We had a full day of travel to get to Chittagong for the second Test, and were very tired when we got to the hotel. I just wanted to lie down in my room. I sat on the bed. *Uh-oh.* It was literally like a table, it was so hard. I lay down and nearly bruised myself. I thought, *It's going to be a long week.*

Better acclimatised than in Fatullah, we bowled first again, and Warne, Gillespie and MacGill had them out for 197 on a pretty good batting pitch. Haydos was out late on the first day, and Ricky copped some stick for sending a night watchman in ahead of him. Dizzy Gillespie was the man, having been brought back into the team for the first time since the 2005 Ashes when many of our fast bowlers had broken down with injury.

If Ricky was worried that he'd given up the chance of scoring runs by sending Dizzy ahead of him, he was ropable when Dizzy ran him out for 52. Rain had disrupted the second day and we were all a bit toey, but when I walked out past Ricky on the third morning, after the run-out, steam was coming out of his ears.

Batting with Gillespie was quite an experience. He had always had a solid defence, but as a tail-ender the good ball would eventually undo him or he would lose patience. I honestly believe that on this day his application and concentration, in very hot conditions, were so impregnable because he was scared of going back to the dressing room and facing up to Ricky. When we went in at tea, I don't remember Ricky saying anything to him, and Dizzy gave him a wide berth.

He kept going and going and going, and was hilarious to bat with, so relaxed and laconic. He kept saying, 'If it's on the stumps, I'll block it. If it's off the stumps, I'll smash it.' I said, 'Yeah, sure mate, whatever you think.'

It was a brilliant batting pitch and there wasn't much spin, pace or bounce. For their bowlers, there wasn't much to rattle Dizzy's simple plan. We batted together for most of the third day, and when he got to 100 in the last overs nobody could believe it. In the middle, he said, 'I can't wait to hear what my mates at home say about this.'

On the fourth morning, he showed no sign of flagging. What kept him going was, he began ticking off the highest scores of some great Test batsmen. He hit a single to fine leg and said, 'That's Mark Waugh.' Then, with a cover drive for a single, he said, 'That's Damien Martyn, got him covered.' I don't think he was motivated to take his score to 200 because of that milestone. It was that he kept saying, 'I desperately want to go past Steve Waugh.' Steve's Test highest was 200.

My innings was more or less forgotten by most people. From the beginning I was pretty nervous, and punched a few off the spinners. The outfield was flying, like lightning. The longer you were there, eventually you could only get yourself out. On the fourth day I got tired, and we were close to declaring. I had a few slogs and got caught on the boundary – the type of thing you'd expect a bowler to do. 182 was my highest Test score at the time, but I probably threw away the opportunity to make a double century.

Not Dizzy. He got to 183, and I thought, *Far out, he's got me covered too!* Ricky showed what a big man he was by allowing Dizzy to get past the 200 mark, which was the icing on the cake. Dizzy was over the moon, as we all were for him. He knew he was coming to the end of his Test career. After every day's play, he sat in the team room and had a few beers and chatted with the boys, soaking it all up. He just wanted to enjoy his last series. He said he knew his time was done. He just thought he would casually score a double-hundred and be the man of the series to sign off from Test cricket!

SEVENTEEN

After a well-earned rest in the winter of 2006, I was gearing up for my first Ashes series. For me, it was simply thrilling to find myself in this position. For the players who had been in England in 2005, there was a hunger for revenge.

In August, we were given sketchy details about flying to Brisbane for some kind of 'camp'. All we were told to bring was the bare minimum: underpants, socks, a couple of T-shirts. We would find out more when we arrived.

So I was a bit nervous about it. We took a bus to a big shed somewhere outside Brisbane. The boys were in good spirits to see each other, but there was a bit of apprehension. What did they have in store for us?

There were 30-odd of us, including the full training squad and support staff. An army guy had us line up and strip down to our underpants. On the floor in front of us there was a backpack with supplies. Everyone was too scared to say something, in case we got a spray from the warrant officer running the show.

We were told that we could put down on the floor any medications. I put down my asthma spray. My asthma had started in a bizarre manner, during adulthood. David had asthma badly as a child and had to go to hospital once or twice, but I'd had nothing. Then, when I was 17 and playing A grade, I did a lap with the team one day and got really wheezy. I said to a teammate, 'Can I borrow your puffer?' The Ventolin worked straight away. I saw a doctor and he said, 'You've got a case of exercise-induced asthma.' Every time I did vigorous exercise, I got tight in the chest and needed the puffer, which opened my chest up. It never really restricted me, as the Ventolin cured it.

For his 'medication', Warnie put down a few packets of cigarettes. The boss guy said he couldn't have them, but Warnie, standing there in his Playboy underpants, managed to persuade them that he was addicted to cigarettes and they were his medication.

We were sorted into five or six groups. Ours had Brett Lee, Gilly, Michael Clarke and Richard McGuinness, our analyst. They put us on another bus, got us out at the bottom of a mountain in the bush, and yelled, 'Get in your formation!' Our task was to cart jerry cans of water up the mountain, staying in a line, precisely 10 metres from the next group. If anyone strayed, we all had to go down for ten push-ups. It was really tough, plus the physicality of going up this bloody great mountain. Sure enough, we had to do push-ups regularly. Three-quarters of the way up, I was asking myself seriously if I could make it. One thing that kept me going was seeing how guys like John Buchanan, Brute Bernard, our media officer Philip Pope and the fielding coach Mike Young, some of them in their fifties, none a professional athlete, were doing it too. I thought, *If they're doing it I've got to keep going.*

It was certainly a shock to the system, having to do this straight-up. We were exhausted at the top. Philip Pope was dry-retching over the side of the mountain, and other guys were lying in agony. And this was just the beginning.

We were sent off in different directions to do exercises in teams, putting the jerry cans on stretchers and transporting them to another location an indeterminate distance away. We rotated the load and held on with different arms, taking turns to have a break, but the boys were very tired. We were only allowed to eat army rations, and it was one activity after another – the next was pushing a four-wheel drive vehicle 4 or 5 kilometres up a dirt track. Then, we just walked and walked, for hours, until sunset on a dirt track. Our army guide said, 'We'll stop here for the night.' I thought, *Stop where?* There was only the dirt track and forest. Our 'camp' was in the forest itself.

Brett Lee, fastidious as always, hung all his clothes on trees to dry them out. We were sitting around and eating dinner: a tin of soup and a loaf of bread to share. We were hungry enough to eat five loaves each. When the sun went down, we crashed quickly. Not far away, Warnie's group had set up, and we could hear Shane complaining about the 'mozzie grand prix'.

I fell into a deep sleep for what seemed like minutes, pitch black, and suddenly: *Boom! Boom!!!*

The guide was packing up his stuff. 'We have ten minutes to get on the road,' he said. 'It's not safe here.' Half-asleep, having been woken by two bomb blasts, it was pitch black, we were scared and desperately trying to roll up our sleeping bags and stuff them into the tiny bags. I couldn't jam mine in, and Pup was having awful trouble. Brett Lee was running around trying to find his clothes hanging on the trees, calling out, 'I can't find my shirt! I can't find my pants!'

We eventually found his clothes and got Pup's sleeping bag into its sack. The guide told us we were twenty minutes too slow getting going, and had to take off at double speed.

There were more exercises that night, but lower intensity than during the day, when they'd really tried to break us down. The focus became more mental than physical. A goal of the camp was to put guys under pressure and and take them out of their comfort zone and see how they'd react when tired and hungry. Would they come together or pull apart? Buchanan had a clear goal, which was to see who would work as a team when things got tough, and who would show the negative side of their character.

The army guys also taught us about the chain of command. Each team had a leader and a 2IC, who you had to go to first if you wanted something from the leader. You had to go through that chain. On this walk, in the middle of the night, I was the 2IC. We took off, not knowing how far we were going. Michael Clarke came up, waddling. 'Huss, I've got that bad chafe, I don't know if I can make it.' I said to the leader, 'Pup's really struggling, he's got bad chafe.' Chafe is a bit like getting hit in the nuts in cricket. Everyone else thinks it's funny, but the guy who's suffering is suffering badly. So we spent a long time with the guide getting some ointment, which finally got passed down to Pup. He reacted like his saviour had come. As he rubbed it on, it was the best day of his life. 'Thanks, Huss, thanks so much!' And I was just the 2IC!

That night, we had to do an orienteering course through a paddock with glow-lights. Our team was racing about, losing members, and having a bit of a disaster. We found our way to a road, and by the side of it Stuart MacGill was on the ground, screaming.

We were saying, 'Are you all right, Magilla?'

He was swearing and cursing everyone in sight.

He'd hurt his knee, and absolutely done his block.

The guide told us to keep going to our rendezvous point, but the whispers were going around about Magilla. We were really worried that he might have injured his knee seriously.

By now, for the rest of us, the fatigue was setting in. Walking for hours and hours, the sleep deprivation, the hunger. The guides told us we could stop and camp for the night as a group on another trail. It was so uncomfortable, there were tyre tracks with a hump in the middle, it was cold, and we were exhausted. We were all worried about getting woken up and having to walk again in the night.

But there were always lighter moments. The whole squad was lying on this track, all in a line, side by side. The next morning I woke up and looked along the line. Somewhere in the middle was a sleeping bag pulled up over someone's head with a tiny hole for his mouth. And out of that hole was a cigarette, alight, the smoke puffing out. Warnie. He was completely covered, except for his cigarette. In a day and night of madness and hunger and fatigue, it's amazing what can make you laugh.

For all the hardship, that camp was awesome, one of my best experiences in the Australian team. We didn't talk cricket. It was more about discovering each other. The next day was a lot of gruelling walking, and then we were transported to a different place to set up tents.

Magilla and Warnie, who was now struggling physically, were kept aside while we did abseiling and treks up another mountain. Because they'd missed the activities, those two had to give a tutorial to the whole squad on leadership, which was really interesting, because they had a curious dynamic. I think, for all the rivalry, they drove each other on. For Warnie, the greatest of all time, having as good a bowler as MacGill on the scene kept pushing him to prove himself the best. Meanwhile, MacGill wanted to compete with the best and be considered up at that level, so when he had an opportunity he was highly motivated. MacGill was very respectful of Warnie and would be the first to admit Warnie was the best we've ever had.

A key activity on the camp was to get in a big circle and, one by one, stand in the centre. When you were there, the others would say things they really liked about you, and things you had to work on. It was confronting being in the middle of your peers, being told things you had to get better at. It was daunting telling guys too, being open enough to say to someone he was a bit selfish. I remember thinking, *I don't know if I've got the balls to tell someone they're a selfish kind of guy.*

There were some home truths. I was told I was too intense and that made other guys feel uncomfortable. They said I should relax a bit. On the positive side, they said my work ethic was good.

The funny thing was, when Glenn McGrath got into the middle, Jason Gillespie got up with a straight face and said, 'Glenn, we think you're a great team man, down to earth and all that. But you wear your pants way too high.'

We were killing ourselves, but the army bosses weren't happy. 'Jason,' his guide said, 'you think this is a serious problem, do you?'

Dizzy said, deadpan: 'Yes. We think it's a serious problem.'

Truth sessions of this kind didn't happen very often in the normal team routine. It started happening among the leaders, bringing in outside consultants to get feedback. When a new player came into the team and we were having a stretch or a warm-up, Gilly would ask the player to tell us all five things we didn't know about him and his family. There were some humorous stories told, like when Mick Lewis joined the team on a one-day tour to New Zealand and described his sister who had some problems with the law. It was a fun exercise and a good way to get to know some of the personal details of guys that we spent so much time with.

Our debriefs stressed that when you get tired and things aren't going well, that's when you've got to come together and look after each other. At the end of the camp, Ricky gave an incredible speech, inspiring us all, and said, looking forward to the Ashes two months away, 'It's up to every individual to get his preparation right. Leave no stone unturned. Make sure you're 100 per cent prepared.' We went straight from the boot camp to the Hyatt resort at Coolum for four or five days of luxury. A soft bed and a shower never felt so good. There were several meetings and our media guys educated us in how big the Ashes series would be, including some schooling in tabloid tactics to get people angry, being set up by people in bars and getting photos in the paper, all the worst-case scenarios. I drank it all in, thinking how the Australian team operated on a different level of professionalism from every other organisation I'd been involved in, and probably from every competing international team.

Our first playing assignment was the DLF Cup in Malaysia, a one-day triangular tournament with the West Indies and India in preparation for the ICC Champions Trophy in India. We took a really big squad to Malaysia, which made people jittery. We had four matches but everyone was only going to be playing two. There was competition within the team for places. Matty Hayden was desperately pushing to get an opening place back from Kato. Everyone was on trial for the Champions Trophy. So it wasn't great for building team spirit. Andrew Symonds was really dirty, saying, 'These are one-day internationals for Australia, I'm not happy games being given away to guys, and I don't want someone coming in and doing well and taking my place.'

But Buchanan and the selectors were adamant. It was great for some of the youngsters, but I was a bit on Simmo's side. Every game for Australia is important and you should have to earn your place. This divide, between those who were looking at planning and the bigger picture and a 'squad' mentality, and those who just thought every game for Australia was sacred, would become bigger and bigger over the next seven years.

But there are swings and roundabouts. Due to the rotation of players, in Malaysia I had the chance to captain Australia for the first time, which made me excited and proud. We were playing the West Indies. I was pumped and made a century, but then Chris Gayle and Brian Lara smashed us around and we lost comfortably. Dan Cullen, the brash young South Australian – an aggressive off-spinner, if there is such a thing – gave us a humorous moment. Dan loved being in the batsman's face. Lara played a ball and Dan was glaring at him, and said, 'You cocky p---k.'

The next five balls, Lara hit for six, four four, four and four. At the end of the over he nodded to Dan, as if to say, *Mate, pull your head in.*

As an aside on sledging, I didn't think the Australian team were as bad as they were made out to be. Haydos, Warnie, Justin, McGrath and Ricky were happy to say a few words to a batsman, but I never heard anything that crossed the line and got too personal. I thought the Aussie team were just copping stick because they were too good, and there had to be some way of bringing them down a notch.

Personally, I didn't sledge. I did it a couple of times early in my career. The first guy I sledged made 150. The second guy I sledged made 100. The third guy I sledged made 150. Something wasn't working. And it wasn't really my thing, I have to admit. I didn't feel right, and was no good at it, so I thought I'd better retire from sledging and let the other guys do it. The funniest sledge I ever heard was in a grade match for Wanneroo. I was at the non-striker's end, and the wicketkeeper was getting stuck into my teammate.

'Gee, you're an ugly player.'

'How can you be so ugly?'

'If there was an ugly eleven, you'd be captain.'

My mate turned around and said, 'Yeah, I've seen your missus, and she's batting number three.'

See, I think if you want to sledge, you have to have the knack of quick repartee, something I never had. When someone sledged me, I preferred not to get caught up in it. The Poms sometimes tried to needle me and get a confrontation going, but I just wouldn't buy into it. Batting was hard enough without having to think up witty comments as well.

When I was captain of teams, I wouldn't sledge, but would encourage the bowlers in ways the batsman could hear. Comments like, 'He's hanging back here,' or 'Don't be scared to bowl bouncers,' were more gamesmanship than sledging. If I could plant some doubts in the batsman's mind, and then set fields to make him think we'd bowl a particular way, that was fair in my book.

If players under my leadership were sledging, I might tell them to rein it in if they'd gone too far, but I like players to express themselves, and if they wanted to play that way, I would back them.

We ended up winning the DLF Cup, beating the West Indies in the final. After the game we had a rare chance to socialise with the West Indians. They were a bit divided on the issue, with some of them wanting to get on the team bus and others preferring to join us for a beer in our dressing room. Chris Gayle was one who came in, and he had the boys in stitches, taking the mickey out of everyone. Leaving the ground that night, my sides were in agony from laughing. It was a nice way to end the tournament.

EIGHTEEN

We got a short break, but just before leaving home for the Champions Trophy, I fell sick with influenza. It was a bad case and I was bed-ridden. I dragged myself up but during the flight I was in a world of pain. The first few days in India were a write-off for me. We also had to take doxycyclin, an antimalaria tablet. I had an allergic reaction to them and got sixteen cold sores: fourteen on my bottom lip and two big ones on my top lip. They were excruciating. At training I couldn't get the zinc off them, and they looked disgusting.

After about ten days I was grumpy and tired and not eating well. In the hotel, I got in a lift with Gilly.

'Huss, they're starting to look a bit better, I think you're on the mend.'

'Thanks Gill, yeah, it's been tough, I'm glad to hear that.'

We got down a few floors and Brad Haddin stepped into the lift. He took one look at me.

'Aaargghh, Huss, that's disgusting!!! Don't make me look at that!'

Oh well, I guess I appreciated Gilly's efforts to pep me up.

Eventually I could start to enjoy the tour. In Jaipur we set ourselves for a big game against England. We didn't say, 'Let's put a marker in the ground for the Ashes,' but most guys thought about it in that way. We particularly wanted to get Kevin Pietersen cheaply, and we didn't want to just win. We wanted to give them a good belting.

McGrath, Shane Watson and Mitchell Johnson bowled brilliantly and everything fell into place. We got Pietersen, continued getting wickets, and then Damien Martyn came out and every single ball was cannoning out of the middle of the bat. I was battling a bit, taking my time with a first real chance in the middle, but it was a joy watching Marto. I hit the winning runs off Steve Harmison, and for the first time I felt like I was really contributing on the tour.

That win kickstarted our campaign. We faced the West Indies in the final, which surprised us as we'd been more worried about South Africa, India or England. We thought the West Indies were dangerous, because of Gayle and Lara, but we were confident after we'd heard that some of them, including Gayle, had suffered a bad bout of gastro. Nathan Bracken did a terrific job with the ball, before Damien Martyn and Shane Watson chased down the target comfortably. We were ecstatic to win the trophy for the first time, and I was very happy to bounce back after such a bad start.

Back home, we had two weeks to get ready for the Ashes, and I had a first-class game against Queensland at the WACA. I was hardly playing any first-class cricket now, which was strange considering I'd played so many before I became a Test player. Prior to my Australian Test debut, I played 174 first-class games in eleven years. In my eight years of cricket as an Australian Test player, I played 79 Test matches and just 13 more first-class matches, seven of them for Western Australia.

The consequence was, I found it tough playing for my state again. The expectation was to score runs, as I was a Test player. I put more pressure on myself, but as I wasn't around the team and didn't know the players or the dynamics between people very well, it was hard to feel comfortable. I batted best when I felt like I was part of a team and could help people. Also, I didn't know the bowlers very well, and lastly, my mind would be drifting a little towards the next Test match. So my performances were not generally very good when I floated back into the West Australian team.

In Brisbane, the hype was on. For our first team meeting, I've never seen an Australian team, before or since, so focused and motivated and intense. In a group that was normally very relaxed, there was definitely an edge.

On the morning of the first Test, it was 32 or 33 degrees outside and Justin Langer went out in a jumper. I thought, *What on earth is he doing? Is he crazy?* JL was always intense, but this was bizarre. Clearly he had some reason, something going on in his mind, but it was another little sign telling me that this was not a normal Test match.

Steve Harmison got ready to bowl the first ball to him. I don't remember anyone saying he was going to bowl a wide. There's always a big call like that, 'Six off the first ball!' and so on, but I was in the viewing area and the call that he was going to bowl a big wide might be an urban myth. At any rate, Harmie charged in and the ball went to second slip. There was an eruption in the viewing area. *Whoa, what happened there?*

I didn't think the Harmison wide set the tone of the series. There were those legends about Michael Slater hitting De Freitas for four off the first ball in 1994–95 and it having a huge impact, but I don't think one ball can do that. Harmison's first ball might have dented his confidence, but it didn't set the tone. In 2010–11, we got Andrew Strauss out in the first over of the series, and then England went on and belted us. In Test cricket, you have so much time to think. You might think, while batting, all the signs are good and things are going your way, it's your day, and the next thing, you're out. It only takes one ball. Another day, you might feel terrible and scratch out good runs. There's too much of a fine line, only millimetres here and there between success and abject failure, for signs and portents to carry any weight.

But at any rate, Justin in his jumper was building momentum on that first morning. Having been an opening batsman for so long, I couldn't believe how he was thrashing away, hitting massive drives. *What are you doing, mate?* He really did want to send a message. As a nervous batsman in the dressing room, it was hard to watch as JL was taking plenty of risks and they were coming off. The scoreboard was rocketing along and it went his way, and our way. His 82 off 98 balls got us off to a great start to the Ashes series.

England were coming at us very hard, however; they were right up for it. They got Haydos, JL and Marto out and the game was right in the balance when I joined Ricky at 3/198.

We put on 209 over the next two sessions. Early in my innings, I was facing Flintoff and he was bowling very fast. I let one go and it flicked my pad. The English appealed, and after I was given not out they were chirpy towards me. I thought, *This is what Ashes cricket's all about.* Then Flintoff pitched up and I drove one past him for four to get off the mark. It felt beautiful being off the mark; I could relax a little. Flintoff gave me a bit of a look – just slightly wide-eyed – like he was thinking, *This didn't happen in 2005.*

But really the partnership was all about Ricky. We were able to take the game away from them. He scored so quickly, all around the ground, that it took all the pressure off me.

When I was 86 and thinking about a hundred, Flintoff got me with a good ball from around the wicket. I felt I played a good forward defence and was disappointed and angry, but he'd got me with a great ball and I was happy to have got some runs early in the series.

We made 602 at almost a run a minute, setting up the match well. Late on the second day, though, I was worried that I'd stuffed everything up. Strauss hooked a McGrath bouncer in the air behind square leg. I was fielding back there, and Brett Lee was at fine leg. We both ran for it and I got there first. But as I took the catch, we made contact and my spike sliced into his leg. I took off, celebrating and waving to the crowd and carrying on a bit, before stopping and seeing Brett lying on the ground. I thought, *I've taken out our opening bowler on the second day of the Ashes series.* I ran back and saw a huge bleeding gash in his leg. *Oh no, what have I done?* Thankfully it wasn't too deep and they were able to tape it up.

Though we bowled England out for 157, Ricky didn't enforce the follow-on. JL batted brilliantly for a hundred and we declared, really confident. We got through their top order quickly but on the fourth afternoon it was getting frustrating when Paul Collingwood and Kevin Pietersen held out for a couple of hours. Pietersen blocked one back to Warnie, who got his throw back to Gilly all wrong and looked like he was trying to hit KP. They were meant to be mates! Pietersen gave Warnie a big spray. Not everyone's confident enough to do that, and the episode fired everyone up. Collingwood charged Warnie and got stumped, and Flintoff pulled a half-tracker to JL at deepish mid-on, but at stumps we knew we still had to get Pietersen. Fortunately, very early on the last day he absolutely belted one off Binga and picked out Damien Martyn at midwicket.

After the Test, Ricky pulled us together and said, 'Enjoy this Test win but remember it's the first match, they'll come back very hard. Look after yourselves and be ready for Adelaide.'

The Adelaide Test started at the end of the same week, so it was going to be a challenge to both sides' endurance. England won the toss and batted really well, Collingwood and Pietersen making massive scores. They belted Warnie everywhere, which was a bit of a worry, and McGrath was struggling with a heel injury. Ricky had been keen for him not to play, but Pigeon had never let him down before and was determined and played with the soreness.

England had us in the field for nearly two days, but had taken a fair while getting to 6/551. We just had to bat well for a couple of days, and we could go to Perth 1–0 up.

It didn't work out that way, initially. We'd lost three quick wickets for 65 when I joined Ricky. We were finding it very difficult to get on top of their bowlers, before Ricky pulled Matthew Hoggard to Ashley Giles at deep square leg and was dropped. It would have been 4 for less than 100, all our best batsmen gone.

I had to work my backside off for every single run. Ricky on the other hand was making it look easy. At the end of one over he said, 'Huss, have a look at this!' There was a big crowd drinking under the scoreboard, and Ricky had spotted a woman on a guy's shoulders, and the crowd was yelling, 'Get your shirt off!' She stopped in the middle of them and whipped her shirt off ... to reveal that she was wearing another shirt underneath. They called for her to get that off, and she did ... and had another shirt on under that. I couldn't believe Ricky and I were standing in the middle of the Adelaide Oval in an Ashes Test, watching her having fun with the crowd, laughing our heads off. But that was the way batting with Ricky could relax you.

England took the second new ball and Hoggard had Ricky caught for 142. Not long after, on 91, I chopped one on. I was so angry at missing out on a hundred again and getting out to a still-new ball, with our score still 260 runs behind, and I remember storming off into the old dressing rooms, which are close to the public. It was the angriest I'd ever been after getting out. I would never throw my bat, but I was chucking my gloves and carrying on a fair bit. I didn't realise people in the viewing area and the public could hear what I was saying. Ricky came in and said, 'Huss, pull your head in, everyone can hear you; you're going to get into trouble.'

Pup, Gilly and Warnie all batted extremely well, which took the wind out of England's sails. Their mentality started to change.

We ended up 38 runs short, a fantastic effort, and figured we had saved the Test match now.

On the fifth morning, England started at 1/59, ahead by 97 runs. It was a draw for all money. But Ricky had a glint in his eye, quite serious and intense. John Buchanan called a team meeting before we went out, which didn't happen often. He and Ricky said, 'We can win this Test match, but we've got to find out a way to do it.' Warnie added, 'We can win it if we believe it.'

John and Ricky were asking us how we should approach it tactically – attacking fields, probably go for a few more runs, and go all out for wickets, or go the other way and strangle them, set defensive fields, bowl dot balls and frustrate them. As a team, that's what we decided to do. Warnie would tie them down from one end and the quicks would attack them from the other. Those three leaders, John, Ricky and Shane, were very confident, and we all got on board.

In my mind, I still thought that if England batted for two sessions we couldn't do it. But Warnie was unbelievable, bowling non-stop for two sessions, hardly sending down a bad ball. England were in survival mode, which worked in our favour as well. We were lucky to get Strauss. I caught him off Shane when he'd missed the ball by at least six inches. The players who liked looking for the signs were saying, 'It's going our way today.' A turning point was the run-out of Ian Bell. We got a sense that they were starting to panic. And then Warnie bowled Pietersen around his legs. The most sceptical among us started to believe. Flintoff recognised this and came out to try to change the momentum of the game: *Stuff this, I'm going to get a quick fifty and take it away.* But our quicks had the ball reversing nicely, and he nicked a big flashing drive. The English definitely started thinking, *Oh no, we're in trouble.*

But Collingwood was surviving, and as it got towards tea, time was becoming an issue and we got nervous again. Even if we got them out, would we have long enough to chase more than 150 runs?

We kept picking up wickets, McGrath getting the tail-enders. When he got James Anderson, I got a big gush of nerves. I'd been hoping we would get a draw, and now it was, *We're a chance to win this. It'll be tough, but we can win this and I may have to bat!*

With a target of 168 in 36 overs, I sat down hoping the guys above me would get the runs and I wouldn't have to bat. But Test cricket rarely works out that way.

Justin slogged Hoggard through midwicket for four off the very first ball, setting the tone, and we were away. Haydos belted a couple. They were both out by the time we were 33, but at least they'd relieved some pressure with a fast start.

Ricky went in for Justin, and when Matty was out I was promoted to number four. The rationale was, the left-armer Giles would be bowling into the rough and it would be difficult for right-handers to score. Ricky wanted a left-right combination to counter him.

As I walked to the centre, I was very nervous. It was a beautiful late afternoon, but suddenly England had a surge of belief, telling each other, 'If we get a couple more wickets here, we might win.'

Ricky said, 'Let's just stabilise, get a partnership going, and think about winning later on.'

I tried to think of it as a one-day innings: get busy, work the ball, run hard between wickets. We put on 83 in 16 overs, a standard one-day partnership. Then, when Ricky got out to Giles, we needed 52 in 14 overs.

Damien Martyn came out. I was geed up, intense – that flaw that the guys had told me I had to work on. I told Marto what the bowlers were trying. He was blank-faced, weirdly calm, detached, unaffected by the situation, as if he wasn't even hearing me. Little did I know what was really going through his mind.

On his first ball from Flintoff, Marto charged and smashed him over mid-off. I thought, *You beauty, come on Marto, do this for twenty minutes and the game is all over.* But the next ball, he charged again, sliced a shot and was unlucky, picking out Strauss at a fine gully.

Pup came out, energised and bouncing around. We needed 47 in 13 overs, but suddenly every run was looking hard again. I wasn't feeling fluent at all. It was a fifth-day pitch. I'd been hoping another guy, Ricky or Marto, could just finish it off. I wondered if I had to take responsibility and up the scoring rate. It was getting stressful again.

We had a bit of luck. Pup played one off his pads and we ran three. It got thrown in to Pietersen for a relay. He hurled it as hard as he could towards the keeper, but it landed in the rough, took a funny bounce and ran off for four overthrows. We'd got seven off that ball and I started thinking, *Yes, this is our day.* It felt like two or three overs' worth of runs, in just that little incident.

As in that long-ago Shield final, people were pouring out of the city down the hill to the oval. They were making an enormous noise, counting the required runs down. I could feel the adrenaline building. When we were 4/163, I pulled Anderson for four, ran down the wicket and punched the air – I couldn't control the emotion. *One more! Come on!* We had three overs up our sleeve but it felt like the last ball. I wanted him to hurry up and bowl. I was just going to hit it and run.

He pitched it up. I cover-drove it into a gap and took off. To this day, it's the best feeling I've had on a cricket field. Pup and I embraced each other, and then I looked up for the boys in the viewing area. Then, I saw something I'd never seen from an Australian team. Often sub-continental teams ran onto the ground after a win, but not Australians. Now they did; they were rushing down the steps and converging on us on the field. Seeing the excitement in their faces, I was overwhelmed. I was hugging everyone. Ricky and Shane said it was the best win they'd played in, after more than 100 Tests. We went in front of the scoreboard and clapped the fans. None of us wanted that moment to end.

By the time I got into the dressing room, I was exhausted, mentally and physically, but didn't know it yet. I did none of the proper recovery, the ice baths and Gatorade and so on. I went straight for a beer and it went straight to my head.

But there was something weird about that evening, too. Within half an hour, Andrew Flintoff and some other English players were coming in for a beer. I sat there thinking, *Wow, they've just lost this amazing Test match. If I was in their shoes I couldn't bring myself to congratulate the opposition so quickly.* But Flintoff seemed happy to have been part of this amazing Test. I would be distraught for days or weeks after losing like that. I thought it was weird that they were taking it so well. Were they putting a brave face on it, or just not hurting so much?

The series was still well and truly alive, and we were the ones who needed to win it to take back the Ashes. Some of our senior players, such as Ricky, Haydos, Marto and JL, didn't want to be drinking with the Poms. So they went off into the physio room and had a few beers on their own there. Ricky said the next day, 'I didn't want to drink with those blokes, we've got a series to win here.'

After a while, JL had great pleasure in coming out of the physio room and telling Flintoff it was time to leave so we could sing our team song. Flintoff was saying, 'Come on, Justin, I'll stay and we can sing your team song together!'

'No chance, get out.'

He was very happy to kick the England captain out, and we sang a particularly boisterous version of *Underneath the Southern Cross*, knowing they were next door listening.

The party continued in our hotel, but I was too tired to stay for long. The rest of the boys stayed for a few hours celebrating. I'd had enough and, exhausted, collapsed onto my bed and let the adrenaline finally run out of me.

I wasn't part of what happened that night with Damien Martyn, but I heard about it later, like everyone else.

Early the next day, we were at the airport and someone mentioned how Marto was nowhere to be seen. I thought he must be in bed after a big night. People were ringing him, but he wasn't answering. Then the word got around that he'd taken off, he was retiring. I thought it was a joke. *No way, he's just sleeping it off, he'll be fine, he'll catch a later flight.*

Then it came to light that he'd snuck off to Sydney, along the way writing a retirement letter to James Sutherland, the CEO of Cricket Australia.

If this talk about him retiring was correct, I was stunned. I tried messaging and ringing him. His phone was off. Nobody could get in touch with him, not even Ricky, who was not only his captain but probably his closest mate in cricket.

I was never close enough to Marto to get to the bottom of his reason for quitting the game in that way. It was said that he was beginning to worry about going through the acid bath of public criticism over his form, and retired so that he wouldn't suffer the pain of being dropped again. I couldn't understand that. I thought he was playing very well, and a big score was around the corner. The selectors generally showed faith in guys in a winning team.

I thought about his strange demeanour when he came out to bat with me in Adelaide. Had he decided to retire already? Was being demoted below me in the batting order part of it? I doubt it but I don't know. Part of the trouble was, he wasn't letting anybody know what was going through his head.

When the team got together in Perth a week later, I was still knocked about by the episode and thought, *Gee I hope this doesn't damage our momentum and have an effect on the team.* I was totally focused on that next Test win that would get us over the line for the Ashes.

The WACA pitch was tending to seam and swing and bounce unevenly on the first day or two. On the first day, we were scoring quite freely, but my old mate Monty Panesar had been brought in for England and he was taking wickets. Batsmen were being deceived by the pace and skid in the wicket. You get out in different ways there from other places. You feel like you're in, but there's that one ball that can bounce a bit more and you're out.

Monty got Justin in the last over before lunch, and once he gets his confidence up he can be a dangerous bowler. For me facing Monty, I wasn't worried about the spin so much as the bounce and skid. He was bowling a wider line trying to get me to drive and nick it to slip. I had the advantage of having played most of my first-class cricket at the ground, but I had to pay extra attention to every ball. I made 74 not out, but it was a real struggle, and we were all out for 244, a similar score to the one we'd made on the first day in Perth against South Africa twelve months previously.

England saw this as their great opportunity to get back into the series. They really believed this was it, if they batted well. We had a great attack, though, so even with a low score we had a lot of confidence. When we turned up for the second day and got them out for 215, that was a huge blow to them. They'd missed their opportunity.

We knew batting was going to be easier in the second innings for both teams, so we needed a really big score. We got off to a horrible start, JL getting out first ball of the innings. Late on that second afternoon, the determination of Haydos and Ricky was immense. Matty hadn't had a big score in the series. He's a very proud man and was desperate for runs. He and Ricky got us through to stumps at 1/119, and sprinted off the field. From the viewing area, I saw how bemused the English were, watching the batting pair sprint off, pumped about what a good day we'd had. It left a deep imprint about how we were here to drive it home.

The third day was a scorcher, about 55 degrees Celsius on the field. Ricky was out quite early for 75, and I had a partnership with Haydos, who was yelling at me between overs, 'Don't give these Pommy bastards anything, grind them into the dirt.' It was intense.

The English were pushing really hard before lunch, and got Haydos before lunch for 92. Monty, his old Northants teammate, was dancing around like a pink flamingo. Haydos went off cursing himself.

Michael Clarke and I batted through the middle session. I really enjoyed batting with Pup, because he was similar to me, very nervous and talkative, and we clicked as a pair. I was having a fair bit of luck, top-edging a hook off Harmison that fell between fine leg and the keeper, nicking a drive between the keeper and first slip, and being caught in close off Monty but given not out.

I said to Pup, 'I'm having a lot of luck today.'

'Mate, just go with it,' he said. 'If it's your lucky day, just ride it.'

I thought, *Stuff it, I will.*

We put on 137 runs in the session, and the English started to wilt in the heat. I certainly was. I made it to my hundred, but was given out caught behind off Monty, a decision I would definitely have reviewed if the DRS had been in place.

Then it turned into the Adam Gilchrist show. I'd been working my backside off all day to get us in a good position, and Gilly scored as many runs as I had in a third of the time. A Test century in 58 balls isn't something you see every day. It was brilliant to watch. Because the day was so hot, a lot of people went home at tea and missed out on one of the great Ashes innings. The amazing thing was, unbeknown to any of us, Gilly had been suffering a crisis of self-doubt during that match and had been considering retiring until his wife, Mel, talked him out of it. I guess self-doubt doesn't discriminate between the supremely gifted few like Gilly and the rest of us.

Ricky called them in, and Brett Lee got Strauss fourth ball that night, lbw shouldering arms. But in the back of my mind, I knew we were in for a tough slog. Jacques Rudolph had resisted us comfortably the previous year. This was a proud English team and they were going to make us fight. A draw would keep the Ashes alive, and in their hands for another match at least.

Ian Bell and Alastair Cook put on 170 the next day, batting almost until tea. We respected Cook highly even though he hadn't made many runs. We thought he had specific areas of strength: a very good cut and good off his pads. He was one English player who pulled well. But he wasn't as good at playing through cover and down the ground, so we pitched up all day and tried to get him to drive. That was where we'd had him before, nicking the new ball, chopping onto his stumps or lbw. We admired his temperament and concentration, and he looked like he could bat forever.

Could they even chase down 557 and win? Records are made to be broken. I had a pessimistic voice saying, *This could be the day.* In Test cricket, there's so much time to think – enough time for doubts and clouds to come into your mind. I was thinking, *Here we go again, are we going to lose? This will be a nightmare.*

But then I'd think, *Hang on, we've got Warne and McGrath, just one wicket and we're through.* Ricky and Gilly always kept the group positive, but you couldn't stop the black thoughts from creeping back.

Warne and McGrath did get the breakthroughs, though. Flintoff was due for a big score, and he and Pietersen threatened to get going, but a good sign for us was that Flintoff was teeing off, trying to hit it over the top even when the fielders were back. Surely he would give us a chance. After Warnie bowled him, it felt like Pietersen gave up hope, not bothering to get the tail-enders to play cat-and-mouse, but just saying, 'You bat, mate, and see how you go.'

By mid-afternoon we had won the match and the Ashes. I couldn't believe what was happening. Two years earlier I had been looking at a lifetime of being in the wrong place at the wrong time, unable to get into the Australian team at its historic high-water mark. Now, I'd played in an Ashes Test at home, scored a hundred, been named man of the match, and won the Ashes. I could die a happy man.

As we did our victory lap, I could see how much it meant to the guys who were in England for the Tests in 2005. Haydos and Justin had tears in their eyes walking around the ground thanking the fans. Ricky, Gilly, Binga, Warnie, Pigeon – I'd never seen them so excited about winning a series. It was a privilege to be part of. And probably Warne, McGrath and Langer knew already that it was their last series.

NINETEEN

When I came into the Australian Test team, there was a feeling of strength we had on the first morning, that sense that in four or five days we would be walking off with a win. The pressure was off me, because we had so many matchwinners. Anything I got was a bonus.

That was about to change.

I wasn't in the loop on the retirements. Warnie was interviewed after the Adelaide game and said, 'This is something I'm definitely going to miss.' I thought, *Hmm, I've never heard him say that.* We knew he was close to the end of his career, but it set me back on my heels. Was he going to retire soon? That was the first time I thought about it.

He didn't call a formal team meeting to announce that he would be retiring. In dribs and drabs he told the boys. That's not to say he didn't like the drama a big scene. In fact, he was setting the stage for it: a Boxing Day Test, needing one wicket for his 700th, before his beloved Melbourne fans.

England's spirit seemed to have shrivelled up in the Perth heat, and they collapsed on Boxing Day, giving Warnie not only his 700th wicket but another four. Then it was the Hayden and Symonds show.

Simmo, who had come in to replace Damien Martyn and had bowled very well in Perth, was loved in the dressing room. Everyone wanted him to do well. His breakthrough century felt like it was meant to be – him and Haydos, great mates, destroying England. I was a bit grumpy in the viewing area after getting out for 6, but I forgot all that when I was watching them. They batted like two boys in the back yard. They were hitting balls so brutally hard that even when it went to long off and long on, they had to scurry for singles. The English had no answers. Simmo hit a short-arm push over mid on that went twenty rows back, off Collingwood, to get to his hundred. I knew what it was like, to prove that you could succeed at the highest level after asking that question for so long, and when Simmo came in I gave him the biggest hug of all time.

Having lost the Ashes, and now copped that onslaught from Symonds and Hayden, England capitulated. Brett Lee did not bowl one loose ball as he tormented Strauss. I could empathise with the English, having had this feeling on a cricket field many times before: it feels like your bowlers are bowling loose balls, and then you bat and you don't know where your next run is coming from. It's a different game. Hayden and Symonds had made batting look like child's play, and now it was impossible. Eventually Strauss lashed at one and got a faint nick. That was how it was: all of our team put England under so much pressure, they had to crack.

Ricky was determined to carry our momentum through to Sydney. There had been talk about how Australia struggled in so-called dead rubbers – not that I considered any Test match a dead rubber. In the team, Ricky and the senior players were still hurting from 2005 and wouldn't be satisfied with anything less than 5–0.

We already had an added motivation to send Shane off well, but the retirements kept coming. McGrath announced his to the boys before training in Sydney. Three or four of us tried to talk him out of it. 'You're not allowed. *We are not allowing you.*' He kept saying, 'No, this is the right time for me, I've had a great time, I'll miss you guys, but this is right for me.'

A day after, JL came to me in the hotel and said, 'I'm going to retire. This'll be my last Test.'

I said, 'We need you to keep going.'

'No, the time's right. We're not playing another Test until the end of the year. I've had enough.'

I'd never had to deal with this. If someone had retired in the past, I was too young to know what they were going through. Now that these guys were going, first Marto and now Warne, McGrath and Langer, it was like a death in the family. I hadn't had any real tragedies in my life. The worst thing that had happened to me was my nanna dying. I wasn't prepared for this sense of loss and didn't know how to react. In hindsight, I wish I'd given more to those guys. For the individual, it's a huge time in his life. In my mind, I was kind of scrambled. I wanted them not to retire – but then I had to re-focus. *We've got a Test to prepare for.* Now, having gone through it myself, I understand better what Justin and the others were feeling.

It's always a long and evenly balanced Test match in Sydney. Bowlers have to work hard for their wickets, but the batsmen don't have it all their own way. This one was evenly poised until an innings from Warnie shifted the momentum our way. He seemed like he was on too much Red Bull. He was teeing off at everything and sledging the fielders right, left and centre. He sledged guys at cover. He sledged Paul Collingwood, who was standing at slip. Paul told me later, in disbelief, 'I didn't even say anything and he started sledging me!'

Warnie's innings turned the tide, and then the bowlers closed in. The Barmy Army put aside their disappointment and added to the great atmosphere coming from the outer. Their team were getting beaten, but they kept turning up and singing their songs.

We respected the Barmy Army, with their songs for different team members; they showed respect for our players and the game as a whole, and showed up in huge numbers.

And finally, when Haydos hit the winning runs, it was over. 5–0. The crowd stayed on after the presentations and we did a lap of honour with the three retirees and their families. It seemed like no-one had left. I felt honoured to be with those three as they received what they deserved.

Capping it all off was going back to the dressing room and seeing Damien Martyn there with a big smile on his face. We were all genuinely delighted to see him. He seemed content, and I thought, *Good on him, he's at peace.* He went out in a bizarre fashion, but he seemed in a good place now.

Our families came into the rooms for a while, which was great for them, to enjoy that experience. After an hour they left and it was time for the boys to be together. We sat and chatted about the series. Steve Harmison came in and got an autographed shirt. I chatted with Alastair Cook for a long time. He said, 'Nah, I didn't play well, I'm disappointed.' I consoled him, saying how tough it would have been to face those bowlers, and forecast that he would be churning out runs for years. He said, 'Let's have a race to ten Test centuries.' At that point, he had four and I had five. By the time of my retirement, he had well and truly outpaced me!

It was good to catch up with the English guys, but as the afternoon wore on it came to a stage where we still hadn't sung the team song. We'd been invited onto James Packer's boat on Sydney Harbour, which we were all very excited about, but the song still hadn't been sung. When I got back to my hotel room to change, under my door was an envelope with my name on it. It was a letter from Justin Langer, saying, 'It's my great honour and duty to hand over the team song to you. I can't think of anyone better to take on this great honour. I want you to take it on with pride and lead it your way and celebrate with the guys.'

My hands started to shake. I couldn't believe he'd handed it on to me.

I went downstairs, where the boys and their wives were waiting, and gave Justin a massive hug. He said, 'Don't say anything yet.'

We had a great time on the boat. When it was very late and very dark, with Sydney Harbour Bridge behind us, Justin called the song. He pumped everyone up, got everyone yelling and screaming, saying something to each individual to make them feel special about things they'd done. He announced he was passing the custodianship of the song to me and dragged me into the middle. He led his last song and pulled me into leading my first. It seemed like he was recognising not only my results, but the values with which I played the game. It was an amazing moment, one of the proudest in my cricket life.

TWENTY

A part of me was saying, *Nothing this good can last forever.* My Test average was hovering around 80 and I was asked all the time, 'How long can you keep this average up? When's it going to stop?' I even got ridiculous questions like, 'Do you think you can beat Bradman's average?'

I couldn't believe myself how well things had gone. I said, 'I'm going to enjoy it while it lasts. There will be times when I don't score runs.' And I was always a realist. The only way to preserve an average of 80 would have been to retire right then.

In the dressing room after that fifth Test, I said to Ricky, 'This has been an awesome series, but looking forward things are going to get a lot tougher.' We both agreed. Ricky said something along the lines of, 'Let's enjoy it while we can.'

The momentum and euphoria of the Ashes carried us a certain way into the one-day series, but then we started to feel jaded. I'd given everything I had, and while I was still trying my best, there wasn't a lot in the tank. It was a long summer. We came off the boil, physically and mentally, and grew complacent after belting England early in the series. And once you slacken a little bit, it's amazing how badly things can go. England found some confidence and were going like a road train at the end of that series. We all felt it and were trying to fight it, but we were exhausted.

The coaches had intensified our training program at the start of the one-day series, hammering us on the fitness side of things, explaining that it was all for the World Cup, but it didn't go down well with the guys. Towards the end, it started to take its toll. The World Cup in the West Indies was still more than a month away, and we hated losing matches here and now in front of our home fans. I never liked the idea of micro-managing the distant future. You don't know what's going to happen with people's form or injuries. We lost Brett Lee and Andrew Symonds, two of our main players, which threw many of the plans into disarray. I understand the theory, but was wary of taking our minds off the present and falling into the losing habit.

Realising we were knackered, the selectors rested a lot of first-choice players for a three-match one-day tour to New Zealand. Michael Brown, the cricket operations manager, rang and told me I would be captain. All of my weariness fell away! Suddenly I was excited about going to New Zealand.

We didn't have much preparation time, but I took the captaincy seriously. I had a team of my own for a tour, and could impress my beliefs on them. I didn't want to change a lot, as I was just filling in for Ricky and Gilly, but it did feel like *my* team. In Wellington, I addressed them at the team hotel before our first match. Wanting to make everyone feel important, I named the team and gave a little spiel about each player, listing their statistics, making a fuss. I wanted them to feel special about being picked for Australia in a one-day international.

The weather was horrendous for the game at Basin Reserve, the 'Cake Tin', icy cold and windy. The curator had put glue into the pitch to hold it together, which was something new. I lost the toss and New Zealand sent us in. *Brilliant*, I thought, *I was going to bat first*. I was happy walking off from the toss, but what I didn't know, because the conditions had been so wet and the pitch was under cover, was that the glue hadn't had time to dry properly.

The ball seamed all over the place and batting was extremely tough. Shane Bond, their excellent fast bowler, pushed the ball across the left-hander but could also bring it back in. His record against Australia was phenomenal. I made forty-odd in a long time, but just as I got out I could feel that the pitch was starting to get better. That glue must have been drying. Alarm bells went off in my head, and sure enough, the Kiwis' top order came out and smashed us everywhere, a pretty horrible start to the series for us.

We wrote that game off because of the conditions, and went to Auckland for the second match. Mike Young, the American fielding coach with a baseball background, stood up to address the team at Eden Park. He's a very passionate guy who loves to speak his mind, and he gave us a 'Run through a brick wall' pump-up speech. He said, 'We've lost Brett Lee, he's a great bowler, but which team can bring in the fastest motherf---er in the world?' We all looked at Sean Tait and cheered. It was hilarious and put us all in a positive mood.

Batting first again, we made 4/336, which I definitely thought was a winning score. I made a hundred off 80 balls, which I guess showed that the captaincy wasn't having a negative effect on my batting.

But while we were bowling, it soon felt like the little things were not going our way. Hoggy had Ross Taylor plumb lbw, but it was given not out. Then Taylor inside-edged one that grazed the stumps. Craig McMillan came out near the end, and we should have had him out for three but Phil Jaques dropped an outfield catch. Taylor made 117 and McMillan 52 off 30 balls, and they passed us with 8 balls to spare.

As it was happening, I was frustrated but philosophical. I was thinking, *This is not quite going to plan, but don't panic, think clearly.* I made a field change and the first ball the bowler bowled was the complete opposite of the plan.

'Er, mate, what happened?'

'Sorry Huss, it was just a bad ball.'

I wasn't the type to get angry or fired up. I saw that we'd tried our best, made some mistakes, but the other team had played well. That's life, move on. So, when we sat down after the game, I didn't say much more than that. Mike Young made another speech, a quieter one, and said, 'Don't worry boys, you've given your best.' I said it was important for us to all meet as a team in the hotel bar and stay together.

The third match was at Hamilton, a small ground, and again we batted first in great conditions. Matthew Hayden batted well, but got to his hundred at slower than a run a ball, which I felt just wasn't quite fast enough. As a stroke of serendipity, he got hit on the toe and broke it, and couldn't run, so he started teeing off. His last 80-odd runs came in no time at all, and he ended up not out on 181 off 166 balls.

But the two earlier losses had made me anxious, and those of us in the middle order didn't get going. In the 49th over I said to someone, 'It's not often you've got 330 on the board and think you really need one more big over.' We got to 346, but I was still concerned.

This was alleviated when we got four early wickets. I thought, *Yes, you beauty, at last!* And there, at 4/41, my tranquillity ended. The New Zealanders clearly decided, *Stuff it, we can't win the match, let's throw caution to the wind, we've already won the series*, and things started going their way. McMillan blasted six after six after six. We tried bowling wide to him, and he still found the gap between two or three guys. The killer blow was when Brendan McCullum came in. In my mind he was the best finisher in world one-day cricket, and from ball one he started smacking us wherever he wanted. I had no clue how to stop the run flow.

I was obviously inexperienced as a captain at that level. Knowing what I know now, I would have done things differently. I tried to be very consultative, supporting the bowlers individually, but I went too far. If the bowler thought differently from me, I let him have his way.

The more New Zealand got away, the more I was second-guessing myself. The field was like a sieve, there were so many holes in it, and I was worried that if I put someone here they'd hit it there, and if I changed the field the bowler wouldn't be happy. In retrospect, I would have gone with my gut instinct and imposed my plans on the bowlers'.

After that loss – on the third-last ball – I was definitely more disappointed and angry. Certainly John Buchanan was. We had now lost seven games in a row and were about to go to the World Cup. The press was saying we were no chance.

It was a disappointing tour and I was relieved to hand the reins back to Ricky and Gilly, but I did think I'd learnt a lot about captaincy. I found it flattering to be seen in a leadership light, and I am honoured to be able to say I was captain of Australia. I don't know if that series had any effect on me being a chance to be captain in the future, but maybe it did, because I wasn't considered again. We were without eight of our first-choice players, and I would have been disappointed if my captaincy credentials were being judged on that. Even our second-string team, without half a dozen first-choice players, almost beat New Zealand at home. If it was seen that I didn't really want the captaincy, then that was incorrect too. I know if I'd been given the job full time, I would have done it well.

TWENTY-ONE

After New Zealand, I felt myself go into a bit of a lull. My first World Cup was coming up, but I probably needed a break. Amy was pregnant with our third child, and I was yearning for some quiet time at home. But we only had about a week and a half before I was on a plane to the Caribbean.

We had three preparation games at our base on the quiet island of St Vincent, and Ricky was very strict on us training properly to pull ourselves out of our trough. The schedule allowed for plenty of time between games, so he was urging us to study the opposition and develop plans for every player. Leading into our practice game against England, he said he wanted to treat it like a proper World Cup match. The English turned up pretty relaxed, and Ricky said, 'We're going to hit them hard and send a message to the rest of the teams about how hard we're going to play.' We went out there and hammered them into submission, and after the game he said, 'That's what I want. We're here and we mean business.'

Our first three Cup games were in Basseterre, St Kitts, another small island away from the action. It felt like we were under the radar, which suited us. We got some confidence from beating

Scotland and the Netherlands, but the third game, against South Africa, would show us where we were at.

It was a great game, it really was. Matty Hayden had won his opening spot back, and I'd never seen him in such a great place, mentally. He came to training and hit a thousand balls, then came back to the hotel and went snorkelling for hours, like he was on holidays. He loved being in the West Indies and it was reflected in his batting. In that match, Shaun Pollock came on and Haydos started walking down the pitch and smacking him back over his head. His 101 off 68 balls gave everyone else confidence. Ricky and Pup both made 90s, and we had an impressive 377.

But we all remembered Johannesburg, and Graeme Smith and AB De Villiers were giving us that feeling, the way they started. At 0/160 in the 21st over, Shane Watson turned the game with a great piece of fielding. He sprinted around the boundary, dived to save the four, picked up, threw it in flat and hard, and hit the wickets to run out De Villiers. Everything changed. Smith had to retire hurt with cramps, which surprised us as it wasn't very hot, and we had the game in check after that.

The Super Eight phase went on for nearly a month, which posed a challenge to team discipline. People can go wayward in the West Indies with time on their hands, but Ricky made sure we planned our downtime well. We went out and enjoyed each other's company, but left enough time to get our preparation right. We trained and planned in the lead-up, and then celebrated a win in style. It was all about picking the right time.

My own batting was beginning to worry me. Most games, I only got in late to have a slog and get out. Mike Young said, 'Keep doing the team thing, don't worry about getting out.' I tried to focus on that, but put pressure on myself when I did get a chance. Against the West Indies in Antigua, I had about 12 overs to bat, and chopped one on for nine. I was disappointed, and growing anxious, but we kept winning so I pushed my own worries under the surface.

We had some unsung heroes in that World Cup. Haydos and McGrath were the stars, and along with Punter were probably the best three players in the tournament. But Michael Clarke also batted really well, Andrew Symonds did brilliantly to come back from a career-threatening bicep injury, and Shaun Tait bowled at his career-best, coming in for Brett Lee. Nathan Bracken and Brad Hogg were phenomenal when we really needed wickets or tight bowling towards the death.

Simmo, as usual, gave us some lighter moments. A few of us had a little fad of writing a reminder word on the shoulder of our bats. For me it was 'Clear mind ', or 'Watch the ball'. Gilly, who also did it, picked up Simmo's bat and looked at the shoulder.

'"SW",' Gilly read. 'What does "SW" mean, Simmo?'

Simmo looked at him as if he was stupid and said: 'Swing Hard.'

I had never been a part of a team that executed its plans so well throughout a whole tournament. It was probably the best cricket I've ever been involved in. The common goal was to win every single game and win the World Cup. No experiments, no rotations, no giving guys a go because they needed it. Just win the World Cup.

We won nine on the trot, but were really tense before playing South Africa at St Lucia. It was a semi-final, and for the first time it was do-or-die. There was talk about South Africa having choked in the past, and so we expected them to come at us very hard.

They batted first. It was a morning game, so there was a little bit of moisture in the pitch. They must have had a preconceived plan of aggression, because Smith got out cheaply swinging at Nathan Bracken, and then Jacques Kallis uncharacteristically charged down and tried to smack McGrath over the top. We were thinking, *What's he doing?* We had them 5/27 in no time, before Herschelle Gibbs and Justin Kemp helped them rally to 149: a low score, but it was still a World Cup semi-final and I was very nervous, having had almost no time in the middle in two months. But our top order, again, made those fears redundant.

Sri Lanka would be playing us in the final in Barbados, and although I was thrilled to be there I was scared the selectors would leave me out. Fortunately, they kept faith.

It was a bizarre day, memorable for the circumstances almost as much as the result. The clouds kept rolling in before the match, and the locals told us they were bringing rain. I was convinced we wouldn't be playing that day. Then, all of a sudden, we had about fifteen minutes' notice to begin the match. Everything was helter-skelter: we were batting in the World Cup final, when we'd been picturing an afternoon of relaxing in our rooms.

Gilly looked amazing from the start. He blazed Chaminda Vaas's first ball to Murali at mid-off. Murali was wringing his fingers as he threw the ball to Chaminda, who said, 'I think we're about to get Gillied.'

I'd been watching Gilly closely through the tournament and even though he had been finding ways to get out cheaply, he had been batting really well. We were hoping Haydos could do it one more time, but he was the one to get out first and Gilly went on an absolute blitz. It was so good to watch. Nothing feels quite like sitting there with your feet up watching an all-time great take your opponent apart. Sri Lanka turned to their superhero, Murali, and two balls in his first over went into the stands. We just wanted it to go on. *Shivers*, I thought, *Gilly's going to make a hundred in a World Cup final. I hope this isn't a dream, I hope the alarm's not about to ring and wake me up and we still have to play the match!*

I wasn't needed as we made 4/281 in our allotted 38 overs. Nathan Bracken got an early wicket for us, but all through the afternoon we couldn't seem to blow the game away. We had the game under control, but Sanath Jayasuriya and Kumar Sangakkara both threatened. The pitch got slower and harder to score, the run rate was going up, and we took crucial wickets.

But then, the threat changed. It wasn't Sri Lanka, but the weather again.

The light began to fade really quickly, as it does near the Equator. We weren't worried about the result, but wanted to complete the match that day and start the celebrations.

Eventually, the umpires came together and said we had to go off for bad light. This set off a massive roar from the Australian supporters, and we were jumping all over each other. But Billy Bowden ran across and said, 'Ricky, it's not over, we have to come back tomorrow.' Ricky just said, 'No, that's rubbish, Billy. It's over.'

We were celebrating as we walked off, but were confused about the rule. Was the game over or not? The umpires were sticking to their guns. There had to be three more overs for an official completion, and if the light didn't improve we would have to come back the next day. It was an absurd situation in everyone's eyes except the officials'. To Mahela Jayawardene's credit, he came in and said to the umpires and Ricky, 'Let's get this game over with tonight. If you guys bowl spinners we can get it done and dusted.'

So we walked out and bowled lollipops for three overs. Fielding at long-on, I was firing the crowd up. Then I looked back to the middle and thought, *I can't see a thing out there! If a ball gets hit towards me I'm going to look like a goose.*

The game ended in the dark, and we were celebrating winning a World Cup a second time on the same day.

Something was always about to happen in the West Indies, though. Australian captains, from Steve Waugh to Ian Chappell, had had infamous run-ins with the local police, who liked to get involved in cricket matters, and later that night we had an incident when we went into the middle of the ground to sing the team song for a second time. Some of the Barbadian police were angry that we were staying to celebrate for so long. When we decided to go onto the field, they wanted to go home and said, 'No, you guys will be arrested. Get off the ground.' We had had a few drinks by then, and were determined to proceed to the wicket, and then we agreed we'd leave straight away.

The police weren't having it. They said they were going to arrest Ricky and put him in jail. Hoggy jumped up over the crew and yelled, 'You can't arrest my captain! I'll take you on!' It was all quite humorous, but history had shown that they weren't afraid to arrest an Australian skipper. Brute Bernard managed to calm things down, though; we sang the song in the middle of Kensington Oval and continued well into the night back at the hotel.

James Packer had organised a boat outing for us the following day, and as Cricket Australia people were coming on, we had to assemble in the morning for a private but compulsory celebration. That was an absolutely brilliant day: we had access to jet skis and speedboats and so on. I personally stayed on a sun lounger for the entire day and did not move. I had one glass of champagne that kept getting filled up. I was spent. I had gone through the World Cup tired without realising it, pushing myself to train harder, worrying about not batting and then not scoring enough runs when I did, and growing over-intense. As I lay on that sun lounger, I realised that none of that mattered. It wasn't about me. Nobody cared about my trials. I was just one part in a beautifully functioning machine. We had won the World Cup.

TWENTY-TWO

When we got home, the Australian fans gave us a brilliant parade in Martin Place in Sydney. Tired as I was, being able to reflect on the season – winning the Ashes and the World Cup, and captaining my country – I didn't have much to complain about.

Things were about to change radically.

Amy and I had planned a family holiday to Fiji before our third baby was born, which was still about twelve weeks away. The day before we were due to leave, Amy had a little bit of bleeding. We weren't too alarmed, but the doctor said, 'You'd better get straight to hospital now.'

They suggested complete bed rest, but she could go home. Although we were obviously canning the Fiji trip, I didn't twig to how serious it could be. Amy was a bit more scared, but didn't let on to me.

Then, when we were at home, she had a massive haemorrhage. I thought the baby was gone, for sure. In the middle of the night I called the ambulance, we got our neighbour to look after Jasmin and William, and I was thinking the worst; there was just so much blood. In the hospital, they did a few tests on Amy and said the baby was okay but Amy would have to stay at the hospital and do nothing but rest. As she was only twenty-eight weeks into her pregnancy, they said the aim was to help her hang onto the baby as long as she could.

I went home, to take charge of Jasmin and William, which was a shock to the system. The World Cup celebration was a distant memory. For a week, I was racing to and from hospital to be with Amy, taking the kids here and there, being a sole parent. I did enjoy looking after the kids, but by 7pm every day I was falling asleep on the couch with dishes everywhere, washing to be hung out, mess everywhere. Just a taste of what Amy had to do every day, week after week, while I was away.

Amy was going stir-crazy in the hospital, so the next Saturday we convinced the doctors to let me take her out for a coffee and to stretch her legs. We had a lovely couple of hours, but towards the end she started saying, 'I don't feel so well.' I said, 'Come on, let's get you back to the hospital.' Later that day, I brought Jas and Will into the hospital to see their Mum before she had to get another scan. The scan showed that for the baby's and Amy's safety, the baby had to come out right now!!

That was a massive shock, and I was very worried. We'd never considered that this might happen. I quickly organised Amy's parents to collect Jas and Will and explained the situation to them. Before we knew it, Amy was on the operating table.

Considering the circumstances, the birth went as well as it could. Just as Amy was going into theatre for an emergency Caesarean, the placenta burst. Blood and fluid covered the obstetrician on duty. Everyone said we were really lucky. If the placenta had burst an hour earlier, the blood would have engulfed the baby and most likely Amy would have passed away as well from the internal bleeding.

As a baby's being born, everything happens too quickly for you to realise the significance of events. About two weeks later, when

I hit the wall with fatigue, it sank in how my close my cricket career had been to finishing. If the children didn't have their mother, I couldn't be away ten months of the year. Everything could end just like that. I was so dependent on Amy, it broke me up to think of her not being there. It put life into perspective, that's for sure.

Molly was born on 19 May 2007 – just twenty-one days after the World Cup final. While Amy recovered, Molly and I were rushed to the neonatal intensive care. Again, we felt like the big fella upstairs was looking after us, as the King Edward Memorial Hospital in Subiaco had neonatal facilities up there with the best in the world.

She was the tiniest human I can imagine ever holding or seeing. I could fit her in my hand. Her head was smaller than a tennis ball, and I could see the bones and veins through her skin, which was almost transparent. She was lying in a humidicrib and had tubes coming out of everywhere, breathing apparatus and eye patches.

Meanwhile, Amy was in the recovery room not knowing if the baby was okay. She was in great pain and getting very emotional. Eventually I sneaked back up there and told her everything was okay, Molly was stable. We had already agreed on the name. Amy said, 'We've chosen Molly, have we? Molly with a "y"?'

Amy had wanted 'Mollie', not 'Molly', but I'd spelt it the wrong way. English was never my strong subject.

Throughout the winter, Amy had to go to the hospital for several hours a day to be with Molly until she was full-term, so I spent another three months as carer for Jasmin and William. I received many messages of support from the cricket community, particularly from older players who had children and understood a bit better what we were going through. To this day, Molly has a fighting spirit and is a blessing to our family.

Those months, full of work and stress and joy, certainly gave me the time and mental space away from cricket that I'd needed, so by the time the new season started I was excited about playing again. We began with the Twenty20 World Cup in South Africa, which was an interesting experience. Nobody really knew how to play the game, so we were treating each innings like it was the last 10 overs of a one-dayer and teeing off. There were so many classy players in the Australian team we were confident of doing well, and despite a rudimentary plan we made it to the semi-final against India. Chasing 189 – we eventually fell just short – I was batting and, when completing a second run, my hamstring went *pop*.

It was the first injury I'd had, which was quite incredible given the amount of cricket I had played. The Australian physio, Alex Kountouris, told me to ice it every few hours, but aside from rest there wasn't much I could do. I flew home where my care was taken over by the Warriors' physio, Rob Colling. It resulted in my missing a one-day series in India, which I was disappointed about, but on the bright side, I could extend my time with Amy and the children, and be fresh for the start of the home summer, in which we had Test series against Sri Lanka, first, and then India, who fancied themselves to win in Australia for the first time ever.

I only had one Shield game to prepare for the first Test in Brisbane. When the Australian team convened, there was a new feeling: Tim Neilsen had come in as coach after John Buchanan had stepped down. John had wanted Tim to come to the World Cup in the West Indies, but Tim let him have his time. Tim and I had a good rapport. He'd throw balls to me all day and wanted to work all the time. He was intense, a contrast to John's Zen calm. I had similar values to Tim when it came to work ethic and putting the team first.

The Gabba pitch was true and flat and didn't give any help to Sri Lanka's spearhead, Murali. Facing him was a nightmare. I could only pick 80 per cent of his balls at best, and he was so accurate, putting so many revs on the ball, I couldn't relax. The Australian crowds kept yelling out 'No ball' when he bowled, which I thought was pretty unsporting. He's quite a sensitive guy and took to heart what people said about him. When I played with him in the IPL the next year, he said he didn't want to come back to Australia. That eventually thawed out, but in 2007 the crowd's taunts had an effect on him.

Hundreds in that Test and the next, in Hobart, settled me down and gave me that comfortable early-season feeling of having runs on the board. I'd had such a tumultuous off-season and before that had tapered off in the West Indies, so I'd been very nervous before those Tests.

In Hobart, Sri Lanka's big guns fired and we were lucky to win. Mahela Jayawardene made a hundred in the first innings. We generally had his measure in Australia, but over the years my respect grew for him as I saw how well he batted in difficult conditions, and how versatile he was in one-dayers and Twenty20. He was a great fighter, and as a Sri Lankan captain, he was dealing with a lot of politics as well as running the team on the field.

Kumar Sangakkara, meanwhile, played one of the best innings I've ever seen in the second dig. We felt like we were going to win, but he kept hitting boundaries at will, so crisply, the sound of the ball coming off the bat just rang through the ground. Lasith Malinga came in and started bombing a few sixes, and I started getting really worried. We had a huge stroke of luck when Sangakkara, on 192, was given out off his shoulder and his head. It was definitely in the top five innings I've seen, and was ended by one of the worst five decisions.

We had a short one-day tour to New Zealand in December, but I began to tense up thinking about the four-Test series against India. I'd had such a great start to my Test career, and the Sri Lankan Tests had gone well for me, but I felt against India that the expectations had ratcheted up. This was the big one; I had to concentrate and work harder. Before I knew it, I had already put more pressure on myself.

Approaching the Boxing Day Test, I felt tighter than ever before. India were hyped up, and there would be big crowds. On the first day, Phil Jaques and Matthew Hayden batted really well but I was the most nervous I'd ever been and got out cheaply, lbw to Anil Kumble.

I felt angry and depressed and my whole world was crashing in – after one innings! Ricky sat next to me at the end of the day and said, 'It's not often the both of us get out cheaply.' His comment defused the tension. It was just another day; next time would be better. No big deal.

Our bowlers did extremely well to win that Test for us, and in the New Year's Test in Sydney I was desperate to get a good score, putting pressure on myself again.

We were 2/27 when I went in, and on my first ball, RP Singh pitched it up. It swung away from me but I went for a huge, nervous cover drive. I happened to catch it right in the middle and it sailed over the field for four. Ricky came up and smirked. 'Great shot!'

'No!' I almost snapped at him. 'It's a terrible shot. What am I doing? First ball!'

Ricky said, 'No, it was great, you just went with your instinct, go for it.'

I fought my way to a nervous 41 but wasn't batting well. Just after lunch, Harbhajan Singh came on and got Ricky out. Harbhajan took off like Cathy Freeman in the Olympic Stadium, he did roly-polies on the ground and played up to the crowd, carrying on. I remember thinking, *What is he doing? The press are going to start on this Harbhajan–Ricky thing.* I wasn't in a great frame of mind, thinking about negative possibilities. Two balls later, I got out to RP Singh.

That day, Simmo batted brilliantly. He was more controlled than the usual Andrew Symonds, playing with great responsibility, and proving to himself that he was an authentic Test batsman. He was lucky, being given not out after nicking one, and surviving a stumping chance that the umpire didn't refer to video, even though it was clearly out. We got to 463 thanks to Simmo's 163 and a feisty 79 from Hoggy, who came into the dressing room with a big smile on his face. I was actually quite disappointed with him, because I rated him very highly as a batsman and this was a chance to make a Test hundred.

We had a couple of long days in the field as Laxman and Tendulkar were in great touch, while Brett Lee, who got on the SCG honour board with five wickets, was all that stood between them and an insurmountable total. When I went in second time, we were two down and about 20 runs ahead. The pitch was turning a bit more, and I was feeling the pressure big time. I was thinking, *I'm not sure where I'm going to score a run. Just hang in there.* It took me a while to get the pace and turn of the pitch, but Haydos was going well at the other end and eventually I got used to it.

My 145 not out set up the match so we could have a crack at bowling India out on the last day, but it was, for me personally, one of my most memorable moments. The team was in a tough spot. The game was in the balance. I'd got myself into a lather over doing well in this series, and was overwhelmed by relief. The SCG is probably my favourite ground in Australia, and I was proud to get a Test match century there.

It all came together for us that afternoon, culminating in Michael Clarke's three wickets in the second-last over of the day. I can't say I wanted the ball to come to me at slip, but two soft catches ballooned, and I was as pumped as anyone to have pulled off the win when it looked for all money like India would save the draw and keep the series alive.

We weren't aware of anything untoward. We enjoyed our celebration and were so hyped up that I decided to lead the song straight away. It was a great rendition. But then, within minutes, several of the team – including Ricky, Haydos, Simmo and Gilly –

were whisked away to a separate part of the SCG. The rest of us were sitting around having a quiet beer trying to enjoy the win, but it wasn't the same. *What's going on? How long are they going to be?* It was a weird feeling in the dressing room. We were overjoyed about winning, but worried – was everything all right? Steve Bernard said they were in a private room being interviewed separately, and could be a while.

Though we hadn't talked about it, we knew the gist of what they were being quizzed on. The tiff between Harbhajan and Simmo was something I'd thought of as a bit of a joke. Australia had gone to India for a one-day series in the spring, and Harbhajan had called Simmo a 'monkey'. Simmo couldn't give a stuff, and wouldn't have taken it as a racial slur. At the end of the game, Harbhajan had come into the dressing room and said, 'I'm sorry, that was terrible, I promise it won't happen again.' Simmo said, 'Don't worry about it, it's nothing.' They shook hands, and that was it.

Then, at the SCG, in India's first innings, Harbhajan came out and swung away and put on 130 with Sachin Tendulkar, and at some point Harbhajan allegedly called Simmo a monkey again. I didn't hear it, but have absolute 100 per cent faith in the guys who did. Unfortunately for them, being witnesses meant they were put through the mill.

On the field, Simmo said to Harbhajan, 'Mate, I thought we'd been through this, you said it was unacceptable and wouldn't happen again. What's going on?'

Haydos and Gilly, who both heard it, immediately reported it to Ricky. There was a set procedure for this, which Ricky followed. He ran off the field and informed the match referee. I didn't think there'd be much of a controversy to it. Obviously I was very wrong.

The evening of the win, we stayed in the rooms until about 11pm. The others were kept in the interviews until two or three o'clock in the morning. I couldn't quite work it out, but the next day's press made it clear. There was a whole rap sheet on us, apparently. In the post-match press conference, Anil Kumble, who was India's captain, accused us of bad sportsmanship. Incidents during that last day were brought up. Even Gilly and Pup were accused of cheating, a ridiculous slur against two players I considered the most ethical in the game. In Pup's case, it came from when Sourav Ganguly nicked Brett Lee to Michael at slip. Sourav said it had bounced, and the umpires were trying to figure it out. The replays were inconclusive. I was right next to Pup when he caught it, and was 100 per cent convinced. I kept telling him, 'Mate, you definitely caught that.'

Was I right or wrong? I believe my instincts were right, as were those of my teammates, and the umpires gave Sourav out. But the thing is, in those situations everyone's under pressure: the batsmen, the fielders, the bowlers, the umpires. You ask the umpire and that's what he's there for, to make that decision. Gilly was accused of unfairly claiming a catch, but all he did was take what he thought was a catch and ask the umpire. He couldn't know for certain, but he thought there was an edge. Then it's up to the umpire. For anyone to question Gilly's integrity in the game, just because a replay showed that the ball might or might not have hit the edge, only made them look silly.

After the Test, I became aware of the 'Sack Ricky' campaign in the press, to make him a scapegoat for people's grievances about many related and unrelated matters. My century, of which I was so happy and proud, didn't get a mention, and nor did this phenomenal SCG Test win. We were being branded as cheats, liars and racists. It was way over the top. I decided not to read this rubbish anymore, but it was hard to escape, particularly as I was asked to front up to the media the next day. I played the straightest bat I could in support of Ricky and the spirit in which we played the game.

The Indian cricket board threatened to boycott the tour if the disciplinary hearings went against Harbhajan, which was another overreaction. I thought there was an element of calculation in it: the Indian team wanting to deflect attention from the fact that they were 2–0 down in the series. The controversy could galvanise them.

We Australian players went our own separate ways after leaving Sydney, and got together a few days later in Perth. At our first team meeting Ricky said, 'There's been a lot of nonsense going around. We have to put it out of our minds and prepare our best for this Test match.' He had an amazing ability to brush off controversy and concentrate on the team goal.

But within the team, there was a lot of resentment towards Cricket Australia. The guys who were witnesses were dragged through the mud and had to sit through hearing after hearing. There was a huge financial implication if the Indians left the tour. But the players felt CA hadn't taken the side of their players. Our team rallied around the guys, and Andrew Symonds in particular. We believed his side and wanted to support him through this difficult situation. CA, on the other hand, were trying to protect their financial interests. The team felt very let down.

A player with the stature of Sachin Tendulkar could have taken control of the crisis and acted as conciliator, standing above it all, so highly was he respected. But for reasons of his own, he chose not to. Obviously I admired Sachin from afar, but I had no relationship with him other than to say hello. Perhaps it was too much to expect of him to be bigger than ordinary mortals. Later, we beat India in a day-night game at the SCG. When they lost, quite often he wouldn't come out and shake the opposition's hand. That used to tick us off, and this night at the SCG, Michael Clarke said to me, 'I wonder if Sachin's going to come out this time?'

Sure enough, no Sachin. Pup decided to draw a line in the sand. He ran up the steps into the Indian dressing room and found Sachin, right at the back, packing away his kit. When Michael asked if he was going to shake hands, Sachin said he'd forgotten. Pup made his point. You don't forget to shake hands after an international match. Perhaps Sachin wasn't a god, just another human like the rest of us.

We were carrying more than just our cricket baggage into Perth. Chris Rogers, who I knew very well from state cricket in Perth, made his debut, which gave the team a different feel. I was used to Justin Langer and Matthew Hayden, two very dominant Australian openers, at the top of the order, and now it was Phil Jaques and Chris Rogers, both very good players who had plundered runs in first-class cricket but not that same experienced, almost impregnable front line. I thought, *Gee, there's a bit of extra responsibility on me, I'm now almost a senior player.*

We lost the Test match and I don't think any of us performed well. I got my first duck in Test cricket – at home, in front of my family and friends.

India had rallied after the Sydney controversy, and as much as we were trying to ignore it I doubt anyone was unaffected. Every player was trying to be on his best behaviour. Nobody wanted to be seen not playing in the right spirit. There is a fine line between trying and trying too hard, and we lacked not only that verbal aggression but also the general aggression and edge that are necessary to Test cricket.

The fourth Test was in Adelaide, and I hated the thought of losing it and drawing the series. I only scored 22, but centuries from Haydos, Ricky and Pup ensured that we were never in danger of losing. I was relieved that we'd won 2–1 but happier that the series had finished. I just wanted it over. There was so much rubbish said and controversy, I wanted to see the back of it. I'd never felt like that about a cricket series before, but there was a sourness to the 2007–08 summer that left a bad taste for everybody involved.

I had no idea that that was going to be Gilly's last Test match. It was heart-wrenching for such a clean sportsman to be dragged into the mire and have his ethics questioned after Sydney, and I wonder if that hastened his retirement. Then, on the first day in

Adelaide, he dropped a straightforward nick off Laxman. I saw a look in Gilly's eye. He's a very proud man and wouldn't want to let his teammates down. Looking back, I realised he was thinking he was ready to go.

But we've all dropped catches, so I didn't think more of it until before breakfast the next day, he pulled me aside.

'Huss, can I have a quick word with you?'

I thought, *Oh no, what's happened?*

He said, 'I've decided to retire. This is my last Test match.'

I didn't know what to say. I was shocked. I was just blinking back the emotions. Then I shook his hand and said, 'Well done, you've had an unbelievable career. Thanks for letting me know.'

He seemed really happy. That's what made me congratulate him. He looked like all the stress had lifted. He was calm and relaxed again. I thought, *Good on you mate, if it makes you this happy you're doing the right thing.* I didn't try to change his mind. He was a new man.

Gilly played the one-day series and got to say goodbye around Australia, including scoring a farewell century in Perth, where he was now a 'local' hero. He'd come a long way since the 'Bring Back Zoehrer' days.

As in most seasons, we'd started to tire. India played very well with some new young players coming over, and Sachin put together some masterful innings in the finals. We all fought as hard as we could, but India had confidence and momentum and they won the series in the second final in Brisbane. The only highlight of that match was when a spectator ran on and Andrew Symonds flattened him with a hip and shoulder. I was in the toilet at the time, though, so I didn't see it live but heard an enormous roar. As with the general course of that summer, it was a disappointment. We had beaten India in the Tests, but the series left scars with a lot of the players.

TWENTY-THREE

During the Australian summer, the players heard the whispers about an 'Indian Premier League' of Twenty20 cricket that was going to start the next autumn. The rumours were wild, mostly focused on the millions of dollars that would be paid at an auction for the players.

Neil Maxwell, my manager by then, was employed by the Board of Control for Cricket in India (BCCI) to get Australians to sign up for the auction. Neil was doing the big sell, and was keen for me and other players to be involved. I trusted him and said I was happy to give it a go as long as it wouldn't cause any drama with CA.

In dressing room discussions, Ricky was sceptical. He might not have trusted the people involved and how it might affect Australian cricket. I was between a rock and a hard place. My captain was saying he wasn't sure about it, whereas my advisor was saying it would be a brilliant opportunity. The Australian Players' Association was working on getting the contracts watertight; the first samples from India had no health benefits if you were injured, and you had to make literally hundreds of appearances. The ACA and Maxwell got the contracts into what they thought would be a good state for player protection, and eventually, once it was ascertained that national commitments took priority, most of the players said yes to being involved. I was relieved in the end that I wasn't out there on my own. There was a safety in numbers. Ricky, Haydos and Gilly were part of it, which made me happy, and also Warne and McGrath, so I felt comfortable in the end.

There was great curiosity as to how much you would go for in an auction. I didn't know who I'd be playing for. We didn't know if players would go for $10,000 or $1 million. The night of the auction, I was at home with the family and checked my computer to find out I was off to the Chennai Super Kings. Australia had a full tour to the West Indies cutting through the IPL season, so I would only be available for four of Chennai's fourteen matches, and I would be paid on a pro-rata basis.

I was excited by the concept of playing with cricketers from around the world, getting to know them and seeing how they prepared and played up close. There was also some anxiety about going to India so soon after the spiteful series in Australia, and concerns about how we would be seen there.

At least I had a buddy going to Chennai in Haydos. And if I was honest, I would say I was grateful for him to be coming, as he would take whatever heat was coming our way.

We arrived for a training camp, where I had a good vibe from the Chennai franchise's friendliness and good organisation. Everything was on a grand scale. In Chennai, we were given thirty training shirts and twelve match shirts – too much! Everything about the tournament was larger than life and full of hype.

Our first visit to the dressing room was hilarious. I was with Haydos and the New Zealanders Stephen Fleming and Jacob Oram. All the Indians were petrified of Haydos. He was big, aggressive and a tough character to play against. As this man-mountain walked into the dressing room, they were seething and almost cowering in the corners. It was a sight to see, and this eerie vibe of *Ssh, there's Hayden!* They disliked him and were terrified of him at the same time.

Suddenly Haydos boomed: 'G'day boys, how ya going?'

With a huge smile, he broke the ice, going around shaking everyone's hand and clapping them on the shoulder. You could see the confusion on their faces: this mean, angry Australian monster was happy to be there and very keen to be everyone's friend. From that moment, they loved having him. It was one example of the way the IPL broke down cultural barriers and helped heal the game.

Our owner was Indian Cements, headed by Mr Srinivasan. As he was also on the board of the BCCI, he gave control of the team to his son-in-law Mr Gurunath. He ran the team along with Kepler Wessels, who was coach, and I assume one of the reasons they chose me to play for them. Chennai was known as a very cricket-focused place, unlike some of the other franchises, which were owned by Bollywood stars and seemed to be as much about showbiz as cricket. I had a great time while I was there, embracing all the excitement of the T20 game and the Bollywood fashion parties, the full IPL experience, but the Chennai Super Kings were always about winning cricket games first and foremost.

The consensus from back in Australia was that the IPL was froth and bubble, and that we were all partying and not enhancing our cricket. I found the opposite: the matches were very competitive and it was a great education playing alongside international stars. MS Dhoni, our captain, was very down to earth and friendly, and the most unflappable player I have ever encountered. This may come across as arrogance to people who don't know him, and when I got together with the Australian boys, who were keen to ask what Dhoni was like, they wouldn't believe me when I told them what a joy he was to play with. Sometimes he mesmerised me with how relaxed he was. Even when we needed 14 runs an over he would say, 'Just play smart cricket, knock it around for twos.' I would be thinking, *We need more than twos!* But he took care of things at the other end – as good a finisher as I ever saw. As a leader, he had a great effect on a lot of Indian players who tended to get very tight and try too hard. He got them to loosen up by not panicking or getting introspective about defeat. He would just say, 'One day you win, one day you lose.' Just relax, smile, enjoy the challenge and do your best.

Possibly my favourite international teammate at CSK was Murali, a world champion I'd always admired. We hit it off from the start. It's a bit embarrassing, but they began to call us Mr and Mrs Cricket. He's just about the only person I've met who loved cricket more than I did. He talked about it non-stop. The team would seat us next to each other on every plane trip, so we could talk about cricket while they slept or read or thought about anything but cricket. We chewed each other's ears off. It was a marriage made in heaven.

In those days, players were still trying to get the hang of the tactical side of T20. Generally the idea was to tee off from the start. We didn't use our brains much. In the very first IPL game, Brendan McCullum belted 158 off 73 balls for Kolkata Knight Riders, and that was how we thought we had to play.

For our first game the next day, we were in Mohali to play the Kings XI Punjab. The conditions were a batsman's dream: flat, fast pitch, an outfield like glass. Haydos and Parthiv Patel got us off to a quick start, and then, coming in at number three, I managed to get a drive away off Brett Lee. Then I clipped one off my toes that raced away for four. That was the settling-in period! Then it was, *Try to bat like McCullum last night and get away with as much as you can.* I had one of those days when everything went right. It was a perfect day and I got 116 not out off 54 balls. I'd never dreamed I could score that fast. I'd spent my life worrying about letting teams down through slow scoring. But now it didn't matter if I got out, so I felt no pressure. It's amazing the effect that can have.

We were to leave after four games, having won them all. But our main focus was playing for Australia. If it had meant not playing games for Australia, I wouldn't have played in the IPL. Haydos and I left for a training camp before going to the West Indies, and CSK lost their next four matches. Matty and I agreed that we must look like legends in Chennai!

There was some regeneration in the Test side in the West Indies, with Brad Haddin coming in for Gilly, and Brad Hodge and Simon Katich making comebacks. It doesn't matter where the West Indies are with their cricket; they always put up a huge fight on their own turf. Shiv Chanderpaul was entering that late phase of his career when he was just about impossible to get out. I enjoyed studying other players' techniques, and there was plenty to look at in Chanderpaul. Before the bowler bowled, he made numerous weird and wonderful movements, but when the ball was released he was in good position to attack the ball off either foot. Like Kato, at the critical moment he was very still.

His concentration defied belief. It was like he didn't care if he went 50 balls without scoring a run. He was happy to bat for three days for a hundred if he had to. This was an education for me, as I'd always struggled with impatience. Every few balls I would get anxious about rotating the strike and put pressure on myself. Chanderpaul, for all his strange-looking hops and fidgets before the ball was delivered, was as implacable as a statue. But he could smash the ball around as well. We would marvel at his patience in scoring a hundred against us, and Ricky would recall a century Chanderpaul hit against Australia off 69 balls.

Suleiman Benn, the 10-foot-tall finger-spinner, was another interesting character. I thought he was a really good bowler, very accurate, with that height and extra bounce. He bowled quickly, so you couldn't use your feet. The pitches were not very true, with varying amounts of bounce, turn and pace, and I couldn't get him away. I caught up with him after the series and he seemed a bit different. He's from Barbados and he said, 'This is my island. I own this island. If you have any trouble with anyone I'll sort them out.'

I laughed nervously and said, 'Mate, I don't think I'll get into any trouble; let's just talk about cricket!'

We won the series 2–0, but it was harder than that. I was the only batsman not to perform. For three years, Test cricket had been fresh to me, and I'd played without fear. But now, teams did more homework on me and showed me more respect, so it became harder. The doubts began to build up. Ricky, Phil Jaques, Kato and Pup all made hundreds, Simmo played some excellent innings, and I was the only one not making a score. In the last Test in Barbados, a Suleiman Benn ball popped off a length and I was caught off the glove. I sat down in the dressing room and said, 'Well, that sums up my damn tour.' Ricky had a little chuckle and said, 'Welcome to Test cricket.' He was right, of course. It wasn't all about peeling off hundreds. He'd been through these cycles a few times, and now it was my turn.

We had a five-match one-day series and, having not performed well in the Tests, I got the feeling that Tim Nielsen was worried about me. I wanted to bat for long periods in the nets until I felt comfortable. It had already been a long tour, it was hot and humid, and Tim pulled me aside and said, 'You're wearing yourself out, you've got to be fresh for the games.' Stubbornly, I said, 'No, I want learn to bat in these conditions.' We clashed a bit and he got angry with me, but by the end of the series I was batting a lot better.

It was a strange tour in some ways. We had quite a few new players for the one-dayers, including my brother David, who had made his international debut during the home summer. Dave and I didn't generally talk cricket at family gatherings. Somehow it was an unspoken agreement. I was really happy he had been given his chance, and wanted him to be free to be himself. I hated the idea that he might be seen as 'Mike's brother'. I don't know if he felt extra pressure because of me, but of course he wanted to be himself, no-one's brother. That was one reason he'd left Western Australia to play in Victoria. So now that he was in the Australian team, I didn't want to take him under my wing or shape him, and nor did he.

With a slight twist of fate, I could easily have spent my career as 'David Hussey's brother', and played in his shadow. I have no idea how I would have felt. It seemed that whenever someone mentioned Dave, my name was mentioned in the same breath, and if that bothered him I would completely understand. It's possible that he's been driven to play a more aggressive brand of cricket than I have because, even if subconsciously, he wanted to distinguish himself. That attacking outlook led to a very good one-day international and T20 career for him, but might have counted against him in the longer form.

The relationship between Dave and me was no issue. Unfortunately there was a bust-up on that tour that came between another pair of 'brothers'.

Andrew Symonds and Michael Clarke were literally best mates. In off-seasons they went camping and fishing and on road trips together. They were inseparable.

After the Test series, Ricky went home with a broken finger, and Michael was called up to stand in as captain for the one-dayers. Simmo was ten minutes late for the team bus to depart for training. He was pulled into a leadership meeting with captain, coach and manager, and was fined for being late. This didn't go down well with him. He was really unhappy that his mate had fined him for what he saw as a very minor indiscretion.

From that moment, they were never the same. If Pup was up one end of the dressing room, Simmo was up the other. They didn't look at each other or talk to each other. New guys in the one-day team wouldn't have noticed, because during training and games, both players were professional. They didn't talk for the whole series. It gave me an uncomfortable feeling, being mates with both of them, and I didn't want to be forced to take sides.

When I look back on our team of that period, I wonder where it went. We had the foundation for a very quick rebuilding phase, the nucleus of a team that could have stayed on top of the world for another five years. I know that there were different reasons for each player, but Phil Jaques, Andrew Symonds, Brett Lee, Brad Hodge and Stuart Clark all ended their careers before their time. Australian cricket should have got more out of them for longer, and we could have kept dominating. While injury and other issues played a part, I began to sense that there was a different mood among the selectors, who were looking well into the future and injecting youth into the Australian team.

For Test cricket, I'm firmly of the belief that you have to pick the best players available at any time. I felt the selectors were starting to look too far into the future. If you look after the now, the future will look after itself. In the next couple of years, they began picking players on a hunch and seeing if they could finish their development as Test players. That's fine if the players were ready. But if they weren't, they wouldn't perform consistently and a losing habit could easily take hold. I felt the selectors were constantly looking for the next Ricky Ponting, rather than letting young players develop at their own speed. I guess this reflects my background of needing to earn your place and not having it handed to you on a platter. Test cricket is a huge shock if you haven't learnt your game inside out and scored a lot of first-class runs.

TWENTY-FOUR

Friendships may have been strained, but cricket went on. Our next engagement was a mid-winter series with Bangladesh in Darwin. We had a lot more cricket coming up later in the year, with a trip to India, home series with New Zealand and South Africa, and then a trip to South Africa before the 2009 Ashes tour. So the fitness staff thought they might use the Darwin series for conditioning. I'd done a fair bit of work so wasn't in bad shape, but when we got there, it was the first time I felt my age. Having just turned thirty-three, I discovered plenty of new aches and pains which didn't go away the next morning.

The series promised to be enjoyable, with an injection of enthusiasm from new players like Shaun Marsh, Cameron White and Brett Geeves. A real enthusiastic feel. The people in Darwin were excited to have the Australian team and bent over backwards to make us feel at home.

But then Simmo went fishing.

I felt for Simmo because he did not set out to do the wrong thing. What happened was, we had an optional training session late one day. At 9 am that morning, we had a team meeting. Simmo had decided not to do the training session, but had overlooked the fact that there was a meeting first – or he thought that was optional too. He had been seen leaving the hotel at 6am to go on a fishing trip with some mates.

He turned up in the late afternoon, and the powers that be were waiting for him at the hotel. He had to go into a disciplinary hearing for missing the team meeting. It didn't help the situation that Pup was captain again. To him, it must have looked like Simmo was challenging him, carrying on what had started in the West Indies. In any case, the leadership group of Pup, Tim Nielsen and Steve Bernard thought Simmo wasn't switched on and didn't want to be there, so he should go home.

I was probably the team member who was close to him, but I didn't see him again after hearing he was going to be in trouble. The disciplinary hearing was in the evening and he was gone the next morning. Only after it had happened did we know he'd been sent home. I tried to contact him, but could not get in touch.

Simmo had been playing the best cricket of his life, but I thought he'd come to a point where he was questioning why he was playing the game. He loved cricket and playing for Australia and the camaraderie in the team. When the last ball was bowled, he was always the first to be sitting on the Esky passing out beers and making people laugh. But the dynamics of the dressing room and culture of the team were changing. He also struggled with the fame side of things. He absolutely hated getting mobbed by young kids or people yelling out his name or wanting photos when he was going down to his corner shop. He was one of the most recognisable sportsmen in Australia at the time, which he didn't find easy. He just wanted to go and play with his mates, which was why we loved him so much. But on top of all that, his familiar friends such as Gilly and Haydos were passing out of the team and he had to build new friendships with new players, a process that takes time, and he didn't know if he had the energy for it when he was already questioning why he was playing the game. Still, he would be part of the Australian team's plans for another year.

Michael was very similar to Andrew in a lot of ways, which was why they had loved each other's company. But in 2008, their careers were headed in opposite directions. While Simmo was drifting away from international cricket, Pup was being groomed as the next Australian captain. As he hadn't had a lot of leadership experience at lower levels – often this is the way with prodigies, as they're usually the youngest player in a team – it was decided to expose him to the captaincy as soon as possible.

We played very well under him in Darwin. He showed himself to be a strong driver who was single-minded about how he wanted the team to play. My view was, you follow the captain. I had no qualms in following his direction. It wasn't a lot different from what Ricky had been doing. I was quite excited about Pup's determination to make the team better by covering more bases in how we prepared. It was a chance to get a little bit better. At my age, the opportunity to learn new ways and improve was exciting.

Ricky was back for the spring tour to India for a four-Test series. There was a lot of talk about how the teams would square up after what had happened in Australia, but I was very friendly with the Indian players I'd been with at CSK, and other Australians had similarly been teammates with Indian internationals in the IPL. Most of them weren't interested in the Harbhajan controversy anyway, and when we got to India I didn't feel any tension between the teams.

After two pretty ordinary Test series, against India and the West Indies, I was very nervous. But a hundred in the warm-up match in Hyderabad set me up well. In India, where the pitches are so dry and the noise, the smell and the behaviour of the ball through the air are so foreign, you need time at the crease. I had marathon net sessions and was extremely happy about those runs in the warm-up.

To get a hundred in the first Test in Bangalore, I was over the moon. I was thrilled to be out there when Ricky posted his ton, putting to bed some demons he'd had about playing in India. On his fourth Test tour, it was a great moment to prove his champion qualities. We controlled the match, but it was a kick in the guts that we couldn't finish them off on the last day. Mitchell Johnson, Stuart Clark and Brett Lee tried very hard, but we were short in the spin department, with the all-rounders Michael Clarke and Cameron White doing the work, and we couldn't get enough breakthroughs.

There was a momentum turnaround in that result. We'd played our best cricket and couldn't penetrate, whereas India knew they hadn't played well and still survived. Their big guns began to fire, and they batted first in Mohali, where Tendulkar passed Lara's Test run record and Ganguly made a hundred. They absolutely pounded us. The pitch was very good and the outfield was fast, and I felt, *Whoa, we're in for a long couple of days*. That was Peter Siddle's first Test match, and he showed everyone what he was made of from the outset. He hit Gautam Gambhir on the head with his first ball, and got Sachin out for his first wicket. But that was the only excitement we had. We copped a thrashing, and were under pressure from there. In the third Test in Delhi we hung on by our fingernails to get a draw. The Indians are a great front-running team, whilst the way we played, we were not very good at being in a defensive frame of mind. They rattled up another 600 and we had to save the Test match. The pitch was turning and we showed a lot of character, particularly Pup, whose century brought him out of a mini-slump.

That brought the series down to the final Test at Nagpur, where a win would have us retain the Border-Gavaskar Trophy, which India hadn't held since 2003–04. Disappointingly, as had been the case throughout the series, the stadium was less than half-full. I love experiencing overseas crowds – the bands, the whistling, the singing, the screams when a player like Sachin comes in – and was looking forward to that in India, but in that series it wasn't loud at all.

Less than the usual spectator noise didn't ease the tension one bit. We were having all sorts of trouble coping with the reverse swing of Ishant Sharma and especially Zaheer Khan. Waiting to bat, I was extremely nervous. I would go up to the analyst and ask, 'Any reverse there?'

Almost invariably he would reply, 'Nah, it's doing nothing.'

But the thing was, when it looked like it was swinging a tiny bit on a TV monitor, when you got out there the truth was that it felt like it was bending around corners. I didn't believe the analyst. When he said, 'Maybe it's doing a tiny bit,' I peered at the monitors and saw terrifying late swing.

Batting at number four, it was easier if early wickets had fallen and I could face the new ball. In India, the new ball can come on nicely and not swing very much. Once it gets older, Sharma and Zaheer could get it reverse swinging very early.

The difference is marked. New-ball swing generally goes quite early, out of the bowler's hand, and you've got time to adjust. When a ball is reverse swinging, it comes down the pitch dead straight and then darts either way, late and radical.

In Nagpur, I was in in the 18th over with Kato going very well at the other end. The Indians had been preparing the ball to reverse, by bowling cross-seam bouncers, throwing the ball hard into the rough and so on, to scuff one side as much as possible while working hard on the other to shine it up. One way of countering it is to watch the ball closely, because when it's reversing you can really see the two different sides. My plan was to pick which way it would swing by watching it in the bowler's hand as he ran in to bowl, and then wait, keeping my backlift low, and play late and straight.

But the Indians foiled this by hiding the ball as they ran in. Zaheer held it in his right hand, hidden, only switching it to his left hand while he was loading up, and still keeping it covered. So as he bowled, I had no idea which way it was going to swing.

When I went out, he was bowling and the ball was reversing. But also, the longer you're there, the easier it becomes to adjust and counter it. The first half-hour is critical. I managed to get through that period quite comfortably, which gave me some confidence and had him taken out of the attack. I was able to thrive, as the outfield was so fast, all I had to do was time the ball and the runs came quickly; there was no need to strain to hit the ball too hard.

Kato and I had a long vigil, and his century was one of the best innings I saw him play. But after he got out, we were under pressure again, and on 90 I was out in the most distressing way. I pushed a ball from Harbhajan into the gap at cover, and Murali Vijay, fielding at silly point, knocked it down. I had just committed forward a fraction too far, and was out of my crease when he flicked it back. The third umpire took a long look before ruling me out. It was my first run-out in Test cricket and couldn't have come at a worse time. I put it down with my most disappointing dismissals ever, as I had worked very hard all day, only to fall short of a hundred and get out at a crucial time in the game.

We were always chasing the game from that point, notwithstanding the amazing 12-wicket debut from Jason Krejza.

'Krazy' was a different kind of bowler, He was an attacking off-spinner, giving the ball plenty of air and putting a lot of revs on the ball. The Indians had our attack on toast, and saw this young spinner as a target. But that offered him opportunities. In both innings he was going at plenty of runs an over, but amongst it he was bowling absolute jaffas. The Indians kept smacking him around and then he'd knock one over. To take 12 wickets on debut, no matter how many runs he went for, was amazing. He was rapt to have the opportunity to play. People would argue later that we should have kept him longer because of the wickets he was taking, but Ricky was very concerned about the number of runs he was leaking. I felt he mainly gave up runs in Nagpur because of the mindset the Indian batsmen were in. But that said, in Australian conditions with less spin, he needed to work on his consistency. When there wasn't rough or uneven bounce, batsmen were able to milk him without taking risks.

Krazy's short stint was part of a long search for the next spinner. Since the retirements of Shane Warne and Stuart MacGill, we had been through about half a dozen spin bowlers. I just wanted us to identify someone who could do a good job. You'll never replace a Warne or a MacGill. In my mind, we weren't searching for that. We wanted someone to come on and keep it tight from one end, then come into the game and help us win when the pitch deteriorated. He needed to complement our pace attack. I thought Nathan Hauritz did a good job for a few years. He didn't give much away and was quite penetrative on wearing pitches. I was quite a fan of his, but the selectors kept searching, chopping and changing, a bit impatient looking for a wicket-taking spinner. When they finally found Nathan Lyon, I was pleading for them to stick with him, because I thought he was the type of bowler we needed.

One thing that stood out, while we slid to defeat in Nagpur, was the confusion going through Haydos's mind. He'd been batting well in the nets, but you don't know what's going on inside. After a lot of past success in India, he was battling this time. In Mohali he started by charging Zaheer in the first over of the second innings of the Test match. I thought, *Why are you doing this?* It was the first time I'd seen him showing the effects of pressure. He was always so confident and dominant and sure of himself, but this time he didn't seem himself.

Coming home from that series felt like coming home from a military campaign. It was so mentally and physically draining, being behind the eight-ball in hot conditions. I'd lost a lot of weight, my face was drawn, and I was spent. But as soon as we got back, we had to race up to Brisbane to prepare for the first Test against New Zealand.

The practice pitches at the Gabba were whizzing all around us. At first we were saying to each other that we felt like how subcontinental teams must feel when they arrive in Brisbane, completely at sea against the bounce and pace. As well as not being attuned to the conditions, we were definitely jaded after India. That made for a good contest with New Zealand, who played at their best. We only prevailed thanks to a good team effort from the bowlers and some terrific batting from Pup, Kato and Hadds, who made his maiden Test century in Adelaide. I went out for pizza with him that night and he was excitedly reliving the highlights, asking me what my favourite shot of his was. It was great to see. If I'm batting with someone in that position, I love sharing it because I know how they feel. When Phil Jaques scored his first Test century, proving he belonged at that level, I was more nervous than if I'd been in the nineties myself.

I'm not surprised that a lot of run-outs happen when a batsman is in the nineties. Often he's so desperate to get to three figures, he loses his head. Sometimes it's his partner who gets over-keen. I was known as a good runner between wickets. I think the first ingredient for this was the sprint training Dad had given us when we were kids – it helps to be fast! The second ingredient is the experience to be able to judge a run. And the third ingredient is to tailor your running to your batting partner at the time. Most of the Australian batsmen of my era were excellent between wickets. Ricky was brilliant, with great awareness, and Michael Clarke and I had a great understanding. At the basis of that was trusting your partner's call, whether you think it's right or wrong. Run-outs occur mainly through indecision and one player not trusting the other's call. If the other guy called, I would go, no questions asked. One in fifty you'll get run out. If players watched the ball and made up their own mind on whether they would run, rather than trusting me, I'd get frustrated with them. I'd call an easy single and they'd send me back. You've got to act as a unit; anything else is a recipe for confusion.

I hadn't been batting well against New Zealand, and the South Africans, who followed them to Australia, were considered a much stronger opponent. In the lead-up to the first Test in Perth, I fell into my bad habit of getting too intense, telling myself this was the series when the great players come to the fore. I put too much pressure on myself, hitting so many balls at practice that even Ricky came up and said, 'Gee, you've hit some balls this week, make sure you save some runs for the middle.' I hadn't even realised. I was absolutely desperate to do well. It was no surprise, then, that I got out for a duck in the first innings to Dale Steyn, and then in the second innings I under-edged a pull onto my stumps off Makhaya Ntini.

We got on top in that Test when Mitch Johnson went bananas for a crazy hour and ended up with eight wickets. Hadds made 94 in our second innings and got us into a good position, but by the last innings the pitch had flattened out, South Africa batted brilliantly, and we didn't ever look like defending what was a record target, which they chased down comfortably.

After the match, there was a lot of discussion about whether the selectors should persevere with the attacking Jason Krejza or replace him with Nathan Hauritz, who would probably keep it tighter. They went with Hauritz. We'll never know if it was right or wrong, which is the unknowable that selectors have to live with and which makes it such a hard job.

I felt under selection pressure myself, not having made any meaningful runs in three home Tests. At 1–0 down, we were in a massive fight. We hadn't lost a series at home for sixteen years, and we were now ranked below South Africa in the ICC standings, so they were entitled to favouritism.

It all hung on the Boxing Day Test in Melbourne, and I chose to have the worst Test match in my whole career. It was just a horror show from the word go. Ricky and Pup batted superbly in our first innings, while I went to let one go off Dale Steyn and it clipped the bottom of my bat. A little unlucky, but out for a duck nonetheless. After three years that were probably too good to be true, I was finding out what Test cricket was really about.

We made a good total of 394, and were in total control of the game when we reduced South Africa to 7/184. Then Paul Harris put on 67 with JP Duminy, which got me a bit worried, but that seemed like nothing when Duminy and Steyn batted together for more than 60 overs, adding 180 for the ninth wicket. Brett Lee broke down and the whole thing slipped through our fingers over by over.

During the partnership, I had my most embarrassing moment on a cricket field. Steyn took a big slog off Hauritz, and I got right underneath it. It was in the sun, so I shuffled this way and that to get it out of that line. The ball ended up landing 2 metres away from me. I was close to Bay 13, who gave me some stick, and it was replayed approximately one million times on the big screen.

For all that, Ricky showed his leadership qualities by remaining amazingly positive. I didn't feel any negativity come in. We were well in the match. There was some frustration around Brett Lee's breakdown, but he would have run in with barbed wire in his feet. We still felt right up for the contest when we finally batted again, trailing by 65.

We were 2/40 when I walked out to join Ricky, who was at his very best again. This was the time to show my worth. I might have made a lot of runs in my first three years in Test cricket, but I really did believe that I was only as good as my last innings, and my head was full of doubts and demons. I heaped a nation's worth of pressure on myself, but I felt like the puny thirteen-year-old again, not knowing where my next run was coming from, facing giant bowlers who easily had my measure.

On 2, I got a brute of a bouncer from Morne Morkel. It hit me on the head and flew to square leg. I couldn't believe the South Africans were appealing at all, and then to my astonishment

Aleem Dar gave me out caught. I was looking at Aleem as if to say, *Surely you saw that that hit me on the head – and nothing else!* Ricky was staring at him in utter disbelief, then staring at me, then staring back at Aleem.

Walking off, it all boiled up inside me, and in the dressing room I got really angry. I threw my helmet. *What on earth have I done? Whose black cat have I stolen, what ladder have I walked under?* Everything in this game was going against me. My confidence was at an all-time low. In the public spotlight, I feared that everyone was talking about what a failure I was.

Thanks to Ricky's 99, we set them 183 to win, which we still thought we could defend. We *had* to win this Test match. We knew it would be hard for them batting last. If we set them 200 we could defend that. A couple of wickets would get us in there. But Binga couldn't bowl, and Graeme Smith, Neil McKenzie and Hashim Amla showed why they were number one in the world.

I was distraught at the end of the game. South Africa had won their first series in Australia, which was hard to take. I'd had a nightmare. In cricket terms, I didn't think life could get any worse.

The Sydney Test match was a big one for us. We came in feeling deflated. For me personally, I had to show a bit of mettle. In a long, drawn-out, tight Test match, I didn't get a lot of runs, only 30 and 45 not out, but at least I could still compete with these guys. I wasn't batting well, but they did have an outstanding attack and were difficult to score runs against.

Yet again, a Sydney Test came down to the wire, and the bowling of Peter Siddle and Mitchell Johnson was instrumental. Mitch bowling at Graeme Smith at the end, the South African captain battling on with a broken finger, will be etched on the memory of everyone who saw it. I was really thankful that we got over the line. But the dramas were only just beginning.

TWENTY-FIVE

The notorious blue between Simon Katich and Michael Clarke was all my fault. I still blame myself.

Soon after the match, Michael Clarke asked me if I could possibly complete the song before midnight. We stayed in the SCG dressing rooms for several hours, enjoying the win. The South Africans, a brilliant bunch of guys who reminded me of Australians in a lot of ways. They came in and had a drink with us, so it went on for quite a while before I could call the guys in and lead the song. The signal was putting John Williamson's 'True Blue' on the stereo. When the boys heard that, everything else stopped, and they would gather for 'Underneath the Southern Cross'.

The South Africans stayed for quite a while, and I enjoyed having a few beers with them. Every half-hour or so, Steve Bernard kept coming up to me and saying, 'Huss, when are you going to sing the song?' I was having a good time, and in the mood to sit for a while, and said, 'Brutus, every time you ask me, I'm going to add another fifteen minutes onto it.'

I didn't realise that Michael Clarke had organised a bar for the post-dressing room celebrations. Feeling under time pressure, he was asking Steve to get me to hurry up and sing the song. I wished in hindsight that he'd come up to me and said, 'Huss, can we sing the song, we need to hurry up and go.' I would have been more than happy to accommodate him, knowing how we all had to juggle team and social commitments, more than ever when it's our hometown Test match. I would have been happy to sing the song straight away and let them go.

While I was completely oblivious to Pup's mounting panic, Kato was on the other side of the room with a clear view of Pup talking to Steve Bernard and getting frustrated. They must have made eye contact, and started making gestures towards each other across the room. I was none the wiser, not looking at either of them.

Then, out of nowhere they came together in the middle of the room. There was a big confrontation and I thought, *What the hell is going on?* This had come out of nowhere. We'd all been having a laugh and a chat.

It got broken up pretty quickly. Kato was put back down in his seat and Pup left the dressing room altogether. We were all in a bit of shock. I certainly didn't know what the hell had gone on. Kato was very apologetic. It was the first Test match for Doug Bollinger and Andrew McDonald – who had, coincidentally, replaced Andrew Symonds, who'd played his last Test in Melbourne. Kato was saying to each of them, 'I'm really sorry for what happened. I just want you to enjoy this win, I'm really sorry, I don't want to ruin your first Test match.'

Andrew McDonald broke the ice beautifully. He said, 'Don't worry, mate, this happens all the time in Victoria.'

Everyone burst out laughing and cheering. We all started drinking again and didn't think about it. I said, 'We'd better get this song done.'

Half an hour later I called it, and asked Brute, 'Where's Pup?'

'He's gone.'

I felt completely responsible. I felt it was a black mark against my name that one of our brothers was missing for the team song. We'd won the Test match together, but he was gone. I felt dreadful about it, and the next morning tried calling him but couldn't get through. I sent him messages. He eventually got back and said it wasn't my fault, don't worry, he'd sort out his differences with Kato.

That set-to had massive repercussions when it got out into the public, and the relationship between the two of them was never the same.

Meanwhile, what was probably a bigger change was brewing the same night. After the song, most of the boys left, except Haydos, who seemed to want to sit and talk for longer. After everything else that had gone on, I was not going to abandon him. Peter Siddle also stayed, and the three of us chatted until well after midnight. Haydos had been getting some stick in the press about his form going back to the Indian tour. There was talk that he should retire, but he'd been making no concessions to that.

But after we'd been chatting for a while, he said, 'Boys, it's been an absolute pleasure playing with you. You never know when it's your last Test.'

Sidds and I both said, 'No way, Haydos, you're fine, keep going.'

What we didn't know was that he'd made the decision in his head. A couple of days later, before the one-day series started, he called a press conference and announced his retirement. So another of the titans was going. It left me with feelings of heightened responsibility and fear. I was really happy I'd been there to spend time with him after his last Test match, but without him, things were only going to get tougher.

The Sydney Test win was a brief flash of brightness in a dismal summer. The triangular one-day series format had been dropped, and we had two five-match series against South Africa and then New Zealand. We lost 4–1 to the Proteas, hitting a low point on Australia Day in Adelaide. It's such a big occasion, with all of the city turning out, and as proud Australians we needed no motivation. At that point we were 2–1 down and needed to win to keep the series alive. Ricky revved us up and won the toss, and on a beautiful batting wicket we made a little more than 200. It was awful. At the change of innings, Ricky said, 'Come on, we can defend this, a couple of early wickets and we're in,' before the South Africans made us look like second-graders and chased down the target in about 35 overs. They won in Perth, and I felt really down again. What made it worse was that there were signs of incoherence from the selectors, a first presentiment of something that was going to spread through the team over the next four years.

Before the one-dayers, the selectors said to me, 'How do you fancy opening the batting?'

I had my doubts, but would do whatever was best by the team. I made it clear that if we were doing it, I needed an extended go. I hadn't opened for a long time, and when I'd done it for Western Australia in one-day cricket I was pretty ordinary. I just said, 'I'll do it. But give it a proper go, don't flick the idea after one or two games.'

I was out early in the first game and then the idea was binned. They changed their minds.

No sooner had we been put away by South Africa than New Zealand beat us twice. This was beyond the pale. We got it from all angles, about Australian cricket being in crisis. Losing can be a habit, and we had it. The Kiwis' coach, Andy Moles, came out in the press saying they wanted to win the series 5–0. I thought, *No worries, mate, we'll show you.*

The third game of the series in Adelaide was my highlight of the summer, because I had my first really good partnership for Australia with Dave, and I hit the winning runs. It was a big turnaround for the team. Dave batted brilliantly, probably his best innings for Australia to that point, and the local boy, Callum Ferguson, came in and finished it off. It was a rare good day that summer.

We won in Sydney to charge back into the series, but a wash-out in Brisbane left it unresolved at 2–2. I was named man of the series, which gave me a little confidence boost after such a tough summer. I just wanted to show people I could be part of the Australian team. Hadn't I done that already? Well, no. It only takes one or two bad innings for the demons of self-doubt to find their way back in. For a long time I thought I was afflicted by this worse than anyone else. But it happened even with the great players like Michael Clarke and Ricky Ponting. They looked calm on the outside, but *only* on the outside. I used to envy guys like Jacques Kallis and Jonathan Trott, who were like stone, nothing seeming to affect them. But once you know the game of Test cricket, you realise they are just hiding it. Trott had a string of superstitious routines between every ball. That's how he kept the demons at bay. Even Kallis must have the same doubts and negative thoughts as most players. I probably didn't suffer any more or less self-doubt than those kinds of players, but because Test cricket is partly about putting on a front, I didn't know that. I thought I was alone.

When we got to South Africa for a return three-match series, I felt like I was carrying an elephant's weight of pressure on my back, and as a team we were rank outsiders. Phil Hughes, Marcus North and Ben Hilfenhaus were brought in, and suddenly the awe-inspiring Australian team were inexperienced. The local media were talking about how good the South Africans were and how they would wipe us away.

We prepared well in Potchefstroom. The new guys were extremely determined to show how good they could be, and we came together quickly as a team. We had some planning sessions, talking about how we were going to play. Somehow I got a really good feeling about this team. I didn't know how we were going to play – South African conditions were very tough and I was nervous about how I'd go – but the preparation was excellent.

At Johannesburg, where we were playing the first Test, there had been some weather and the pitch was underprepared. The day before, they'd had a tent over the pitch and some hot air blowers were going full tilt. When I saw them I thought, *Gee, this is going to be fun, an underprepared wicket at the Wanderers.*

I have hardly a critical word to say about Ricky's captaincy for the six years I played under him. But his dogmatic approach to batting first was the worst thing for a batsman's nerves. He won the toss and, on a surface that was sketchy at best, decided to bat. I thought, *You've got to be bloody kidding me. We're batting first on this?*

Inevitably, we lost wickets quickly before, equally inevitably, Ricky and Pup batted brilliantly, counter-attacking, hitting boundaries as if for fun, and throwing the pressure back on the bowlers. Marcus North, on debut, and Brad Haddin joined the party. It was magical batting and it rocked the South Africans. Then Mitchell Johnson, a real confidence player, teed off and made 96. I was disappointed for him, thinking the opportunity to rack up a hundred might not come up again. But we had 466, a score that would have stunned the Proteas.

Then Mitch, who was oozing self-belief, set the tone magnificently with the ball. He's been much maligned, but when he gets it right he can swing the ball back into the right-handers at great pace and be next to unplayable. Conditions were perfect, a little bit overcast with a bit of juice in the pitch, and he got his action right. He got Graeme Smith early, a beautiful ball swinging away late from the left-hander. I could feel that their batsmen were unsure. Mitch's pace was well up too. He was a massive threat. He did it again in the second innings, with great support from Pete Siddle, and we won.

No-one could believe it, least of all the shell-shocked South Africans. We stayed in the dressing room for a few hours, and then I took the team out into the middle of the Wanderers for one of the most memorable renditions of our song. The press were still there, and the South African players, but we didn't care.

We rode that wave into Durban. Mitch took so much confidence from that Johannesburg match, he could have taken apart any batting order, the mood he was in. The whole team was bristling with self-belief. And then there was me.

My return at the Wanderers was 4 and a first-baller, cramped up by a Kallis bouncer, spooning the ball meekly to square leg. It was horrible, grotesque. On top of the fractious Indian series at home, a more or less barren tour to the West Indies, a couple of fighting innings in India, and then two poor series in the Australian summer, I was plumbing the depths. This Test cricket wasn't so fun anymore! I didn't know how to pull myself out of it. And that was the state of mind I was in when Dale Steyn decided to bomb me in Durban.

TWENTY-SIX

Looking back on my encounter with Steyn at Kingsmead, when I lost my bottle and started screaming abuse at him, is one of my favourite stories from my Test career. Whenever I think of it, I'm reminded that this is a tough game that I often found literally impossible. But I guess I can afford to be fond of it, because I know I pulled myself out of that trough and eventually rediscovered my touch. Test cricket would become fun again. But it took a while!

In South Africa, I was able to treat my personal anxieties with the best tonic of all: team success. Peter Siddle, an unsung hero of that tour, bowled like a genius in the second innings, and Kato revived his left-arm wrist-spinners to take three vital wickets at the end. Against all predictions, we had won the series, turned the tables on the all-conquering South African team in their own back yard. It meant so much to our team, and at the end of that Durban Test we celebrated like we'd won the World Cup. The South Africans, who were banished back to first-class cricket for a game after Durban, gave us a touch-up in the third Test in Cape Town, but honestly it didn't matter. Mitch Johnson showed that he could become an all-rounder in scoring that first Test hundred that had slipped by in Johannesburg. But all in all, we were probably in party mode, even if subconsciously. It only takes a slip of 1 or 2 per cent in Test cricket, and suddenly you're being belted.

It's the same in one-day cricket. We let our standards slip in the five-match series, winning only the first and last games. We were losing while chasing targets, and three games in a row I wasn't able to fulfil my middle-order brief. I began wondering if people would think I couldn't do it anymore. No-one spoke to me about it, but there was a first doubt in my own mind about my one-day career. We'd lost two one-day series in a row, and I felt the selectors might be looking for a change.

All the same, it had been a great Test series win for us there, and the tour was rightly judged a success. Even now, I can't quite believe how things fell away so badly after that. We looked like we had a world-beating Test team for years to come. Phil Hughes, Michael Clarke, Marcus North, Peter Siddle, Mitch Johnson, Ben Hilfenhaus and Andrew McDonald were young and coming into their prime. There were still plenty of years left in Punter, Kato, Brad Haddin and me. I still find it difficult to contemplate how it all went wrong. But it started with the 2009 Ashes tour.

As is common nowadays, the Ashes tour started as something else, in this case a Twenty20 World Cup in England. It proved a disappointing start to a bloody disappointing tour.

It started okay with a practice match against New Zealand, which we won. English conditions require more getting used to than others – I believe it needs a month to feel comfortable there – so a two-match preparation was a bit rushed. Probably, though, the powers thought that we would be in England for a long time, and the Ashes series was the prime objective.

Around the time of that practice match Simmo decided to catch up with some mates in London, and they went out for a couple of beers. The next morning, the rugby league State of Origin was on TV, and a few of the team went to a pub to watch it. Simmo was a very passionate Queensland supporter and decided to get into the spirit with a few more beers, even though it was still the morning in England.

In the afternoon we had recovery – a bit of a fitness session, testing our energy and so on. Simmo turned up in less than a great state. Stuart Karppinen, the fitness coach, said, 'Don't worry about it, Simmo, I think you should just go.' So Simmo went off to bed back at the hotel.

Later, Tim Nielsen and Ricky met with him and it was decided that he'd better go home. As in Darwin, it was only the next day that the rest of us realised he'd gone. I was trying to call him but couldn't get in touch.

It was a shame for his career, and a big blow to our team, but part of me thought, *Good on him*. If he didn't enjoy playing for Australia, he shouldn't be doing it. I wish he could have gone out a better way, but he was disillusioned with the environment around the team, cricket wasn't the way he wanted it to be – how it used to be – and he'd had enough.

For my part, I didn't see it coming. I'm hopeless with this sort of stuff, reading what was going on beneath the surface, and was routinely the last to hear any gossip. Thinking back, there must have been ongoing issues. An international cricket team has different guys from different walks of life, often with big personalities and big egos. It's a competitive group, and you've got to expect there'll be some conflicts. I, however, am hopeless at reading them.

I missed him. We weren't as close as when we were first in the team, but we were still mates. He said the culture of the team had changed too much for him: too much structure, no room for personalities, too many young guys who preferred to sit in their rooms playing PlayStations rather than coming to the bar and yarning with him. But I didn't play video games in my room or go to the pub during the week, and we were still friends. It wasn't an either/or. The best times we had together were when we were letting our hair down after a win. We always got on well at training and while playing. It didn't change much through the whole journey. But clearly, we were not close enough for him to confide in me when he was battling with those doubts. Possibly he saw me as someone who was very happy with the way the team was being changed, but that wasn't quite right. I was certainly not as disillusioned as he was, but things were not 100 per cent either.

We were bumped out of the Twenty20 tournament in two games. Chris Gayle took us apart in London, and we were tight in the game against Sri Lanka in Nottingham. Afterwards, Brad Haddin came up and asked, 'Do you think that's the last T20 game you'll play for Australia?'

I said, 'I bloody hope not!' It took me aback, but the rumours were about. I was thirty-three, and T20 was looking like a young man's game. David Warner had made his debut in Melbourne the previous summer. We hadn't heard too much about him, but he absolutely destroyed them, starting with Dale Steyn. We were blown away. If that was the future, I would have to adapt fast in order to keep up.

T20 cricket was new and exciting, but that was adding to my self-doubt. I thought the selectors would start looking at new and younger players. But part of me was optimistic. I thought players who had been successful in Test cricket might be able to adapt to T20 cricket. You needed experience to think your way through certain situations. It wasn't just going to be young powerful hitters, specialists even, to dominate T20. How were they going to recover when they start to struggle? Mental ability is the key, no matter what the format of the game.

There were two weeks to kill while the T20 was still on, and we holed up in Leicester where the training facilities were outstanding. We had two weeks of nets and fielding and bonding sessions, and a couple of games of golf. It was good to relax. The

Ashes tour proper started in Sussex, where we were given a task, as individuals, to make a presentation to the group about what the Ashes meant to each of us. It was a really good exercise, and got guys thinking about the history.

Speaking of (recent) history, Gilly happened to be there, so he got us in a huddle and spoke about his Ashes experience. What came out above all was to keep your 'eyes in'. That is, look after your mates, don't worry about what the opposition are doing, don't be distracted by everything on the periphery. He felt that in 2005 the team had lost that internal focus and care.

I was one of the last to present. I wrote and delivered a light-hearted poem about the team, taking the mickey out of each of the boys. Everyone had been saying serious things, so I wanted to lighten things up. I'd never forgotten being told I was too intense back in 2006!

Finally Ricky gave a stirring speech, bringing everything together. I felt the team was in a good place. Most of us had been there for several weeks now. We had games in Sussex and Worcestershire, a good preparation. The spirit reminded me of the beginning of our South Africa tour.

In my opinion, we had a really good squad. We didn't bowl teams out in the lead-up matches, but that didn't worry me. I was keen to get runs under my belt after what felt like an eternal lean trot, but some of the guys were a bit casual about these games. We might have taken them more seriously.

In a four-day match at Worcester, I made 150 against the England Lions, my first big score for a while. They had a good attack and the pitch was doing a bit early, so it left me feeling well prepared and hungry for the challenge going to the first Test in Cardiff.

I'd played a few county games at Sophia Gardens, and the wicket was always an absolute belter. There was a lot of stress around the first Ashes Test, as always, but the pitch played beautifully and England made 435 before our batsmen cashed in massively –

except me. It's an embarrassing scorecard, from a personal point of view. Hughes 36, Katich 122, Ponting 150, Clarke 83, North 125 not out, Haddin 121 ... and Hussey 3.

Sometimes when you sit and watch a partnership for a very long time with the pads on, you play your innings in your head. I had that while watching Kato and Ricky put on 239 in about two sessions. When I found myself in the middle, everything was quicker and the ball was doing more off the seam and in the air than it had looked like. I went for a drive and got a nick and was on my way back.

But the team was in a great position, and on the last day, starting with Cook and Ravi Bopara already out for 20, we were confident. Ben Hilfenhaus snared Pietersen, and then Nathan Hauritz got Strauss out with a long hop that he should have pasted to the boundary. We felt it was going our way. But slowly the momentum changed. Mitchell Johnson started to spray a few and lost his mojo. Paul Collingwood dug in. The crowd got into us. Late in the day, when we were getting desperate, Graeme Swann was hit on the fingers and called the physio, who strolled out, whistling 'Dixie'. We were saying to the umpires, 'Come on, they're wasting time.' Swanny had treatment, then got hit again, and the same charade was repeated. As a group, we got angry. Then they started running messages out, trying every trick in the book. Ricky was growing very frustrated, telling England's support staff to get off. The umpires stepped in. But ultimately, Monty Panesar, of all people, hung in there with Jimmy Anderson for 12 overs and we couldn't get the breakthrough.

Not finishing the job when you've totally dominated a match can be demoralising. Being able to finish a Test match is the X-factor, and often you see teams that do a lot of good things but can't quite get over that line. We'd done everything we could to win, but they'd hung on. We let out a great scream of frustration, whereas England felt like they'd had a bit of a win.

In the second Test at Lord's, having dominated the previous week, we needed to go that hard again, whereas the opposition knew they had to lift their level. In a counter-intuitive way, although we'd been the better team in Cardiff, England went into the second Test with a mental advantage.

The first day at Lord's was pivotal. I'll never forget walking through the Long Room for the first time in a Test match, and it was packed. You could feel that every spectator in their suit and tie was desperate to be walking onto that field. The English batsmen came down their stairs, Cook and Strauss, and the roar shook the Long Room from the inside out. That rattled us, all that emotion. It's a great experience, but it was daunting.

We were horrible on the field. Cook and Strauss were 0/150 in the blink of an eye. We never looked like turning it around. Even if they stuffed up and got 400, we would be under pressure. It was the worst imaginable start. They were hitting boundary after boundary and we couldn't change their momentum. Whatever Ricky tried couldn't slow them down. It was out of control. There were players in our team who could remember Edgbaston in 2005, but nobody mentioned it in the dressing room. You don't want to bring up bad memories. I just thought, *We're going to have to bat well in the first innings.*

England did stuff up a bit, only making 425. But that was more than enough. We were hanging on to save the game before we could think about winning it.

I had such a point to prove, after what seemed like years since I'd made a decent Test score. What better place? What better circumstances? Hughesy and Ricky had gone early, but Kato and I were – well, determined isn't the word. It was quite overcast. On a clear day in London, Lord's can be a wonderful place to bat, but if it's cloudy, the ball swings and seams. Unfortunately for us it was grey and drizzling, and the lights were on. They'd got early wickets and their tails were up. Kato and I got a good partnership going, just nibbling our way above the hundred, before Flintoff bowled an unbelievably good spell. I glanced up at the scoreboard and noticed he was nudging 150kmh. *Gee, he's really putting in.* The crowd was very much behind him, as you'd expect.

Kato holed out off Graham Onions, but still, I was defending well, enjoying the battle and rotating the strike. I generally struggled with the Lord's slope. Generally if they were bowling from the pavilion end, the ball went down the slope away from me. In county cricket, I got caught behind many times to balls running down the slope. I'd been told by other players to adapt and play outside what I thought the line was, which was hard, but I was trying. But then, Flintoff got a ball that pitched on my off-stump. I let it go, to run down the slope, but it seamed back the other way, up the slope, and cannoned into the stump. He did his flamboyant celebration. I was *desperate* to get a big score, but sometimes you're undone by an amazing piece of bowling. So I trudged off Lord's, very disappointed, but forced to give credit to the bowler.

We battled, but in the end we had two days to survive. It was always going to be tough. We lost Hughes and Katich early. To believe you can bat two days, you normally need to get a good start. This time we were under serious pressure, always just one mistake away.

I batted pretty well for 27 and went for a drive off Swanny. It spun massively and went to first slip. The English started celebrating. The umpire put his finger up. As I walked off, I suddenly thought, *I didn't hit that.* I turned around. *I must have hit it, it went to first slip and he gave it out straight away.*

My disappointment turned to rage when I climbed into the dressing room and saw the replay, which showed I'd missed the ball, not by a little bit but by several inches. I felt the fury build up. I was taking my shoes off as I watched it. You could have driven a London cab through the gap between my bat and the ball, and the commentators were saying, 'No, he's definitely missed that.'

I lost it. What happened next is quite shameful. I threw down my boot, and it bounced up off my bag and put a hole ... in the wall ... *of the Lord's dressing room.* I was absolutely distraught. *This is the home of cricket and I've put a hole in the wall.*

I sobered up quickly and went to the room attendant, Pete.

'I'm really sorry, mate, my shoe has put a hole in the wall. Any damage that's done, I'm happy to pay for, I'm so embarrassed, this is the worst day ever.'

He said, 'Don't worry, Huss, it'll be taken care of. No-one will ever know.'

Next day, it was fixed. But I felt terrible to have desecrated the most famous cricket ground in the world. No injustice out in the middle was worth that.

Meanwhile, Pup's incredible second-innings 136 was unfolding. In my mind, it was as good as his triple hundred against India in Sydney and his 150 against South Africa at Newlands. He was in amazing form for that whole Ashes series. But truth be told, I wasn't in a great state to appreciate it. Brad Haddin played really well too. It was tough to watch, knowing how well they were playing but also how futile it was, after all the work we'd left for them. The second new ball brought things to an end, and England were one up.

Their players didn't carry on too much in the post-match presentations. Strauss kept saying, 'There's a long way to go in the series.' They were gracious in victory, the players that is. I didn't take too much notice of the fans and I certainly wasn't reading any press.

I wasn't the only one whose game was being picked apart on public view. Mitch Johnson was being alternately ridiculed and over-coached. He had enough going on in his head without me getting in there. I was trying to be as supportive as I could, but I didn't know what was wrong. Was it mental, technical or what? He was probably getting a dozen other people giving him advice, so the last thing he needed was me confusing him any more. I thought he needed to relax, focus on a couple of things that had worked for him in the past, and let it go. You can get as much or as little help as you think you need, but at the end of the day you're the one who has to sort it out.

Phil Hughes was going through something similar. It seemed almost like a concerted campaign, targeting Phil and Mitch so soon after their great series in South Africa. It's part and parcel of international cricket – your technique is scrutinised to death – and if you're not comfortable with your own game and experienced enough to know what works for you, you'll be under a lot of pressure.

My message to any new player was the same as Warnie had given me in November 2005. You can't fail if you play your way. *Your* game is the game that got you here. I understand that you can't score runs all the time. Phil had done so well. I wanted to say, 'You'll be fine, mate, you've scored runs before.'

But, as with Mitch, I didn't want to be another distraction, and I was hardly in a position to offer advice. I was on the receiving end every day. People were saying to me, 'For what it's worth, I've noticed this small thing about your batting ...' I was like, 'Thanks, but I've heard that from a dozen other places.' My plan when I encountered this stuff was to read no press, stick to my own short list of things that work for me, and believe things would turn around. When you're playing your best, your mind is clear. The challenge, when you're playing badly, is to find a way back to that clarity.

We went to Northampton, where Ricky and Pup were rested and I was captain of Australia. I loved that game, back at my old county where I had fond memories and good friends. The Northants squad had changed out of sight since I'd been there, but I knew the administrators and staff. To catch up and reminisce was fantastic. I was determined to do well in the game, too. We all got some runs, and ended up winning in the last half-hour.

Andrew McDonald took four wickets after scoring 75. I've always been a huge fan of Ronnie. He loves the game and thinks about it a lot and I enjoy having a beer with him and talking cricket for hours. He's a very honest bloke, and an underrated player. Every time he's played for Australia he's done a bloody good job, and it's a shame that injuries have since put a brake on his career.

The win gave us a lift for the third Test at Edgbaston. Phil Hughes was dropped for Shane Watson to come in as opener (and then got into hot water for leaking his disappointment to his mates and the world on Twitter), Graham Manou came in after Hadds broke his finger during the warm-up, and I made my now-regulation first-ball duck. And then it rained and rained. I played a lot of 500 on the first day. It was a frustrating and weird day. You're always nervous when the pitch has been under cover, but Watto batted brilliantly. Coming in at 2/126, I left my first ball from Onions and it cannoned into the top of off stump. We had the worst day yet, losing seven wickets in the first session, and again put ourselves under pressure.

Our 263 began to look okay until Flintoff got away from us, and, with more rain around, we were under the pump again in our second dig. We couldn't afford to drop this Test match, whereas England were in position to attack and attack and attack.

In at 2/52, I felt that I was playing for my position. It was hard to filter out the chatter that I didn't know where my off stump was anymore. Thankfully, I punched a four down the ground off Onions to start. But if I got out we were under serious threat of losing. I battled my way to 64, just enough to keep the wolf from the door, but even then felt things were going against me. I played forward to a ball from Stuart Broad that bounced and seamed away, and I nicked it. I thought, *I only need a little bit of luck*. That ball had come out of nowhere. I wasn't ever getting a second chance. But Pup and Northy got together and batted out the match, so at least we'd staved off falling 2–0 behind.

That half-century shook something loose inside my head. Between the third and fourth Tests, I came to a resolution.

We usually studied the opposition very closely, and I had been watching all the footage of Swann, Broad, Anderson and the others. The selected footage was of them bowling beautiful outswingers and inswingers and balls spinning square, and put me in a defensive and negative frame of mind. Because I'd been watching all this, I was expecting them to be moving it all over the place all the time.

My mental routine, while I was batting, hadn't been working for me. I would think, *Stance, relax arms, clear mind, watch the ball* … But eventually, you say it so many times it loses its power and might as well be saying, *Throw the pillow against the wall.* I tried to mix it up and say to myself, *Watch the seam.* But it wasn't working either. Other guys liked to tinker with their routines to keep it fresh. Justin Langer, for instance, was one who needed something different all the time. I, on the other hand, liked the comfort of my proven routine. I was having too many negative thoughts for *any* routine to work, and it was driving me up the wall.

I decided to put all that aside and just go out there and be positive. I went through all my dismissals from the summer against South Africa, the tour of South Africa, and so far in this Ashes series. I'd had a rough run with bad luck, but the other theme was that I'd got out being tentative. I was sure part of it came from watching this footage – *When's the big inswinger or outswinger or quick bouncer coming?* I had too many preconceived ideas. I decided not to watch the footage anymore. I would be positive, no matter what.

That was a big turning point in my career, though it didn't bear fruit immediately.

Headingley always felt like our Test match. In Edgbaston we'd had the Haddin injury, and here Matt Prior had back spasms during the warm-up and this caused confusion among their squad, as they were ringing around for someone else before he ended up playing. Strauss batted after winning the toss – fortunately, because Ricky would have done the same – and we got on a roll. In the fourth over, Marcus North took a blinding catch of Strauss at third slip. He never even saw it but stuck his hand out, and the ball was there. We got what we wanted, bowling England out for 102 in 34 overs. In our reply I was very positive, smacking my first couple of balls for four. Then Broad came in from around the wicket. I took a big step forward, and the ball seamed back and hit me. I had to be too far forward or outside the line, but I was fired out yet again.

As an aside on umpires, I had a good rapport with them generally. But I had my opinions on some. The umpires in that match were Billy Bowden and Asad Rauf. Billy was a nice guy but like all umpires gave some incorrect decisions and even if he had clearly stuffed up he would never admit he'd made a mistake. Also, I felt he was constantly worrying about side issues such as batsmen running on pitches, and fielders walking backwards to change position, rather than just trying to get his decisions right.

Rauf was was also a very nice guy, though his decision-making lapsed at times. South Africa's Rudi Koertzen had been a good umpire for a long time but was making more bad decisions by the end.

The best during my career was probably Simon Taufel, though because he was Australian we didn't have him for Test matches. Aleem Dar, who like Rauf was from Pakistan, gave me some bad decisions early in my career but improved out of sight and was close to the best in the world by the end. And a couple of the English guys, Mark Benson and Ian Gould, were very good. If Gould made a blunder, he put up his hand and said he'd made a shocking decision.

Gould was a former Test player. In county cricket, most of the umpires were retired first-class players and had a great understanding of the game. They knew what was going through players' minds. They'd been in every situation, and tended to make good decisions due to that experience.

Australia has begun to train up some ex-players as umpires, and it's going well. Paul Wilson and Rod Tucker are easier to respect, as distinguished past players, and Paul Reiffel's decision-making is pretty good, though I did have one quite amusing run-in with him.

In a Shield game against Victoria, we had two shocking decisions against us before lunch, one by Pistol. We were in line to get our lunch and the Victorians were taking the mickey out of us, which made me even angrier. After lunch I went into the umpires' room and said, 'We can't afford these stuff-ups, the game's too tight.'

Pistol opened up both barrels: 'Mate, why don't you get stuffed? There's a forum for this after the game. Bring it up then. Now's not the right time, so bugger off out of our room.'

I wandered back to the WA dressing room with my tail between my legs, having been put well and truly in my place.

Meanwhile in Headingley, Northy made another unbelievably good century, and Michael Clarke got 93. We were very confident of winning, but England had fought well in Cardiff when we'd been on top. *Please*, I thought, *can we do it one more time!*

Mitchell Johnson had one of those days when he got it right. He looked like getting a wicket every single ball. Swinging it into the right-handers at great pace, he bowled like a genius. Ben Hilfenhaus got four wickets and we won the Test match. What a great feeling: our first win, 1–1 going into the last match. We celebrated really well that night, staying in the dressing room for hours. Headingley had a weird, small, rectangular room with a low roof, like a little box. We sang the song, throwing beer and champagne all over each other. The floor was like a bath, various fluids flowing up around our ankles. This was why we played the game. After weeks of collective self-doubt, we'd proved to ourselves that we could compete.

For the whole tour, there had been conjecture and criticism around our bowling attack. At Headingley, on a seaming wicket, we had played four quicks: Peter Siddle, Mitch Johnson, Ben Hilfenhaus and Stuart Clark. There was a school of thought that these were our best four bowlers and we should stick with a winning team.

On the other hand, the wicket we came upon at the Oval looked very bare, tailor-made for spin. The choice was between Stuey Clark or Nathan Hauritz, and it was weird for those two. The morning of the match, they were standing together before the warm-up. Jamie Cox was the selector on duty. He walked over towards them. Stuey, always a straight shooter, said, 'Come on, Coxy, who is it?'

Jamie pointed to Stuey and said, 'You're it. Sorry, Haury, you're out.'

That was a real gamble, and we knew it. We bowled first and England put together a solid first day to be 8/307 at stumps. We'd stuck at our task, but the pitch was taking a fair bit of turn even with Northy bowling his tweakers. Maybe we should have gone in with a spinner? Stuey didn't get any wickets, and it was only going to spin more.

England got to 332 the next morning. Watto and Kato both started well again, but just before lunch, some drizzle started to fall. The umpires were wanting to get the game to lunch and prolonged it, letting more rain fall on the wicket. They took forever to get the covers on the pitch. I was standing on the balcony saying, 'Get the covers on, for goodness sake!'

For half an hour, that moisture on the pitch made the ball seam wildly. I know it sounds like an excuse, but it just seemed like the gods, together with some inattention from the umpires, were conspiring against us. We lost Watto straight after lunch, then Ricky, and then I was lbw third ball. I rated Broad highly as a bowler, aggressive and tall and prepared to try things, and with the assistance of that fresh shower on the wicket he was running through us. The dampness also helped the ball grip and spin, and Swanny took wickets at the other end. By tea we were eight down, and under enormous pressure. It was the session that turned the series.

I was close to breaking point. Although I'd tried to be more positive, I had responded with more of the same: 10 and 0. Ian Chappell was saying that this had to be my last Test match. I was finished, I was past it, they had to bring in new players. After I got out for a duck, he was repeating that I definitely had to go.

The television commentary was saying the same thing that afternoon. Michael Clarke was in the dressing room, and in my earshot he was saying to a few of the guys, 'I don't want to jinx anything, but I've seen this before.'

What he was saying was, when someone is completely written off they come out and score a hundred and save their career. That's all he said, but I knew he was referring to me. Very subtly, it felt like a vote of confidence.

In the second innings, Strauss left his bowlers two and a bit days to bowl us out. We had next to no chance of winning, but we had no choice but to try. On the third night, when Shane Watson and Simon Katich were not out and we had this mountain to climb, I was thinking, *If this is going to be my last Test innings, then stuff it, what will be will be, I'm going to enjoy it. I'm not going to let my last memory of Test cricket be tense and agonising. If I get out, who cares, it's my last game anyway.*

On the fourth morning, both openers were out early and as I walked out to bat, winning the game wasn't in my mind, I was just soaking it all in: my last Test match. It had been a great four years. I'd never expected it to happen, so I could only regard it as a bonus. There were so many great memories. I was thankful to have had the chance, when so many others had gone close but missed out.

Under no pressure and feeling no tension at all, funnily enough, I found that the little things started going my way. I got to 50, and Paul Collingwood dropped me. In a philosophical, almost dreamy mood, I thought, *That's amazing; the difference between a great series and a poor one is a little bit of luck. That would have been the end. Now, for some reason, the luck has gone my way.*

Soon after, I was involved in the most gut-wrenching moment for our team. I hit a ball to mid-on and thought there was a run there. Ricky and I had a great understanding between wickets. Andrew Flintoff, the fieldsman, was injured, basically on one leg. He had no chance. Ricky went, Flintoff picked up and hurled the ball wildly, and when Ricky's bat was millimetres short of safety, the ball broke the stumps at his end.

Against the odds, Michael Clarke was proved right: I batted on and made a century. We lost wickets at the other end, though, and I was the last to fall. It was a bittersweet day. I'd saved my career, but it's a horrible feeling to be out there when you're losing the Ashes. The English spectators and players were going nuts, and I just wanted to get off the field.

In the dressing room, only Ben Hilfenhaus, the number eleven, was with me, the other players having gone out to shake hands and endure the presentation. My head was in my hands as the pain sank in. I was fighting back tears. Scoring that hundred was no consolation. We'd lost the Ashes. I was glad none of my other teammates were in there. It felt like the worst day in my life.

At length, I had to take a deep breath, get my gear off, go down there and cop it on the chin. England had copped it for so many years, and now it was our turn. We just had to take it graciously.

TWENTY-SEVEN

With the Ashes behind us, I made a pact with myself: I would stop putting too much pressure on myself and carry that attitude of freedom with which I'd batted at the Oval for the rest of my career.

Easier said than done. We had three one-day series straight after the Ashes: against England in England, the ICC Champions Trophy in South Africa, and then against India in India. It speaks volumes of the Australian team's resilience that after the despair of losing the Ashes, we won all three. But I was still up and down.

During the one-dayers in England, I had a chat with Mike Young at Nottingham. Essentially the message was the same.

'Far out, Youngy, where am I at? I'm really worried I'm going to get dropped.'

'Huss, if you're to go out, go out swinging. Swing the lumber, man!'

Some things translate easily from baseball. I started swinging the lumber, and my form trickled back.

In the Champions Trophy, we were missing six to eight first-choice players and had basically a brand-new team, with only Ricky and Brett Lee as the senior luminaries. For some reason, though, we had a relaxed and happy atmosphere, a bit of joy in our lives, and we played like it. We got used to Centurion, where we had most of our games, and got on a roll. Our last qualifier was against Pakistan. They batted first, and their batsmen didn't take the initiative, instead knocking it around without taking risks. We were cruising in the run chase until a mid-innings collapse. It was a really exciting match, and we got a bye on the last ball to win. Because of Pakistan's batting, the boys started talking about the match-fixing side of things. That's the problem with Pakistan's past behaviour: it leaves question marks over what might be innocent vagaries in the game. In the lift going up to our rooms, the fast bowler Mohammad Asif said to me, 'It's nice for you guys to be challenged about match fixing rather than us all the time.' I laughed as if he was joking, but I think he was serious! He might have thought we were trying to fix the game by losing wickets quickly. Later, looking back, knowing that Asif was convicted over match-fixing, it seems even more surreal.

For the semi-final and the final, Watto took charge at the top of the order, much as Matthew Hayden had done in the 2007 World Cup. Against England in the semi, I could kick back and enjoy the brutality. England simply didn't know where to bowl. Every ball was sailing away to, or over, the boundary. He did it again in the final against New Zealand. He just targeted a bowler and tried to hit every ball for six. He got all his weight on his back foot and pounced forward, launching himself into the ball, as intimidating as a batsman can be.

Over the years, it became one of the most talked-about issues in Australian cricket, how Watto was so devastating in the short formats but couldn't convert in Test cricket. The difference, in my view, had to be mental. He had just done a great job in 2009 opening the batting. That he got so many starts, so consistently, yet couldn't turn them into big scores, had to derive from lapses in concentration. We certainly didn't want to make an issue of it – we just stayed supportive, as with all players who were struggling – but it's not as if Watto was struggling. It was a strange situation where he was doing a fine job for Australia, but seemed under pressure because his average remained in the 30s and, at the time of writing, he had been playing Test cricket for eight years while making just two centuries.

For a few series, he kept getting out in the 90s. People measure a batsman by his centuries, not his nineties. I didn't think he would care so much, but now that I've retired, I get the sense that you do care a lot more after you've stopped playing. I suspect that if things don't change, it will nag at Watto later.

But the more pressing question was that he would inevitably become vulnerable to selectors. There wouldn't be much debate if he'd made ten centuries, or if selectors talked about 90-plus scores as the measure, but the reality was that they were talking about the lack of centuries and the comparatively low average. As a supporter of Shane, I felt that your average was not always a fair reflection of your usefulness to the team. Your average went up when you converted 60s and 70s into 150s. You might make just as many starts and just as many failures, but one series your starts turn into 50s, and another series your starts turn into 200s. That's what gets your average up. But my view on Watto was that in the three Ashes Tests he played in 2009, for instance, he was one of our best batsmen because he was safe and consistent at the top of the order. He always did the job for us. His not making any centuries didn't change that fact.

The tour to India after the Champions Trophy was also very enjoyable, and our young team played enthusiastic, powerful cricket. I had a highlight in the match in Hyderabad, when Sachin Tendulkar was tearing us apart as only he could. You could bowl the ball in the same place four times, and he'd hit boundaries in four different quadrants of the field, all out of the middle of the bat. Whatever we tried, he had a counter-plan and read our minds.

We were getting back into the match, thanks to a great long-range run-out by Nathan Hauritz, but Sachin was still in. Out of nowhere, Ricky asked me to have a bowl. Like a man going to the gallows, I trundled up to Sachin. To my surprise, I only went for four off the over. He must have been thinking, *I can't get out to this quality of bowling*, so he treated me with more respect than I warranted.

I thought, *Great, I can be taken off now, I've done my job.*

But to my horror, Ricky said, 'No, that was a great over, let's go again.'

In my second over, Sachin whacked two fours. I reckon he was thinking, *This guy has to go, but not too much, if I don't belt him too hard I might get him another over.*

At the end of it, I thought, *That's me done. Two overs for twelve, that's pretty good, I'm happy with that.*

But Ricky wanted me to bowl another over. I thought, *Are you serious?*

Sure enough, in my last over they smashed me for fourteen, and Sachin was hitting me wherever he wanted to. I'd been 'Tendulkared'.

What was great about having several youngsters in the team, including Callum Ferguson, Adam Voges, Doug Bollinger, Shaun Marsh and Cameron White, was that they were all too keen and bubbly to allow any negative thoughts to take hold. The second-last game was a day match in Guwahati, an out-of-the-way place that took a day to get to. The hotel beds were like rock, the phones had no reception, and the food was iffie at best. We had to wake up for the game at five-thirty in the morning. First ball, Virender Sehwag hit Mitch Johnson for a six over point. It would have been natural to fall into pessimistic thinking, but this group didn't allow it to happen, and we won again. That trio of one-day series victories – England, the Champions Trophy and India – was one of my happiest and proudest periods playing for Australia, and lifted the spirit of the whole team after the Ashes.

But when we got home, we were straight into a Test series with the West Indies. The Australian audience and commentators hadn't paid much attention to our one-day wins. Their minds were still on the Ashes, and on who had to go. At thirty-four, I was under the microscope. I had to score runs or else I'd be dropped, despite the fact that I'd scored Australia's last Test century. Surely, I thought, my place wasn't up for grabs? But the commentary was all *Get rid of Hussey, he's too old, let's look to the future.*

John Buchanan got in touch. With his usual quiet insight, he said, 'Huss, if you continue trying to protect what you've done, you'll get these results. Let go of what you've done. The sky's your limit. Look ahead, not backwards. Forget about protecting what you've done in the past. Let the tension out of your body and the thoughts out of your mind.'

It was great advice. I *had* been protecting what I'd done; my first three years in Test cricket had been so good, it felt like I had to fight to maintain that record. I'd been looking backwards. Armed with that advice, I batted okay in the first Test at the Gabba and made 60. Walking off, I was thinking, *Phew, that felt good … but is that enough?* I'd let a big opportunity go. I could have kept the doomsayers at bay if I'd turned that into 150.

They were still after my head when we went to Adelaide, and again I played okay. It was reverse-swinging and Dwayne Bravo got me.

When the ball is reversing, it swings very late. My response is to keep my backlift low and avoid committing my footwork too early. Thrusting forward along the line of the ball is how you get out lbw. So I had a deliberate plan to use less, rather than more, footwork. Unfortunately I nicked one while we were trying to hang on for a draw, and past players were saying my footwork was terrible. I was really disappointed, because people who've played reverse-swing bowling should know you adjust your technique. People criticising my footwork were taking a cheap shot and it wasn't true.

RIGHT: As captain of the Australian team playing against the West Indies at Kannara Oval Stadium during an unbeaten 109 run innings on the fourth one-day of the DLF triangular series in Kuala Lumpur on 18 September 2006. (Photo by Saeed Khan/AFP/Getty Images)

BELOW: Leaving the field with Andrew Symonds after the team's win in the ICC Champions Trophy match between Australia and England in Jaipur, India on 21 October 2006. (Photo by Hamish Blair/ Getty Images)

ABOVE: (L–R) Me, Matthew Hayden, Adam Gilchrist, Brett Lee, Stuart Clark, Ricky Ponting, Shane Warne and Michael Clarke after securing the Ashes with a win on the fifth day of the third Ashes Test match between Australia and England at the WACA in Perth on 18 December 2006. (Photo by Paul Kane/Getty Images)

LEFT: Celebrating a century during the second day of the first Test match between India and Australia at the M Chinnaswamy Stadium in Bangalore on 10 October 2008. (Photo by Dibyangshu Sarkar/AFP/Getty Images)

ABOVE: The team cheers me on to score the winning run at the end of the ICC World Twenty20 second semi-final match between Australia and Pakistan at the Beausejour Cricket Ground in St Lucia on 14 May 2010. Australia won by 3 wickets with one ball remaining to qualify for the final. (Photo by Emmanuel Dunand/AFP/Getty Images)

RIGHT: Leaving Brisbane's Gabba after scoring 195 during the third day of the first Ashes Test match between Australia and England on 27 November 2010. (Photo by Tom Shaw/Getty Images)

ABOVE: Paul Collingwood of England just fails to get to a bat pad chance from me during the second day of the fifth Ashes Test match between Australia and England at the Sydney Cricket Ground on 4 January 2011.

(Photo by Hamish Blair/Getty Images)

RIGHT: Winning the match in the third One Day International match between South Africa and Australia at the Sahara Stadium Kingsmead in Durban, South Africa on 28 October 2011. I was also awarded Man of the Series.

(Photo by Steve Haag/Gallo Images/ Getty Images)

ABOVE: Ricky Ponting and I take more runs on the third day of the first Test match between Australia and India at the Melbourne Cricket Ground on 28 December 2011. (Photo William West/AFP/Getty Images)
BELOW: Celebrating 150 runs during the third day of the second Test match between Australia and India at the Sydney Cricket Ground on 5 January 2012. (Photo by Mark Nolan/Getty Images)

ABOVE: Playing for the Chennai Super Kings against Kolkata Knight Riders during the Indian Premier League (IPL) T20 final at the M A Chidambaram Stadium on 27 May 2012 in Chennai, India. (Photo by Santosh Harhare/ Hindustan Times via Getty Images) BELOW: A view of the scoreboard shows the score for Michael Clarke and me, near the end of play, during the first day of the second Test match between Australia and South Africa at Adelaide Oval on 22 November 2012. (Photo by Morne de Klerk/Getty Images)

ABOVE: The family poses for a photo. (L–R) Molly, William, me, Jasmin, Amy and baby Oscar before the team's Christmas lunch at Melbourne's Crown Casino on 25 December 2012. (Photo by Scott Barbour/ Getty Images) BELOW: Playing cricket with William after Australia defeated Sri Lanka on the third day of the second Test match at the Melbourne Cricket Ground on 28 December 2012. (Photo by Robert Cianflone/Getty Images)

ABOVE: Walking through a guard of honour onto the pitch in my last Test match during the second day of the third Test match between Australia and Sri Lanka at the Sydney Cricket Ground on 4 January 2013. (Photo by Cameron Spencer/Getty Images)

BELOW: Being chaired from the field by Mitchell Johnson and Peter Siddle after my retirement from international cricket on the fourth day of the third Test match between Australia and Sri Lanka at the Sydney Cricket Ground on 6 January 2013. (Photo by Mark Kolbe/Getty Images)

So I was under the pump coming to the third Test at the WACA. Chris Gayle said to me after Adelaide,' Why do these people hate you so much, why do they want to get rid of you?'

I said, 'I don't know, mate.'

He said, 'You're a really good player, they can't drop you.'

I said, 'Good, well, can you go and tell them?'

In Perth, I hit one of my first balls through cover for four, always a good sign. Bravo looked at me as if to say, *Gee, he's on today.* I got to 82 – adequate again, but desperately disappointing too.

Maybe I was being oversensitive, but it now seemed that every summer was starting with the question of 'How long can they hold on to Hussey?' I didn't read the newspapers – another distraction I could do without – but it's difficult to filter everything out when you're the one who's under the pump. On television, a past player would be saying, 'Hussey has to go.' Or on an opinion show, panellists who knew nothing about cricket would be jumping on the bandwagon. I would lunge for the remote to switch it to something else. Or, friends and family would mention an article about you. 'Oh, bloody Ian Healy, I can't believe what he was saying about you.' Without having read the article myself, I got the gist of what was being said.

When I was interviewed myself, my response every single time was the same boring thing: 'I have the backing of the captain, I know if I keep believing in my game it will come around.' I thought that if I said the same message over and over and over, they would get bored with me and go off in a new direction. It was a skill that Dad, as a communications official with the West Australian government, had perfected when I was a kid: holding long, amicable conversations with journalists, speaking a lot while actually saying nothing at all.

In that Perth Test match, I think the razor gang did get bored with me. Also, they found a new target. Throughout that series, Ricky was starting to struggle with the pace and fire of Kemar

Roach. I hadn't noticed anything until he was hit on the arm at the WACA. We'd never seen Ricky get hit, or when he did, he shrugged it off instantly. Even broken fingers didn't worry him. This one hit him and hurt him. He was in the physio's hands for a very long time, so we knew it had to be serious.

I didn't think he was in decline as a batsman, but, having had my struggles, I empathised with him when the discussion of 'When's Ricky going to go?' began, he's a great player, but he's still just a man. Things weren't going to plan for him that summer; it happens to everyone. I never worried about it being irreversible though. A quality player, even if he has a run of outs, will come back to the top. That's how the game works.

After we beat the West Indies 2–0, we started our series against Pakistan. In the first innings, Shane Watson was on 93 when he got into an embarrassing mix-up with Simon Katich; they both ended up at the same end and Watto was ruled out. That was just the latest in a string of agonising nineties. But then, in the second innings, Watto finally made his first Test hundred – just. He should have been out on 99. Pakistan's captain, Mohammad Yousuf, had put Abdur Rauf, a debutant fast bowler, at point, a critical position for Watto. We couldn't believe it when we saw Rauf fielding there. On 99, Watto sliced a catch to him. Rauf spilt it, and Watto sneaked through for a single. What a place to do it, on the MCG in front of his mum and dad. I was really happy for him, knowing how he would be feeling, and wanting him to experience that. I hoped it would inspire him to many more.

After a 170-run win, we went to Sydney where the pitch was very green and on a gloomy morning the floodlights were on. When Ricky went out to toss, I said in the dressing room, 'Is he going to bat or bowl?'

Someone said, 'Surely he's going to bowl first.'

'I don't know,' I said. 'He batted first in Johannesburg on a pitch like plasticine. I don't think he's ever bowled since Edgbaston in 2005.'

Sure enough, he won the toss and batted first. I thought, *Oh, hell.*

Pakistan had a very good bowling attack with Umar Gul, Mohammad Sami, Mohammad Asif and Danish Kaneria. They could even afford to leave out the quick left-armed teenager, Mohammad Aamer. They all gave me an awful amount of trouble. Throughout my career, I struggled against all sorts of bowlers, often not the predictable ones. I've had plenty of bowlers come on and thought, *Oh no, I hate facing this guy.* For some reason, there are a lot of Pakistanis on that list: Gul, Asif, Aamer, Sohail Tanvir, Shoaib Akhtar. I'm glad I didn't play in the eras of Wasim Akram or Imran Khan!

They knocked us over for 127 and we hoped to do the same to them, but the pitch steadily improved and they led by 206. It should have been a lot more, but when they had us on toast we took some late wickets. But we had a mountain to climb; you're not often going to win a Test match when you're 200 behind on the first innings.

We batted a bit better, but kept losing wickets at the wrong time. Watto made another score in the nineties. Danish Kaneria was getting it to turn a lot and got a run of middle-order wickets, and the game looked gone. When Peter Siddle came out to join me at 8/257, we were all but dead in the water.

Pete was a good number ten, though, and showed a lot of character. He said, 'Come on, let's get stuck in and see how we go.' He got us through that night, and the next morning we enjoyed our batting. Our chat was reasonably relaxed: 'Just keep going, you never know.' Sidds was more relaxed than me – my 'reasonably relaxed' is probably mega-intense for anyone else.

Mohammad Yousuf was playing the cat-and-mouse game with us, moving the field in and out depending on whether Sids or I was on strike. Sids became more determined to survive his two balls per over, and each time he did, his confidence grew.

Pakistan put down some catches. The wicketkeeper, Kamran Akmal, put me down twice and Sids once. But I didn't see how they could be intentional, as was later insinuated. The ones I nicked were off the spinner Kaneria, and those either go in or they don't. I don't think there's enough time, for a keeper standing up to the stumps, to deliberately drop nicks that go into his gloves. I've spoken to wicketkeepers who've supported that reasoning, and said that if he did it on purpose, he's a bloody good actor.

When Yousuf didn't change his tactics, leaving the field well back for me, I felt it was a little bit strange, but no more than that. Their tactics were passive, but I couldn't sense anything more sinister than that. The bowlers were still coming in hard. Umar Gul was charging in trying to knock us over, and Kaneria was ripping it. It was a good battle.

By the end, I made my first home century in two years – the first since that notorious India Test at the SCG. It felt like a great weight off my shoulders, though I would have loved to score a hundred earlier in the season too. We led by 175, which exceeded our expectations by a mile. It was a pretty good batting pitch, but you never know.

Pakistan got off to a positive, confident start, but we got a lucky wicket when Yousuf, their best batsman, absolutely creamed a drive down the wicket and it nearly took Nathan Hauritz with it, but he held onto the caught-and-bowled. Haury then spun us to victory. I was really proud to be part of a win and to score a hundred in a winning cause. I sometimes got frustrated by scoring runs in a losing cause. Some of my best innings were in losses, and it's a horrible feeling. In this game, I felt extremely happy and proud because of that partnership with Peter Siddle contributing to yet another amazing Sydney Test match win. It was a stab back at my critics too. They'd been on my back all summer. I hoped, in vain, that they'd admit they'd been wrong.

When we were celebrating, no-one even thought about the legality of the match or the genuineness of Pakistan's efforts. It never came up until the next year, when Asif, Aamer and Salman Butt were caught match-fixing, and there were claims that that Sydney Test match was named as being fixed. That was the first time we went over it and thought about it. Having been in the middle in the contentious period, I honestly didn't suspect anything. As I've said, Kamran's dropped catches and Yousuf's tactics appeared to me to be just part of the game. In the fourth innings, the Pakistan batsman appeared to be doing everything possible to win, but it didn't come off for them. I would still take convincing that there was anything corrupt about that Test match.

That said, it was incredibly disappointing to hear what Asif, Aamer and Butt did. Spot-fixing clearly does happen, and like anyone else I'm distressed to hear these stories and agree with the strongest sanctions against players found guilty. It's the worst kind of attack on our game.

But this is my personal story, and in my experience I saw nothing of it. I was never, ever approached by anyone. A curious part of me would like to be, to see what they do! But I never was. No offers of gifts by mysterious gentlemen, no phone calls about weather and team information, no inducements or invitations of any kind. Later in 2010, Watto and Hadds said they'd received phone calls in England, which they reported immediately. Each season we were given education sessions where we were told what to expect – a guy will ring up and say he's a huge fan and wants to offer a business opportunity and meet you for a drink, or knock on your hotel room door. We were simply told to report any approach to the team manager straight away. If you didn't report the approach, you could be in strife as well.

Maybe I'm a bit Pollyanna about this, but I like to think Australian players are not seen as good targets for bookmakers;

our culture isn't mixed up in that sort of stuff. For myself, I find the game so hard as it is, without having this added complication! Just playing international cricket is challenging enough. I wouldn't be able to concentrate on something like having to get out between 20 and 30. I'd be petrified about getting out for 16. I don't know how they do it. For the bowlers it may be easier, but I still don't know how they handle the stress.

It came up in the 2013 IPL season too, where there were allegations made against three players, and also against an owner of my own team, the Chennai Super Kings. Again, I knew nothing about this and at the date of writing no information has been made public to suggest that there is anything to it. I'll wait and watch with great interest.

What perplexes a lot of us is, how can you do this when you are playing for your country? How can you undermine everything you believe in? How can you betray the trust of supporters, teammates, your family? I can only speculate, but in the case of the Pakistan players, they were not paid well, and perhaps the guilty ones were trying to make up for that. In the case of well-paid players like Shantha Sreesanth, who was suspended from the IPL for alleged match-fixing, I can only wonder if they were being blackmailed by someone threatening to destroy them or their family if they didn't cooperate. I can't see any player being willing to do things against the spirit of the game. Being threatened is the only reasonable motivation I can think of, but as I say, I'm only guessing.

In Australia, as well as being constantly educated on anti-corruption issues, we are also well paid, which should take out the greed factor. There will always be greedy people out there who want more, though, and whenever I hear about corruption I feel really sad for those involved. I believe that when you do the wrong thing, it will come out eventually. And then your name will be ruined forever.

TWENTY-EIGHT

We completed a clean sweep of Pakistan in the third Test in Hobart. For the first time in my experience, Ricky hadn't been making a massive contribution to the team with his bat, and the talk – outside the team, never inside – was growing that he wasn't up to it. He never showed any sign of anxiety to the team, but I knew from talking to Justin Langer, who had become our batting coach, that Ricky was really beating himself up over it. JL was saying to him, 'Mate, don't worry, you'll be fine.' But Ricky kept fretting about it.

Before he'd made a run in Hobart, he top-edged a hook to fine leg. If he'd been caught, it would have been interesting to see what would have happened next and how he'd have handled going through a summer without any big scores. But Aamer bungled it, Ricky scored 200 and everyone said it was back to normal. One catch going down was the difference between a lot of mental anguish and talk in the public, and the resumption of normal service. It's a knife-edge.

Amy knew what a fine line it was. She saw how, the night before a Test match, I went into a weird state, with her but not with her. She saw me become a different person on that night. I would be robotic in my responses, polite but not interested or engaged. That was how I was before every Test match, but when things weren't going well for me, it was exponentially magnified. Sometimes she had to pull me aside and say, 'I know it's the night before a Test, but you're too stressed, you've got to find a way of relaxing.' She was good at identifying when I was so tense I wouldn't be able to perform. Beneath it all, I knew that I could only control so much, and luck would play a decisive role in whether I made a duck or a big score. It's a hard thing to live with.

And it was getting harder. When Molly was a year old, we'd discovered that she had a mild case of cerebral palsy. Because of her premature birth, she had been subjected to regular testing for developmental stages, and after about a year they detected some tightness in her legs. She wasn't as flexible as normal. It was at that stage a mild case, so she could still functcion well. But the treatment involved is regular, extensive and often invasive, which she doesn't enjoy. Cerebral palsy is not curable, but if you work hard in the formative years you can manage it as best as you can.

It was a constant source of wonder to me, how Amy handled all of this while I was away ten months of the year, hardly ever uttering a word of complaint. She had the responsibility of getting Jasmin and William ready for school every day, plus running the household, shopping and paying the bills and everything else. Her family was very helpful, but most of the time she did it by herself. What she missed most was being able to sit down at the end of the day and offload it all to her husband. It's a lonely life, not being able to have those daily adult conversations, and it takes a very special character to do without that basic need.

I was not a fully functioning family member. On tour, it was often difficult to speak at the right time for both partners. When she really wanted to talk with me about her day, the time difference might mean I was out on the cricket field or sleeping. In the middle of tours, when we did speak, I often didn't have a lot to contribute:

just cricket, which couldn't interest her all that much when she had domestic concerns pressing on her all the time. It was hard to find a common ground until, in the last phase of a tour, we could get excited about planning what we'd do when I got home.

But even then, once I was back, there was always a transitional period. I came back home and messed up all the routines that Amy had set. Because I only had a short stint with the kids, I wanted to squeeze too much in. The kids would get home from school and I'd be wanting to take them to the river, the beach or the park. Amy would say, 'Well, first they have to do their homework and other normal parts of their routine, and maybe then they can do what you want.'

Towards the end of my career, from about 2010, all of this was accumulating bit by bit. If I didn't still love cricket, I couldn't have kept performing. But more important than that was the unwavering support I received from Amy and the family. She might have wished I had a normal job, but she never ever put pressure on me by saying she couldn't manage. She's a strong believer in taking whatever life throws at her, and getting on top of it. But I would be lying if I said there weren't times when the sadness of being away got all too much for me.

We won all ten of our one-day internationals that summer, but our crowds were quite low. Evidently the West Indies and Pakistan weren't as big a drawcard as India or England, but there was another change happening very rapidly. The state-based Twenty20 Big Bash was starting, and there was some talk, for the first time, about how 50-over cricket might be overtaken by T20.

I really wanted the 50-over comp to flourish. Some of my great memories are of playing in Australia before packed crowds in ODIs. I also thought it was important that that form continued to prosper. Australia is hosting the World Cup in 2015 so we need to promote that format.

In 2010, I grew disappointed that there wasn't as much promotion for the one-day international series as the domestic competition. That became even worse in the years after, when the Big Bash was re-formatted in city-based franchises with a more open recruitment system. As international players, we were disappointed. It seemed they were giving more priority to a domestic competition than to promoting the World Cup, the biggest tournament in the sport. And then, in 2012, they began scheduling Big Bash games at night. The Big Bash should have fitted around the Australian games, but it felt like it was the other way around.

Back to 2010: we went to New Zealand for another successful one-day series, before the Test preparation was overshadowed by Michael Clarke having to go home to sort out his personal issues, namely the breakup of his engagement to Lara Bingle. That was all a bit bizarre and happened very quickly. We didn't hear anything apart from what was on television, and he was gone before we knew it. When he came back, on Test eve, we had a team meeting where our message to him was, 'We don't want to know the details but we're 100 per cent behind you if you need us.' Pup was our mate and we saw he was going through a difficult time. It all being in the public domain would have added to the stress. I don't know what it was like in the old days, but when I was in the Australian team most of the guys had families and there was great understanding for their lives outside cricket. The senior players incorporated family with cricket life. Everyone respected what families went through, and the stress on partners and children. There was a lot of empathy for him.

Then we had to put it aside and get on with our cricket, which wasn't simple either. Ricky was very agitated because the Test players who hadn't been in the one-day series were flying over very late. Marcus North was really struggling. He'd gone back to Western Australia for some state cricket, and Ricky was upset that players were getting into horrendous form with their states before coming back into the Australian team. He had to upskill them again for Test cricket. Ricky spent hours with Northy getting his technique back to where it had been.

I knew Marcus very well. We grew up one suburb apart, played a lot of our junior cricket together, and were both at Wanneroo. When I was working my way into the state team, Marcus was the next big thing. He left Wanneroo after a couple of years but we reconnected when we were both in the West Australian team. I really liked Northy and we got on very well. He had the ability to go anywhere, but he was very insecure mentally, and I worried that that would undo him. In his very first Shield game he made 16 and I said, 'Well done! How do you feel?' He said, 'I really want a score, I don't want to disappoint, I want to feel settled in the team.' I said, 'Relax, no-one's expecting you to cement your place in one game.' But he seemed very insecure in himself. It's a perfectly natural thing, as I well know, being insecure too. Yet Northy was a very different person from me in how he addressed his anxiety, as became apparent when he was in the Australian team.

When he got selected for the Test tour of South Africa in 2009, I thought it was a very good choice. He was taking over Simmo's number six position, and like Simmo was a handy part-time bowler. He was experienced by now, and had a good understanding of his game and of himself as a person. His time had come. Could he get over his personal insecurities?

He seemed destined for great success. He made a century on debut in South Africa, another in his first Test in England, and several other good scores. His start couldn't have been better for his self-confidence. When he had confidence, he was unstoppable. But I knew from Western Australian cricket that he could also have long runs where his confidence absolutely deserted him. His ups and downs were extreme and long-lasting. Some guys smooth out that roller-coaster, but Northy had too much going on in his mind.

By 2009–10, he was still playing well, but all of a sudden he was saying to me, 'I need some runs or else I'll be gone.' I said, 'Come off it, you've made a century just recently, you're batting really well.' But Northy was hard to convince. He needed to know everything that was written about him in the press, and was sensitive to every question mark.

So it was going to be intriguing, coming into the first Test in New Zealand, how Northy and Pup, coming out of two very different crises, would bat. Would their off-field problems distract them, or focus and release them? In the event, they both batted out of this world. Pup played as well as I'd ever seen, which is saying something. He put his head down and put all the dramas behind him. He batted like a man just let out of prison. And then Northy went out and absolutely smashed them. I don't think there was anything quite as satisfying as seeing a teammate rise out of difficult times and prove himself, whether it's for the first time or after five or ten years in Test cricket.

In that Trans-Tasman series, which we won 2–0, Simon Katich, my best man, and I played our fiftieth Test match in the same game in Hamilton. It gave me a moment of reflection. Having got to thirty years of age without playing a Test, it was a real milestone to get to fifty. We had a few photos together, and Amy came over. Kato and I had a bit of a chuckle together about how far we'd come, and what a nice coincidence it was to be reaching this mark together. We looked forward to playing together for several more years. Sadly, it wasn't to turn out that way.

TWENTY-NINE

Once World Cups came in, Australia started to take international Twenty20 cricket more seriously. After the New Zealand tour in 2010, I went to India for a handful of IPL games with Chennai Super Kings, and then flew to join the boys in the West Indies for the third T20 World Cup.

We weren't among the favourites, which gave us an element of surprise. We had dangerous batsmen such as Warner and Watson, pace in Dirk Nannes and Shaun Tait, and pretty good players all down the list. And the nature of T20 cricket makes each contest a bit of a lottery – one player can win a game on any given day. We certainly had the tools to beat some of the good teams.

My role was to come in when we were in trouble. I liked that role, feeling I had nothing to lose. I could save the day and be a hero, or if I got out, we could say that everyone above me should have done the job.

Personally, the highlight was the semi-final in St Lucia, against Pakistan, the title-holders. They amassed 191, and we needed 90 to win off 45 balls when I came in at fifth wicket down. Cameron White was going well at the other end. I can't smack my first ball out of the park like a Warner or a Gayle. My plan was to get busy, assess the pitch and the pace, get the senior partner on strike, and then go for it. Cameron hit a couple of sixes but then got out. I thought, *That's it, the game's pretty much over.* Steve Smith came and went, and then Mitchell Johnson came out. We needed 50 runs off the last three overs. The pressure was right off. As far as I was concerned, the game was gone. So Mitch and I just said, 'Stuff it, let's have a go.'

A couple went for four, but I still thought it was impossible to get 50 off three overs. In the second-last over we got a four early, and I got some ones and twos and a four off the last ball. That left 18 to win off the last over, to be bowled by the off-spinner Saeed Ajmal, one of the best T20 bowlers in the world.

I said to Mitch, 'I think he's going to fire in fast yorkers.' Mitch got a pad on the first one and we took a leg bye. Seventeen needed off five balls.

My tactic was to go back deep into my crease and hope Ajmal would miss his length, so I could get underneath it and hoist it over the top. To my amazement, his next ball was a slow half-tracker. For the left-hander, the boundary was short on the leg-side, with a strong wind carrying that way. I pulled this long-hop and it went for six. Behind me, Kamran screamed at Ajmal in Urdu, I assumed something like *What the heck are you doing?*

Eleven off four. I expected the fast yorker now, and, going back, got underneath it. It went for six as well. We only needed five runs off three balls. *Shivers! Could we win this?* That's when the fears and nervousness came back – it was the first time I thought we could win. *What do I do now? What's he going to bowl?* My mind was whirring.

Ajmal bowled another slow one, wide of off stump, quite a clever ball. I tried to slice it behind point where it might spin off for four. I didn't quite get it right and it flew off the edge. Better than the planned shot, it ran away to the boundary.

Now we needed one run off two balls. I thought, *What if I get out? A new batsman will need one off one.* Pakistan brought the field in and I just thought, *Hit it in the middle, wherever it goes we'll run.* He bowled a good ball and I swung, and it came out of the middle, sailing high for another six. We'd got those 50 runs, and hadn't even needed the full three overs. I'd got 60 off 24 balls, with 48 of my runs coming in sixes and fours. So much for my belief that I was a nicker and nudger!

There's been a lot of talk about how changes in bat-making have transformed players' ability to hit sixes. I don't agree. Cricket bats didn't improve all that much while I played top-level cricket. Manufacturers played around with the shape and took the moisture out, which expanded the size of the bats. Older bats were denser, but were still good wood. Bat quality may have improved a little bit, but they're still the same pieces of wood coming out of the same forests.

Where the increased size of the bats made a difference was in your head. When you're wielding what looks like a great big club, you believe you can hit the ball further. And this occurred alongside changes in practice – what I really think caused the bigger hitting.

When I first played Shield cricket, my whole game was based around defence: batting for time, letting balls go. I learnt that from Geoff Marsh, Graeme Wood, Mike Veletta, Justin Langer, the top players in the game. Six-hitting batsmen like Damien Martyn and Adam Gilchrist, just coming through, were rarities. We certainly didn't practise smashing sixes, and those guys did it because they were naturals.

Once Twenty20 arrived, all of us would start practising six-hitting every single day. Reverse-sweeps, paddles, ramp shots – crazy shots we'd never have dreamt of before, we were now practising routinely. So our intent as batsmen became to hit sixes *all the time.* Obviously, once you're thinking that way, and practising it constantly, you do it in the middle. So I think it's more the players' confidence that has changed, rather than the bats we use.

While I'm on the subject of bats, I can't resist going into one of my favourite subjects.

As a young first-class player, I'd been sponsored by Gray-Nicolls, but as I was one of their lesser lights, I eventually received bats of dubious quality, the rejects from the other players, so I signed with Kookaburra, who remained my bat sponsor for the rest of my career. The first couple of years, frankly the bats were pretty ordinary. Again, I was at the low end of their list. But Ricky, who was sponsored by them, was instrumental in talking with their bat makers about changing the shapes. He developed some fantastic bats with them.

In my opinion a good bat for Australian conditions will have the middle quite high. In India, by contrast, bats need to be bottom-heavy. In Australia you want it higher because of the bounce. It balances the bat out really well. Ricky did a lot of work and they began developing darned good bats.

I was always specific on my bat weights – embarrassingly so. I used a 2lb 8oz or 2lb 9oz. I used the Kookaburra bat with the graphite backing briefly – that was when I hit the roof at the Dome in Melbourne – but they were banned. Those bats were a bit heavier, so for a while my bats went up to 2lb 10oz. I'm a player who likes to control the blade, work the ball into gaps rather than going for pure power, however, and eventually I felt the bats were a bit heavy. I couldn't control my cross-bat shots. So I brought the weight back down to 2lb 8oz or a fraction more. I was that anal about weight, I carried a set of scales with me and weighed it. If it was too heavy, I took off some string or changed the grip to bring its weight down. People say it's more about the pickup than the weight, but it got in my head that I needed the weight to be exact.

At the start of each summer, Kookaburra sent me six bats. I went through them and picked out the one I really liked. I kept two or three match bats and two or three practice bats on the go. Once I got a good match bat in my hand, I used it until it broke. I've had some magic bats. Sometimes you know the first time you tap it down. Every now and then, every few seasons, you just know it's perfect for you. I had a couple of bats that scored three Test centuries each, and I wished they could have gone forever. I've kept all my Test century bats, and written who they scored hundreds against. That's about the only thing I keep as memorabilia – a cabinet with my Test century bats. It was a sad day when I had to retire one of my best bats. Sometimes they got bat-old: the middle started to go, and their performance died. Sometimes I re-handled them to extend their life.

When I didn't like them, or had a bad run with them, I gave them away. Who to? There were always bowlers floating around the batsmen looking for bats.

In St Lucia, after I took 22 runs off those last four balls, my teammates were so excited, they burst out of the bunker and charged onto the field. Seeing the looks on their faces, I shared their ecstasy. It was a great buzz, to prove that we could contend under pressure in Twenty20, but the euphoria also clouded the fact that we hadn't played well in that semi-final and were probably coming off the boil. In the final at Bridgetown, England didn't allow us to play anywhere near our best and were deserving winners.

After a short break, we went to England for a collection of T20, one-day and Test matches against Pakistan. Having been to Pakistan as a kid, I was very disappointed not to play Test cricket there. The political situation obviously made it hard to tour in the early 2000s, and then the attack on the Sri Lankan cricketers in Lahore in 2009 put the country off-limits. I hope international cricket will soon resume there, both for the sake of the Pakistanis, one of the most fervent cricket nations on earth, and for players from other countries, who I'm sure would love to sample the hospitality and cricket conditions in that great country.

That said, we were delighted to get the chance to play a Test again at Lord's. I got a fifty and a first-ball duck and we won the Test match when Marcus North took six wickets, but as usual there was weird stuff going on in the Pakistan team. Shahid Afridi, who had been made captain, was trying to clear the fence in a Test match every ball. I couldn't understand what on earth was going on. Obviously his mind wasn't working well. Inevitably, he skied one, and then resigned as Pakistan captain.

But nothing is as certain as their unpredictability, and at Headingley they bowled us out for 88. It was terrible to go down for less than three figures, but the ball was moving around a hell of a lot after the wicket had been covered for several days and Asif, Aamer and Gul were fantastic bowlers in those conditions. Ricky won the toss and batted, again. There wasn't much we could do. Watto got us back into the match with six wickets in their first innings, and we tried to get them under some pressure when they had to chase 180 in the fourth innings. They made a strange decision, though, on the third night of the match. They were 3/140 and had us on toast. Azhar Ali, the tall young right-hander, was belting us. We were gone, and they could have won it that night, but decided not to take the extra half-hour. It seemed like a mistake, and the next morning the mood had changed. They wanted the win badly and didn't know how to go about doing it, and batted so nervously, with such tension, after being so free the night before, that they very nearly did not get there. In the end, they fell over the line with three wickets to spare. But that was the last of the joy for them. They stayed on to play a series with England, and the scandal broke about the three players involved in spot-fixing. After they'd played so well against us, Pakistan cricket was again in a dark place.

Since the beginning of the IPL, and with the spread of Twenty20 cricket more generally, many in the cricket community were worried about its potential to harm Test cricket. I will talk about some of these aspects later. But initially, the fear was that players would choose the big money in IPL in preference to playing for their country. For me, that was never an issue: my Chennai Super Kings commitments would always play second fiddle to national duties. I would never have signed with CSK if I thought there would be any conflict. Yet against my wishes, in late 2010 I was dragged into exactly that situation, though in a most bizarre way.

In September that year, I had to go to South Africa to play with CSK in the Champions League, the competition between the top T20 domestic teams from India, Australia, South Africa, the West Indies, Sri Lanka and New Zealand. Even though I had also played for the Western Warriors, the Australian champions who had qualified for the Champions League, my prior commitment was to CSK.

But when it came to clashes with the Australian team, my CSK contract was crystal-clear. Any Australian national commitments took priority over IPL commitments. In my view, when the Australian team took off for India, a few days after my first Champions League game in South Africa, that's when the Test tour started and that's when I was due to be in India. I talked to Cricket Australia to arrange to fly out and meet the team as soon as they got to India.

This didn't go down well. Cricket Australia said, 'No, you can't leave.'

I said, 'What do you mean? I have a Test series.'

For two weeks, I had a running argument with Michael Brown and James Sutherland at Cricket Australia. They said, 'It's okay, finish the Champions League and then join the team, you'll be in India a couple of days before the first Test.'

I said, 'No, this is horrendous preparation, I need time to be over there before the series. I need to get over there.'

But they stood firm and said, 'No, you're not going.'

This was completely upside down. The conflict I'd expected was for Cricket Australia to be on my side, arguing to the Chennai Super Kings that they had to let me go to play for my country.

I told Chennai, 'I should be going but am being told I'm not allowed to go.' Some of the CSK players who would be representing India, such as MS Dhoni and Suresh Raina, were in the same boat, as was Doug Bollinger. It's possible there was a quid pro quo between the Australian and Indian boards: if Dhoni and Raina had to stay in South Africa and be unprepared for the Test series, then it was somehow evened out by the same rule being applied to Doug and me. Poor Dougie, who had only just broken into the Australian team, was completely confused. He kept saying, 'What are we doing?' I said, 'I'm trying to sort it out.' He said, 'Okay, I'll do whatever you do.' We could have just booked our own flights to India. But I didn't think there would be any winners if we chose that route.

I was absolutely livid. So, over in India, were Ricky and Tim Neilsen. They knew you had to take time to acclimatise to Indian conditions and were increasingly agitated that they did not have their full squad. For Ricky, it seemed to confirm all his initial reservations about the IPL.

To make matters worse, in the media it was represented that I was greedy and refusing to leave – the exact opposite of the truth. The spokesman for CA, Peter Young, said it was my choice to play IPL and I was doing it for the money.

When I heard this, I was ropable. I wrote a strongly worded letter to James Sutherland, telling him Peter Young had got it completely wrong and they had to issue a retraction. They did, saying it was their decision, not mine, to keep me in South Africa, and acknowledging that I wanted to go and join the team in India.

But I felt the damage was done, a suspicion confirmed the next year when Steve Waugh interviewed me for the Argus Review into Australian cricket. I was surprised by how wrong he was on the Champions League issue. He questioned me closely about why I'd stayed in South Africa, and clearly didn't know that I'd wanted to go to India. It annoyed me that that story, which was completely wrong, was still going around. He said he thought I was staying in South Africa for the money. It was frustrating to still be setting the record straight a year later.

Making the best of what was on offer, I found refuge on the cricket field, and batted quite well for CSK. I got an unbeaten fifty in the final, which we won, against the Warriors from Port Elizabeth. But my mind was definitely on the Test series in India.

The process of getting there was farcical. The Champions League final was in Johannesburg on the night of 26 September. The first Test was starting in Mohali on 1 October. We flew out on 27 September, but, unable to get a direct flight, we had to sit for eight hours in Dubai. From there we flew to Mumbai, then took another flight to Mohali, and had a one-hour drive. It took two days to get there, a week later than I'd wanted. The administrators couldn't even manage a decent route for us.

When we arrived, Doug and I only had time for one training session. I had a strong feeling that the team were angry at the two of us, and didn't know what had been going on. They felt we weren't committed to the Test team. It was only when I explained how hard I'd been fighting to get to them that they understood. I felt that it lingered over things, however, for the next six months.

Ricky won the toss in Mohali, and we made 428, but I felt terrible. It was one of the best batting pitches you could imagine, and the ball was doing nothing, but I took a session to eke out 17 runs. I was blocking ball after ball, my eyes and mind not working properly. MS Dhoni, who'd been in the same predicament as me, dropped two catches that day.

I felt better as the Test wore on, and it evolved into a situation where we had to take six wickets on the last day, while India had to get 176 runs to win. The game was right on the line and Dougie was bowling really well, dismissing Rahul Dravid, Sachin Tendulkar and Harbhajan Singh. VVS Laxman was holding out with the tail, and just when we needed that final push, Dougie tore his side. I felt that it cost us the Test match, and Ricky was furious. That injury came at the crucial time. Without Doug, we just couldn't get the final wicket and India won. It's probably as disappointed as I've ever been after a Test match. I thought our preparation had not been enough. I really felt let down by CA.

We regrouped for the second Test in Bangalore, where Northy made another century and Ricky also batted very well. I got a terrible lbw decision, to follow another in the second innings in Mohali. Ian Gould, who gave me out, said in the bar after the game, 'Oh, Huss, I'm so sorry, I've given you two shocking decisions, I hope you get another chance, I'd hate your career to end because of my two bad decisions.'

My future was being determined by factors beyond my control. I appreciated Ian apologising. I was filthy, I was feeling myself going into the familiar downhill spiral where everyone would be questioning my place in the Australian team.

In that Test, Murali Vijay scored a hundred and Sachin Tendulkar was at his unbelievable best. His bat looked like it was three bats wide. He toyed with Nathan Hauritz, who bowled to some good fields and plans, but Sachin played with his mind, hitting the ball to wherever the field wasn't. Cheteshwar Pujara came in and batted well on debut, a real quality player. It looked like when the great players went, India had a strong list coming in behind them.

As usual, a spring tour of India was not the ideal preparation for a home summer, and we had an Ashes series coming up. In two Sheffield Shield matches, I had great difficulty adapting from slow to fast pitches, the pace and bounce. There was a lot of speculation about the Ashes team. It seemed that every summer now, my name was in the firing line. I hadn't got any runs in the first Shield game and went to Melbourne for the second. Greg Chappell, who was on the national selection panel, made me very nervous. Every time I'd heard Greg talk, publicly or privately, it was how important youth was and how we had to look to the future. When he was coach of India, he'd done his best to phase out the older players and expose young players at international level. I fundamentally disagreed with this. I thought young players needed to be seasoned for years in first-class cricket, as I had been, with the only exceptions the bona fide freaks like Ricky Ponting or Michael Clarke – or, going back further, Greg Chappell himself. For the rest of us mortals, I believed in experience and earning your stripes.

But Greg was obviously extremely well respected, and, from what I heard, quite dominant in selection meetings. Before the Shield match in Melbourne, he came up to me and said, 'Huss, there's a lot of good young players around, but at the moment the position's yours. They've got to take it off you.' That felt good. I appreciated the vote of confidence. But then he got this look on his face and said, 'But for goodness sake, can you please score some runs ... and just bat normally?'

That undid everything. I thought, *Thanks a lot, Greg, I'm trying.*

In the first innings, I faced 18 or 20 balls for a duck and wandered off. I sat in the dressing room wondering what was going on. Meanwhile, a young Australia A team was playing England in Hobart. There was a lot of talk about who should be dropped to make way for the new players.

That night, I got on the phone to Amy.

'What do you reckon?' I said. 'Do you think I can still do this? If you've lost faith in me, I'm not sure I can do it. Everyone else seems to have lost faith. Every commentator wants me to go. I feel like Greg wants me to go.'

Amy said that she believed 100 per cent that I could do it. It took a little while for me to really hear her, but it gave me a tremendous boost to know that at least there was one person who shared my hope that I was still a Test cricketer.

In our second innings, we lost a wicket in the first over and I was in, ten minutes before lunch. My first ball I wafted at, outside off stump. Then I edged one along the ground for four: not the most convincing start. During the break, I sat in the dressing room. The Australia A game was on TV right next to where I was sitting, and Michael Slater was commentating, saying, 'It's too late for Hussey, nothing short of three figures will save him, but I think he's got to go.'

I thought, *Stuff you, Michael Slater.*

After lunch, the pitch was really good and I had one of those days when everything clicked. I punched one down the ground off Damien Wright, and once again, one good shot literally turned things around. I don't know why. I hadn't changed anything about my preparation or my technique. I stuck to my trusted routines, and this day it all fell into place. Marcus North was batting with me, and when I reached my hundred he raced down the pitch and was screaming for joy. I had no emotion. He said, 'Get excited, you're in the Test team!' I took a deep breath. Just relief, and a bit of anger. There was still no guarantee I'd be selected.

They did select me, but it didn't alleviate any of the pressure. It would all be on again if I made low scores in Brisbane. I was tense and negative. It seemed that every person in Australia didn't want me in the Test team, not a good feeling going into an Ashes series.

The team were really good to me, very encouraging, almost proud of me after the pressure I'd been under. When we got together in Brisbane, we had a ritual of congratulating each other for being in the first Test team. Training was always good with the Australian team. We hit ball after ball at Allan Border field, and I felt I was hitting the ball well, despite what the whole world thought.

But it was the Ashes – it doesn't matter how confident you're feeling, you have to find a way of doing it in the middle.

I had a worrying conversation that week with Northy. All the pressure was on me, but he was very agitated about his place in the team. I said, 'What are you worrying about? You've just made a hundred in India.'

He said, 'Just give me two Tests, if I don't score runs you can get rid of me.'

I said, 'Why are you even thinking like this?'

He felt that if he wasn't making a hundred, he was under pressure. And that had been the case throughout his career. His hundreds were frequently followed by failures. He tried to work very hard on it over the years. At Western Australia, he would peel off a magnificent hundred but then next innings, find himself marooned. He focused a lot on his nerves at the start of his innings. The more he focused on it and the harder he tried, the worse it became. He worked really hard with Sandy Gordon on mental skills in Perth, but in the end, it was about to desert him.

We got a great start, dismissing Strauss in the first over. The Gabba pitch was doing a bit on the first day, and all the bowlers did well, climaxing with Peter Siddle's hat-trick. Getting England out for 260 put us ahead in the game, and our openers gave us a good start until we lost three quick wickets either side of lunch on the second day and I was in.

I was beside myself with nerves. My first ball, off Stephen Finn, I nicked and it dropped all of 5 centimetres short of second slip. That was all the difference it took between despair and euphoria.

Every single time I tapped my bat, I said, *Stuff you, Michael Slater*. It sort of gave me a calming rhythm and provided extra motivation to keep going. Hadds came in, and we got a stand going. When he was first in the Australian side, he got frustrated with my intensity in the middle. I would be worried about everything the bowlers were trying, while Hadds preferred to relax and tell jokes and keep each other entertained. By now, I was learning to go with him and have fun.

We batted for a whole day together, and put on 307 for the sixth wicket. That comment from Slats kept driving me on. When I got to 140, I was saying my personal mantra louder, to get it into the stump mikes. Every ball: *Stuff you, Michael Slater.*

He didn't hear it, as far as I know, though I later told him he was a source of inspiration throughout that Test. I continued saying it throughout the series, as it certainly worked for me in Brisbane. I ended up making my highest Test score, 195 – six runs short of Jason Gillespie's!

We got into a commanding position, but the pitch didn't really crack up and play any tricks. Instead, it flattened out and turned into a road. We knew it was going to be a hard graft getting England out, but Strauss, Cook and Trott showed their class and we didn't even look like getting them out. As in Cardiff, it was a kick in the teeth that we couldn't convert a dominant position and go one up in the series, but we put it down to the flatness of the pitch and moved to Adelaide in a positive frame of mind.

Adelaide is my favourite Test match in the calendar: the whole city comes out, there's a great social atmosphere, and the pitch is a dream to bat on. Ricky won the toss, and I was thinking, *Beautiful, if history's any guide I won't be batting before tea.*

I found a spot in the dressing room to lie down on the floor. I set my pads up as pillows. I was all comfy, ready to watch the first session and chill out.

Fourth ball, Simon Katich and Shane Watson got confused between wickets again, and Kato was run out without facing a ball. I thought, *That's a shame, I'll have to put my boots on.* But Ricky was going out and the pitch was so good, I still thought I wouldn't have to bat for a long time. *We'll be fine.*

Next ball, Ricky nicked off to slip. All of a sudden, I was thinking, *I'm next in.* From a state of complacent relaxation, I was rushing around like a headless chook trying to get my gear on. I ran up to the viewing area. As soon as I got there, Pup was also out. A minute ago I was totally relaxed, lying on the floor to enjoy the game, and now suddenly I was walking on, and we were 3 for 2 off 2 overs and 1 ball. At least I hadn't have time to get nervous.

Jimmy Anderson was bowling brilliantly. His improvement from four years previously had been extraordinary. In 2006–07, he couldn't get the ball to move much and lacked discipline and confidence. Now he was the complete bowler. He was high in confidence, with great control and skill, and was moving the ball laterally both ways.

I tried to stick to my same plans and routines. A dose of luck helped. I went for a big drive and nicked it, but it landed just short of third slip. From there I got through that initial period, and it really was a beautiful batting pitch. Watto and Northy both made starts, but we couldn't find that big partnership. Desperate to make a hundred, I worked my backside off all day, concentrating and building another stand with Hadds, before Graeme Swann bowled a fuller and wider ball late in the day that undid me. I tried to knock it to deep point, and it was the first one that really turned. I nicked it to slip.

Digging your team out of a mess gives you enormous satisfaction as a player. But my 93 had only done part of the job; the team required someone to get 150 or more. We got 245, probably half of what we needed.

England built up a huge lead, and we didn't have the fortitude to fight it out and get a draw. Pup and I were doing our best late on the fourth afternoon, and he was very determined, amid a rare lean trot. In the last over of the day, he was out to Kevin Pietersen. Next morning, I was first to go. The loss was crushing.

There were some bad signs that we had to address quickly if we were going to get back into the series. The leadership called a team meeting, talking about addressing parts of our preparation. These were generic things. Our preparation was good. There seemed to be issues brewing beneath the surface. I couldn't put my finger on it. It just felt like there were fractures within the team. It comes when things aren't quite going right. People think the wrong decisions are being made, and don't want to stand up and say it. I thought a social occasion might give us the chance to do that.

A lot of players had organised flights home that night after the match to get away from it all for a few days. I spoke up and said, 'I don't think we should go home tonight, I think we should relax together here, socially. It's important when things have gone horribly wrong that we stick together and show our unity.'

But that was overruled. The other guys couldn't wait to board flights and get home the same day. I was disappointed with that. We'd just lost a Test match. If we stayed together for a team dinner socially, it might have been an opportunity for players to get things off their chest and clear the air.

Only the West Australian contingent stayed overnight, plus Ryan Harris, who was catching up with family and friends in Adelaide, where he'd lived before moving to Queensland.

I had dinner with the other West Australians, Justin Langer and Marcus North. During dinner, while Northy was in the toilet I said to Justin they should stick with Marcus; he'd scored a hundred in Bangalore two Tests back.

Justin just looked at me and said, 'He's gone, mate.'

Maybe some of the leadership felt awkward, knowing Northy was about to be dropped, and that was why they didn't insist on everyone staying in Adelaide. But in my view, that was another reason the boys should have stayed together. You never know when it's going to be someone's last Test match. Marcus's last experience as a Test cricketer would be that we lost a match and the guys didn't stick with him. Dinner with Justin Langer and Mike Hussey doesn't quite cut it. I felt that the whole team should care for their mates.

We had another tough, green pitch in Perth, which was becoming the norm. We scored 268 in the first innings, in line with the trend in recent WACA Tests, and Hadds and I were among the runs again. I had the advantage of having played a lot of cricket there, but it was still an ordeal just to survive, and I had a slice or two of luck. Mitchell Johnson, who swung the bat late and top-scored, then got it completely right with the ball. I felt that it didn't matter who was batting, they were going to get out. He was unstoppable. Ryan Harris was a good inclusion in those conditions, too, so relentless, never bowling a bad ball. After barely taking a wicket since the first day in Brisbane, we bowled England out for 187.

The pitch was still doing a bit when we batted again, but I was loving my cricket again and felt in control. A desperate situation improved my concentration, and with some of the other senior players out of touch I enjoyed the responsibility of being the man Australia was relying on. Watto made 95 and and I got to my hundred with Ryan Harris as my batting partner. He's a champion bloke. What everyone likes about him is that he's honest and will do everything for the team, 100 per cent every single time. He's old school, without any airs and graces. When I got to my hundred, I said to him, 'This is the best feeling of all, an Ashes hundred on your home ground.'

Our lead was more than 380, a big advantage on a pitch that was still playing up. But we had a few scars. England had batted so well in the first two Tests, for days without losing a wicket, and we had no illusions about how hard it would be to get them out. In the event, we went through them quickly. Ryan Harris was the star, with six wickets. As we walked off, he said, 'You know how you said yesterday getting that hundred was the best feeling in the world? Well, I reckon getting five wickets and winning this Test is the best feeling in the world for me.' It was a nice moment we had together.

The buildup to Boxing Day was huge. The Ashes were on the line. We were confident from Perth, but, in retrospect, maybe a bit over-confident. We talked about being aggressive and taking it to them. Maybe we didn't pay attention to the little things. It seems odd that a team that had been outplayed in Adelaide and much of the Brisbane Test would be over-confident, but the overall mood had that instability to it: we were either down in the dumps or over the top. It wasn't the calm confidence of earlier years.

There was some moisture in the MCG wicket but Ricky was always going to bat first and we thought we'd take England apart again. On the first morning, when the ball was moving around, we were horrendous, playing big shots and carrying on as if we could attack our way out of any situation. We were knocked over for 98. Even then, we were bubbling with that brittle, possibly false, confidence, and went out sure we were going to roll them. By stumps, they were 0/157.

It was a horrible feeling walking off like that after such a crucial day in the series. We'd been completely outplayed, to a degree where getting back into the Test match appeared more or less impossible. It was worse than depressing. At the hotel, Amy said, 'I've never seen you so down after a day of cricket. You've got to lighten up and take the pressure off yourself.'

The next two days, it just got worse. Jonathan Trott never seemed rushed, relentlessly sticking to his game. The best teams in the world had experienced, hardened international players who knew their games inside and out. It was a lesson Australia didn't seem to be learning. If you want to get rid of experienced players, you develop a soft culture and also a losing culture, because young players who don't know their game can't perform well on a consistent basis. Even a freak like Ricky Ponting was inconsistent in his first five years of Test cricket. When you fill a team with players picked on potential talent, you're up and down and riding your moods. England were the better team in that series because they had much more seasoning and therefore a steadiness under pressure.

Our batsmen all tried hard in the second innings, but England had the ball swinging whether it was new or old. It took us a long time to score runs because of the challenge of a moving ball. By the end of the third day, in a match of such high importance, we had capitulated.

We were devastated, because the Ashes were gone again. We'd let ourselves and the whole country down. During an Ashes series, everyone talks about how you've got to beat those Poms. The rivalry is unique. The thrill in winning in 2006–07 was the greatest I'd experienced, and the despair in 2010–11 was correspondingly low. I don't think I've ever felt as miserable about cricket as I felt that week in Melbourne.

To make matters worse, we would be without our captain in Sydney. Ricky was copping a lot of criticism for his form, and then he had broken his finger catching Trott in the Perth Test. He only played in Melbourne because it was such a crucial Test, and fielded at mid-off. Every time he touched the ball he was getting lightning bolts of pain, for which he needed injections every session. By each meal break they'd worn off and he was in agony. He shouldn't have played.

If anyone was getting more stick than Ricky, it was Michael Clarke – and now he was going to be Australian captain. The razor gang had moved from me to Ricky to Pup, and in his case, the tabloid media went after him with a mean, personal edge. I certainly believed he was one of our best batsmen, and knew his form would come back. But it was hard for him to become captain under those circumstances. He didn't say much in the lead-up – just prepare well and give it our best shot. Then, when he walked out to bat on the first morning in Sydney, sections of his home crowd booed him. I didn't hear it from inside the dressing room, but when

I was told about it I thought it was really ordinary behaviour from a home crowd.

I don't know what real depression feels like, but I was close to it in Sydney. I was exhausted physically and mentally, and we only made 280. In the field, we hung in there at first, reducing them to 5/226, but after Ian Bell came in it seemed like England were batting for a week. The Barmy Army was singing. We'd had to scrounge for every single run, whereas for them it was just a cruise. I kept saying to myself, *You've got to cop it, and this is when you learn the most about a bloke's character.* I thought it was important to stick together and keep our heads up and try our hardest, but the truth was that by then I was just running on fumes. In the end, England were a lot better than us and deserved to win it.

THIRTY

It was hard to get over losing the Ashes so badly, but sometimes the unstoppable flow of international cricket can be a blessing. There were times in my career when I felt that we didn't get enough time to celebrate a big win, as we had to move on to a new venue or a new tournament. In January 2011, the arrival of the one-day series was perfectly timed, as we didn't have time to sit around and mope about the Ashes. The World Cup, in the subcontinent, was coming up in the autumn, and that gave us a good diversion from our unhappiness after the Tests.

One-day cricket had been our salvation in recent times, too. In the first match at the MCG, Watto played an unbelievable 161 not out as we were chasing a total of 295. I was supporting him, running hard between wickets. Then, as I stretched for a second run, my leg went *Ping!*

What was that? But there wasn't any pain. It felt weird, sort of weak and numb, but didn't hurt, so I kept batting and running between wickets. I kept stretching it and thought maybe it was all right.

When I got out I told Alex Kountouris, the physio, what I felt. Alex did a few tests and was trying to remain positive. He said, 'I hope you will be okay, it might be a little strain in your hamstring.' The next day I went for an MRI scan. The doctor said, 'I'm sorry, but it's worse than we thought.'

I said, 'One game, two games?'

He sighed. 'No, you'll need an operation, your tendon has come away from where it's meant to be joined to the knee. We have to go in and find it and reattach it.' He explained that the tendon is like an elastic band from the knee to the buttock, and mine had snapped off.

My immediate thought was of the World Cup. 'How long am I out?'

'Eight to twelve weeks.'

That was cutting it extremely fine. I was absolutely desperate to play in my second World Cup. The first had been such great fun, one of the best memories of my career to play in a team that functioned so cohesively. We had a meeting with the surgeon, David Young, who was really positive, saying, 'I can get you back within eight to ten weeks and you'll be ready for the second or third game in the World Cup.'

Alex, who was a more conservative character, said, 'You've got no chance.'

David said, 'I'm telling you now, he'll be fine.'

I got excited and said, 'Let's get it done and get right for the World Cup. Whatever it takes, I'll do.'

Rehabilitation became as much of an obsession for me as any other part of cricket. This was my first very serious injury and I was dead-set going to get it fixed by the World Cup. But then I was rocked. I had to go to the MCG to meet with Andrew Hilditch, the chairman of selectors. He said, 'Our policy's going to be that if you're not fit for the start of the first game, you won't be selected in the squad.'

I argued my case. 'I don't agree with you. World Cups are not won in the first and second games. They're won at the end of the tournament. That's when you want your best team. We're playing minnows to start with, and those are the only games I'll miss. It's not a five-Test series where you have to start by winning. It's about the end.'

He wasn't having it. 'If you're not available for the first game, you won't be in the squad.'

I walked away shattered.

The next day I was lying on my bed in the hotel and seeing his name on the phone I felt sick. He was just ringing to confirm the bad news. 'If you're not fit for the first game,' he said, 'you can't be part of the squad.'

I was in tears. My World Cup dream was taken away for what I thought was no good reason, just inflexibility.

While I was still in Melbourne I had the operation, and Amy came over to look after me and get me back to Perth. The first ten days were extremely painful. David Young had mapped out a plan for my comeback and I wanted to get it done even quicker, to make the selectors look bad for not picking me.

At first I could hardly get off the couch for the swelling, but David told me this was to be expected. Bit by bit, I was able to walk, then stretch, then do physio, then jog, run and bat. In the end, my recovery went almost to the day to how David had forecast it.

My first game was a Shield match against Queensland at the WACA starting on 3 March, almost eight weeks to the day since the injury. I was rusty and weak, but was able to let go and run fast if not flat out.

Meanwhile, the World Cup squad was in Bangalore, preparing for their first game. Out of the blue, I got a call from Michael Brown at Cricket Australia, saying, 'Huss, there's been a change in the rules. If someone gets sent home, we can replace them with a player from outside the squad. If that happens, we can select you.'

I thought it was a weird call, because all I'd heard was that the selected squad was final. At any rate, I wasn't getting my hopes up. Only a bad injury would send someone home. But a week later the phone rang again. Doug Bollinger was coming home with an ankle injury and I would be replacing him. I really couldn't believe it. As I boarded the plane, I was extremely excited and couldn't wait to join the boys, but it also seemed surreal how things had fallen into place and the eligibility had apparently been changed.

With a Shield match and some one-day cricket for Western Australia, I'd actually had more game time than the boys in India. However, there was the challenge of getting used to Indian conditions double-quick, and I was still nervous about my hamstring holding up. David Young kept reassuring me, saying it would be stronger than before. He'd sewn it onto a second hamstring. He kept saying, 'You can let go.' But I had to do it, under pressure, before I could fully believe him.

Everyone was watching me like a hawk. 'Is he going to be okay?' I kept up a brave front, saying I'd be fine. Alex put me through some rigorous tests, and scrutinised me sceptically. I got through with flying colours. I didn't run as fast as I possibly could, but fast was enough to prove that I could play.

When I was named to play Kenya, I was that happy I texted David Young about ten times to thank him. I was in the World Cup, obviously my last chance in the premier one-day tournament. I felt like a kid again.

Despite losing to Pakistan, we got through to the quarter-finals. As a team we weren't quite clicking, but I didn't mind. I was ecstatic to be there. But then we ran into what had become an Indian juggernaut in Ahmedabad. It was their time. Ricky made a courageous hundred on a big-turning pitch. My brother Dave, who now really belonged in the Australian one-day team, batted powerfully and with maturity to finish our innings, and bowled well too, but Yuvraj Singh, a guy we'd had the wood on in the past, was having the tournament of his life and put us away in the end. We were never quite good enough in that tournament, but personally I was happy to have proven people wrong and come back from the injury.

After the World Cup, Ricky stood down as one-day captain, and Michael Clarke took over as full-time captain. His first assignment was a short one-day series in Bangladesh on the heels of the World Cup. These series can seem interminable and irrelevant from the outside, but for me, every game for Australia was important. Without exception. After a couple of months on the couch and doing rehab, I was refreshed. So I went to Bangladesh full of beans.

As a captain, Pup was a very strong driver and had a clear path that he wanted to take the team on. You were either on it or you were off it. I was behind the captain, as always. What he was bringing in wasn't a lot different from Ricky, but Michael brought a lot of intensity to it, not leaving a stone unturned when it came to fitness and preparation. He wanted to bring his personal philosophies and professionalism into the team structure. Quite often, a change in leadership brings on a honeymoon period when everyone's keen to impress. Michael set the tone with a brilliant hundred in the first game, and in the second, Watto smashed 170-odd with a world record number of sixes. In the third game I noodled out a hundred on a great batting pitch, which I didn't often get a chance to do in one-day cricket.

We were motivated by a number of factors. You don't like to be criticised, and we were stung by being knocked out of the World Cup. And everyone's career was on the line. You could lose it in a blink. So even though there might not have seemed a lot at stake, with a new captain and effectively a new era, we had plenty to play for.

After Bangladesh, I went back to India for my first full season in the IPL. I'd played only four games for CSK in 2008 and three games in 2010, so I was looking forward to the challenge of a fourteen-match tournament.

IPL was definitely more relaxed than international cricket, but you don't stop learning, especially when you're seeing the top players from around the world every week. I felt I could play with freedom at Chennai, and we had a terrific year, going through and winning the final. It made so many people happy: the players, the fans, the people at the franchise. It was a fantastic way to end what had been a long and tumultuous season. The family came over for about ten days, at CSK's expense, which was brilliant. I'd always wanted the children to come and see how people in India live, and to give them a glimpse of how lucky they are. Every time I went to India, I sat the kids down and asked them to give me a bag of toys to give to Indian children who were not as fortunate as them. They were incredibly generous. But when we were there, they were scared by the noise and heat and volume of people and how busy it was, and maybe weren't quite old enough to appreciate the lesson! But I still felt it was important to expose them. I'd had such an insular childhood myself, never knowing much about the world beyond Mullaloo, and wanted to equip my children for the very different kind of life they would emerge into.

Finally, at the end of the IPL, I could put my feet up. That year had had so many ups and downs, with the Champions League, the Test tour of India, successful one-day tours, then the Ashes and the World Cup and getting injured; among the disappointments were also some personal highs. I could be proud of my Ashes series, as a batsman. I was elated to have overcome a serious injury and played in the World Cup. I felt I'd answered my critics, for the moment anyway.

THIRTY-ONE

Personal goals are one thing, but in cricket they always have to interact with the bigger picture: your team's progress, the state of the greater game. During the winter, Cricket Australia began its review into the sport, chaired by Don Argus.

I was interviewed twice, by an American consultant in Sydney and then at the WACA by Steve Waugh and a couple of CA officials. I found myself talking openly, and was assured that everything would be confidential. I've mentioned Steve Waugh's misinformation about me playing in the Champions League. Other than that, it felt like a good process at the time. But when the results of the review came out, Cricket Australia went in the other direction from pretty much everything I'd suggested.

One example was whether the captain and coach should be selectors. I said it had worked for me in county cricket, being able to get the team I wanted. When I was West Australian captain, allowed to have input into selections but not as a selector, I found it frustrating, because there were times when I would say my piece and then find out that the selectors had gone the opposite way. So I did have sympathy for the idea of the captain being a selector.

However, the Australian team was completely different again. To be a selector puts the captain into too much of a compromising position when he has to leave players out and the next week needs them to play for him. How can they be sure they have his backing? How does Michael Clarke, when he wants Ricky Ponting in his team and is fighting tooth and nail to keep him, cope when all the selectors don't agree? Does he come back to Ricky and say, 'Sorry, the selectors have said you're out, and here are the reasons why'? He can't really say, 'Mate, I disagreed, I was voting to keep you.' He can't betray the confidence of the selection room.

So Ricky thinks, 'This captain doesn't want me,' when the captain may well have wanted him.

It affects relationships between players on the fringe and the captain. You become more guarded in the dressing room. *Michael Clarke is watching how I prepare, how I am in here, and that might impact on my selection.* I noticed, during that period, that when Michael was around, everyone went a bit quieter and kept their head down. It's not a comfortable feeling; people aren't being themselves. Overall, I just felt that it drove a wedge between the players and their leader, and it wasn't fair to either side.

When it came to the coach, I was even more certain that he shouldn't be a selector. If I was a player and was really struggling, I would like to feel confident in going to the coach and baring my heart. But if he's a selector, I might be guarded about what I say to him. He's there for you to share your problems with. But can you? I raised it with Mickey Arthur later, and he said, 'I know if you're struggling, don't worry about that.' To a degree he was right. He would know when someone was struggling. But what he couldn't know was whether there were other problems in the player's mind that were not of a technical nature. Maybe there was something personal. A player should have been able to confide those issues to his coach, but if the coach was also a selector, he probably wouldn't.

It also comes down to the individual in question. There again I was ignored. I was a big Tim Neilsen fan. I admired his love for cricket, his backing of the players, his work ethic and his understanding of the game. He could have improved some facets of player management, but otherwise I thought he was absolutely brilliant and was disappointed when he was let go and replaced by Mickey Arthur, who had had success as coach of South Africa.

Another area I was concerned about was the rush to get teenagers and other youngsters into first-class cricket. I thought the Sheffield Shield should be hard and uncompromising, not a finishing school. If you start playing youngsters who aren't quite good enough yet, it will lower the standards and intensity and make the jump to Test level so much bigger. I opposed any concerted push to get rid of guys in their late twenties and early thirties. We're all formed by our own experiences, and I was living proof that you could start playing Test cricket at 30 and still have a long career. As a batsman, you don't hit your prime until your late twenties, so why were they looking at players that age and moving them on for twenty-year-olds?

Anyway, this was yet another area in which they did the opposite of what I suggested. A very clear sign of this came in the first series of the new season, a tour to India, when Simon Katich was dropped.

I was very surprised, to say the least. Kato had ruptured his Achilles tendon in Adelaide during the Ashes series, but he was fit again now and I saw him as one of the best batsmen in Australia. If the selectors formed adverse opinions about Simon's contribution to the dressing room, I felt they were completely wrong. Kato was an excellent team man. They selected Phil Hughes and Usman Khawaja, both of whom I felt were very promising young batsmen, but I thought it would have been more beneficial to them and the team that they spent more time dominating first-class cricket before stepping in for someone as accomplished as Kato. For a young player in this position, it's inevitable that his focus is turned inward, as he tries to cement his place. By contrast, Kato was a strong, confident presence around the group, and had been just about our best-performed batsman in the previous two or three years. I had tremendous respect for him and thought it was wrong that he was dropped. It sent a destabilising message, I felt. If they left Simon Katich out, what did that mean for the rest of us? We already know we're accountable. We live with that insecurity every day. But to dump such a good player, apparently only because of his age, put us under more pressure, and entrenched the culture of looking after number one. The thing about so much change – new captain, coach, players, selectors, administrators – is that everyone keeps his head down and just worries about doing his job, and can become quite insular, I guess. A team culture takes time to develop as relationships develop and trust is built up.

Then, as is well documented, Kato called a press conference and highlighted many faults in and around the team set-up.

So we went to Sri Lanka with all eyes on Pup. When a new captain takes over, you watch the type of leader he's going to be and follow the way he goes. Michael didn't openly dictate our program in meetings, but he was adamant that if anyone wasn't being professional or wanted to let off steam in the way he didn't see fit, he'd come down hard on it.

Ricky was such a hard act to follow, and it was going to be difficult for anybody to take over from him.

In my view, there should have been so much more driving you to become captain, such as motivating the guys to get better, taking the team forward and inspiring them.

I was also nervous about his lack of experience. All through his career, because he was such a gifted batsman, Michael had graduated above his age group and been playing with senior guys who could look after him. This has happened throughout history, from Ricky Ponting back to Don Bradman. When they're that good, they spend a lot of their junior cricket as child prodigies playing among men. This means that when they become Australian captain, it might be one of the first teams they have led. So they have to learn on the job.

In recognition of this, CA had been grooming Michael as vice-captain ever since Gilly's retirement. Since 2008, he'd been doing a kind of apprenticeship under Ricky. Michael wanted to learn from Ricky, but also challenge Ricky. That can be a good element of vice-captaincy, to challenge the captain's ideas, and it was the way Pup saw his learning process.

If I had doubts about Michael becoming captain, I didn't have any ready-made alternatives. It had been decided that I, being the same age as Ricky, was expected to leave the game at around the same time as him and they needed to look at the next generation. I had no problem with that. I thought I could have been a good vice-captain, because I had a good rapport with other players, building friendships, particularly with newer members to make them feel comfortable. I would do whatever my captain asked, without question. But then, I understood why they made Pup vice-captain, and then Brad Haddin and Shane Watson. That was part of the planning for the future. And I didn't have to have the VC by my name to play that leadership role. I'd support the captain and be a conduit between him and the young guys, whether I had a formal leadership position or not. There are many ways to be a leader in a cricket team.

We started the Sri Lankan tour with a five-match one-day series, which we won. At the end of it, Pup came up to me and said, 'You haven't made as many runs as you would have liked, Huss, but I back you and think you've got a big role to play in this team going forwards.'

But the wonderful thing about cricket is, it's full of surprises. Whatever my feelings at the start of that series, I played some of my best cricket under Pup's captaincy over the next eighteen months. I don't know quite what the chemistry was, but it worked, and in the end that's what matters.

The Galle wicket was like a beach, one of the most challenging I've ever played on. The sandy soil had the ball turning viciously. I got 95 in the first innings, which put me in a better frame of mind. The funny thing was, I didn't worry much about just missing out on a century at the time. Ninety-five runs in a Test match is still an awesome effort. But at the end of my career, I have niggles about having 19 Test centuries, not converting that 95. I can only imagine how someone like Michael Slater feels – he would have had 23 Test centuries, not 14, if he hadn't got out in the nineties nine times, and with those stats he probably wouldn't ever have been dropped. It's something you think about more when it's all over.

When we went into the field in Galle, our off-spinner Nathan Lyon, in his first Test innings, took 5/34 and we were in control of the match. I was particularly happy for Nathan. Whoever came into the Australian team to bowl spin post-Warne and MacGill was under pressure, and for Nathan to come in and bowl beautifully was great to see. He was clearly an out-and-out team man, who loved supporting the others and enjoyed their success, and I clicked with him from the start.

Meanwhile, Michael was leading the team very well on the field. He was always thinking outside the box, throwing in an unconventional fielding position or new bowler to plant a doubt in the batsmen's mind if ever he thought the game was drifting. After we won the first Test comfortably, we went to Pallekele, where we took some early wickets but Kumar Sangakkara threatened to get away. In those Sri Lankan Tests, everything I touched seemed to turn to gold, so Pup thought it might be like that with the ball too.

He asked me to bowl, and as usual I thought, *Are you serious?* But I trundled in, and ... to be honest, I don't know how I got Kumar. I wish I could say it swung in and seamed away and caught the edge. But in my first over, I floated up a big wide juicy half-volley that he smashed right out of the middle of the bat. Phil Hughes took a great catch at short cover. Then Pup took me off.

But after I made 142 in our first innings, Pup thought he might develop me into a secret weapon. I bowled a loosener to the opener, Paranavitana, and he played and missed – or at least I thought he did. I didn't appeal. Brad Haddin appealed quite confidently, though. The umpire gave it not out. Brad was adamant, and we referred it to the video. Something was picked up, and he was out, even though I never thought he was. Everything was going my way. And it was a really good part of Michael's captaincy to go with his gut instinct.

We drew that match and the next, so the new skipper was off to a winning start, and quite rightly he got a lot of the credit. Shaun Marsh had made a century on debut, in front of his dad, and Phil Hughes belted a fighting hundred in the third Test. As for me, I was pinching myself. I made two centuries and totalled 462 runs at 92.6, average-wise the most successful Test series in my whole career. I was man of the match in all three Tests, which was a great feeling. For all my doubts leading into it, something was going right. I felt hugely excited to be part of the team's future.

THIRTY-TWO

We wedged in a brief visit home before a tour to South Africa that spring. Under Michael Clarke, a new demand for off-field discipline was coming in. After a win in the first of a three-match one-day series, we lost in Port Elizabeth, but as it was Brad Haddin's birthday, some of us got together for a beer. South African players were there as well, and the next morning we were in trouble for drinking too late with the opposition. I thought it was a great opportunity to enjoy each other's company socially. Unfortunately, the powers that be didn't agree. In Durban the next day we were grilled about our conduct and preparation by Michael Clarke and Troy Cooley, who was standing in as coach. Their message was to pick your times. We thought we'd picked our time pretty well – we didn't have a match for another week – but there was a strong objection to going out and having a drink after losing a match.

We were all sheepish, but later we talked amongst ourselves and felt aggrieved. We didn't think we were doing anything wrong. We were treated like naughty schoolboys, and it put us on edge.

Sometimes these things can bring you together, though. Michael said, 'When we win the series, we can party as hard as anyone.'

We did that, and had a great celebration. It's not easy to beat South Africa at home, and we played really well in that last game. I was there at the end with the Sydney teenager Pat Cummins, who played well under pressure, and the feeling in the team was buoyant after we squeaked home.

South African pitches, as I well knew, were sporty, but most of all in springtime. In our warm-up game at Potchefstroom, a young kid called Marchant De Lange bowled like the wind and was hitting everyone in the head or body. It was a tough initiation into red-ball cricket, but I thought it was good, because if we could get through this we could get through anything.

The Cape Town pitch looked pretty spicy too. I was one of several Australians to fail on the first morning, as Dale Steyn, Vernon Philander and Morne Morkel gave us a torrid workout. But Michael Clarke played one of the most phenomenal captain's innings of all time. Other than his 329 in Sydney two months later, his 151 in Cape Town was the best I've seen him play, and on a much more difficult pitch. I watched most of it from the pavilion. For his first half-hour he looked uncomfortable against the short ball and they peppered him, hitting him on the head and all over his body. But he counter-attacked as only he can. It was a big statement that he wouldn't bow down, and would dictate to the bowlers even on the hardest wickets. Of our total of 284, he scored more than half the runs.

Conditions for bowling were a lot like Headingley, and it was tailor-made for bowlers of fast-medium pace, accurate but with natural variation, such as Ryan Harris and Shane Watson. They bowled great spells, doing just enough both ways to get the nicks. They absolutely routed South Africa for 96. Halfway into the second day, we had a fantastic lead and were excited about the way the Test match was going.

Did I say routed? I guess that wasn't a real rout. From midway through the day, when we started our second innings, that Test match turned into a bad dream. The wicket started doing a bit less, so instead of playing and missing as we had in the first innings, we started to nick them. Philander's big hooping swingers were hitting us in front rather than curving too much.

In seven overs before tea, we lost Watto, Ricky and Phil Hughes. I came out first ball after tea in a positive frame of mind. Morkel served up what I thought was an inviting half-volley, and I went for the biggest cover-drive of all time. I nicked it to slip – *first ball*. It was a terrible shot, just terrible. We were 4/13. But plenty of teams have picked themselves up from there and made good scores. I sat down, feeling very low about the shot I'd played, when there was a big roar and all of a sudden Pup was sitting down beside me, taking his gear off.

Then Hadds came back. Then Ryan Harris. Then Mitch Johnson. When Shaun Marsh came back – he'd gone in at number ten after suffering an injury – we were 9/21. There was just silence and disbelief in the dressing room. Was this really happening? We were about to wake up, right?

On the television screen, the lowest scores in Test cricket were being posted. New Zealand's all-time low of 26 seemed like a mile away. Finally, Peter Siddle and Nathan Lyon put on a partnership for the last wicket – and got us to 47. I don't think the South Africans could believe it either.

I wasn't thinking so much about the overall collapse as cursing myself for my own performance. It was blatantly obvious that I'd played an awful shot. I'd seen it and gone for it, and it didn't go right. Quite a few of the wickets were through good bowling, but not mine. We only needed to put 150 on the board to be in a great position.

Still, even with 47 we led by 235, and South Africa would have to exceed their first innings by a long way. Conditions seemed to be getting better for batting, but we still had every expectation of bowling them out.

But suddenly, Graeme Smith was finding batting easy, and Hashim Amla, coming in at number three, flicked a switch to show us how good he was. They were getting away from us until, on the last ball of the day, Amla sliced a drive to me at gully. It was an absolute dolly, and I put it down.

First ball duck, all out 47, dropped their best player on the last ball: all in all, probably my worst day in Test cricket.

The next morning, they cruised home. It was no contest. Smith and Amla both made centuries and it didn't seem the same pitch as the previous day. We were in shock. How had it turned to this?

After the game, it was the first time I'd ever seen panic in the Australian team. We had a batters' meeting for an hour and a half. The bowlers also held a meeting, thrashing it all out. I thought, *It's been an ordinary game, but for the first half some of the guys played really well.* The boys said to me, 'What the hell were you thinking, playing that shot first ball?' It can be good to be hear your teammates say what they're thinking, rather than being told what you want to hear. But it's also confronting. I had the chance to say what I was feeling. I said, 'I know it was a terrible shot. It was instinctive, I felt I was in good position, I went for it, and I just stuffed it up.' There were a lot of home truths spoken, and guys were being very honest with themselves. Brad Haddin said, 'I'm really struggling at the moment.' I think it was a weight off his shoulders to be able to say that. It saved someone else from going up to him and saying, 'Mate, you look like you're struggling.' It cleared the air for him to confess how he was feeling. For Hadds, like the rest of us, the only way was up.

Ryan Harris picked up an injury in that match, so Pat Cummins came in for his first Test in Johannesburg. He was a fantastic young bloke, who loved the team environment and had a maturity beyond his years. And Usman Khawaja, who'd been unlucky to be left out of the team since the Sri Lankan Tests, got his chance after Shaun Marsh's injury.

We had another bowler-friendly wicket, but the team showed a lot of character, fighting tooth and nail. Our pride was hurt by what happened in Cape Town. This Test was going to show our fighting qualities.

The first innings were pretty much on parity, but in South Africa's second dig Pat Cummins just bowled amazingly, with fire and penetration, really worrying all the batsmen. I would have loved to play more cricket with him, as he promised to give the team that sense of having a frightening pace spearhead. I had strong opinions about players needing to be seasoned in Shield cricket before coming into the Test team, but it was different with bowlers. Pat, like James Pattinson and Mitchell Starc after him, was a very special, precocious talent, and bowlers mature at an earlier age than batsmen. Even though none of them had had much first-class experience, I was right behind their selections.

The match came down to us needing 310 to win on a wearing Wanderers pitch. We lost the openers early, but there was a spirit in the team that just would not accept defeat. Ricky and Usman put on a resolute stand, and then I had a good partnership with Brad Haddin. I wasn't really happy with how I was batting. Vernon Philander was unplayable. Early in my innings I played and missed four balls in an over. I thought I'd be able to get my runs off him, if I could survive Steyn and Morkel, but now I wondered how I'd get bat on ball. I was going for big shots, feeling loose, but they weren't there. Shot selection was a problem. I nicked a couple through slips. Just as I felt like I was settling down and getting the situation under control, my nemesis Steyn got me out. I don't know how many times he got me over the years, but it was more than I care to remember.

But we kept inching forward, in partnerships. We couldn't quite get someone to bat all the way through, but that's the nature of South African conditions. The fighting qualities of all the boys was a really good sign about the characters we had. Finally Pat

Cummins and Mitch Johnson got together with 30 runs needed, and it was excruciating watching from the pavilion, with balls lobbing just beside and over the fielders. But Pat and Mitch found a way, and we had – by two wickets – one of our most exhilarating and memorable wins for many years.

THIRTY-THREE

When you start your Test career at thirty, one thing that comes with the territory is that your age always seems to be a factor. If you have a rough trot when you're young, everyone just says, 'He's out of form, he'll be okay.' When you're in your thirties, it's 'He's too old, he's lost it, they have to bring in someone young.'

I'd been putting up with that at the start of the previous three or four Australian summers, but it didn't get any easier. We started the 2011–12 season with a two-Test series at home against New Zealand, and when I didn't make any big scores it was on again. 'Hussey's time is up.' It was incredibly disappointing, two or three matches after I'd had my most productive series and won the man-of-the-match award in every game. But I was used to it. I needed runs to keep the wolf from the door.

We beat New Zealand easily in Brisbane, but on a poppy wicket in Hobart we batted poorly and lost. David Warner, formerly seen as a Twenty20 specialist, proved he was a Test batsman by carrying his bat on the last day, but we fell short. I felt the speculation intensify around my position. So I left Hobart in a bad mood, which only worsened when I made a duck in the Twenty20 Big Bash League for Perth Scorchers that followed.

Coming into the Boxing Day Test, then, I was in what seemed like an annual state of stress. Amy and I found out we were going to have another baby, which was exciting. But I'd be lying if I said I wasn't stressed about cricket. Amy said I had to find a way to get my mind off it. I wasn't fun to be around.

After the Hobart debacle, we had a batting camp in Melbourne. We hit lots of balls and got together for dinner as a batting group. I really enjoyed it. But unfortunately, it doesn't matter how well you hit the ball in the nets. On Boxing Day, I came in at 4/205, a solid position, to face Zaheer Khan. He was a very wily bowler, and his first ball, a short one, caught me by surprise. I went to play at it, dropped my hands and thankfully missed it. To my dismay, the umpire put his finger up. To my absolute despair, India weren't allowing DRS so there was no going back, when I knew a replay would show that I was not out. To be under all that pressure and get a first-ball duck – as I walked off the MCG, I was screaming, *Give me a break!* Some people said they hadn't ever seen me so animated. I was screaming at the cricket gods. Against New Zealand in Hobart, I'd been hit on the pad first ball but the umpire gave it not out; yet, because they had DRS, the Kiwis referred it and I was given out. Even DRS seemed to have a mind of its own, biased against me. That's what I was screaming at.

That night, I went through my usual battle with nerves and the dumps. It's a horrible feeling, sitting in your hotel room, really tense with negative thoughts, knowing you are one mistake away from the end of your career for Australia. Everyone was saying I had to go. One good ball, one bit of bad luck, and I was finished.

The Test match was an arm-wrestle, which turned our way on the third day when Peter Siddle and Ben Hilfenhaus wrecked the Indian middle order with a great spell of bowling. But then it swung the other way as our top order were out quickly. I came in at 4/27 to join Ricky, who was under the same age-related pressure as I was. It wasn't something we talked about; we didn't need to. But it annoyed me hugely that people could question Ricky Ponting's selection, after all he'd done and the champion he was. After a handful of bad games, they wanted to get rid of him straightaway. People didn't see how much he gave the team off the field, working with the young guys or chipping in with wise words in team meetings. It angered me almost as much as the questioning of my own selection. At any rate, Ricky was about to rise to the challenge.

My mood was a lot like it had been in the Oval Test in 2009. When I hit rock-bottom, I just thought, *See the ball, and what will be will be.* As so often happened, one shot unlocked me. Off my first ball, I clipped Ishant Sharma off my pads for three. I relaxed. The gods had decided I'd had enough, and the wheel turned for me. I had some good luck when Dravid dropped me at slip off Ravi Ashwin. Ricky made 60 and I got to 89 before Zaheer got me again, but we'd batted the team into a good position.

India had 292 to win in plenty of time, not out of reach for a batting order of Sehwag, Gambhir, Dravid, Tendulkar, Laxman, Virat Kohli and Dhoni. Sachin was batting particularly well. What excited me was how well our bowlers bowled to them. Granted, some of the Indians weren't comfortable on the bouncy wicket, but Craig McDermott, our bowling coach, had encouraged the guys to pitch the ball up and find the nicks. Our guys executed it ball after ball. James Pattinson sustained the pressure, bowling with enormous heart, charging in all day. He looked like the finished article already. It was great to watch all the bowlers dismantle the world's most prolific batting order.

More wickets fell on the first day in Sydney, continuing the pattern. India fell for 191, and we were 3/37 when Pup joined Ricky. They got through to stumps, but it was the second day when they put on a show. I was overjoyed for Ricky, to see him silence his critics. People were speaking absolute rubbish about him. At the other end, the way Michael was playing, I've never seen better. How hard was he hitting the ball off his pads! It was super for him as captain, at his home ground, to bat like this, and great for the public to see he was a serious player and could pile up huge scores as captain of Australia.

The bad thing was, I couldn't sit back and enjoy it. It's quite a roller-coaster when you're the next man in, watching a partnership like that unfold. I went through different stages – sleeping, buzzing around, comfortable, really nervous … I would have had twenty or thirty toilet breaks. I got so nervous, Mickey said, 'Do you want to have a break and take your pads off for twenty minutes? We'll send Hadds in next.' No way was I going to let that happen. It's part of the game. I was just trying to relax and not live every single ball that was happening out there.

When Ricky finally got out for 134, after a partnership of 288, I was out there. The applause for Ricky was tumultuous. As I approached the wicket, Virat Kohli walked past me and said, 'It always happens, after a long partnership a quick wicket always falls.' I gave him a little smile, but inside I was saying, *Bugger off*.

My first ball, from Ishant Sharma, was the same kind of wide full one that Morne Morkel had bowled me at Cape Town. I went for it, and instead of nicking it to third slip I got it in the middle and it went for four. Pup came up and said, 'That's a great start, Huss!'

I shook my head. 'It's a shocking shot, it's the ball I nicked in Cape Town.'

He said, 'Don't worry about it, follow your instincts, back yourself.'

There was something imperious about him. He was supremely confident, with a kind of glow. I always enjoyed batting with him. Normally, this was because we were similarly nervous early in our innings. We were on the same wavelength. Usually, when Pup came to the crease he was a very nervous starter. I would try to calm him down, but he'd just look at me and say, 'Just back up and get ready to run.' He wanted to get off the mark that desperately.

Observers would say how in control we looked during our partnerships. Looking back, that's hilarious. It was the opposite! Our conversations were so insecure: 'I don't know how I'm going to get a run off this guy.' 'I feel like I'm going to get out every ball.' 'What are we going to do now? It's reverse swinging!' 'Now they're putting this guy on; I hate facing him!' Our conversations were so negative and tense. People outside had no idea.

But this time, in Sydney against India, there was a serenity about him, and a degree of determination I'd never seen. 'I don't want to give these guys anything,' he was saying. 'I want to keep grinding them. Don't give them a thing.' He wanted to grind them into the dirt.

I had the best seat in the house. Those shots coming off his pads, I'll never forget the sound of bat on ball. And I love the Sydney Test match. It's a good pitch because it has some grass but comes onto the bat, you get full value from the outfield, the crowds like that they're very close to you, and there's the historic feel of the old grandstands. The players' dressing rooms make it feel like a historic occasion every time you play there.

All this added up to one of my favourite cricketing moments. We put on 334 by the time Pup declared. He kindly waited for me to make my 150, but he didn't care about setting records himself, finishing on 329.

The match was far from over. We knew their batting order was going to fight hard. Sachin was still batting well, but there was so much talk about his hundredth international hundred. He was batting brilliantly in Sydney in both innings, but then you could almost see him start to think about it. As the pressure built up, he went into his shell, after dominating our attack. He was starting to protect what he'd done and just edge towards the milestone. In the second innings, when Sachin was 80, Michael Clarke got him, an edge onto Brad Haddin's pad that ballooned to me. It changed the momentum of their whole innings and put it into its terminal phase.

Having gone 2–0 up in the series, we still had to take back the Border-Gavaskar Trophy which India had won in 2010. They'd beaten us in Perth in 2007–08, so we weren't making any assumptions about the third Test. It ended up being quite an extraordinary scorecard, with the bowlers having total ascendancy in the game except for a two-and-a-half-hour period when David Warner and Ed Cowan batted. The WACA wicket was as foreign to India as you can imagine, with lots of seam and swing, but even when we bowled them out for 161 I thought it was going to be really hard work to get a lead. Very often in Perth, whatever the team batting first has scored, the team batting second is bowled out cheaper.

And so it was. Most of us failed with the bat. But for a little space on the first afternoon and the second morning, Davie and Eddie got on a roll. Davie's 180, off 159 balls, reminded me of Gilly's ton in the 2006–07 Ashes, hitting the opening bowlers over their head and into the crowd. Eddie was the rock beside him, and once they'd put on 214 in 38 overs we could see the Indians drop their heads.

A Test match that finished in two and a half days was not what the WACA needed. But we were happy to take it. Ben Hilfenhaus had one of his best matches, taking eight wickets, as part of the career-best season he was having.

There was a great feeling in the team. As a new captain, Pup was big on maintaining our intensity through the series, and we had the exuberance of youth in players such as Warner, Cowan, Pattinson, Starc, Harris and Siddle, who were so keen to play. When something's new, you go as hard as you can all the time. Our bowlers certainly were. Ricky and I were motivated by the desire to show we still had a place out there. It was all going beautifully.

We carried it through to Adelaide, where Ricky and Pup again played massive innings and Nathan Lyon, brought back into the team after missing the Perth Test match, bowled us to a win on the last day. It didn't matter to me how many wickets he took – what impressed me was that he knew his art well for a young player. I knew there would be challenges along the way, but that didn't bother me because I knew he was a man of great character. His wickets were a bonus, but I saw him as a long-term investment, more than twenty or thirty Tests, before he reached full maturity.

As songmaster I wanted to give the younger guys a special experience, so they could go away and say, 'I was part of the Australian Test team song, what a thrill.' In Adelaide, we walked to the southern end of the ground and sang the song inside the scoreboard. James Pattinson had missed the last two Tests with injury, but we got him on the phone. I wanted him to be part of it. We quite often did that. We went into the team huddle and he was in Melbourne, on the video link, dressed up in his whites and his baggy green cap.

Eighteen months later, after Australia beat India 4–0 in Australia, India returned the favour, 4–0 in India. People wonder how this can be so. But if you play Test cricket, you know that experience in foreign conditions is crucial. As a batsman, you need to figure out where you'll score runs. In Australia, for instance, I scored mainly through cover and with my pull shot, whereas in India I had to learn more about deflections and playing with the spin. Australia also has a great home ground advantage partly because of the vast differences between Brisbane, Perth, Adelaide, Sydney, Melbourne and Hobart. It takes an adjustment in each place. We've had a great advantage, historically, due to that diversity. But I know how hard it is both ways, and if teams are very even in talent, experience in the conditions can make the 5 per cent difference that results in a 4–0 scoreline. I didn't watch the Australian tour of India in 2013 with any sense that

I'd have been able to make a difference. I empathised greatly with the Australian players and, having retired, I was rather glad that I wasn't having to fight my way out from that suffocating pressure. There were comments about 'Bringing back Hussey', but I never felt that I would have made a difference to the result.

During that Adelaide Test match, for the first time I put my growing unease into words and started questioning whether I wanted to keep playing. I had a chat with the team psychologist, saying, 'I'm not sure if I want to keep playing. I've written down the pros and cons.' The main pro was that I still loved the game itself, was satisfied with my batting, and having waited so long to play for Australia I didn't want to give it up in a hurry. The main con was the amount of time I was away from home. Life was severely out of balance. The kids and Amy were finding it increasingly hard, and the whole family was under strain.

The psychologist was quite taken aback and gave me the impression that it would be the wrong thing to do to walk away now.

But during the one-day series following the Tests, I started to detect more warning signs about the team environment. I felt relaxed about my game after making some runs, but I felt that all the structures being built up around coaching, managing and selecting the team were so new, it would take time to build up the trust in those structures that is essential to getting yourself into the right frame of mind to play Test cricket.

One of the first of those warning signs was after we put in a dominant performance against India in the first one-dayer in Melbourne. Before the second game, Mickey Arthur said to the team, 'We're going to reward you guys by not making any changes.'

I thought, *Reward? Does that mean if we don't play so well we'll be punished, and dropped?* What was going on? I believed in sticking with players who've done well, giving them a chance to deliver. We'd played a near-perfect game and were being 'rewarded' with another game. It sent a bad message to the team – no-one is safe. We already know that. Nobody has a right to his place. What we needed from our coach was a degree of backing and help with our games, not a veiled threat that if we didn't keep playing outstanding games, our heads were on the block.

We got through the one-day series with a narrow win over Sri Lanka in the finals, and a week later, after a huge summer in Australia following two intense spring tours to Sri Lanka and South Africa, we were in St Vincent, starting a marathon series against the West Indies.

In the finals in Adelaide, I had Bob Carter over from New Zealand. We had a long heart-to-heart in which I told him I'd been thinking about retiring. Bob, who knows me as a cricketer as well as anyone, said I should keep playing for as long as I could. He thought I would regret it if I retired before my time, and in his opinion I was still before my time.

But it was hard to take, having come through such an emotional summer, starting with the highs of Sri Lanka and the lows of South Africa, but ultimately battling my way through, being on a plane to the West Indies the day after it all finished. I'd been away for five months, and now I was looking at another three and a half, including another commitment to a season in the IPL. For the first time, my mind was clouded with doubt over how much cricket I was prepared to take on.

The cricket in the West Indies, one-day and Test, was tough and gruelling. In 50-over cricket, the wickets were so slow and uneven, 200 was a good score. I didn't actually mind that too much. For the younger guys who'd been playing first-class cricket, to find international cricket a struggle was a good thing. For people like David Warner, Matthew Wade, Ed Cowan and James Pattinson to experience how tough it was around the world, it was a great education for them personally, but also they would then take that message back to their peers in first-class cricket.

Having hurt his hamstring in Australia, Pup didn't come for the one-day matches, handing Watto the reins. I thought he did a brilliant job as captain. His philosophy was about being confident, putting pressure on the opposition, backing his players, making you feel like he valued you personally.

Pup was back for the Tests, and our win in the first match in Barbados was a testament to the skill and persistence of Ryan Harris and Ben Hilfenhaus, who did it with the ball and then, maybe surprisingly, with the bat in the first innings. When he didn't have problems with his left knee, Hilfy was a tremendous bowler, very accurate and smart, always thinking about batsmen and scheming how to get them out. When his knee was sore, though, he couldn't quite get over his front leg and get his arm high enough to swing the ball, and this began to affect him the next season in Australia when he lost his place in the team.

While I wasn't making any big scores, I felt like I was contributing well and was a valued member of the team. It had taken me so long to get an opportunity to play for Australia, I didn't want to wish it away. As Bob Carter had said, if I pulled the pin, I didn't want to regret it two or three years down the track. But on the other side of the coin, it was an increasing strain for the family. I felt as though I wasn't part of the family in any useful sense. I was missing so many things, and was unable to contribute to them. And what could I say to Amy about my days? Training, hotel, beach, dinner with the boys – it's a good life for a young guy, but when your heart is back home, it can feel a bit empty emotionally. By the time I was ready to go home, complete exhaustion had set in for Amy.

While in the West Indies, I became concerned at a deeper level about how much I was enjoying being in the team.

My view was always that in cricket you have to be genuinely happy for your teammates' success. If it wasn't happening, was it a team culture, or just a few players? I was a bit nervous about that, and organised a meeting with Mickey. I sat down with him and got all my concerns out in the open. 'We need to foster a culture that makes them want to think about other people and play for the team,' I said. 'Get them out of insular thinking and bring in team activities. It's about caring for each other. There's too much insular thinking, about number one only.'

Was I overreacting? I did question myself. Perhaps I was just an old guy pining for the good old days. This was a new team and it takes time for a new culture to develop. I shouldn't be comparing them to a former group that had developed friendships over a long time. It will take time for these guys to feel comfortable about their place in the team.

Did Mickey see it as something that could be improved?

In our chat, I don't think anything I said went in. Mickey definitely listened, but he was in tunnel vision mode too. He had specific things he wanted to focus on, and anything from left field didn't register.

I walked away from the meeting thinking I was glad to have got it off my chest, but it didn't go anywhere.

It was understandable how Mickey had his specific plans, and Michael too. But for me it was a big early warning sign that this team had problems ahead of it. We were fostering an environment where guys only cared about their own positions and didn't think about the team.

The dressing room became just as stressful and tense as out in the middle. It should be a sanctuary, where you can let go and have a joke with your teammates. Our dressing room wasn't relaxed or calm, or conducive to good play. I didn't enjoy that tension and

I'm sure some of the guys weren't enjoying it. It was a far cry from having people like Gilly and McGrath and Simmo and Haydos. New guys, of course, wanted to keep their heads down and do the right thing. So maybe over time the friendships and trust will develop. But I began to sense that if this happened, it would have to happen after my time.

THIRTY-FOUR

After another IPL stint, I finally got home in late May. Our baby wasn't due until September, and we went to Margaret River for a family holiday and had a fantastic five or six days. On the last day, we were about to come back to Perth and Amy said she wasn't feeling right. As we drove back, she wasn't getting better, and went straight to bed when we got home. That was unusual for her, and I was alarmed. She was in pain all night, and first thing the next morning she said, 'I feel like I'm having contractions.'

My stomach flipped. Was it happening again? I said, 'You can't be, that's ridiculous,' knowing it wasn't ridiculous at all. We had to rush to the hospital again, and sure enough, Oscar was coming out. That was another massive shock. Having been through a premature birth with Molly I knew what to expect, but was very scared about complications affecting both Oscar and Amy.

Oscar was taken into intensive care straight away. It being winter, he wasn't allowed any visitors for three months other than Amy and me. Amy was very sick for ten days from the infection, and I was looking after the other three, with some help from Amy's auntie Deb, who was a godsend, Amy's mum and sister and my mum. It reminded me of what Amy had to contend with to do it herself all the time. It hit me pretty hard. I don't know how she did it. Physically, mentally, emotionally, I was battling to cope.

It was awful for me, seeing Amy go through so much suffering with the birth and the infection. You wouldn't wish anyone to have to go through those premature births. Unless you've seen it, you don't realise how difficult it is.

And then, within weeks, I was going away again. How long could this go on? I was still getting a buzz out of cricket, but things were preying on my mind. I began to think about options, how to phase myself out of the different formats. Test cricket meant the most to me, I'd give that up last. But I was still enjoying the other formats. I thought I would be left out of the Australian T20 team after the upcoming World Cup, so that decision would be taken away from me, as the selectors would be looking for players for the future. That was fine.

Amy and I got a big whiteboard out, drew up a list of the future tours, and came up with a number of options. Other than the Australian summer, it was pretty much all Test cricket coming up – big tours to India and then England. In one-day cricket, I didn't see myself getting to the Champions Trophy in England. I talked with Neil Maxwell, and we started piecing together a plan. With one-day cricket, I thought I'd like to retire at the end of the 2012–13 Australian summer. Depending on how I was feeling with Test cricket, I would retire either at the start of the Australian summer, the end of the Australian summer, or at the end of the Ashes tour to England. Those were the three options in my mind. Neil said, 'Just go away and think about it, take some time.'

My mind was very much on family when we flew out to the United Arab Emirates for games against Afghanistan and Pakistan.

It was hard to comprehend the importance of the Afghanistan match, their first against Australia. We prepared for it as a normal one-day international, and a chance to get used to conditions before playing the established opponent. But for the Afghanis, it was a momentous occasion. On the political side, with so much conflict in the area and Australian troops being there for the best part of ten years, it was important for relations between the two countries. I don't think much about politics in sport, but it was good to play that game and make that statement of friendship and support.

We went to an Australian military base in the Gulf and saw their mission control centres, which was interesting for all of us. International players live in a bubble – airport, hotel, cricket ground – without getting out and seeing the world we live in. it was brilliant to meet the military people and see how their lives worked. I suggested to Pat Howard, the high performance manager at Cricket Australia, that they should take the guys to Gallipoli before the Ashes tour, as had been done in 2001. But they didn't have time. It would have been great to give the players a reference point, to put their cricket struggles into perspective, in the way that the Middle East did for us in 2012.

The Afghani cricketers didn't speak much English and we only socialised at one function before the game, having a group photo. But they had some really good players and gave us a tough game. Michael Clarke approached every game as if it was really important, and said we had to be on our guard. The conditions were more familiar to them than to us. They'd been preparing for the World T20, and it was our first game. I was nervous, and Afghanistan pushed us hard, but we had a bit too much polish for them in the end.

Their new-ball bowlers and spinners were all very impressive, while a couple of their batsmen had amazing natural hitting ability. There's plenty of talent to work with. Their next step is a holistic approach to the game, more than just batting/bowling/fielding. They were having a real crack at us skills-wise, but I got the sense that they were in awe of some of the Australian players. They had a lot of room for improvement, not so much in cricket skills, but in fitness and the mental side.

When we played T20s and ODIs with Pakistan, the conditions were definitely the most challenging I've ever faced. The daytime temperatures were 57–58 degrees. We were starting matches at 8pm and playing till 3am. At 10.30pm one night, I remember seeing on the scoreboard that it was 38 degrees! I really struggle in the humidity, and I was in a world of pain during all those games, particularly the ODIs. It was a tough series, but our team showed amazing work ethic and character to get through.

In the last game, the series was on the line and we were in trouble chasing a decent score. It was so hot, I thought, *How on earth are we going to get these runs?* I was chipping away, and then Glenn Maxwell hit 50 off 30 balls. He was hitting Saeed Ajmal over cover against the spin. It brilliant to see a young player come through and just take command like that in the most challenging conditions, and gave me renewed hope for the future. Not my future, however; for reasons beyond my control, my 65 that night would be my last one-day international innings, and that would be my last match.

We followed the one-dayers with a three-match T20 series with Pakistan in Dubai, perfect preparation for the World T20 in Sri Lanka. We'd made the semis of the first World T20, but it remained one trophy Australia hadn't won. Michael Clarke having stood down from T20 cricket, Tasmania's George Bailey was the captain. We had a strange start. The batters were sat down before the first game and told, 'We want to stick with this batting order for the foreseeable future. We want you guys to have the confidence to go out there and play for the team, you're not under pressure to keep your wickets.'

I thought that was fantastic to know. Put the team first, yourself last – a brilliant philosophy.

So we played the first two games, and then my brother Dave was dropped. I said to George, 'What happened to the philosophy of sticking by guys and giving them a long run?'

He said, 'Yeah, I know, but we're not sure what our best team is.' Suddenly they'd dropped one of our best players after two games. We were all under pressure. I could understand they weren't sure about what was the best team, but saying one thing and doing the other created some doubt amongst the players.

The preparation settled down after that. We were used to subcontinental conditions by the time of the tournament proper, and Watto turned up in brilliant touch. He was like Matthew Hayden in the 2007 World Cup, capable of taking a game by the scruff of the neck. He scored his runs so fast, it helped all our attitudes. I didn't feel like I had a lot of pressure on me to score quickly. I could knock it around and pick up boundaries here and there.

But T20, as I've said, can be a lottery due to the influence of one player – there can be just one turning point in a game. We found that with Chris Gayle and Kieron Pollard in the final. They obliterated us, and that was that. That last trophy remained tantalisingly out of reach, and I bowed out of international T20 cricket without any announcement or fanfare.

Between the end of the World T20 and the start of the Australian season, I went to South Africa for another Champions League tournament with the Chennai Super Kings. Faf du Plessis, the talented South African all-rounder, and I were fighting for one place allocated to a foreign player, and as he was batting extremely well in his home conditions, I only played one game.

I never much enjoyed not playing cricket while I was away – if I was to be apart from my family, I wanted there to be an immediate reason – and I was cooling my heels, watching the matches, when Amy rang and told me that Oscar had to go into hospital for a double hernia operation. I asked CSK for permission to leave the tournament before our last two matches and the finals, and they were fine with that.

When I woke up one morning, just before I left, a statement with the blinding clarity of truth hit me in the face. It was my first thought of the day: *I don't have to do this anymore.*

I lay there in shock. It seemed so unfamiliar yet also obvious. *I've exceeded everything I've dreamt of doing in the game. I'm going to play the Aussie summer, but I don't want to go away on long tours anymore.*

Straight away, I rang Amy. I was going to retire! She was lost for words. I flew home, where I couldn't do a lot directly for Oscar, but it was great to have some more time with the other kids and to help Amy out. She kept asking if I was sure about retiring, and every time I said, 'I'm sure, this is what I want to do.'

So I went into the Australian summer feeling strangely calm, but also with the nagging fear that my decision to retire would affect my batting adversely. We had a three-Test home series against South Africa to start the summer. Considering my past record against their bowlers, there was every chance that my future could be taken out of my hands.

The summer started with a Shield game against Victoria. My brother Dave, who was renowned for enjoying a chat on the field with his opponents, never sledged me in all our years of state cricket. After all the fighting as kids, we never said anything. I never said anything to him because I thought he thrived on it. Maybe he felt the same way about me: we didn't not sledge because we were good brothers, but because we didn't think it would work!

For the first Test, the Gabba pitch was dry and lacked pace and bounce. Our bowlers struggled to work their way through the South African batsmen on the first day, and then the second was rained out.

The apparent ease of batting on the first day didn't give me any comfort. Steyn, Morkel and Philander would come very hard at us regardless. When we started batting on the third afternoon, we went three down in no time and I was very, very nervous. Michael Clarke joined Ed Cowan, and they both had some luck. Pup was caught off a no ball, and Eddie nicked one down the leg side that the South Africans didn't refer. I thought I'd be out there any moment. But through that evening and the next day, they built a fantastic partnership of 259. When I came out in the early afternoon, the bowlers had had to do a lot of hard work, but we were still 151 runs in arrears.

Pup was in such phenomenal form, I considered myself privileged to be out there watching him pulling off some outrageous shots, hitting Dale Steyn over his head for a one-bounce four and treating the best pace attack in the world with disdain. We found our rhythm together. He liked that I was very busy and talked a lot and ran hard between wickets when I came out. As in Sydney, he was in a calm, confident headspace, in complete control.

Pup and I put on 228, of which I got an even hundred. It put us in position to have a great crack at South Africa on the last day. We took five wickets, but the 68 overs we had to play with, and a lead of just over 100, were not enough. It was disappointing not to finish them off, but they were hot favourites and we'd outperformed them through the match.

In the second Test in Adelaide, Pup was again at his brutal best. David Warner had thrashed a hundred in the morning, but it was only just past lunch when I came in after he was the fourth out. I simply couldn't believe the way Pup batted through that afternoon. Facing Morne Morkel is one of the toughest challenges – he's tall, he's quick, he gets bounce and seam movement and reverse swing – and whenever he came on, I was at the non-striker's end hoping Michael would take all six balls. He kept hitting Morne over his head for four: smashing him. It created a swell of momentum and I could just go with it. I made another hundred, but again it was very much in a supporting role to Michael's 230, his fourth double-century of the year, a feat that not even Don Bradman achieved.

As the match unfolded, we got into what we thought could be a winning position. I had that personal seed of doubt in my mind – they were the best team in the world, and we'd lost James Pattinson to injury in the first innings. It's easily forgotten that in a match when we went within inches of knocking off the world number-one Test team, our spearhead bowled a total of nine overs.

In the fourth innings, we'd set it up so we had almost five sessions to bowl South Africa out. I was confident, but expected it to be a hard slog. Our bowlers, one short, got four wickets in the first 20 overs and we looked set. But on the last day, AB De Villiers, Jacques Kallis and Faf Du Plessis dug in and gave us a lesson in pure defence. It was a bit like that last day of the Shield final in Adelaide, when Jamie Siddons and crew forgot about scoring runs and just challenged us to get them out. Our bowlers worked like Trojans, and we still felt that one lapse was all it would take. Their dressing room would have been full of nervous batsmen, petrified about going in. We just had to get them into the middle, but Kallis batted for a long time even with a torn hamstring, and AB batted completely against his stereotype as a blaster.

Throughout, the heat was like a furnace. We missed a couple of chances, which is inevitable in a long stint in the field. Pete Siddle was exhausted, but kept on running in and trying, as did Ben Hilfenhaus. We wrested the initiative back in the last hour, but the bowlers were exhausted. We just didn't quite have the reserves to get those last two wickets.

It was bitterly disappointing. South Africa had showed their number-one status as a great fighting team, but to me it felt like the Ashes Test at Cardiff in 2009 when we couldn't bowl England out at the end. Good teams take those great feats of survival and turn them into fuel.

With two centuries and a fifty in three innings, I had papered over that hole in my record against South Africa. I don't know if my decision to retire influenced my batting, but I probably was a tiny bit more relaxed. On the other hand, I was executing what had been my plan since the 2009 Ashes: to bat as if every innings could be my last, to soak it up and not worry so much. When I was batting so well, Amy kept asking, 'Are you sure you want to give this up?'

I was, but she kept asking. It got to the point where I joked, 'Don't you want me to retire?'

She said, 'Yes, I do, but I want you to be totally sure and not regret it later. If it's what you want, I'm 100 per cent behind you.'

It didn't change through that summer. I was content with my decision.

The media were off my back, so that settled my emotions. Not so for Ricky, who was facing daily questions over how long he was going to go on. Although he seemed in decent touch, he wasn't making scores, so there was also a real possibility that he might be dropped.

When we flew to Perth, I was nervous about the effect of the Adelaide draw. I sat next to the manager, Gavin Dovey, in the plane, and said, 'I'm worried about this Test. I've seen it before, at Lord's in '09.' We'd put so much effort into Adelaide and got to the end without a result, whereas South Africa would get a lift out of surviving. The match was being billed as our 'grand final', and it felt that way: if we won, we could knock South Africa off their perch as the number one–ranked Test team.

But that was soon overshadowed by two big pre-match developments.

Before the first practice, a team meeting was called at the hotel. I was staying at home, so I raced in to East Perth. I didn't know what the meeting was about. Ricky got up and told us this would be his last Test match. He said how difficult it had been recently, and then turned to what he stood for in the game and what legacy he wanted to leave. We were all stunned. Then it was, 'Let's get training and prepare for this Test match.'

It was a weird feeling, hearing this while knowing I was going to retire three Test matches later. I didn't say anything. Personally, I thought, *Good on you, you must be so relieved, no more pressure to perform, no more speculation about your place in the team. You can go and spend more time with family and friends.*

Ricky's announcement gave us more motivation to push hard in the match, but a confusing signal was sent out when Peter Siddle and Ben Hilfenhaus, our two leading pace bowlers after James Pattinson's injury, were omitted. The pitch looked green, the two guys didn't have to train in the lead-up, and they really wanted to play. They'd done so much hard work in Adelaide on a flat pitch, the conditions in Perth would have suited them. They deserved the right to play on a conducive wicket. It would be more fun for them, but they were pulled out of the game.

As a member of the team, I was bewildered. Different rationales were coming out all the time. First I was hearing they were exhausted and couldn't recover in time. The next day the story was that they had injury niggles. Then I heard a third version, which was that they'd been dropped. I didn't know what was going on.

The selection confusion also hardened my resolve to keep my decision to myself. For a start, I didn't want to tell anyone in case I changed my mind. I was *pretty* sure, but not absolutely. There was also a slightly selfish side to it. With so much important cricket coming up, a lot of the planning and preparation was around the Indian and Ashes series. The idea of forward planning was so strong amongst the management, I feared that if I let them know I was considering retirement they would flick me straight away and bring someone else in to blood him. I wanted to finish in the last Test of the summer, at the SCG, and if I was still good enough to be picked for Australia, I felt I'd earned that right. It was a statement of principle: I thought they should just pick the best team.

My fears about the Perth Test match proved to be well founded. We had a good start with the ball, on the typically green WACA wicket, but on the second morning we lost five wickets in fifteen overs. This was the first pitch of the summer that was helping the fast bowlers, and Steyn, Philander and Morkel bowled well as a unit. We were getting the nicks when we'd previously been playing and missing. Then Smith, Amla and De Villiers hammered us into submission. We'd competed so well against the number-one team for ten days of cricket, but then we were undone in one.

I was philosophical. They were the better team at this stage. We had a good team but had a lot of improving to do; we weren't the finished article. It was a huge mountain to climb, trying to recreate our effort from Adelaide, and while our performance dropped a bit, the South Africans' went up. In effect, we had lost the Perth Test on the last day in Adelaide.

Although I was extremely disappointed that we'd lost, I was proud of the way we'd competed. It was only a couple of sessions that had cost us the result. But it was over now, and so was Ricky's career, which was particularly hard for me to come to terms with. Having admired him for so long, and knowing I was harbouring this secret about my own future, I didn't know what to say to him. We had a great celebration at Gilly's house after the Perth Test match, but I didn't have the chance to talk to Ricky one-on-one. I didn't have the right words. Was I sad for his ending or happy about his career? I couldn't do my feelings justice. I would have to write down a speech and prepare for a week to be able to say what I thought of him as a person.

For me, nothing had happened to alter my decision. After eight years, I was dreading any more long tours away. I felt guiltier than ever for leaving Amy. I was providing for her and the kids, but not in a way I should be providing. Did I want to go through ten or eleven months away, facing extremely tough cricket challenges? No – I was dreading it. That was the defining factor in my decision to retire, and the recent weeks had confirmed it.

THIRTY-FIVE

O ne thing Michael Clarke's captaincy style had in common with Ricky's was to focus completely on the coming match and go hard. He kept talking about becoming the number-one team in the world, which was clearly his obsession. We had to keep getting better, he said, every single time we trained and played.

The first Test against Sri Lanka in Hobart was the beginning of life without Ricky. Phil Hughes came in, desperate to cement his place in what was his fourth crack at Test cricket. I wanted to go out on a high and keep my standards up. We all had something to play for.

Sri Lanka had a very strong and experienced batting order and it was a tough, traditional Test match. I made another hundred on the first day, and Tillekeratne Dilshan got a ton for the Sri Lankans. We got into a winning position again, and had a day and a half's play to bowl them out in the fourth innings. Since Adelaide, the questions had sharpened over whether we could lay that killer blow. Could we finish a team off? Did we have the bowlers to do it?

A lot of pressure was placed on Nathan Lyon, which frustrated me on his behalf. I kept telling him, 'You won't be judged on one day's play, it's all part of a journey you go through. There will always be ups and downs.' He was bowling well, and through the summer had five or six catches go down off his bowling. If those had been taken, there would be no doubts about his position. As a batsman, nobody knew better than I that a millimetre changes your whole life. When I was struggling at the start of the 2010–11 Ashes, I nicked one a few centimetres from slip first ball and went on to make 195. It's a very fine line between completely opposite outcomes.

On the last day in Hobart, the little things eventually tilted our way. Mitchell Starc bowled out of his skin. His pace was really good, his accuracy was getting better, he swung the ball, and when everyone was tired he kept pushing and got the breakthroughs. Peter Siddle's persistence was enormous too. It was a huge relief to get over the line, even if we left it until the last few overs.

Mitchell Starc, after getting the key wickets in Hobart, was given a 'rest' from the Melbourne Test match. I really felt for him. It's every kid's dream to play in a Boxing Day Test match. He was desperate to play and in great form. Management sold it to him as needing him to be fresh for all the big cricket coming up. I thought that was planning way too far ahead. You never know if you're going to get another chance. And three Tests down the track, in India, he would be dropped. Plus, his omission gave other guys opportunities to come in and do well. I understood the thinking behind it, and the need to preserve our bowlers, but it didn't sit well with me. This was a Test match for Australia. It was Boxing Day.

Jackson Bird came in for his debut, Mitchell Johnson got a chance on a sporty wicket, and they took their chance to show off their skill on a bouncy wicket. Melbourne was a fantastic Test match for us, and a convincing win, helped along by yet another hundred from Pup, who showed that not even a strained hamstring could slow him down.

For myself, knowing that D-Day was fast approaching, I'd felt like I'd lost control a bit mentally while I was batting. I couldn't score freely and felt like everything I did was in a rush. I just couldn't settle. I couldn't rotate the strike, and the Sri Lankans were diving on the ball and cutting off singles. I told myself to swing the lumber against Dilshan's off-breaks, and tried to hit one over deep midwicket. It went a bit straight. Rangana Herath ran around the boundary, stuck out his hand and caught it between his fingertips. He then did about fourteen rolls. He looked around like he couldn't believe what he'd done. I wasn't surprised; it pretty much summed up my day.

I was happier than ever with my decision, but now that I had to let people know, I was getting edgy. I'd spoken to Maxi about the actual announcement. My preference was to leave it until the end of the summer. I was worried that they'd drop me from the team, and I didn't want to be the centre of attention, with all the fuss that entailed. But Neil was adamant that I announce it before the Sydney Test match. He said, 'If I'm an Australian cricket fan and I don't get the chance to come and say goodbye to you in a Test match, I'll be annoyed about that.'

I hadn't thought about it that way. I'd only been worried about how it would affect my preparation. But he said it was important to consider all those people who came to watch the game. Gradually, though I was very reluctant about being in the spotlight, I came around to his way of thinking.

In Melbourne, after the Test match, Amy and I went onto the MCG and had a play with the kids – a pretty rare opportunity, which I thought I should take before it was too late. No-one watching knew how much meaning this moment had for me.

In the dressing room, I joined the team for some beers and a celebration. I felt a little bit bad with my decision hanging over my head. I had to let them know, but there were so many meetings going on. Michael, Mickey and the selectors were trying to plan for the Sydney Test match, for the one-day series, for who would go to India early, who would go later, and so on. Mickey and Michael seemed to be in meetings for about three hours.

Finally, Mickey sat down next to me, grabbed a beer and sighed, 'Finally I can relax.'

'Er, Mickey.'

'Yeah?'

'When you get a moment, would you mind if we had a word?'

'Sure,' he said brightly. 'Let's do it now.' He probably thought after all the meetings he'd sat through that this would be something minor.

We grabbed Pup and went into a meeting room.

I was dreading this so much, I didn't know if I could do it. I took a deep breath and blurted out: 'Sydney's going to be my last Test match.'

Michael said, 'Huss, are you telling us you're retiring or are you asking us for our opinion?'

'I'm retiring.'

They were both stunned. Michael's head dropped. He didn't say anything. Mickey's eyes were wide. *Wow*, I thought. *I didn't expect that.*

Pup finally gathered himself and said, 'Good on you, mate, congratulations, you've had an amazing career. I hope when I retire that I can go out the same way, on my own terms.'

Mickey said, 'We respect your decision, Huss. Good luck with your future.'

It was all very quick and, after what I'd readied myself for, comparatively unemotional. I added: 'I'd like to play out the summer in as many one-dayers as you see fit.'

Pup said, 'From my point of view, you've earnt the right to play in as many of the one-dayers as you can. We'll have some meetings in the next couple of days and let you know what we come up with.'

That was how it finished. When I walked out of the room, I thought, *That was a lot easier than I thought it was going to be.*

When we came out, some of the boys were saying, 'What was that about?'

Not wanting to turn it into a full-blown announcement that took the shine off the Test match win, I mumbled something about the one-dayers. That night's celebration was about the team, not me. Jackson Bird had done really well in his first Test, and I wanted the song to be special for the new guys. I took them into the middle of the MCG and led it with gusto. The only ones in the team who knew were Michael, Mickey and me.

Afterwards, I felt relieved that I'd gone through with it. It was becoming a bit more real. I also had a little feeling in my stomach: *I hope I don't wake up tomorrow worried that I haven't done the right thing.*

Before it got out, I wanted to tell the boys that night. I travelled back to the hotel in a van with Nathan Lyon and Shane Watson, two players I was particularly close to. As we pulled up, I said, 'Just so you know, Sydney's going to be my last Test.'

They were in complete shock and tried to talk me out of it. I explained that I was happy with the decision and wanted to spend more time at home.

Nathan was almost in tears. Once we walked into the hotel I pulled him aside.

'Mate, if you're willing, I want you to be the man I pass the song onto. I think you're the best man for the job, you play for the right reasons. I'm keeping it a secret at the moment, but I can't think of a better person.'

I don't know if it registered with him. He wandered away in a daze, and I went off to have dinner with family and friends. I felt pleased to give him this vote of confidence in his longevity in the Test team. When things aren't going his way, he will have legions either bagging him or giving him advice. He's got to figure out who he trusts, and what he's got to do, and have faith that it will get him through. He'll be fine. Of all the younger cricketers I've played with, Nathan is the one who most reminds me of myself. I certainly have faith in him.

Giving the song to Nathan was definitely a statement I was making about values I was trying to pass on and preserve. I wanted to find someone who was going to be in the team, which was hard at that time, as so many people were coming in and out and Nathan could easily fall out of favour. Who else was definitely going to be in the team? But that itself wasn't a good reason. I wanted to choose the right character. Nathan plays the game for the right reasons, as I see it. I played because I loved the game and wanted to wear the baggy green cap. Nathan played with passion, with love of country.

While I was still in Melbourne I finished telling the boys, either in person or over the phone. I didn't know how to announce it publicly, but Maxi's plan was to do an exclusive with Channel Nine, perhaps cultivating a relationship that might lead to post-career work. But just as I was about to go into the studio, news came through that Tony Greig had passed away. That was obviously more important than my retirement interview. Part of me was relieved to be slipping into the background, while another part was feeling bad for Tony's family. Like Kerry Packer, he had been a key figure in making the game what it was for players of my generation and we owed him a great debt.

I was dizzy with conflicting emotions when we moved up to Sydney for the last Test match. It was extremely tough, not having been through it before. Maxi guided me through the media interviews, photo shoots and public appearances. I was still fighting him, saying it was interfering with my preparation for the Test match and this was exactly why I hadn't wanted to be the centre of attention. But he kept saying, 'In years to come you'll appreciate doing it this way, and other people will appreciate it.'

I put my trust and faith in him, and eventually agreed that it was the right thing to do. *Embrace it, it's never going to happen again.* I had nothing else to prove. I could enjoy my cricket and enjoy the crowd. Channel Nine put together some great footage that we can keep and look back on for the rest of our lives. I have fantastic memories of my last Test, and I was grateful to Maxi for pulling me out of my bubble and showing me the bigger picture.

I was grateful that Pup had lost the toss and we were fielding first. I'd have been too nervous to hold a bat, let alone use it. Just before we went out, Pup said, 'I want you to lead the team out.'

'No, no, come on mate, I want to play the Test as normally as possible, I've had all the stuff about me.'

He said, 'I'm not going out there until you lead the team out.'

'No, I really don't want to lead the team.'

Pup set his jaw in that way that only he can. He said, 'Well, okay, I'll stand here and the whole world will wait.'

Eventually I gave in. 'Ah, bugger you, okay.' It was a really nice gesture on his part. The reception from the public was overwhelming, far exceeding what I'd expected. Walking out onto the field, I was keeping it at arm's length, to preserve my cricket-concentration bubble, while also soaking it up, taking a look around and listening to what people were shouting out. The crowd had come out to say goodbye, and it was a way for me to say goodbye to them. It was a great feeling to be going out on my own terms. People often say it's good to go out when they're asking 'Why?' I had seen so many players, even some of the greatest, leave the game with bitterness and scars, and I was happy that I was walking away from the team with none of that, nothing but a sense of satisfaction about what I'd achieved.

We took the whole of the first day to dismiss Sri Lanka, and I waited 41 overs on the second before I had to bat. Steve Waugh had been at training in the lead-up to the Test. He said, 'I found I just wanted to get out there as quickly as I could and get on with it. If you take your time you might get too emotional and think too much about it all.'

With his words ringing in my ears, I bustled out there. As in my one-day debut, I didn't hear the crowd. In my head I was going through my mental routine for batting.

Suddenly I saw a guard of honour forming in the middle, among the Sri Lankans. I thought, *Oh no, I really don't want this, I just want to get on with the job.* Then I thought it was weird that they were doing this in the first innings. I might bat again in the second! But it was a very nice gesture. The last guy in the guard was Mahela Jayawardene, the skipper, and he shook my hand. He said, 'Good on you, mate.'

I said, 'If you really want to help, you can serve up a couple of half-volleys for me.'

He had a bit of a laugh, and then I got down to business as usual, trying to build a partnership with Pup. He'd been struggling with his back and hamstring. Normally we liked to run really hard, but this time he was saying, 'Just be careful on the quick ones, I'm struggling.'

We put on 56, and things were looking good for a last big stand. But then Pup called a quick single. I was shocked at first, after what he'd said, but, as always, I went on my partner's call. I charged and put in a big dive, but thought I was just short when the throw broke the wicket.

I went down the other end while we waited for the video umpire's decision. Pup was absolutely distraught, down on his haunches, moaning and shaking his head. 'Oh no, what have I done? What have I done?'

I said, 'Mate, don't worry about it, these things happen.'

When it came up as out, I gave him a pat on the back and said again, 'Don't worry about it, it's fine.'

And it really was. For once, when I got out, I was calm. I didn't feel like I had anything to prove to anyone. Poor Pup was really upset and even later he was down on himself about it. I did my best to make him feel better. He'd wanted to make it a big one for my last Test, and also to commemorate Tony Greig with a hundred, but cricket doesn't always reward your hopes.

Matty Wade's hundred gave us a good lead, and we worked our way through the Sri Lankan top order. As Sangakkara had injured himself in Melbourne and couldn't play, things were easier than normal, but a couple of their youngsters, Chandimal and Thirimanne, showed that there would be plenty of life in Sri Lankan cricket after their batting big guns retire.

On the fourth morning of the Test, I was hit with a bombshell. John Inverarity, the chairman of selectors, came up to me in the dressing room with Mickey Arthur and Michael Clarke at his side. They had just finalised the side for the one-day series.

John said, 'We're not playing you in the one-dayers.'

I was in shock. I don't think I said anything. John went on, 'We're happy to give you a farewell match in Perth.'

We went out to field. I was at second slip, my thoughts racing. When I could focus on the play, I thought, *Please don't hit it to me, I'm a 50 per cent chance at best of catching it.*

As the day went on and we battled to pick up the last wickets, I thought, *I don't want a charity match. Playing for Australia isn't a charity. I want to be in the team to win the series. I don't want to come in and distract and disrupt the whole team for one match.*

We finally got the Sri Lankans out and entered the fourth innings with a target of 141. It shouldn't have been a problem, but the pitch was wearing and Herath and Dilshan were the type of accurate, dangerous spin bowlers who could exploit our nerves.

I was desperately hoping not to bat. I wanted us to win no-wickets-down. But David Warner was out in the second over, Phil Hughes batted well but got out, and then Pup and Ed Cowan were grafting their way towards the target. I was sitting next to Mickey Arthur in the viewing area, next in, saying, 'Please guys, you do it!'

When we had about 40 to win, the crowd started yelling out, 'One of youse get out! We want Hussey!'

I *really* didn't want to bat now. I said to Mickey, 'Can you get someone on the loudspeaker to tell them to be quiet?'

When Pup got out, I felt bad, because he was the Australian captain and people were cheering. I didn't think that was right.

The game was there to be won, or lost. I raced out there and got on with it. Unlike in my previous couple of innings, I had the feeling that this was my day. The ball was finding the middle of the bat, even though it was spinning a lot. I was in control of my thoughts. I really enjoyed it.

We played some extra time to get the result before tea, but Mitch Johnson and I couldn't quite get there. I wasn't fussed. I enjoyed the twenty minutes off. In the break, Channel Nine played a tribute piece. I didn't want to watch it and get emotional, so I walked into another room and spent the break alone. All the boys were watching it, except me.

Soon after we went back out into the middle, I was facing Herath. They'd left cover open to tempt me into the big drive and get bowled by a ball spinning in out of the rough. I didn't want to expose one of the other guys waiting to bat, by trying to finish it with one big blow. Herath put one there, and I pushed it for a quick single. That would be the last ball I faced in Test cricket, and I finished how I got a lot of my runs, just wanting to get the job done in a professional manner.

Mitch came down the wicket. 'Huss, I don't want to hit the winning runs.'

I said, 'I don't care. If the ball's there, get it over with.'

That didn't go down well with him. He pushed one into a gap, but didn't want to run. I charged through anyway. Mitch felt a bit bad but I said, 'I just wanted it over.'

The Sri Lankan players and umpires came and said some very nice words of congratulation, and I got the chance to walk around and say goodbye to the crowd. I gave our team and support staff a hug, and then went to do media. It was over. I had my last chance to sing the team song.

While Sri Lanka were batting in their second innings, I found John Inverarity and said I didn't want the charity match in Perth. 'I want to be available for the whole one-day series or not at all.'

He said, 'That's a good choice. Okay, well, you're not playing then.'

I said, 'Oh, Okay.' I felt a bit let down, but I thought, *I've had a great finish in Sydney, for the sake of a few one-dayers it doesn't matter in the whole scheme of things.* It was a magical week and I didn't want to taint it by wondering about the politics underneath the situation.

I found Michael Clarke later, and told him my decision about the Perth one-dayer. He was very supportive, but still in shock about John telling me I wouldn't be picked.

'How did you not say anything?' he said. 'How did you not argue or disagree with him?'

'I was in shock,' I said.

He said, 'I was in shock too, but I couldn't believe you didn't say anything.'

'Mate, I didn't know what to say.'

It was good to talk with him about it. He couldn't say he agreed or disagreed with the selectors, which made it difficult for him. He had to present a united front. I certainly didn't hold it against him, but it was another confirmation of my opinion that the captain is too divided in his loyalties when he is on the selection panel. Later in the year, Michael came to the view that being a selector took up too much of a captain's time, and stood down.

If only the aftermath of the Test match had finished there, and we'd gone on and had a routine celebration! What happened over the next few hours and days didn't detract one iota from the joy and satisfaction I gained from my last day with the Australian team. I want to make that clear. Nothing was blemished. But there was a matter that became annoying, because it showed a disappointing side of a very small minority of the Australian public.

During the last Test, Gavin Dovey told me Pup had organised a night out on James Packer's boat several months in advance. It was a reward for the boys at the end of the summer, to thank them for their efforts and go out and celebrate in style on Sydney Harbour. When the arrangement was made, of course nobody had known it would be my last Test. I hadn't known it myself.

It turned out that no children would be allowed on the boat, for safety reasons. That was quite understandable. Partners were allowed, but we had all four of our kids in Sydney, and extended family and friends too. Amy and I both wanted to be with them and didn't want to leave the kids.

All this was pretty straightforward to me. I said to Gavin, 'I just want some hours to celebrate with the boys in the dressing room. I don't want to stop them from having the celebration on the boat.' It was a great opportunity for the team. We did it in 2006–07, and it was brilliant. I said, 'I reckon the boat will be great for the boys, but after we have our time in the dressing room as a team, I'll have my time with the family.'

We had a fantastic time in the dressing room. The team had organised for John Williamson to come in and sing 'True Blue' to us. It was a live-in-person way of calling the team song.

Afterwards, the team presented me with a watch and had organised another gift. A few people spoke some really nice words, and then the time came for everyone to go: the team to the boat, and me to my family.

When we got back to the hotel, the boys had to be downstairs in half an hour to assemble for the boat trip. A few of the support staff had children, so we were all going to meet at the mezzanine and have some pizzas.

Unfortunately, when they came down to leave, some of the boys didn't know about my conversation with Gavin and assumed I was going on the boat. Peter Siddle and Nathan Lyon came up to the mezzanine and said, 'What's going on? Aren't you coming?'

I said, 'I'm staying with the family, but I want you to go, you'll have a great time.'

Sidds, who was now a teetotaller, decided to stay at the hotel. I talked Nathan into going. 'It'll be a great experience, you're part of the team going forward, go on, have a good time.'

As far as the celebrations were concerned, I was more than happy. We'd had our time in the dressing room. The night came and went, and I went to bed a very happy man. Everything had turned out as I wanted.

Or had it? The next morning, I woke up to a phone message from Gavin saying, 'I really want to talk to you in the morning.'

I thought, *Oh no, what's happened*, and called him in a panic to ask what it was about.

'Come and have a chat,' he said.

I had no idea what had gone on, and was quite flustered when I met him downstairs at the hotel.

Gavin said, 'I'm a bit concerned that a couple of the players were really disappointed that you didn't go on the boat. They thought the team should have stayed with you, whereas others thought they should have gone on the boat.'

Shane Watson and Peter Siddle, he said, had told him the team shouldn't have gone on the boat without me. I said, 'We've been through this, I've told you I had no problems with the guys going on the boat.'

He said, 'We both know that, but the boys didn't know that, and we're worried it'll cause divisions in the team going forward.'

I agreed that we needed them all on the same page, so I spoke to Watto and Sidds and calmly explained the process, telling them the boat had been arranged months before, I didn't have any issues and it was all above board. Sidds was fine. He said it was a bit disappointing that the whole team didn't stay with me, but he accepted it. Watto was not so accepting. He was adamant that the team should have changed its plans and stuck with me.

I kept telling him, 'Look, I had no problems, it was fine.'

It shouldn't have been an issue. But a week or so later an email turned up, written by someone who clearly had it in for Michael Clarke.

For what it's worth, here's an edited version of the relevant parts of the email:

Mike [Hussey] apparently was promised at a minimum two one-dayers in the ODI series, in Perth. He was promised this on the back of 'best available' talk. It is probably worth mentioning that a lot of the players are a bit scared of Clarke in terms of the fact that he is a selector now, so they avoid trying to piss him off. Anyways at some point Clarke called Mike over (after the end of play) and asked if he could have a word. In this discussion he told Mike that he wouldn't be playing because they were 'looking to the future'. Mike asked about best available side and all that shit and Clarke said, 'You can have a lap of honour before we play the ODI in Perth', to which Mike told him to shove his lap up his ass.

Cricket Australia didn't want to announce the axing, but certain members of the Hussey camp 'accidentally' dropped the hint to journos around the country. Clarkey wasn't happy about this and I guess it set the tone for the following couple of days (this was after play day 3 from memory).

So then the day before the game finished, Mike was asked by Clarke what he wanted to do for his last game, and he said that he wanted to just sit in the change rooms and get pissed with the team and the entire support staff. Michael Clarke then proceeded the following day to organise to go on James Packer's massive boat (which they could do any time for the next 3 days) but he wanted to go that evening the Test ended.

As a side note, they all get pretty expensive retirement gifts from the team, and Mike (being in charge of the song) will change the ipod to John Williamson's 'True Blue' – this is when the team knows to get in a huddle to sing the team song. Anyways, someone turned the music off, and Mike started complaining that someone had f---ed the ipod up ... next minute John Williamson walks in singing 'True Blue' ... thought that was pretty cool. So anyway, Clarke tried to turn it and say 'I did this for you, Mike' (the boat) when he already knew Mike didn't want to go to the boat, he wanted to get pissed in the change rooms. So at the end of the day everyone is in the change room drinking, Clarke had left early because he wanted to go on the boat, and some players (including Warner) left as well. When it was time to leave for the boat a couple of players asked Mike if he was coming, and Mike was like, 'Nah, go have fun, I will stay and celebrate with my family and the support staff'. Nathan Lyon (Mike's best friend in the team) said 'F--- that, if Huss isn't going, I'm not going'. Then Watto said the same. As vice-captain, that meant that a lot, because the players came back to the room and were gonna bail on the boat, because they weren't worried as much about Clarke losing it.

So the next minute they get word that Clarke has made the boat an 'official Cricket Australia function', which means the players get in trouble for not attending. This forced a lot of the players to leave. Siddle and Lyon and the support staff were the only ones left from what I understand, absolutely petty and s--- form from Clarke considering that they could have gone on the boat the following night.

So in the end Mike, his family and the support staff stayed in the rooms. Mike then woke up with a voicemail from Clarke which abused the s--- out of him for leaking to the media and about how he didn't go on the boat with the players. Then Clarke put David Warner on the phone, who abused the s--- out of him as well. Mike just took it in his stride and didn't respond, and the next morning in the lobby of the hotel Clarke wouldn't even look at him. Mike apparently said, 'Hey Clarkey, one day you'll know,' and that was the last words they had exchanged.

Mike was referring to the fact that Clarke ... can't understand why Mike is retiring (young family etc).

The next thing I knew, I got a call from Paul Marsh at the ACA saying, 'This email's been circulating. Is there any merit in it?'

The point in reprinting it is to show how wrong it was. I've been asked about it by so many people, it's worthwhile to address thoroughly.

First, I was never 'promised' a 'victory lap' at the WACA or two one-dayers.

Second, it was John Inverarity, not Michael Clarke, who made the offer of a one-day match as a farewell. As I recounted above, the conversations were between me and John. Michael was very empathetic to my situation, and I certainly did not tell him to stick anything up his ass.

Third, there was no 'leak' from the 'Hussey camp' to anyone. I didn't even know there was a 'Hussey camp'! The email named the source as Amy's brother, who's a lovely twenty-year-old knockabout kid. He had been on the trip to help us out with the children, and was drawn into this innocently.

Fourth, the boat trip had been organised months in advance, not the same day, and there was no flexibility. By no means was it arranged in defiance of my wishes to spend time with the team in the dressing room.

Fifth, there was no call from Michael Clarke (or David Warner) abusing me about leaking information. The only call I had from anyone in the team was on the night, when a few of them got on the phone after a few more beers and said they wished I was there. It was all very light-hearted.

Sixth, there was no conversation or encounter of any kind between me and Michael Clarke the following day. That was pure fiction.

I could just ignore the whole thing and consign the email to the trash bin, where it belongs. But I'd never been targeted like that before, so it was an upsetting thing to have to go through.

It was hurtful on a number of levels. It put a dampener on what was otherwise a great time for me and the team. And I was worried it would affect my relationship with Michael. As soon as I saw it, I rang him and left a message and said, 'There's this email floating around; it's a pack of lies and I had nothing to do with it.'

When we eventually spoke, he was angry about this email. He's had his image attacked at different times and is used to it, but he was angry to see that someone close to the team had been a source, giving the writer enough grains of truth – the John Williamson story, the boat, and so on – for them to think they were onto something. It must have come from someone close to the team, and that was what worried him. Michael's manager tracked it back to a guy in the Sydney financial markets who'd been at the cricket getting drunk every day, heard some gossip and decided to write this email. I didn't know this guy, and nor did anyone in my family. He was just using my situation as a vehicle to drive a grudge he had against Michael.

If it wasn't hurtful, and public knowledge, it would be laughable. This person had a few dots, but when he joined them, he formed a picture that was wildly off the mark.

I don't want to hide from it because I know the truth. The truth doesn't reflect badly on everyone – we were all trying to do the right thing. There was a miscommunication about what I wanted to do on the night, but these things happen. If it said anything, the whole affair confirmed, first of all, that there are some nasty pieces of work out there, and secondly, that communications and trust among the close cricket fraternity were not what they could have been. This lack of trust came to the surface when the team went to India and England later in the year.

THIRTY-SIX

When the Australian team went to India and lost the Test series 4–0, there were calls to 'Bring back Hussey'. I find this flattering, but they were probably coming from the same people who, if I'd gone and struggled with the bat, would have been calling 'Hussey's got to go.' That's the nature of the game. All I knew was that I was finished with international cricket. When I saw the boys struggling with the spin of Ravi Ashwin and Ravindra Jadeja, I wasn't missing it and certainly didn't think I could have done any better. When each wicket fell, I was thinking, *Gee it looks like really hard work out there.*

I haven't had a moment's regret about retiring. Perhaps the timing could have been better from the team's point of view, but that's only if I was still eager to play. I wasn't anymore. The 2013 year could easily have turned into a cricketing nightmare for me. Being away from home for months on end playing some really tough cricket where you need to be 100 per cent committed to the training, travel and games is something I was not prepared to do. My worry was that I would let myself, the team and the country down if my heart was not fully up for those challenges.

My thoughts were turning to life after cricket. I was playing another season with the Chennai Super Kings, which I thought would be my last. It may seem strange that I quit international cricket to spend time with my family, only to go to India for two months. But it was two months of hard work, and then I could spend all of the winter months at home while the boys would be locked in a massive Ashes battle in England.

Amy also agreed that going cold turkey on cricket mightn't be the best thing for me. I've given my life to this great game. To suddenly turn the switch off might be too big a shock. So the IPL, and the Big Bash League, are my ways of phasing out gradually, as I've seen players such as Gilly and Warnie do.

I've loved all my seasons with CSK. The Twenty20 game fascinates me, which is a surprise. I've seen the format evolve and improve. When we started, it was, 'Go out there and swing, play it like it's the last five overs of an ODI.'

These days, a lot more thought goes into it. At CSK my plan was for the first two overs just to play normally and get ourselves in, and then go hard on the last four overs of the first powerplay. Then we would consolidate again until the 12th or 13th overs, from which it was, 'Hit out or get out, as we have some fantastic hitters like Dhoni, Bravo, Morkel and Jadeja to come in and finish the innings off.' That's how we set up our batting plan. The bowlers have become a lot smarter too and have brought the scores down by experimenting with different types of balls like wide yorkers, slower-ball bouncers, and slower balls. You don't know what's coming next.

I tend to agree that the interests of the crowds are put above those of the players – you don't spend your life playing and training so that you can bowl for four overs or bat for 20 balls – but Twenty20 has been fantastic for the game by introducing cricket to young kids, women, and people who like a short, fun format. Once they've fallen in love with that format, they might follow the longer game. It gets a volume of people in. In Australia, the competition from other sports is so high, you need to keep working to attract audiences.

In the last five years, Twenty20 tournaments have become a lot more serious too. They've moved from entertainment to a very seriously contested competition. The coaches and players want to keep their jobs, by winning, and the supporters want success. Even though it's fun, it's not a circus.

I was planning to join the CSK coaching staff as a batting coach for 2014. I was a bit nervous about not playing much cricket and then going straight into IPL and having to perform under pressure, but Stephen Fleming and the owners have encouraged me to play another year as a batsman, where they think I'll provide more value to them.

At time of writing, I am waiting to see. All IPL contracts ended after the 2013 season, and it's up to the franchises to retain their players at the next auction. I'm hoping Chennai will buy me back. Meanwhile, I've signed up with the Sydney Thunder in the BBL to help that team get to the top. I look forward to a couple of months in a city that has given me so many great memories. It was an extremely tough decision to leave Perth Scorchers and one I agonised over for a long time, but it's a great opportunity to join a team that has been struggling and to try and help their revival as a respected team in the competition.

The idea of a life after cricket is strange. Like any professional sportsman, I have lived two lives: one in cricket and one outside. This book has been mainly about my cricket life. Now my focus is on my 'real' life. But when I think of how much I love the game, I can't imagine cutting that life off completely.

I have consulted a lot of retired players about how to deal with the next stage. Some want to get away from cricket altogether.

Others want to keep a 'cricket fix' through playing. Justin Langer and Allan Border were two greats who went on in Sheffield Shield cricket as they weaned themselves off their playing careers. Justin really wanted to keep playing, but he needed a project – to lead a team. When I played my last few games for Western Australia in early 2013, I didn't want the burden of leadership. The challenge of bat versus ball was motivation enough. I don't know if I want to go through all the rigours of leading a team. Others have gone into coaching, the media and management. Stephen Fleming, my coach at CSK in recent years, went from being captain of the New Zealand cricket team, making important decisions every day, to not having his phone ring. He found that tough, like a retiring CEO.

The best advice seems to be to try a bit of everything and see what I enjoy. People say, 'Figure out what you want to do. It's like batting. Figure out what you do best.' I understand that. I'm doing an institute of directors course, as I'm already on a couple of boards. I would like to do some media work. I hope to help coach some of the West Australian boys, but informally, not in a structured role, as I'm not ready to take on a full-time commitment involving travel.

As far as the wider game is concerned, I feel that it is in good shape in Australia and internationally. I have lost touch with grassroots cricket, having not been part of it for a decade or more, but as William grows older I am sure I will re-connect. He is playing Into Cricket, the first stage, which is popular with kids.

At grade cricket level, my one concern is that it doesn't have as many 28- to 35-year-olds playing as when I was with Wanneroo. Changes in society have meant that men that age are spending more time with their families, or working, and don't have the ability to give their weekends to a cricket club. The result is that there aren't so many good hard blokes to teach youngsters how to play. When I started playing A-grade, there were only two young guys like me, and the rest were much older. Now the proportion has been reversed. It's had a detrimental effect on the standard of play, which has been reflected at the next level. And then in state cricket, the same push for youth has affected the standards there, and made the jump to international cricket bigger than ever.

Internationally, I think the game is in pretty good shape. The ICC are spending a lot of money on developing new areas like China, Japan, South-East Asia and elsewhere. I applaud that, but would also like them to spend the majority of their money on making sure the core countries are strong. Some of them are having financial troubles and have weak first-class structures. Effort and money has to be put in to maintain that core.

An issue that international administrators have to face is suspect bowling actions. A lot of bowlers around the world have bad actions and some things need to be done. Players are thinking, 'He's getting away with it so I'll try to get away with it.' It's a common topic in dressing rooms and greatly frustrating. If you get out to a chucker, you feel you've been personally disadvantaged. It may cost your career. Authorities need to monitor suspect actions a lot closer.

I've spoken highly of T20 cricket and the good it's brought to the game. It's been brilliant in enticing young athletes to play cricket, which is paramount when other sporting codes are competing to sign them up from a young age. T20 has brought many more numbers to the game, and opened the door for more families, women and children to fall in love with cricket. But I do think it will have an impact on Test cricket. In T20 you're trying to clear the front leg and get the arms free. My grounding was in getting in line, batting for long periods and building scores. I'm already seeing first-class players whose techniques have been weakened, worldwide. And the mental capabilities are going out of the game. Now it's, 'Get on with it, get to 40 or 50 quickly, get the game moving.' With more and more T20 cricket being played, I believe that the emphasis is more on scoring quickly, hitting boundaries and power play. This could have an effect on Test cricket where defensive technique is so important; batting for long periods of time and building innings are skills that take years and years of practice to learn and execute, under pressure, in the middle.

After the allegations surrounding the 2013 IPL, it's hard to talk about Twenty20 cricket without mentioning the spectre of corruption. Cricket corruption sounds to me like it has been around throughout the history of the game and will possibly have a presence in years to come, but the game is doing a lot to educate and deter players. In my whole career in the Australian team I've never been approached by anyone with any corruption in mind. Players weren't paid that well in the past, whereas they are paid very well now. So the temptation is a lot lower. At the IPL and all international matches, there is a blanket rule to hand our phones in on the team bus before we arrive at the ground. There are devices detecting if mobile phones are being used in dressing rooms. But I'm not naïve to the fact that it still happens. Even if there's only be a tiny, tiny percentage of players who aren't competing in a great spirit and giving of their best. In all sports, a minority that causes scandals doesn't wreck the whole sport in the long term, but, that said, every step needs to be taken to rub out cheats with absolute finality.

I've made no secret of the fact that I always found batting a mental and emotional struggle. I don't know how I'll feel about not playing as time goes by. But I know for sure that I'm looking forward to not having that sick feeling in my stomach as I'm waiting to bat. I'm looking forward to no more stress about losing. I'm looking forward to no more public scrutiny and pressure on my batting.

I'm not a deep thinker about whether it's all been worthwhile. Obviously I'll never get back those months I missed of my children's early years, and all the time I missed with Amy. That was the price we paid. I have no regrets about it, but it's a high price. The honour of representing Australia in a game that I love gives me enormous pride and makes the sacrifices along the way worthwhile.

For so long, I was committed to my dream to play for Western Australia. Then there was a dream to play for Australia. Once I'd made it, there was a transition to: How do I keep playing for Australia? And finally it was: How do I want to be remembered?

I wanted to be a respected player and a respected team man and respected for how I played the game. When I was young I didn't think about that – it was about getting to the destination. But I hope I ended up achieving those goals in my years as an international player.

The main thing I want to be remembered for is as a good team man. The respect of my peers was everything. When I was given that guard of honour by the Sri Lankan players in Sydney, I was shocked. I didn't expect it or feel I deserved it, not compared to someone like Ricky Ponting. But maybe they and the public see me as someone who's played the game with good values. If that's so, I would feel hugely honoured.

During that last Test, a few people said that what encapsulated me was that whenever Australia was in trouble, they could depend on me to come out and save the team. That touched me. To be seen as a man for a dire situation makes me feel really good inside.

But you know what? On the inside, when those crises were happening and I was the next man in, I absolutely hated it! And I didn't feel like a dependable type. Nobody was more nervous than I was. But when I hear that at the other end of the struggle, people respected me for getting the job done, it does feel worthwhile.

My most precious memory of cricket at all levels is the time I've spent in the dressing room with the team after a good game. That's what it's all about. Everyone can be himself and show his true personality, and let go. That's what I really love, and where the laughter and fun is. The Australian dressing room is a sacred place. Not many people get to go in there, so I treasure that and will never forget what a privilege it was.

MICHAEL EDWARD KILLEEN HUSSEY

Born: May 27, 1975 Mount Lawley (Western Australia)
Left hand batsman – Right arm medium

CRICKET CAREER

Summary	M	Inn	NO	Runs	HS	0s	50	100	Avrge	Ct	Balls	Mdns	Runs	Wkts	Avrge	Best
Test Cricket	79	137	16	6235	195	12	29	19	51.53	85	588	11	306	7	43.71	1–0
Sheffield Shield	112	207	12	8007	223*	14	41	16	41.06	114	948	29	507	14	36.21	3–34
Other First-Class	82	142	21	8541	331*	5	33	26	70.59	108	516	22	280	6	46.67	1–5
First-Class	273	486	49	22783	331*	31	103	61	52.14	307	2052	62	1093	27	40.48	3–34
International One Day	185	157	44	5442	109*	3	39	3	48.16	105	240	1	235	2	117.50	1–22
Australian Domestic One Day	84	80	10	2720	106	5	21	3	38.86	46	276	–	329	10	32.90	3–52
International Twenty/20	38	30	11	721	60*	1	4	–	37.95	20	6	–	5	–	–	–
Indian Premier League	46	45	7	1691	116*	1	12	1	44.50	22	–	–	–	–	–	–
Big Bash Twenty/20	4	4	1	35	21*	1	–	–	11.67		–	–	–	–	–	–
Twenty/20 Career	105	96	21	3102	116*	3	22	1	41.36	55	6	–	5	–	–	–

HIGHEST BATTING AVERAGE FOR AUSTRALIA (Test cricket - Qualification 20 innings)

Batsman	Career	M	Inn	NO	Runs	HS	0s	50	100	Avrge
Don Bradman	1928–1948	52	80	10	6996	334	7	13	29	99.94
Greg Chappell	1970–1984	88	151	19	7110	247*	12	31	24	53.86
Michael Clarke	2004–2013	97	164	17	7656	329*	8	27	24	52.08
Ricky Ponting	1995–2012	168	287	29	13378	257	17	62	41	51.85
Jack Ryder	1920–1929	20	32	5	1394	201*	1	9	3	51.62
Michael Hussey	2005–2013	79	137	16	6235	195	12	29	19	51.53

FIRST CLASS TRIPLE CENTURIES BY AUSTRALIANS

Runs	Team	Opponent	Venue	Season
Don Bradman (6)				
340*	New South Wales	Victoria	Sydney	1928–29
452*	New South Wales	Queensland	Sydney	1929–30
334	AUSTRALIA	ENGLAND	Leeds	1930
304	AUSTRALIA	ENGLAND	Leeds	1934
357	South Australia	Victoria	Melbourne	1935–36
369	South Australia	Tasmania	Adelaide	1935–36
Bill Ponsford (4)				
429	Victoria	Tasmania	Melbourne	1922–23
352	Victoria	New South Wales	Melbourne	1926–27
437	Victoria	Queensland	Melbourne	1927–28
336	Victoria	South Australia	Melbourne	1927–28
Michael Hussey (3)				
329*	Northamptonshire	Essex	Northampton	2001
310*	Northamptonshire	Gloucestershire	Bristol	2002
331*	Northamptonshire	Somerset	Taunton	2003
Bobby Simpson (2)				
359	New South Wales	Queensland	Brisbane	1963–64
311	AUSTRALIA	ENGLAND	Manchester	1964
Justin Langer (2)				
342	Somerset	Surrey	Guildford	2006
315	Somerset	Middlesex	Taunton	2007

FOUR OR MORE CENTURIES IN CONSECUTIVE INNINGS

100s	Batsman	Centuries	Team	Opponent	Venue	Season
6	Don Bradman	118	DG Bradman's XI	KE Rigg's XI	Melbourne	1938–39
		143	South Australia	New South Wales	Adelaide	1938–39
		225	South Australia	Queensland	Adelaide	1938–39
		107	South Australia	Victoria	Melbourne	1938–39
		186	South Australia	Queensland	Brisbane	1938–39
		135*	South Australia	New South Wales	Sydney	1938–39
5	Michael Hussey	100	Northamptonshire	Hampshire	Southampton	2003
		331*	Northamptonshire	Somerset	Taunton	2003
		115	Northamptonshire	Derbyshire	Derby	2003
		187	Northamptonshire	Durham	Northampton	2003
		147	Northamptonshire	Glamorgan	Cardiff	2003

HIGHEST WICKET PARTNERSHIPS

Runs	Wkt	Batsmen	Team	Opponent	Venue	Season
334*	5th	Michael Clarke (329*) & Michael Hussey (150*)	AUSTRALIA	INDIA	Sydney	2011–12
320	4th	Jason Gillespie (201*) & Michael Hussey (182)	AUSTRALIA	BANGLADESH	Chittagong	2005–06
307	6th	Michael Hussey (195) & Brad Haddin (136)	AUSTRALIA	ENGLAND	Brisbane	2010–11

UNDERNEATH THE SOUTHERN CROSS

LONGEST INNINGS BY AUSTRALIANS

Mins	Batsman	Team	Opponent	Venue	Season
766	Michael Veletta (262)	Western Australia	Victoria	Perth	1986–87
762	Bobby Simpson (311)	AUSTRALIA	ENGLAND	Manchester	1964
727	Bob Cowper (307	AUSTRALIA	ENGLAND	Melbourne	1965–66
720	Mark Taylor (334*)	AUSTRALIA	PAKISTAN	Peshawar	1998–99
716	Graham Yallop (268)	AUSTRALIA	PAKISTAN	Melbourne	1983–84
708	Greg Shipperd (200*)	Tasmania	Western Australia	Perth	1989–90
653	Michael Hussey (310*)	Northamptonshire	Gloucestershire	Bristol	2002
651	Michael Hussey (331*)	Northamptonshire	Somerset	Taunton	2003

MOST RUNS FOR AUSTRALIA (Test cricket)

Batsman	Career	M	Inn	NO	Runs	HS	0s	50	100	Avrge
Ricky Ponting	1995–2012	168	287	29	13378	257	17	62	41	51.85
Allan Border	1978–1994	156	265	44	11174	205	11	63	27	50.56
Steve Waugh	1985–2004	168	260	46	10927	200	22	50	32	51.06
Matthew Hayden	1994–2009	103	184	14	8625	380	14	29	30	50.73
Mark Waugh	1991–2002	128	209	17	8029	153*	19	47	20	41.81
Justin Langer	1993–2007	105	182	12	7696	250	11	30	23	45.27
Michael Clarke	2004–2013	97	164	17	7656	329*	8	27	24	52.08
Mark Taylor	1989–1999	104	186	13	7525	334*	5	40	19	43.49
David Boon	1984–1986	107	190	20	7422	200	16	32	21	43.65
Greg Chappell	1970–1984	88	151	19	7110	247*	12	31	24	53.86
Don Bradman	1928–1948	52	80	10	6996	334	7	13	29	99.94
Michael Hussey	2005–2013	79	137	16	6235	195	12	29	19	51.53

MOST RUNS FOR AUSTRALIA (International One-days)

Batsman	Career	M	Inn	NO	Runs	HS	0s	50	100	Avrge
Ricky Ponting	1995–2012	374	364	39	13589	164	20	82	29	41.81
Adam Gilchrist	1996–2008	286	278	11	9595	172	19	55	16	35.93
Mark Waugh	1988–2002	244	236	20	8500	173	16	50	18	39.35
Steve Waugh	1986–2002	325	288	58	7569	120*	15	45	3	32.90
Michael Clarke	2003–2013	227	207	42	7375	130	10	54	7	44.69
Michael Bevan	1994–2004	232	196	67	6912	108*	5	46	6	53.58
Allan Border	1979–1994	273	252	39	6524	127*	11	39	3	30.62
Matthew Hayden	1993–2008	160	154	15	6131	181*	9	36	10	44.10
Dean Jones	1984–1994	164	161	25	6068	145	6	46	7	44.61
David Boon	1984–1995	181	177	16	5964	122	6	37	5	37.04
Michael Hussey	2004–2012	185	157	44	5442	109*	3	39	3	48.16

HIGHEST BATTING AVERAGE FOR AUSTRALIA (International One-days - Qualification 20 innings)

Batsman	Career	M	Inn	NO	Runs	HS	0s	50	100	Avrge
Michael Bevan	1994–2004	232	196	67	6912	108*	5	46	6	53.58
Michael Hussey	2004–2012	185	157	44	5442	109*	3	39	3	48.16
Michael Clarke	2003–2013	227	207	42	7375	130	10	54	7	44.69
Dean Jones	1984–1994	164	161	25	6068	145	6	46	7	44.61
Matthew Hayden	1993–2008	160	154	15	6131	181*	9	36	10	44.10

LEAST DAYS TO REACH 100 TEST RUNS

165	Michael Hussey (Australia)
229	Andrew Strauss (England)
244	Bert Sutcliffe (England)
268	Brian Luckhurst (England)
291	Michael Slater (Australia)
295	Kevin Pietersen (England)
300	Alistair Cook (England)
304	Rahaul Dravid (India)
320	Mark Taylor (Australia)
340	Michael Clarke (Australia)

LEAST INNINGS TO REACH 100 TEST RUNS

12	Bert Sutcliffe (England)	17	Graeme Smith (South Africa)
12	Everton Weekes (West Indies)	18	Bert Collins (Australia)
13	Don Bradman (Australia)	18	Wally Hammond (England)
14	Neil Harvey (Australia)	18	Doug Walters (Australia)
14	Vinod Kambli (India)	18	Mark Taylor (Australia)
16	Len Hutton (England)	18	Jimmy Adams (West Indies)
16	Frank Worrell (West Indies)	18	Cheteshwar Pujara (India)
16	Lawrence Rowe (West Indies)	19	Arthur Morris (Australia)
17	George Headley (West Indies)	19	Andrew Strauss (England)
17	Sid Barnes (Australia)	19	Michael Hussey (Australia)

MOST FIRST-CLASS CAREER RUNS BY AUSTRALIANS

Batsman	Career	M	Inn	NO	Runs	HS	0s	50	100	Avrge
Justin Langer	1991–2009	360	622	57	28382	342	38	110	86	50.23
Don Bradman	1927–1949	234	338	43	28067	452*	16	69	117	95.14
Allan Border	1976–1996	385	625	97	27131	205	32	142	70	51.38
Stuart Law	1988–2009	367	601	65	27069	263	39	128	79	50.50
Mark Waugh	1985–2004	368	591	75	26855	229*	47	133	81	52.04
Darren Lehmann	1987–2007	284	479	33	25795	339	20	111	82	57.84
Michael Di Venuto	1991–2012	335	589	42	25078	254*	42	145	60	45.85
Matthew Hayden	1991–2009	295	515	47	24603	380	28	100	79	52.57
Greg Chappell	1966–1984	322	542	73	24535	247*	28	111	74	52.31
Ricky Ponting	1992–2013	289	494	62	24150	257	22	106	82	55.90
Steve Waugh	1984–2004	356	551	88	24052	216*	39	97	79	51.95
David Boon	1978–1999	350	585	53	23413	227	35	114	68	44.01
Michael Hussey	1994–2012	273	486	50	22783	331*	31	103	61	52.25

FIRST-CLASS CAREER

Debut:- 1994–95 Western Australia v Tasmania, Hobart

Season	Country	M	Inn	NO	Runs	HS	0s	50	100	Avrge	Ct	Balls	Mdns	Runs	Wkts	Avrge	Best
1994–95	Australia	1	1	–	16	16	–	–	–	16.00	–	–	–	–	–	–	–
1995–96	Australia	12	24	1	945	146	–	3	2	41.09	9	–	–	–	–	–	–
1996–97	Australia	12	22	2	928	147	–	5	2	46.40	5	6	–	2	–	–	–
1997–98	Australia	12	21	2	915	134	1	3	3	48.16	3	–	–	–	–	–	–
1998–99	Scotland	1	1	–	67	67	–	1	–	67.00	–	–	–	–	–	–	–
1998–99	Ireland	1	1	1	125	125*	–	–	1	–	–	–	–	–	–	–	–
1998–99	Australia	12	22	–	907	187	1	7	1	41.23	8	130	6	61	2	30.50	2–21
1999–00	Australia	10	18	1	874	172*	2	3	3	51.41	13	90	4	44	1	44.00	1–11
2000–01	Australia	11	21	1	605	137	1	1	1	30.25	13	102	4	63	–	–	–
2001	England	16	30	4	2055	329*	–	9	5	79.04	19	108	2	78	2	39.00	1–14
2001–02	Australia	11	19	1	621	100	2	4	1	34.50	16	42	1	21	–	–	–
2002	England	13	23	3	1442	310*	2	4	5	72.10	21	–	–	–	–	–	–
2002–03	Australia	10	17	1	610	145	2	4	1	38.13	13	–	–	–	–	–	–
2003	England	14	21	2	1697	331*	–	5	6	89.32	17	84	2	52	1	52.00	1–5
2003–04	Australia	11	22	–	920	138	1	8	1	41.82	17	264	15	124	3	41.33	1–10
2004	England	7	13	1	442	78	2	2	–	36.83	10	48	2	22	–	–	–
2004–05	Australia	9	17	3	851	223*	1	2	3	60.79	11	386	13	167	8	20.88	3–34
2005	England	10	18	4	1074	253	1	5	3	76.71	19	72	–	59	1	59.00	1–36
2005–06	Pakistan	2	4	1	129	101*	–	–	1	43.00	3	–	–	–	–	–	–
2005–06	Australia	7	13	3	730	137	–	2	3	73.00	4	48	1	33	1	33.00	1–21
2005–06	South Africa	3	5	1	257	89	–	3	–	64.25	2	12	–	6	–	–	–
2005–06	Bangladesh	2	3	–	242	182	–	–	1	80.67	–	–	–	–	–	–	–
2006–07	Australia	6	9	2	504	103	1	4	1	72.00	6	48	1	30	1	30.00	1–25
2007–08	Australia	8	14	3	716	145*	2	2	3	65.09	13	30	–	33	–	–	–
2007–08	West Indies	4	7	–	156	56	–	1	–	22.29	5	36	2	14	–	–	–
2008–09	India	5	8	1	520	146	–	3	2	74.29	4	72	2	41	–	–	–
2008–09	Australia	5	9	1	190	70	3	1	–	23.75	3	30	–	22	1	22.00	1–22
2008–09	South Africa	3	6	–	132	50	1	1	–	22.00	1	–	–	–	–	–	–
2009	England	7	12	2	572	150	2	4	2	57.20	7	–	–	–	–	–	–
2009–10	Australia	6	11	2	502	134*	–	3	1	55.78	8	12	–	3	1	3.00	1–3
2009–10	New Zealand	2	3	–	93	67	–	1	–	31.00	2	–	–	–	–	–	–
2010	England	2	4	1	69	56*	1	1	–	23.00	3	–	–	–	–	–	–
2010–11	India	2	4	–	99	34	–	–	–	24.75	2	–	–	–	–	–	–
2010–11	Australia	8	15	–	721	195	3	3	3	48.07	8	6	–	2	–	–	–
2011–12	Sri Lanka	4	6	–	491	142	–	2	2	81.83	4	42	4	7	2	3.50	1–0
2011–12	South Africa	3	5	1	101	41*	1	–	–	25.25	1	66	–	31	–	–	–
2011–12	Australia	6	9	1	316	150*	2	1	1	39.50	11	180	1	79	2	39.50	1–7
2011–12	West Indies	3	6	–	219	73	–	1	–	36.50	3	48	1	25	1	25.00	1–19
2012–13	Australia	12	22	4	930	115*	–	4	3	51.67	23	90	1	74	–	–	–
Test Cricket		79	137	16	6235	195	12	29	19	51.53	85	588	11	306	7	43.71	1–0
Sheffield Shield		112	207	12	8007	223*	14	41	16	41.06	114	948	29	507	14	36.21	3–34
Others		82	142	21	8541	331*	5	33	26	70.59	108	516	22	280	6	46.67	1–5
Total		273	486	49	22783	331*	31	103	61	52.14	307	2052	62	1093	27	40.48	3–34

	Inn	NO	Runs	HS	0s	50	100	Avrge	Ct	Balls	Mdns	Runs	Wkts	Avrge	Best
First Innings	136	5	7234	329*	10	29	23	55.22	88	564	11	355	9	39.44	2–21
Second Innings	136	12	7516	331*	6	25	24	60.61	95	600	27	281	7	40.14	3–49
Third Innings	132	12	5127	150	12	32	11	42.73	56	216	6	121	1	121.00	1–20
Fourth Innings	82	20	2906	121	3	17	3	46.87	68	672	18	336	10	33.60	3–34

Batting Position	Inn	NO	Runs	HS	0s	50	100	Avrge
1/2	304	25	15009	331*	13	65	40	53.80
3	27	1	797	118	5	3	1	30.65
4	76	10	3187	150	8	18	9	48.29
5	45	7	2272	195	3	11	6	59.79
6	29	4	1364	150*	2	5	5	54.56
7	5	2	154	54	–	1	–	51.33

Highest Score: 331* Northamptonshire v Somerset, Taunton, 2003
Best Bowling:- 3–34 Western Australia v Queensland, Brisbane, 2004–05

Team	M	Inn	NO	Runs	HS	0s	50	100	Avrge	Ct	Balls	Mdns	Runs	Wkts	Avrge	Best
Australia A	7	12	2	643	145	–	3	3	64.30	8	–	–	–	–	–	–
AUSTRALIA	79	137	16	6235	195	12	29	19	51.53	85	588	11	306	7	43.71	1–0
Australian XI	6	8	4	510	150	–	2	2	127.50	6	12	–	7	–	–	–
Durham	10	18	4	1074	253	1	5	3	76.71	19	72	–	59	1	59.00	1–36
Gloucestershire	7	13	1	442	78	2	2	–	36.83	10	48	2	22	–	–	–
Northamptonshire	43	74	8	5194	331*	1	18	16	78.70	57	192	4	130	3	43.33	1–5
Western Australia	121	224	14	8685	223*	15	44	18	41.36	122	1140	45	569	16	35.56	3–34

100s	Team	Opponent	Venue	Season
146*	Western Australia	Pakistanis	Perth	1995–96
105	Western Australia	New South Wales	Sydney	1995–96
147	Western Australia	Victoria	Perth	1996–97
138	Western Australia	Victoria	Melbourne	1996–97
108	Western Australia	Tasmania	Hobart	1997–98
134	Western Australia	South Australia	Adelaide	1997–98
120	Western Australia	New South Wales	Perth	1997–98
125*	Australia A	Ireland	Dublin	1998–99
187	Western Australia	Tasmania	Perth	1998–99
112	Western Australia	Tasmania	Perth	1999–00
172*	Western Australia	South Australia	Perth	1999–00
172	Western Australia	New South Wales	Sydney	1999–00
137	Western Australia	Victoria	Melbourne	2000–01
159	Northamptonshire	Glamorgan	Cardiff	2001
122	Northamptonshire	Yorkshire	Northampton	2001
329*	Northamptonshire	Essex	Northampton	2001
232	Northamptonshire	Leicestershire	Northampton	2001
208	Northamptonshire	Somerset	Taunton	2001
100	Western Australia	New South Wales	Sydney	2001–02

100s	Team	Opponent	Venue	Season
170	Northamptonshire	Worcestershire	Northampton	2002
150	Northamptonshire	Derbyshire	Derby	2002
140	Northamptonshire	Essex	Northampton	2002
174	Northamptonshire	Worcestershire	Worcester	2002
310*	Northamptonshire	Gloucestershire	Bristol	2002
145	Australia A	South Africa A	Perth	2002–03
264	Northamptonshire	Gloucestershire	Gloucester	2003
100	Northamptonshire	Hampshire	Southampton	2003
331*	Northamptonshire	Somerset	Taunton	2003
115	Northamptonshire	Derbyshire	Derby	2003
187	Northamptonshire	Durham	Northampton	2003
147	Northamptonshire	Glamorgan	Cardiff	2003
138	Western Australia	Tasmania	Perth	2003–04
210	Western Australia	Tasmania	Perth	2004–05
124	Western Australia	Pakistanis	Perth	2004–05
223*	Western Australia	Victoria	Perth	2004–05
253	Durham	Leicestershire	Leicester	2005
144*	Durham	Lancashire	Manchester	2005
146	Durham	Leicestershire	Chester-le-Street	2005
101*	Australia A	Pakistan A	Rawalpindi	2005–06
137	AUSTRALIA	WEST INDIES	Hobart	2005–06
133*	AUSTRALIA	WEST INDIES	Adelaide	2005–06
122	AUSTRALIA	SOUTH AFRICA	Melbourne	2005–06
182	AUSTRALIA	BANGLADESH	Chittagong	2005–06
103	AUSTRALIA	ENGLAND	Perth	2006–07
133	AUSTRALIA	SRI LANKA	Brisbane	2007–08
132	AUSTRALIA	SRI LANKA	Hobart	2007–08
145*	AUSTRALIA	INDIA	Sydney	2007–08
126*	Australian XI	Indian Board President's XI	Hyderabad	2008–09
146	AUSTRALIA	INDIA	Bangalore	2008–09
150	Australian XI	England Lions	Worcester	2009
121	AUSTRALIA	ENGLAND	The Oval	2009
134*	AUSTRALIA	PAKISTAN	Sydney	2009–10
118	Western Australia	Victoria	Melbourne	2010–11
195	AUSTRALIA	ENGLAND	Brisbane	2010–11
116	AUSTRALIA	ENGLAND	Perth	2010–11
142	AUSTRALIA	SRI LANKA	Pallekele	2011–12
118	AUSTRALIA	SRI LANKA	Colombo	2011–12
150*	AUSTRALIA	INDIA	Sydney	2011–12
100	AUSTRALIA	SOUTH AFRICA	Brisbane	2012–13
103	AUSTRALIA	SOUTH AFRICA	Adelaide	2012–13
115*	AUSTRALIA	SRI LANKA	Hobart	2012–13

TEST CAREER

Debut:- 2005–06 Australia v West Indies, Brisbane

Series	Opponent	Venue	M	Inn	NO	Runs	HS	0s	50	100	Avrge	Ct	Balls	Mdns	Runs	Wkts	Avrge	Best
2005–06	West Indies	Australia	3	6	3	361	137	–	–	2	120.33	–	–	–	–	–	–	–
2005–06	South Africa	Australia	3	5	–	279	122	–	1	1	55.80	1	12	–	12	–	–	–
2005–06	South Africa	South Africa	3	5	1	257	89	–	3	–	64.25	2	12	–	6	–	–	–
2005–06	Bangladesh	Bangladesh	2	3	–	242	182	–	–	1	80.67	–	–	–	–	–	–	–
2006–07	England	Australia	5	7	2	458	103	–	4	1	91.60	5	6	–	5	–	–	–
2007–08	Sri Lanka	Australia	2	3	1	299	133	–	–	2	149.50	3	–	–	–	–	–	–
2007–08	India	Australia	4	7	1	292	145*	1	–	1	48.67	9	–	–	–	–	–	–
2007–08	West Indies	West Indies	3	6	–	137	56	–	1	–	22.83	5	36	2	14	–	–	–
2008–09	India	India	4	7	–	394	146	–	3	1	56.29	2	72	2	41	–	–	–
2008–09	New Zealand	Australia	5	9	1	190	70	3	1	–	23.75	3	30	–	22	1	22.00	1–22
2008–09	South Africa	South Africa	3	6	–	132	50	1	1	–	22.00	1	–	–	–	–	–	–
2009	England	England	5	8	–	276	121	2	2	1	34.50	6	–	–	–	–	–	–
2009–10	West Indies	Australia	3	5	–	235	82	–	2	–	47.00	5	12	–	3	1	3.00	1–3
2009–10	Pakistan	Australia	3	6	2	267	134*	–	1	1	66.75	3	–	–	–	–	–	–
2009–10	New Zealand	New Zealand	2	3	–	93	67	–	1	–	31.00	2	–	–	–	–	–	–
2010	Pakistan	England	2	4	1	69	56*	1	1	–	23.00	3	–	–	–	–	–	–
2010–11	India	India	2	4	–	99	34	–	–	–	24.75	2	–	–	–	–	–	–
2010–11	England	Australia	5	9	–	570	195	1	3	2	63.33	5	6	–	2	–	–	–
2011–12	Sri Lanka	Sri Lanka	3	5	–	463	142	–	2	2	92.60	2	42	4	7	2	3.50	1–0
2011–12	South Africa	South Africa	2	4	–	60	39	1	–	–	15.00	–	54	–	24	–	–	–
2011–12	New Zealand	Australia	2	3	–	23	15	1	–	–	7.67	4	66	1	27	2	13.50	1–7
2011–12	India	Australia	4	6	1	293	150*	1	1	1	58.60	7	114	–	52	–	–	–
2011–12	West Indies	West Indies	3	6	–	219	73	–	1	–	36.50	3	48	1	25	1	25.00	1–19
2012–13	South Africa	Australia	3	5	–	295	103	–	1	2	59.00	3	54	–	54	–	–	–
2012–13	Sri Lanka	Australia	3	5	3	232	115*	–	–	1	116.00	9	24	1	12	–	–	–
Total			79	137	16	6235	195	12	29	19	51.53	85	588	11	306	7	43.71	1–0

	Inn	NO	Runs	HS	0s	50	100	Avrge	Ct	Balls	Mdns	Runs	Wkts	Avrge	Best
First Innings	46	3	2189	146	4	13	7	50.91	24	162	2	90	2	45.00	1–19
Second Innings	33	2	1890	195	2	7	7	60.97	21	114	2	63	1	63.00	1–0
Third Innings	41	6	1527	145*	5	7	4	43.63	23	66	2	31	–	–	–
Fourth Innings	17	5	629	121	1	2	1	52.42	17	246	5	122	4	30.50	1–2

Batting Position	Inn	NO	Runs	HS	0s	50	100	Avrge
1/2	8	1	387	137	–	1	1	55.29
4	62	7	2531	146	7	14	7	46.02
5	38	5	1978	195	3	9	6	59.94
6	26	2	1242	150*	2	4	5	51.75
7	3	1	97	54	–	1	–	48.50

Highest Score:- 195 Australia v England, Brisbane, 2010–11

Best Bowling:- 1–0 Australia v Sri Lanka, Pallekele, 2011–12

SHEFFIELD SHIELD CAREER

Debut:- 1994–95 Western Australia v Tasmania, Hobart

Season	Team	M	Inn	NO	Runs	HS	0s	50	100	Avrge	Ct	Balls	Mdns	Runs	Wkts	Avrge	Best
1994–95	West Australia	1	1	–	16	16	–	–	–	16.00	–	–	–	–	–	–	–
1995–96	West Australia	11	22	1	782	105	–	3	1	37.24	8	–	–	–	–	–	–
1996–97	West Australia	11	20	2	887	147	–	5	2	49.28	5	6	–	2	–	–	–
1997–98	West Australia	11	19	1	782	134	1	1	3	43.44	3	–	–	–	–	–	–
1998–99	West Australia	11	20	–	877	187	1	7	1	43.85	8	130	6	61	2	30.50	2–21
1999–00	West Australia	10	18	1	874	172*	2	3	3	51.41	13	90	4	44	1	44.00	1–11
2000–01	West Australia	10	19	1	553	137	1	1	1	30.72	12	90	4	56	–	–	–
2001–02	West Australia	10	18	1	600	100	2	4	1	35.29	16	18	1	6	–	–	–
2002–03	West Australia	7	11	1	348	90	1	3	–	34.80	7	–	–	–	–	–	–
2003–04	West Australia	9	18	–	752	138	1	6	1	41.78	14	198	7	114	2	57.00	1–20
2004–05	West Australia	8	15	2	721	223*	1	2	2	55.46	9	296	5	137	7	19.57	3–34
2005–06	West Australia	1	2	–	90	86	–	1	–	45.00	3	36	1	21	1	21.00	1–21
2006–07	West Australia	1	2	–	46	46	1	–	–	23.00	1	42	1	25	1	25.00	1–25
2007–08	West Australia	2	4	1	125	59*	1	2	–	41.67	1	30	–	33	–	–	–
2010–11	West Australia	3	6	–	151	118	2	–	1	25.17	3	–	–	–	–	–	–
2012–13	West Australia	6	12	1	403	99*	–	3	–	36.64	11	12	–	8	–	–	–
Total		112	207	12	8007	223*	14	41	16	41.06	114	948	29	507	14	36.21	3–34

	Inn	NO	Runs	HS	0s	50	100	Avrge	Ct	Balls	Mdns	Runs	Wkts	Avrge	Best
First Innings	50	–	1910	187	4	8	4	38.20	26	300	8	189	5	37.80	2–21
Second Innings	62	4	2945	223*	4	12	8	50.78	41	264	7	140	3	46.67	3–49
Third Innings	52	1	1662	137	5	12	3	32.59	16	108	3	68	1	68.00	1–20
Fourth Innings	43	7	1490	108	1	9	1	41.39	31	276	11	110	5	22.00	3–34

Batting Position	Inn	NO	Runs	HS	0s	50	100	Avrge
1/2	176	8	7033	223*	11	35	15	41.86
3	13	–	327	118	3	1	1	25.15
4	9	2	286	90	–	3	–	40.86
5	6	1	285	99*	–	2	–	57.00
6	1	–	19	19	–	–	–	19.00
7	2	1	57	32	–	–	–	57.00

Highest Score:- 223* Western Australia v Victoria, Perth, 2004–05

Best Bowling:- 3–34 Western Australia v Queensland, Brisbane, 2004–05

MICHAEL HUSSEY

INTERNATIONAL LIMITED-OVERS CAREER

Debut:- 2003–04 Australia v India, Perth

Opponents	M	Inn	NO	Runs	HS	0s	50	100	Avrge	Ct	Balls	Mdns	Runs	Wkts	Avrge	Best
Afghanistan	1	1	–	49	49	–	–	–	49.00	1	–	–	–	–	–	–
Bangladesh	13	8	4	376	108	–	2	1	94.00	4	108	1	72	1	72.00	1–22
Canada	1	–	–	–	–	–	–	–	–	–	–	–	–	–	–	–
England	29	22	5	663	84	1	4	–	39.00	13	48	–	65	1	65.00	1–31
India	21	19	6	770	81*	–	7	–	59.23	11	36	–	41	–	–	–
Ireland	2	2	1	38	30*	–	–	–	38.00	–	–	–	–	–	–	–
Kenya	1	1	–	54	54	–	1	–	54.00	–	–	–	–	–	–	–
New Zealand	30	27	10	1038	105	–	8	1	61.06	27	18	–	22	–	–	–
Netherlands	1	1	–	2	2	–	–	–	2.00	1	–	–	–	–	–	–
Pakistan	10	10	2	427	67	–	4	–	53.38	2	18	–	20	–	–	–
Sri Lanka	28	23	8	477	71*	2	3	–	31.80	16	–	–	–	–	–	–
South Africa	24	23	5	807	83*	–	6	–	44.83	15	12	–	15	–	–	–
Scotland	1	1	–	4	4	–	–	–	4.00	–	–	–	–	–	–	–
West Indies	20	17	2	630	109*	–	3	1	42.00	13	–	–	–	–	–	–
World XI	3	2	1	107	75*	–	1	–	107.00	2	–	–	–	–	–	–
Total	185	157	44	5442	109*	3	39	3	48.16	105	240	1	235	2	117.50	1–22

	Inn	NO	Runs	HS	0s	50	100	Avrge	Ct	Balls	Mdns	Runs	Wkts	Avrge	Best
First Innings	112	27	4245	109*	–	32	3	49.94	68	138	–	155	2	77.50	1–22
Second Innings	45	17	1197	78	3	7	–	42.75	37	102	1	80	–	–	–

	Inn	NO	Runs	HS	0s	50	100	Avrge	Ct	Balls	Mdns	Runs	Wkts	Avrge	Best
Daylight	47	9	1691	105	–	13	1	44.50	29	144	1	125	2	62.50	1–22
Under Lights	110	35	3751	109*	3	26	2	50.01	76	96	–	110	–	–	–

Batting Position	Inn	NO	Runs	HS	0s	50	100	Avrge
1/2	2	1	36	30*	–	–	–	36.00
3	2	1	118	81*	–	1	–	118.00
4	27	5	1077	105	–	10	1	48.95
5	42	7	1544	108	1	12	1	44.11
6	63	15	1942	109*	2	11	1	40.46
7	21	15	725	88*	–	5	–	120.83

Highest Score:- 109* Australia v West Indies, Kinrara, 2006–07

Best Bowling:- 1–22 Australia v Bangladesh, Fatullah, 2005–06

100s	Team	Opponent	Venue	Season
109*	Australia	West Indies	Kinrara	2006–07
105	Australia	New Zealand	Auckland	2006–07
108	Australia	Bangladesh	Mirpur	2010–11

DOMESTIC LIMITED-OVERS CAREER

Debut:- 1996–97 Western Australia v Victoria, Perth

Season	Team	M	Inn	NO	Runs	HS	0s	50	100	Avrge	Ct	Balls	Mdns	Runs	Wkts	Avrge	Best
1996–97	Western Australia	4	4	–	119	82	1	1	–	29.75	2	–	–	–	–	–	–
1997–98	Western Australia	7	6	–	95	49	1	–	–	15.83	4	–	–	–	–	–	–
1998–99	Western Australia	6	6	–	126	51	1	1	–	21.00	2	–	–	–	–	–	–
1999–00	Western Australia	7	7	2	330	100*	–	2	1	66.00	7	69	–	71	3	23.67	3–52
2000–01	Western Australia	11	9	1	428	94	–	5	–	53.50	3	–	–	–	–	–	–
2001–02	Western Australia	10	10	2	440	103*	–	2	1	55.00	9	–	–	–	–	–	–
2002–03	Western Australia	11	11	4	256	65*	–	2	–	36.57	7	12	–	14	–	–	–
2003–04	Western Australia	9	8	1	426	106	1	4	1	60.86	6	165	–	202	7	28.86	2–38
2004–05	Western Australia	10	10	–	383	79	–	4	–	38.30	–	18	–	34	–	–	–
2005–06	Western Australia	3	3	–	61	35	–	–	–	20.33	2	12	–	8	–	–	–
2006–07	Western Australia	1	1	–	9	9	–	–	–	9.00	2	–	–	–	–	–	–
2007–08	Western Australia	2	2	–	12	12	1	–	–	6.00	–	–	–	–	–	–	–
2012–13	Western Australia	3	3	–	35	30	–	–	–	11.67	2	–	–	–	–	–	–
Total		84	80	10	2720	106	5	21	3	38.86	46	276	–	329	10	32.90	3–52

	Inn	NO	Runs	HS	0s	50	100	Avrge	Ct	Balls	Mdns	Runs	Wkts	Avrge	Best
First Innings	45	3	1608	106	2	12	2	38.29	26	156	–	171	8	21.38	3–52
Second Innings	35	7	1112	103*	3	9	1	39.71	20	120	–	158	2	79.00	1–36

Batting Position	Inn	NO	Runs	HS	0s	50	100	Avrge
1/2	11	–	225	82	3	2	–	20.45
3	2	1	54	50*	–	1	–	54.00
4	26	2	987	106	2	9	1	41.13
5	26	5	1007	103*	–	6	2	47.95
6	13	2	440	84*	–	3	–	40.00
7	2	–	7	5	–	–	–	3.50

Highest Score:- 106 Western Australia v New South Wales, North Sydney, 2003–04

Best Bowling:- 3–52 Western Australia v Victoria, Melbourne, 1999–00

100s	Team	Opponent	Venue	Season
100*	Western Australia	Victoria	Melbourne	1999–00
103*	Western Australia	Tasmania	Hobart	2001–02
106	Western Australia	New South Wales	North Sydney	2003–04

INTERNATIONAL TWENTY/20 CAREER

Debut:- 2004–05 Australia v New Zealand, Auckland

Opponent	M	Inn	NO	Runs	HS	0s	50	100	Avrge	Ct	Balls	Mdns	Runs	Wkts	Avrge	Best
Bangladesh	2	1	1	47	47*	–	–	–	–	4	–	–	–	–	–	–
England	4	3	1	36	18	–	–	–	18.00	4	–	–	–	–	–	–
India	4	2	–	21	13	–	–	–	10.50	2	–	–	–	–	–	–
Ireland	1	1	–	10	10	–	–	–	10.00	–	–	–	–	–	–	–
New Zealand	2	2	1	53	31*	–	–	–	53.00	1	–	–	–	–	–	–
Pakistan	9	9	2	247	60*	–	2	–	35.29	3	–	–	–	–	–	–
Sri Lanka	3	2	1	40	39*	–	–	–	40.00	1	–	–	–	–	–	–
South Africa	5	4	2	105	53*	1	1	–	52.50	3	6	–	5	–	–	–
West Indies	7	5	3	147	59*	–	1	–	73.50	2	–	–	–	–	–	–
Zimbabwe	1	1	–	15	15	–	–	–	15.00	–	–	–	–	–	–	–
Total	38	30	11	721	60*	1	4	–	37.95	20	6	–	5	–	–	–

	Inn	NO	Runs	HS	0s	50	100	Avrge	Ct	Balls	Mdns	Runs	Wkts	Avrge	Best
First Innings	16	5	300	47*	1	–	–	27.27	12	–	–	–	–	–	–
Second Innings	14	6	421	60*	–	4	–	52.63	8	6	–	5	–	–	–

Batting Position	Inn	NO	Runs	HS	0s	50	100	Avrge
3	9	4	260	59*	–	2	–	52.00
4	4	1	97	53*	–	1	–	32.33
5	6	–	83	37	1	–	–	13.83
6	3	–	33	18	–	–	–	11.00
7	8	6	248	60*	–	1	–	124.00

Highest Score:- 60* Australia v Pakistan, Gros Islet, 2009–10

INDIAN PREMIER LEAGUE CAREER

Debut:- 2007–08 Chennai Super Kings v Kings XI Punjab, Mohali

Season	M	Inn	NO	Runs	HS	0s	50	100	Avrge	Ct	Balls	Mdns	Runs	Wkts	Avrge	Best
2007–08	4	3	1	168	116*	–	–	1	84.00	2	–	–	–	–	–	–
2009–10	3	3	1	37	15	–	–	–	18.50	–	–	–	–	–	–	–
2010–11	14	14	2	492	83*	1	4	–	41.00	6	–	–	–	–	–	–
2011–12	8	8	–	261	56	–	2	–	32.63	4	–	–	–	–	–	–
2012–13	17	17	3	733	95	–	6	–	52.36	10	–	–	–	–	–	–
Total	46	45	7	1691	116*	1	12	1	44.50	22	–	–	–	–	–	–

	Inn	NO	Runs	HS	0s	50	100	Avrge	Ct	Balls	Mdns	Runs	Wkts	Avrge	Best
First Innings	29	5	1135	116*	–	8	1	47.29	11	–	–	–	–	–	–
Second Innings	16	2	556	88	1	4	–	39.71	11	–	–	–	–	–	–

Batting Position	Inn	NO	Runs	HS	0s	50	100	Avrge
1/2	39	5	1486	95	1	12	–	43.71
3	3	1	168	116*	–	–	1	84.00
5	3	1	37	15	–	–	–	18.50

Highest Score:- 116* Chennai Super Kings v Kings XI Punjab, Mohali, 2007–08

Innings by Innings

Start Date	Grade	Team	Opponent	Venue	Inn	Pos	How Out	Runs	(Balls)	O	M	R	W	C
1999–00														
27/02/2000	Dom OD	Western Australia	Queensland	Perth	1	5	c Seccombe b Kasprowicz....	28	(29)	–	–	–	–	1
02/03/2000	Shield	Western Australia	Queensland	Perth	1	1	c Seccombe b Dawes..	33	(118)	–	–	–	–	2
02/03/2000	Shield	Western Australia	Queensland	Perth	4	1	–	–	–	–	–	–	–	–
09/03/2000	Shield	Western Australia	New South Wales	Sydney	2	1	c Heath b Johnston..	172	(242)	–	–	–	–	2
09/03/2000	Shield	Western Australia	New South Wales	Sydney	4	1	–	–	–	6.0	0	11	1	–
2000–01														
13/10/2000	Shield	Western Australia	Queensland	Perth	2	1	c Seccombe b Nofke.	41	(146)	–	–	–	–	1
13/10/2000	Shield	Western Australia	Queensland	Perth	3	2	c Perren b Bichel...	5	(13)	–	–	–	–	–
20/10/2000	Dom OD	Western Australia	South Australia	Perth	1	6	c Vaughan b Wilson..	35	(20)	–	–	–	–	–
26/10/2000	Shield	Western Australia	South Australia	Adelaide	1	1	c Gillespie b Wilson	48	(131)	–	–	–	–	–
26/10/2000	Shield	Western Australia	South Australia	Adelaide	4	1	–	–	–	4.0	1	16	0	–
09/11/2000	Fclass	Western Australia	West Indians	Perth	2	1	c Browne b Black....	41	(101)	1.0	0	1	0	1
09/11/2000	Fclass	Western Australia	West Indians	Perth	4	2	c Browne b Dillon....	11	(29)	1.0	0	6	0	–
15/11/2000	Dom OD	Western Australia	Queensland	Perth	2	1	–	–	–	–	–	–	–	–
18/11/2000	Dom OD	Western Australia	Tasmania	Hobart	1	7	c Ponting b Marsh...	5	(9)	–	–	–	–	1
19/11/2000	Shield	Western Australia	Tasmania	Hobart	2	1	c Hills b Denton....	35	(86)	5.0	1	17	0	–
19/11/2000	Shield	Western Australia	Tasmania	Hobart	4	2	c Di Venuto b Saker.	5	(11)	–	–	–	–	2
01/12/2000	Shield	Western Australia	New South Wales	North Sydney	2	1	b Bracken	1	(14)	–	–	–	–	–
01/12/2000	Shield	Western Australia	New South Wales	North Sydney	4	2	lbw b Nash....	4	(22)	–	–	–	–	–
09/12/2000	Dom OD	Western Australia	South Australia	Adelaide	2	7	c Davies b Blewett.	2	(3)	–	–	–	–	–
15/12/2000	Shield	Western Australia	New South Wales	Perth	2	1	c Haddin b Clark....	13	(53)	–	–	–	–	3
15/12/2000	Shield	Western Australia	New South Wales	Perth	4	1	not out.	29*	(53)	–	–	–	–	1
02/01/2001	Dom OD	Western Australia	Victoria	Perth	1	5	b Fleming	79	(118)	–	–	–	–	1
04/01/2001	Shield	Western Australia	Victoria	Perth	2	1	lbw b Warne...	35	(56)	–	–	–	–	1
04/01/2001	Shield	Western Australia	Victoria	Perth	4	1	c Berry b Lewis	42	(72)	–	–	–	–	2

Start Date	Grade	Team	Opponent	Venue	Inn	Pos	How Out	Runs	(Balls)	O	M	R	W	Ct
16/01/2001	Dom OD	Western Australia	Victoria	Melbourne	2	8	-	-	-	-	-	-	-	1
19/01/2001	Dom OD	Western Australia	New South Wales	Perth	1	4	c and b Higgs.	94	(104)	-	-	-	-	-
26/01/2001	Dom OD	Western Australia	Tasmania	Perth	1	5	c Marsh b Kremerskothen…	53	(64)	-	-	-	-	1
04/02/2001	Dom OD	Western Australia	New South Wales	North Sydney	2	6	c MacGill b Higgs…	19	(22)	-	-	-	-	-
16/02/2001	Dom OD	Western Australia	Queensland	Brisbane	2	5	c Carseldine b Hauritz…	57	(74)	-	-	-	-	-
18/02/2001	Shield	Western Australia	Queensland	Brisbane	1	1	c and b Bichel	7	(34)	-	-	-	-	1
18/02/2001	Shield	Western Australia	Queensland	Brisbane	3	1	c Seccombe b Bichel.	0	(1)	-	-	-	-	-
25/02/2001	Dom OD	Western Australia	New South Wales	Perth	1	6	not out.	84*	(68)	-	-	-	-	1
02/03/2001	Shield	Western Australia	South Australia	Perth	1	1	c Smith b Harrity…	9	(17)	4.0	2	6	0	-
02/03/2001	Shield	Western Australia	South Australia	Perth	3	1	c Blewett b Smith…	35	(78)	-	-	-	-	1
09/03/2001	Shield	Western Australia	Tasmania	Perth	1	1	c Clingeleffer b Wright…	90	(240)	2.0	0	17	0	-
09/03/2001	Shield	Western Australia	Tasmania	Perth	3	2	c Di Venuto b Saker.	15	(37)	-	-	-	-	-
15/03/2001	Shield	Western Australia	Victoria	Melbourne	1	1	c Elliott b Inness.	2	(18)	-	-	-	-	-
15/03/2001	Shield	Western Australia	Victoria	Melbourne	3	2	c Roach b Lewis	137	(216)	-	-	-	-	-
2001														
20/04/2001	Fclass	Northamptonshire	Glamorgan	Northampton	2	1	c Evans b Wharf	18	(19)	2.0	0	11	0	-
20/04/2001	Fclass	Northamptonshire	Glamorgan	Northampton	4	1	-	-	-	-	-	-	-	-
25/04/2001	Fclass	Northamptonshire	Essex	Chelmsford	2	1	c Hyam b Anderson…	21	(56)	-	-	-	-	2
25/04/2001	Fclass	Northamptonshire	Essex	Chelmsford	4	1	lbw b Cowan…	3	(8)	-	-	-	-	-
09/05/2001	Fclass	Northamptonshire	Surrey	Northampton	1	1	b Salisbury…	75	(149)	-	-	-	-	-
09/05/2001	Fclass	Northamptonshire	Surrey	Northampton	3	1	c Hollioake b Butcher	67	(112)	-	-	-	-	1
25/05/2001	Fclass	Northamptonshire	Yorkshire	Leeds	2	1	lbw b Silverwood….	22	(34)	-	-	-	-	-
25/05/2001	Fclass	Northamptonshire	Yorkshire	Leeds	3	1	c Blakey b Hoggard..	17	(67)	-	-	-	-	-
30/05/2001	Fclass	Northamptonshire	Lancashire	Northampton	1	1	c Hegg b Muralidaran	70	(113)	-	-	-	-	-
30/05/2001	Fclass	Northamptonshire	Lancashire	Northampton	3	1	c Hegg b Muralidaran	82	(188)	-	-	-	-	1
13/06/2001	Fclass	Northamptonshire	Leicestershire	Maidstone	1	1	lbw b Malcolm.	10	(30)	-	-	-	-	-
13/06/2001	Fclass	Northamptonshire	Leicestershire	Maidstone	3	1	c Burns b Maddy	45	(80)	-	-	-	-	1

Start Date	Grade	Team	Opponent	Venue	Inn	Pos	How Out	Runs	(Balls)	O	M	R	W	Ct
20/06/2001	Fclass	Northamptonshire	Somerset	Northampton	2	1	lbw b Johnson.	12	(19)	-	-	-	-	-
20/06/2001	Fclass	Northamptonshire	Somerset	Northampton	4	1	-			3.0	0	14	1	1
29/06/2001	Fclass	Northamptonshire	Glamorgan	Cardiff	2	1	b Croft.	159	(295)	-	-	-	-	1
29/06/2001	Fclass	Northamptonshire	Glamorgan	Cardiff	3	1	b Croft.	68	(162)	-	-	-	-	-
04/07/2001	Fclass	Northamptonshire	Yorkshire	Northampton	1	1	c Byas b Lehmann....	64	(112)	-	-	-	-	-
04/07/2001	Fclass	Northamptonshire	Yorkshire	Northampton	3	1	lbw b Kirby....	122	(273)	-	-	-	-	-
18/07/2001	Fclass	Northamptonshire	Surrey	Guildford	1	1	c Batty b Giddins....	15	(38)	2.0	0	9	0	2
18/07/2001	Fclass	Northamptonshire	Surrey	Guildford	3	1	c Batty b Bicknell....	41	(97)	-	-	-	-	-
27/07/2001	Fclass	Northamptonshire	Essex	Northampton	1	1	not out.	329*	(444)	2.0	0	14	0	2
27/07/2001	Fclass	Northamptonshire	Essex	Northampton	4	1	not out.	70*	(33)	-	-	-	-	1
08/08/2001	Fclass	Northamptonshire	Kent	Northampton	1	1	run out.	35	(50)	5.0	1	15	1	-
08/08/2001	Fclass	Northamptonshire	Kent	Northampton	3	1	not out.	7*	(14)	-	-	-	-	-
15/08/2001	Fclass	Northamptonshire	Lancashire	Manchester	2	1	lbw b Schofield	93	(116)	3.0	0	15	0	1
15/08/2001	Fclass	Northamptonshire	Lancashire	Manchester	4	1	not out.	10*	(28)	1.0	1	0	0	-
23/08/2001	Fclass	Northamptonshire	Leicestershire	Northampton	1	1	b Malcolm	232	(298)	-	-	-	-	2
23/08/2001	Fclass	Northamptonshire	Leicestershire	Northampton	3	1	c Malcolm b Davis....	82	(101)	-	-	-	-	1
05/09/2001	Fclass	Northamptonshire	Kent	Canterbury	2	1	lbw b Trott....	7	(15)	-	-	-	-	1
05/09/2001	Fclass	Northamptonshire	Kent	Canterbury	4	1	c Symonds b Trott....	23	(20)	-	-	-	-	1
12/09/2001	Fclass	Northamptonshire	Somerset	Taunton	1	1	c Turner b Johnson....	208	(358)	-	-	-	-	-
12/09/2001	Fclass	Northamptonshire	Somerset	Taunton	3	1	c Lathwell b Blackwell....	48	(90)	-	-	-	-	1
2001–02														
12/10/2001	Dom OD	Western Australia	South Australia	Perth	1	6	not out.	36*	(37)	-	-	-	-	2
17/10/2001	Shield	Western Australia	Queensland	Brisbane	1	2	c Seccombe b Dale....	0	(17)	-	-	-	-	1
17/10/2001	Shield	Western Australia	Queensland	Brisbane	3	2	c and b Noffke	66	(176)	-	-	-	-	-
21/10/2001	Dom OD	Western Australia	Queensland	Brisbane	1	5	b Hauritz	24	(38)	-	-	-	-	-
24/10/2001	Dom OD	Western Australia	Tasmania	Perth	1	6	c Clingeleffer b Polkinghorne…	29	(59)	-	-	-	-	1
26/10/2001	Shield	Western Australia	Tasmania	Perth	2	2	c Marsh b Wright....	9	(43)	-	-	-	-	-

Start Date	Grade	Team	Opponent	Venue	Inn	Pos	How Out	Runs	(Balls)	O	M	R	W	Ct
26/10/2001	Shield	Western Australia	Tasmania	Perth	4	2	-	1.0	1	0	0	-	-	-
03/11/2001	Dom OD	Western Australia	Tasmania	Hobart	2	5	not out.	103*	(109)	-	-	-	-	-
08/11/2001	Shield	Western Australia	Queensland	Perth	1	1	c Symonds b Noffke..	2	(10)	-	-	-	-	-
08/11/2001	Shield	Western Australia	Queensland	Perth	3	1	c Maher b Hopes	35	(104)	-	-	-	-	-
25/11/2001	Shield	Western Australia	South Australia	Adelaide	1	1	c Manou b Johnson....	40	(85)	-	-	-	-	-
25/11/2001	Shield	Western Australia	South Australia	Adelaide	3	2	c Johnson b Rofe....	11	(71)	-	-	-	-	-
30/11/2001	Dom OD	Western Australia	South Australia	Adelaide	2	5	c Vaughan b Young....	45	(50)	-	-	-	-	1
07/12/2001	Fclass	Western Australia	South Africans	Perth	2	1	c Kirsten b Ntini...	21	(62)	-	-	-	-	-
07/12/2001	Fclass	Western Australia	South Africans	Perth	4	1	-	4.0	0	15	0	-	-	1
14/12/2001	Shield	Western Australia	New South Wales	Sydney	2	1	b Bracken	100	(262)	-	-	-	-	1
14/12/2001	Shield	Western Australia	New South Wales	Sydney	4	1	-	2.0	0	6	0	-	-	-
23/12/2001	Dom OD	Western Australia	Victoria	Melbourne	2	4	b Hewett	6	(17)	-	-	-	-	1
04/01/2002	Dom OD	Western Australia	Queensland	Perth	1	5	lbw b Noffke..	28	(40)	-	-	-	-	1
16/01/2002	Dom OD	Western Australia	Victoria	Perth	1	5	c Moss b Lewis	61	(87)	-	-	-	-	2
18/01/2002	Shield	Western Australia	Victoria	Perth	2	1	b Lewis.	18	(70)	-	-	-	-	3
18/01/2002	Shield	Western Australia	Victoria	Perth	4	2	not out.	22*	(61)	-	-	-	-	4
25/01/2002	Shield	Western Australia	Tasmania	Hobart	2	2	c Clingeleffer b Jurgensen	33	(71)	-	-	-	-	-
25/01/2002	Shield	Western Australia	Tasmania	Hobart	3	2	lbw b Saker...	2	(7)	-	-	-	-	-
03/02/2002	Dom OD	Western Australia	New South Wales	Sydney	1	6	c Rummans b Bracken.	63	(64)	-	-	-	-	1
13/02/2002	Dom OD	Western Australia	New South Wales	Perth	2	4	b Bracken	45	(51)	-	-	-	-	-
15/02/2002	Shield	Western Australia	New South Wales	Perth	1	1	c and b Higgs.	86	(161)	-	-	-	-	1
15/02/2002	Shield	Western Australia	New South Wales	Perth	3	2	c Lee b Nash..	60	(82)	-	-	-	-	1
28/02/2002	Shield	Western Australia	Victoria	Melbourne	2	1	c Mott b Harvey	0	(10)	-	-	-	-	-
28/02/2002	Shield	Western Australia	Victoria	Melbourne	3	2	c Berry b Moss	61	(134)	-	-	-	-	2
13/03/2002	Shield	Western Australia	South Australia	Perth	1	1	c Johnson b Rofe...	39	(150)	-	-	-	-	2
13/03/2002	Shield	Western Australia	South Australia	Perth	3	2	c Adcock b Wilson....	16	(46)	-	-	-	-	1

Start Date	Grade	Team	Opponent	Venue	Inn	Pos	How Out	Runs	(Balls)	O	M	R	W	Ct
2002														
18/04/2002	Fclass	Northamptonshire	Oxford	Oxford	1	1	c Jones b Sharpe....	11	(28)	–	–	–	–	2
18/04/2002	Fclass	Northamptonshire	Oxford	Oxford	3	1	retired.	52	(101)	–	–	–	–	5
24/04/2002	Fclass	Northamptonshire	Worcestershire	Northampton	2	1	c Batty b Kabir Ali.	170	(309)	–	–	–	–	–
08/05/2002	Fclass	Northamptonshire	Derbyshire	Derby	2	1	lbw b Cork....	13	(23)	–	–	–	–	1
08/05/2002	Fclass	Northamptonshire	Derbyshire	Derby	3	1	c Di Venuto b Welch.	150	(277)	–	–	–	–	–
15/05/2002	Fclass	Northamptonshire	Middlesex	Northampton	2	1	c Nash b Cook.	84	(106)	–	–	–	–	–
15/05/2002	Fclass	Northamptonshire	Middlesex	Northampton	3	2	lbw b Laraman.	27	(44)	–	–	–	–	2
24/05/2002	Fclass	Northamptonshire	Nottinghamshire	Nottingham	1	1	c Read b Logan	10	(34)	–	–	–	–	–
24/05/2002	Fclass	Northamptonshire	Nottinghamshire	Nottingham	3	2	c Read b Smith	36	(31)	–	–	–	–	2
31/05/2002	Fclass	Northamptonshire	Essex	Northampton	1	1	b Sharif	140	(185)	–	–	–	–	1
31/05/2002	Fclass	Northamptonshire	Essex	Northampton	3	2	c Stephenson b Ilott	41	(73)	–	–	–	–	–
12/06/2002	Fclass	Northamptonshire	Essex	Ilford	2	1	c Middlebrook b Stephenson	67	(124)	–	–	–	–	1
12/06/2002	Fclass	Northamptonshire	Essex	Ilford	3	2	c Flower b Middlebrook....	71	(155)	–	–	–	–	2
26/06/2002	Fclass	Northamptonshire	Nottinghamshire	Northampton	2	1	c Johnson b Logan....	39	(45)	–	–	–	–	–
26/06/2002	Fclass	Northamptonshire	Nottinghamshire	Northampton	4	2	lbw b Harris..	4	(8)	–	–	–	–	1
03/07/2002	Fclass	Northamptonshire	Durham	Northampton	2	1	not out.	0*	(6)	–	–	–	–	2
03/07/2002	Fclass	Northamptonshire	Durham	Northampton	4	1	b Hunter	15	(35)	–	–	–	–	–
19/07/2002	Fclass	Northamptonshire	Worcestershire	Worcester	1	1	c Rhodes b Bichel....	174	(291)	–	–	–	–	1
19/07/2002	Fclass	Northamptonshire	Worcestershire	Worcester	3	1	c Rhodes b Sheriyar.	6	(30)	–	–	–	–	–
25/07/2002	Fclass	Northamptonshire	Derbyshire	Northampton	2	1	lbw b Cork....	13	(29)	–	–	–	–	2
25/07/2002	Fclass	Northamptonshire	Derbyshire	Northampton	4	1	c Lungley b Cork....	0	(1)	–	–	–	–	–
07/08/2002	Fclass	Northamptonshire	Middlesex	Lord's	2	1	c Alleyne b Laraman.	9	(36)	–	–	–	–	–
15/08/2002	Fclass	Northamptonshire	Gloucestershire	Bristol	2	1	not out.	310*	(433)	–	–	–	–	–
15/08/2002	Fclass	Northamptonshire	Gloucestershire	Bristol	4	1	–	–	–	–	–	1	–	–
2002–03														
28/10/2002	Fclass	Western Australia	England XI	Perth	1	4	c Trescothick b Caddick....	0	(14)	–	–	–	–	3

Start Date	Grade	Team	Opponent	Venue	Inn	Pos	How Out	Runs	(Balls)	O	M	R	W	C
28/10/2002	Fclass	Western Australia	England XI	Perth	3	1	c Caddick b Jones…	14	(34)	-	-	-	-	1
06/11/2002	Dom OD	Western Australia	South Australia	Perth	2	4	c Miller b Harris…	11	(33)	-	-	-	-	1
08/11/2002	Shield	Western Australia	South Australia	Perth	2	1	c Fitzgerald b Harris	48	(144)	-	-	-	-	-
08/11/2002	Shield	Western Australia	South Australia	Perth	4	2	lbw b Harris…	9	(32)	-	-	-	-	1
14/11/2002	Shield	Western Australia	Victoria	Perth	2	1	lbw b White…	56	(88)	-	-	-	-	-
14/11/2002	Shield	Western Australia	Victoria	Perth	4	1	-	-	-	-	-	-	-	-
24/11/2002	Shield	Western Australia	Queensland	Brisbane	1	1	c Seccombe b Kasprowicz…	33	(40)	-	-	-	-	-
24/11/2002	Shield	Western Australia	Queensland	Brisbane	3	2	c Law b Kasprowicz..	0	(13)	-	-	-	-	1
29/11/2002	Dom OD	Western Australia	Queensland	Brisbane	2	5	not out.	23*	(29)	-	-	-	-	2
06/12/2002	Dom OD	Western Australia	Tasmania	Perth	1	6	run out (Di Venuto/Marsh).	38	(71)	-	-	-	-	1
19/12/2002	Shield	Western Australia	South Australia	Adelaide	2	4	c Deitz b Smith	62	(128)	-	-	-	-	1
19/12/2002	Shield	Western Australia	South Australia	Adelaide	4	4	-	-	-	-	-	-	-	-
02/01/2003	Dom OD	Western Australia	Queensland	Perth	1	4	c Hopes b Hauritz…	10	(18)	-	-	-	-	-
10/01/2003	Dom OD	Western Australia	Victoria	Melbourne	1	5	c Elliott b Warne…	7	(14)	-	-	-	-	-
19/01/2003	Dom OD	Western Australia	New South Wales	Coffs Harbour	2	3	not out.	50*	(87)	-	-	-	-	2
23/01/2003	Shield	Western Australia	New South Wales	Newcastle	2	4	c Haddin b Bollinger	90	(206)	-	-	-	-	-
23/01/2003	Shield	Western Australia	New South Wales	Newcastle	4	6	c Mail b Katich	19	(23)	-	-	-	-	-
01/02/2003	Dom OD	Western Australia	South Australia	Adelaide	2	4	not out.	37*	(70)	-	-	-	-	-
05/02/2003	Shield	Western Australia	Tasmania	Hobart	2	4	not out.	5*	(14)	-	-	-	-	-
09/02/2003	Dom OD	Western Australia	Tasmania	Hobart	2	5	not out.	65*	(93)	2.0	0	14	0	-
12/02/2003	Dom OD	Western Australia	New South Wales	Perth	1	5	b Bollinger…	5	(15)	-	-	-	-	-
14/02/2003	Dom OD	Western Australia	Victoria	Perth	1	6	c Harwood b McDonald	6	(10)	-	-	-	-	1
23/02/2003	Dom OD	Western Australia	New South Wales	Perth	1	4	c Katich b Clark….	4	(11)	-	-	-	-	-
27/02/2003	Shield	Western Australia	New South Wales	Perth	2	4	b Nash..	14	(31)	-	-	-	-	1
27/02/2003	Shield	Western Australia	New South Wales	Perth	3	4	c Haddin b Bollinger	12	(25)	-	-	-	-	2
13/04/2003	Fclass	Australia A	South Africa A	Adelaide	1	2	b Pretorius…	15	(46)	-	-	-	-	-
13/04/2003	Fclass	Australia A	South Africa A	Adelaide	3	1	b Boje..	84	(203)	-	-	-	-	1

Start Date	Grade	Team	Opponent	Venue	Inn	Pos	How Out	Runs	(Balls)	O	M	R	W	C
19/04/2003	Fclass	Australia A	South Africa A	Perth	1	2	c Tsolekile b Langeveldt...	4	(7)	-	-	-	-	-
19/04/2003	Fclass	Australia A	South Africa A	Perth	3	1	c Amla b Bacher	145	(183)	-	-	-	-	2
2003														
30/04/2003	Fclass	Northamptonshire	Worcestershire	Worcester	2	1	c Rhodes b Mason....	45	(113)	-	-	-	-	1
14/05/2003	Fclass	Northamptonshire	Yorkshire	Northampton	2	1	c Lumb b Gray.	65	(196)	-	-	-	-	1
14/05/2003	Fclass	Northamptonshire	Yorkshire	Northampton	4	2	-	3.0	0	32	0	-	-	-
30/05/2003	Fclass	Northamptonshire	Glamorgan	Northampton	2	1	c Wallace b Kasprowicz....	39	(85)	-	-	-	-	-
30/05/2003	Fclass	Northamptonshire	Glamorgan	Northampton	4	1	c Cosker b Kasprowicz	14	(40)	-	-	-	-	1
04/06/2003	Fclass	Northamptonshire	Gloucestershire	Gloucester	1	1	c Hancock b Lewis...	264	(436)	-	-	-	-	-
04/06/2003	Fclass	Northamptonshire	Gloucestershire	Gloucester	4	1	-	-	-	-	-	1	-	-
13/06/2003	Dom T20	Northamptonshire	Worcestershire	Worcester	1	1	c Smith b Hall	67	(59)	-	-	-	-	2
16/06/2003	Dom T20	Northamptonshire	Glamorgan	Cardiff	1	3	not out.	79*	(58)	-	-	-	-	1
19/06/2003	Dom T20	Northamptonshire	Gloucestershire	Bristol	1	3	c Windows b Harvey..	32	(40)	-	-	-	-	-
20/06/2003	Dom T20	Northamptonshire	Somerset	Northampton	1	3	c Gazzard b Francis.	88	(58)	-	-	-	-	2
24/06/2003	Dom T20	Northamptonshire	Warwickshire	Northampton	2	3	c Obuya b Wagg	13	(13)	-	-	-	-	-
27/06/2003	Fclass	Northamptonshire	Derbyshire	Northampton	1	1	st Sutton b Dumelow.	59	(113)	-	-	-	-	1
27/06/2003	Fclass	Northamptonshire	Derbyshire	Northampton	3	1	c Sutton b Dumelow.	28	(61)	-	-	-	-	1
02/07/2003	Fclass	Northamptonshire	Hampshire	Northampton	2	1	c Pothas b Bruce....	4	(11)	-	-	-	-	-
02/07/2003	Fclass	Northamptonshire	Hampshire	Northampton	4	2	lbw b Tomlinson	18	(39)	-	-	-	-	-
09/07/2003	Fclass	Northamptonshire	Durham	Chester-le-St	2	1	c Mustard b Shoaib Akhtar.	43	(89)	-	-	-	-	-
09/07/2003	Fclass	Northamptonshire	Durham	Chester-le-St	4	2	not out.	72*	(106)	-	-	-	-	-
23/07/2003	Fclass	Northamptonshire	Somerset	Northampton	1	1	b Blackwell....	20	(49)	-	-	-	-	-
23/07/2003	Fclass	Northamptonshire	Somerset	Northampton	4	1	-	-	-	-	-	1	-	-
31/07/2003	Fclass	Northamptonshire	Hampshire	Southampton	2	1	c Katich b Tremlett.	13	(37)	-	-	-	-	-
31/07/2003	Fclass	Northamptonshire	Hampshire	Southampton	4	2	c Tremlett b Bruce..	100	(207)	-	-	-	-	-
14/08/2003	Fclass	Northamptonshire	Somerset	Taunton	2	1	not out.	331*	(471)	-	-	-	-	2
14/08/2003	Fclass	Northamptonshire	Somerset	Taunton	4	1	-	5.0	1	6	0	-	-	-

Start Date	Grade	Team	Opponent	Venue	Inn	Pos	How Out	Runs	(Balls)	O	M	R	W	Ct
20/08/2003	Fclass	Northamptonshire	Derbyshire	Derby	2	1	run out.	115	(208)	-	-	-	-	-
20/08/2003	Fclass	Northamptonshire	Derbyshire	Derby	4	1		-		-	-	-	-	-
03/09/2003	Fclass	Northamptonshire	Durham	Northampton	2	1	b Bridge	187	(340)	3.0	1	5	1	1
03/09/2003	Fclass	Northamptonshire	Durham	Northampton	4	1		-		-	-	2	-	-
10/09/2003	Fclass	Northamptonshire	Glamorgan	Cardiff	1	1	b Croft.	147	(11)	-	-	-	-	2
10/09/2003	Fclass	Northamptonshire	Glamorgan	Cardiff	3	2	c Maynard b Croft...	50	(130)	3.0	0	9	0	-
17/09/2003	Fclass	Northamptonshire	Worcestershire	Northampton	1	1	run out.	4	(16)	-	-	-	-	1
17/09/2003	Fclass	Northamptonshire	Worcestershire	Northampton	3	2	c Pipe b Batty	79	(188)	-	-	-	-	-

2003–04

Start Date	Grade	Team	Opponent	Venue	Inn	Pos	How Out	Runs	(Balls)	O	M	R	W	Ct
03/10/2003	Fclass	Western Australia	Zimbabweans	Perth	2	1	lbw b Streak.	15	(24)	11.0	8	10	1	1
03/10/2003	Fclass	Western Australia	Zimbabweans	Perth	4	2	c Ervine b Gripper..	79	(79)	-	-	-	-	-
19/10/2003	Shield	Western Australia	South Australia	Perth	2	1	c Manou b Rofe	20	(44)	4.0	1	30	0	1
19/10/2003	Shield	Western Australia	South Australia	Perth	4	2	b Cleary	30	(78)	11.0	5	25	1	1
24/10/2003	Dom OD	Western Australia	South Australia	Perth	1	4	run out (Johnson)...	67	(61)	-	-	-	-	-
02/11/2003	Dom OD	Western Australia	New South Wales	North Sydney	1	4	run out (Nicholson).	106	(94)	5.3	0	38	2	-
04/11/2003	Shield	Western Australia	New South Wales	Sydney	1	2	lbw b Nicholson	0	(2)	-	-	-	-	2
04/11/2003	Shield	Western Australia	New South Wales	Sydney	3	2	c Jaques b Waugh.....	53	(112)	-	-	-	-	-
09/11/2003	Dom OD	Western Australia	South Australia	Adelaide	2	4	not out.	84*	(74)	4.0	0	29	0	1
19/11/2003	Shield	Western Australia	Victoria	St Kilda	1	2	lbw b Wise...	23	(45)	8.0	1	24	0	1
19/11/2003	Shield	Western Australia	Victoria	St Kilda	3	1	c Elliott b Lewis...	57	(123)	-	-	-	-	-
05/12/2003	Dom OD	Western Australia	Tasmania	Perth	2	4	lbw b Geeves.	0	(4)	-	-	-	-	1
07/12/2003	Shield	Western Australia	Tasmania	Perth	1	1	c Clingeleffer b Wright...	138	(259)	1.0	0	3	0	1
07/12/2003	Shield	Western Australia	Tasmania	Perth	3	2	c Denton b Marsh...	61	(71)	-	-	-	-	-
19/12/2003	Fclass	Australia A	Indians	Hobart	1	1	c Ganguly b Nehra...	67	(158)	-	-	-	-	1
19/12/2003	Fclass	Australia A	Indians	Hobart	3	2	c Tendulkar b Pathan	7	(6)	-	-	-	-	1
09/01/2004	Dom OD	Western Australia	Queensland	Perth	2	6	-			7.0	0	41	1	-
11/01/2004	Shield	Western Australia	Queensland	Perth	1	2	c Law b Dawes.	10	(55)	-	-	-	-	-

Start Date	Grade	Team	Opponent	Venue	Inn	Pos	How Out	Runs	(Balls)	O	M	R	W	Ct
11/01/2004	Shield	Western Australia	Queensland	Perth	3	2	c Simpson b Hopes…	15	(45)	-	-	-	-	-
21/01/2004	Dom OD	Western Australia	New South Wales	Perth	1	4	c Thorney b Nicholson……	69	(97)	5.0	0	41	2	1
23/01/2004	Shield	Western Australia	New South Wales	Perth	1	2	c Pilon b Thornely..	76	(207)	-	-	-	-	3
23/01/2004	Shield	Western Australia	New South Wales	Perth	3	2	b Bracken	71	(90)	-	-	-	-	3
01/02/2004	Int OD	Australia	India	Perth	2	7	not out.	17*	(23)	3.0	0	15	0	1
04/02/2004	Shield	Western Australia	Tasmania	Hobart	1	2	lbw b Downton.	82	(165)	-	-	-	-	-
04/02/2004	Shield	Western Australia	Tasmania	Hobart	3	2	run out (Cox/Watson/Clingeleffer)	9	(34)	5.0	0	20	1	-
13/02/2004	Dom OD	Western Australia	Queensland	Brisbane	2	4	c Maher b Hauritz…	66	(83)	4.0	0	36	1	-
15/02/2004	Shield	Western Australia	Queensland	Brisbane	2	3	b Noffke	49	(116)	4.0	0	12	0	1
15/02/2004	Shield	Western Australia	Queensland	Brisbane	4	1	run out (Hauritz)…	23	(32)	-	-	-	-	2
21/02/2004	Dom OD	Western Australia	Victoria	Melbourne	1	5	b Warne.	28	(47)	2.0	0	17	1	1
29/02/2004	Dom OD	Western Australia	Queensland	Brisbane	2	5	c Hopes b Hauritz…	6	(15)	-	-	-	-	-
04/03/2004	Shield	Western Australia	South Australia	Adelaide	1	1	c Higgs b Cleary….	28	(66)	-	-	-	-	-
04/03/2004	Shield	Western Australia	South Australia	Adelaide	3	2	c (S)Harris b Tait..	7	(9)	-	-	-	-	-
2004														
14/07/2004	Dom T20	Gloucestershire	Glamorgan	Cardiff	2	4	b Wharf.	15	(13)	-	-	-	-	-
15/07/2004	Dom T20	Gloucestershire	Warwickshire	Bristol	1	1	lbw b Giles…	32	(27)	-	-	-	-	-
21/07/2004	F-class	Gloucestershire	Lancashire	Cheltenham	2	3	lbw b Martin..	5	(17)	-	-	-	-	1
21/07/2004	F-class	Gloucestershire	Lancashire	Cheltenham	4	3	c Chilton b Hooper..	44	(122)	-	-	-	-	1
28/07/2004	F-class	Gloucestershire	Worcestershire	Cheltenham	1	3	c Hall b Mason	0	(1)	-	-	-	-	-
28/07/2004	F-class	Gloucestershire	Worcestershire	Cheltenham	3	3	lbw b Kabir Ali	68	(160)	-	-	-	-	-
03/08/2004	F-class	Gloucestershire	Middlesex	Lord's	1	3	c Koenig b Agarkar..	43	(78)	1.0	0	2	0	1
03/08/2004	F-class	Gloucestershire	Middlesex	Lord's	3	3	c Shah b Agarkar….	0	(4)	-	-	-	-	-
19/08/2004	F-class	Gloucestershire	Warwickshire	Bristol	2	3	lbw b Troughton	26	(59)	-	-	-	-	2
19/08/2004	F-class	Gloucestershire	Warwickshire	Bristol	4	3	–			1.0	0	1	0	-
24/08/2004	F-class	Gloucestershire	Northamptonshire	Northampton	2	3	c Sales b Cook	78	(216)	2.0	1	6	0	2
24/08/2004	F-class	Gloucestershire	Northamptonshire	Northampton	4	3	not out.	49*	(143)	-	-	-	-	-

Start Date	Grade	Team	Opponent	Venue	Inn	Pos	How Out	Runs	(Balls)	O	M	R	W	C
09/09/2004	Fclass	Gloucestershire	Sussex	Bristol	1	3	b Lewry.	1	(10)	-	-	-	-	2
09/09/2004	Fclass	Gloucestershire	Sussex	Bristol	3	3	lbw b Davis...	37	(75)	-	-	-	-	-
16/09/2004	Fclass	Gloucestershire	Lancashire	Manchester	1	3	c Law b Keedy.	46	(81)	-	-	-	-	1
16/09/2004	Fclass	Gloucestershire	Lancashire	Manchester	3	3	b Keedy.	45	(78)	4.0	1	13	0	-
2004-05														
15/10/2004	Dom OD	Western Australia	Tasmania	Perth	2	4	c Bailey b Kremerskothen..	79	(96)	1.0	0	19	0	-
17/10/2004	Shield	Western Australia	Tasmania	Perth	2	1	c Cox b Wright	210	(333)	-	-	-	-	2
17/10/2004	Shield	Western Australia	Tasmania	Perth	4	1	not out.	7*	(18)	3.0	0	9	0	-
31/10/2004	Dom OD	Western Australia	New South Wales	North Sydney	1	4	c Haddin b Bradstreet	13	(18)	-	-	-	-	-
02/11/2004	Shield	Western Australia	New South Wales	Sydney	2	1	c Haddin b Nicholson	8	(21)	1.0	0	1	0	-
02/11/2004	Shield	Western Australia	New South Wales	Sydney	3	2	lbw b MacGill.	5	(46)	-	-	-	-	-
14/11/2004	Dom OD	Western Australia	Victoria	St Kilda	1	4	c Lewis b White	60	(57)	-	-	-	-	1
19/11/2004	Dom OD	Western Australia	Queensland	Perth	2	4	c and b Hopes.	21	(40)	-	-	-	-	-
21/11/2004	Shield	Western Australia	Queensland	Perth	1	1	c Hartley b Dawes...	16	(46)	5.0	1	17	1	-
21/11/2004	Shield	Western Australia	Queensland	Perth	3	2	c Noffke b Dawes.....	6	(40)	-	-	-	-	-
01/12/2004	Shield	Western Australia	Victoria	St Kilda	1	1	b Wise.	24	(32)	-	-	-	-	-
01/12/2004	Shield	Western Australia	Victoria	St Kilda	3	2	c Roach b Harvey....	36	(58)	1.0	0	2	0	1
09/12/2004	Fclass	Western Australia	Pakistanis	Perth	2	2	c Mohammad Yousuf b Shoaib Akhtar	124	(203)	15.0	8	30	1	2
09/12/2004	Fclass	Western Australia	Pakistanis	Perth	4	2	not out.	6*	(17)	-	-	-	-	-
17/12/2004	Dom OD	Western Australia	South Australia	Adelaide	1	4	lbw b Cullen..	69	(96)	2.0	0	15	0	-
19/12/2004	Shield	Western Australia	South Australia	Adelaide	1	1	c Manou b Tait	5	(19)	-	-	-	-	1
19/12/2004	Shield	Western Australia	South Australia	Adelaide	3	2	c Manou b Rofe	0	(7)	-	-	-	-	-
02/01/2005	Dom OD	Western Australia	New South Wales	Perth	1	4	c Haddin b Bradstreet	59	(92)	-	-	-	-	-
13/01/2005	Dom T20	Australia A	Pakistanis	Adelaide	1	4	c Azhar Mahmood b Iftikhar Anjum	21	(17)	-	-	-	-	1
14/01/2005	Dom OD	Western Australia	Victoria	Perth	1	5	lbw b White...	28	(29)	-	-	-	-	-
16/01/2005	Shield	Western Australia	Victoria	Perth	2	2	not out.	223*	(406)	-	-	-	-	1
16/01/2005	Shield	Western Australia	Victoria	Perth	4	2	-	-	-	-	-	-	-	-

Start Date	Grade	Team	Opponent	Venue	Inn	Pos	How Out	Runs	(Balls)	O	M	R	W	Ct
23/01/2005	Dom OD	Western Australia	Tasmania	Devonport	1	5	c Bailey b Doherty..	26	(63)	–	–	–	–	1
28/01/2005	Shield	Western Australia	Tasmania	Hobart	2	1	c Clingeleffer b Griffith.	19	(52)	10.0	0	25	0	1
28/01/2005	Shield	Western Australia	Tasmania	Hobart	4	2	lbw b Marsh...	95	(136)	–	–	–	–	1
04/02/2005	Dom OD	Western Australia	South Australia	Perth	2	4	c Manou b Harris....	7	(14)	–	–	–	–	–
11/02/2005	Dom OD	Western Australia	Queensland	Brisbane	1	4	c Nash b Kasprowicz.	21	(43)	–	–	–	–	1
17/02/2005	Int T20	Australia	New Zealand	Auckland	1	7	not out.	31*	(15)	–	–	–	–	–
22/02/2005	Int OD	Australia	New Zealand	Christchurch	1	7	not out.	32*	(20)	–	–	–	–	–
26/02/2005	Int OD	Australia	New Zealand	Auckland	1	7	not out.	65*	(73)	3.0	0	22	0	3
01/03/2005	Int OD	Australia	New Zealand	Wellington	2	7	–	–	–	–	–	–	–	–
05/03/2005	Int OD	Australia	New Zealand	Napier	1	7	not out.	0*	(0)	–	–	–	–	–
10/03/2005	Shield	Western Australia	Queensland	Brisbane	2	1	b Dawes.	13	(18)	14.2	2	49	3	–
10/03/2005	Shield	Western Australia	Queensland	Brisbane	4	2	lbw b Hopes....	54	(83)	15.0	2	34	3	2

2005

Start Date	Grade	Team	Opponent	Venue	Inn	Pos	How Out	Runs	(Balls)	O	M	R	W	Ct
13/04/2005	Fclass	Durham	Leicestershire	Leicester	1	1	c Habib b Masters...	253	(426)	–	–	–	–	1
13/04/2005	Fclass	Durham	Leicestershire	Leicester	4	1	–	–	–	–	–	2	–	–
20/04/2005	Fclass	Durham	Worcestershire	Chester-le-St	2	1	b Vaas.	2	(24)	–	–	–	–	1
20/04/2005	Fclass	Durham	Worcestershire	Chester-le-St	4	1	lbw b Mason...	15	(21)	–	–	–	–	–
06/05/2005	Fclass	Durham	Somerset	Stockton-on-Tees	2	1	c Trescothick b Caddick...	47	(71)	–	–	–	–	1
06/05/2005	Fclass	Durham	Somerset	Stockton-on-Tees	4	1	c Turner b Caddick.	51	(65)	–	–	–	–	1
11/05/2005	Fclass	Durham	Lancashire	Manchester	2	1	not out.	144*	(285)	–	–	–	–	–
11/05/2005	Fclass	Durham	Lancashire	Manchester	4	1	not out.	26*	(29)	–	–	–	–	1
20/05/2005	Fclass	Durham	Yorkshire	Chester-le-St	2	1	b Bresnan	26	(38)	–	–	–	–	2
20/05/2005	Fclass	Durham	Yorkshire	Chester-le-St	4	1	c Jaques b Kruis....	61	(137)	–	–	–	–	2
13/06/2005	Int T20	Australia	England	Southampton	2	5	c Flintoff b Gough..	1	(6)	5.0	0	24	0	–
18/06/2005	Int OD	Australia	Bangladesh	Cardiff	1	6	not out.	31*	(21)	–	–	–	–	–
19/06/2005	Int OD	Australia	England	Bristol	1	6	b Harmison....	84	(83)	–	–	–	–	–
23/06/2005	Int OD	Australia	England	Chester-le-St	1	6	c Collingwood b Flintoff..	5	(10)	–	–	–	–	2

Start Date	Grade	Team	Opponent	Venue	Inn	Pos	How Out	Runs	(Balls)	O	M	R	W	C
25/06/2005	Int OD	Australia	Bangladesh	Manchester	2	6	–	–		–	–	–	–	–
28/06/2005	Int OD	Australia	England	Birmingham	1	6	c Jones b Harmison…	45	(42)	–	–	–	–	2
30/06/2005	Int OD	Australia	Bangladesh	Canterbury	2	7	–	–		–	–	–	–	1
02/07/2005	Int OD	Australia	England	Lord's	1	7	not out.	62*	(81)	4.0	0	31	1	–
07/07/2005	Int OD	Australia	England	Leeds	1	7	not out.	46*	(52)	–	–	–	–	1
10/07/2005	Int OD	Australia	England	Lord's	2	7	–	–		–	–	–	–	1
12/07/2005	Int OD	Australia	England	The Oval	2	7	–	–		–	–	–	–	–
21/07/2005	Fclass	Durham	Derbyshire	Derby	1	1	lbw b Welch….	10	(40)	–	–	–	–	2
21/07/2005	Fclass	Durham	Derbyshire	Derby	4	1	not out.	42*	(96)	5.0	0	23	0	1
26/07/2005	Fclass	Durham	Somerset	Taunton	1	1	lbw b Caddick.	63	(136)	–	–	–	–	3
26/07/2005	Fclass	Durham	Somerset	Taunton	3	1	c Parsons b Smith…	27	(35)	–	–	–	–	1
03/08/2005	Fclass	Durham	Essex	Southend-on-Sea	1	1	c Foster b Adams…..	8	(28)	–	–	–	–	1
03/08/2005	Fclass	Durham	Essex	Southend-on-Sea	3	1	c Irani b Adams	0	(7)	–	–	–	–	1
12/08/2005	Fclass	Durham	Leicestershire	Chester-le-St	1	1	lbw b Masters.	146	(287)	–	–	–	–	–
12/08/2005	Fclass	Durham	Leicestershire	Chester-le-St	3	1	not out.	61*	(119)	–	–	–	–	1
24/08/2005	Fclass	Durham	Yorkshire	Scarborough	1	1	lbw b Bresnan.	92	(147)	7.0	0	36	1	1
2005–06														
11/09/2005	Fclass	Australia A	Pakistan A	Rawalpindi	1	1	b Shahid Nazir	2	(0)	–	–	–	–	1
11/09/2005	Fclass	Australia A	Pakistan A	Rawalpindi	3	2	c Zulqarnain Haider b Mohammad Sami…	11	(0)	–	–	–	–	–
17/09/2005	Fclass	Australia A	Pakistan A	Rawalpindi	1	1	lbw b Mohammad Asif.	15	(0)	–	–	–	–	–
17/09/2005	Fclass	Australia A	Pakistan A	Rawalpindi	3	1	not out.	101*	(0)	–	–	–	–	2
05/10/2005	Int OD	Australia	World XI	Melbourne	1	7	c Pietersen b Vettori	32	(44)	–	–	–	–	1
07/10/2005	Int OD	Australia	World XI	Melbourne	1	7	–	–		–	–	–	–	–
09/10/2005	Int OD	Australia	World XI	Melbourne	1	6	not out.	75*	(74)	–	–	–	–	1
18/10/2005	Shield	Western Australia	Victoria	Perth	1	1	c Crosthwaite b Lewis	4	(21)	6.0	1	21	1	2
18/10/2005	Shield	Western Australia	Victoria	Perth	3	2	c Crosthwaite b Wise	86	(190)	–	–	–	–	1
23/10/2005	Dom OD	Western Australia	Victoria	Perth	2	5	c Crosthwaite b Wise	35	(44)	–	–	–	–	2

Start Date	Grade	Team	Opponent	Venue	Inn	Pos	How Out	Runs	(Balls)	O	M	R	W	Ct
29/10/2005	Dom OD	Western Australia	Victoria	St Kilda	1	5	c Klinger b Lewis....	17	(29)	2.0	0	8	0	0
03/11/2005	Tests	Australia	West Indies	Brisbane	1	2	c Ramdin b Powell...	1	(14)	-	-	-	-	-
03/11/2005	Tests	Australia	West Indies	Brisbane	3	1	c Collymore b Gayle.	29	(65)	-	-	-	-	-
12/11/2005	Dom OD	Western Australia	South Australia	Adelaide	2	4	c Manou b Cleary....	9	(27)	-	-	-	-	1
17/11/2005	Tests	Australia	West Indies	Hobart	2	2	c Sarwan b Bravo....	137	(235)	-	-	-	-	1
17/11/2005	Tests	Australia	West Indies	Hobart	4	5	not out.	31*	(82)	-	-	-	-	1
25/11/2005	Tests	Australia	West Indies	Adelaide	2	5	not out.	133*	(215)	-	-	-	-	-
25/11/2005	Tests	Australia	West Indies	Adelaide	4	5	not out.	30*	(62)	-	-	-	-	1
03/12/2005	Int OD	Australia	New Zealand	Auckland	1	7	not out.	21*	(20)	-	-	-	-	1
07/12/2005	Int OD	Australia	New Zealand	Wellington	1	7	not out.	1*	(1)	-	-	-	-	1
10/12/2005	Int OD	Australia	New Zealand	Christchurch	1	7	not out.	88*	(56)	-	-	-	-	-
16/12/2005	Tests	Australia	South Africa	Perth	1	5	c Langeveldt b Ntini	23	(51)	-	-	-	-	-
16/12/2005	Tests	Australia	South Africa	Perth	3	6	c Boucher b Pollock.	58	(121)	-	-	-	-	-
26/12/2005	Tests	Australia	South Africa	Melbourne	1	5	b Ntini.	122	(203)	-	-	-	-	1
26/12/2005	Tests	Australia	South Africa	Melbourne	3	5	c Kallis b Smith....	31	(74)	-	-	-	-	-
02/01/2006	Tests	Australia	South Africa	Sydney	2	5	c Boucher b Botha...	45	(111)	2.0	0	12	0	-
02/01/2006	Tests	Australia	South Africa	Sydney	4	5	-	-	-	-	-	-	-	-
09/01/2006	Int T20	Australia	South Africa	Brisbane	1	6	-	-	-	-	-	1	-	1
13/01/2006	Int OD	Australia	Sri Lanka	Melbourne	1	7	not out.	34*	(30)	-	-	-	-	-
15/01/2006	Int OD	Australia	South Africa	Brisbane	1	7	b Kruger	73	(107)	-	-	-	-	1
20/01/2006	Int OD	Australia	South Africa	Melbourne	1	6	c Kruger b Hall	18	(31)	-	-	-	-	-
22/01/2006	Int OD	Australia	Sri Lanka	Sydney	2	6	run out (Vaas)	0	(1)	-	-	-	-	1
26/01/2006	Int OD	Australia	Sri Lanka	Adelaide	2	7	not out.	25*	(30)	-	-	-	-	-
29/01/2006	Int OD	Australia	Sri Lanka	Perth	2	7	-	-	-	-	-	-	-	-
03/02/2006	Int OD	Australia	South Africa	Melbourne	1	7	b Van Der Wath	62	(44)	-	-	-	-	-
05/02/2006	Int OD	Australia	South Africa	Sydney	1	7	not out.	47*	(33)	-	-	-	-	1
10/02/2006	Int OD	Australia	Sri Lanka	Adelaide	2	7	run out (Dilshan/Sangakkara)....	16	(21)	-	-	-	-	-

Start Date	Grade	Team	Opponent	Venue	Inn	Pos	How Out	Runs	(Balls)	O	M	R	W	C
12/02/2006	Int OD	Australia	Sri Lanka	Sydney	1	7	not out.	23*	(8)	-	-	-	-	-
14/02/2006	Int OD	Australia	Sri Lanka	Brisbane	2	7	-	-	-	-	-	1	-	-
26/02/2006	Int OD	Australia	South Africa	Centurion	1	5	c Dippenaar b Pollock	56	(73)	-	-	-	-	-
03/03/2006	Int OD	Australia	South Africa	Cape Town	2	6	c Kemp b Nel..	22	(48)	-	-	-	-	-
05/03/2006	Int OD	Australia	South Africa	Port Elizabeth	1	6	c Gibbs b Hall	22	(10)	-	-	-	-	-
10/03/2006	Int OD	Australia	South Africa	Durban	2	7	run out (Hall)	19	(24)	2.0	0	15	0	1
12/03/2006	Int OD	Australia	South Africa	Johannesburg	1	4	c Ntini b Hall	81	(51)	-	-	-	-	2
16/03/2006	Tests	Australia	South Africa	Cape Town	2	5	c Boucher b Hall....	6	(23)	-	-	-	-	-
16/03/2006	Tests	Australia	South Africa	Cape Town	4	5	not out.	14*	(20)	-	-	-	-	-
24/03/2006	Tests	Australia	South Africa	Durban	1	5	lbw b Kallis..	75	(155)	1.0	0	2	0	1
24/03/2006	Tests	Australia	South Africa	Durban	3	7	-	1.0	0	4	0	1	-	-
31/03/2006	Tests	Australia	South Africa	Johannesburg	2	5	lbw b Boje....	73	(153)	-	-	-	-	-
31/03/2006	Tests	Australia	South Africa	Johannesburg	4	2	lbw b Boje....	89	(197)	-	-	-	-	1
09/04/2006	Tests	Australia	Bangladesh	Fatullah	2	2	b Mohammad Rafique.	23	(65)	-	-	-	-	-
09/04/2006	Tests	Australia	Bangladesh	Fatullah	4	2	b Enamul Haque jr...	37	(79)	-	-	-	-	-
16/04/2006	Tests	Australia	Bangladesh	Chittagong	2	5	c Shahadat Hossain b Aftab Ahmed	182	(203)	-	-	-	-	-
16/04/2006	Tests	Australia	Bangladesh	Chittagong	4	4	-	-	-	-	-	-	-	-
23/04/2006	Int OD	Australia	Bangladesh	Chittagong	2	6	not out.	36*	(61)	3.0	0	13	0	-
26/04/2006	Int OD	Australia	Bangladesh	Fatullah	1	6	b Abdur Razzak	18	(15)	5.0	0	22	1	2
28/04/2006	Int OD	Australia	Bangladesh	Fatullah	2	6	-	5.0	1	13	0	-	-	-
2006-07														
18/09/2006	Int OD	Australia	West Indies	Kinrara	1	6	not out.	109*	(90)	-	-	-	-	2
22/09/2006	Int OD	Australia	India	Kinrara	1	6	c Dravid b Harbhajan Singh	13	(20)	-	-	-	-	2
24/09/2006	Int OD	Australia	West Indies	Kinrara	1	7	not out.	30*	(24)	-	-	-	-	-
18/10/2006	Int OD	Australia	West Indies	Mumbai	2	7	b Taylor	13	(16)	-	-	-	-	-
21/10/2006	Int OD	Australia	England	Jaipur	2	5	not out.	32*	(85)	-	-	-	-	2
29/10/2006	Int OD	Australia	India	Mohali	2	7	-	-	-	-	-	-	1	-

Start Date	Grade	Team	Opponent	Venue	Inn	Pos	How Out	Runs	(Balls)	O	M	R	W	Ct
01/11/2006	Int OD	Australia	New Zealand	Mohali	1	5	c Marshall b Franklin	35	(52)	-	-	-	-	-
05/11/2006	Int OD	Australia	West Indies	Mumbai	2	5		-	-	-	-	-	-	1
12/11/2006	Shield	Western Australia	Queensland	Perth	1	3	c Hayden b Johnson...	46	(87)	7.0	1	25	1	1
12/11/2006	Shield	Western Australia	Queensland	Perth	3	3	c Hartley b Hopes...	0	(5)	-	-	-	-	1
17/11/2006	Dom OD	Western Australia	Queensland	Perth	1	4	c Hartley b Hopes...	9	(12)	-	-	-	-	2
23/11/2006	Tests	Australia	England	Brisbane	1	5	b Flintoff....	86	(187)	-	-	-	-	1
23/11/2006	Tests	Australia	England	Brisbane	3	5	-	-	-	5.0	0	1	0	-
01/12/2006	Tests	Australia	England	Adelaide	2	5	b Hoggard	91	(212)	-	-	-	-	-
01/12/2006	Tests	Australia	England	Adelaide	4	4	not out.	61*	(66)	-	-	-	-	1
14/12/2006	Tests	Australia	England	Perth	1	4	not out.	74*	(161)	-	-	-	-	-
14/12/2006	Tests	Australia	England	Perth	3	4	c Jones b Panesar...	103	(156)	-	-	-	-	-
26/12/2006	Tests	Australia	England	Melbourne	2	5	b Hoggard	6	(20)	-	-	-	-	-
26/12/2006	Tests	Australia	England	Melbourne	4	4	-	-	-	-	-	-	-	-
02/01/2007	Tests	Australia	England	Sydney	2	4	c Read b Anderson....	37	(100)	-	-	1	-	1
02/01/2007	Tests	Australia	England	Sydney	4	4	-	-	-	-	-	-	-	-
09/01/2007	Int T20	Australia	England	Sydney	1	4	st Nixon b Panesar...	18	(9)	-	-	-	-	1
12/01/2007	Int OD	Australia	England	Melbourne	2	5	-	-	-	-	-	-	-	-
14/01/2007	Int OD	Australia	New Zealand	Hobart	1	6	c (S)Marshall b McMillan..	20	(32)	-	-	-	-	1
19/01/2007	Int OD	Australia	England	Brisbane	2	6	not out.	46*	(73)	-	-	-	-	-
21/01/2007	Int OD	Australia	New Zealand	Sydney	2	6	not out.	65*	(73)	-	-	-	-	2
26/01/2007	Int OD	Australia	England	Adelaide	2	4	-	-	-	-	-	-	-	-
28/01/2007	Int OD	Australia	New Zealand	Perth	1	6	not out.	29*	(16)	-	-	-	-	-
02/02/2007	Int OD	Australia	England	Sydney	2	6	b Bopara	6	(14)	-	-	-	-	-
04/02/2007	Int OD	Australia	New Zealand	Melbourne	2	6	run out (Vincent/Oram)....	8	(5)	-	-	-	-	2
09/02/2007	Int OD	Australia	England	Melbourne	1	6	c Nixon b Flintoff..	17	(19)	-	-	-	-	-
11/02/2007	Int OD	Australia	England	Sydney	2	6	c Strauss b Flintoff	0	(10)	2.0	0	12	0	-
16/02/2007	Int OD	Australia	New Zealand	Wellington	1	4	c Taylor b McMillan.	42	(96)	-	-	-	-	-

MICHAEL HUSSEY

Start Date	Grade	Team	Opponent	Venue	Inn	Pos	How Out	Runs	(Balls)	O	M	R	W	C
18/02/2007	Int OD	Australia	New Zealand	Auckland	1	4	c Taylor b McMillan.	105	(84)	-	-	-	-	3
20/02/2007	Int OD	Australia	New Zealand	Hamilton	1	5	c McCullum b Gillespie.....	13	(8)	-	-	-	-	1
14/03/2007	Int OD	Australia	Scotland	Basseterre	1	6	st Smith b Hoffmann.	4	(6)	-	-	-	-	-
18/03/2007	Int OD	Australia	Netherlands	Basseterre	1	6	c (S)Mohammad Kashif b Ten Doeschate..	2	(4)	-	-	-	-	1
24/03/2007	Int OD	Australia	South Africa	Basseterre	1	6	c Kallis b Hall	5	(3)	-	-	-	-	-
27/03/2007	Int OD	Australia	West Indies	North Sound	1	6	b Powell	9	(18)	-	-	-	-	-
31/03/2007	Int OD	Australia	Bangladesh	North Sound	2	6	-	-	-	-	-	-	-	-
08/04/2007	Int OD	Australia	England	North Sound	2	6	-	-	-	-	-	-	-	-
13/04/2007	Int OD	Australia	Ireland	Bridgetown	2	2	not out.	30*	(41)	-	-	2	-	-
16/04/2007	Int OD	Australia	Sri Lanka	St George's	2	6	-	-	-	-	-	-	-	-
20/04/2007	Int OD	Australia	New Zealand	St George's	1	5	c Styris b Franklin.	37	(44)	-	-	-	-	2
25/04/2007	Int OD	Australia	South Africa	Gros Islet	2	6	-	-	-	-	-	-	-	-
28/04/2007	Int OD	Australia	Sri Lanka	Bridgetown	1	7	-	-	-	-	-	-	-	-
2007–08														
12/09/2007	Int T20	Australia	Zimbabwe	Cape Town	1	5	run out (Sibanda)...	15	(23)	-	-	-	-	-
14/09/2007	Int T20	Australia	England	Cape Town	2	5	-	-	-	-	-	1	-	-
16/09/2007	Int T20	Australia	Bangladesh	Cape Town	2	5	-	-	-	-	-	1	-	-
18/09/2007	Int T20	Australia	Pakistan	Johannesburg	1	5	c Imran Nazir b Sohail Tanvir...	37	(25)	-	-	-	-	-
20/09/2007	Int T20	Australia	Sri Lanka	Cape Town	2	5	-	-	-	-	-	-	-	-
22/09/2007	Int T20	Australia	India	Durban	2	5	c Yuvraj Singh b Joginder Sharma	13	(12)	-	-	-	-	1
26/10/2007	Shield	Western Australia	Victoria	Melbourne	1	1	lbw b Denton.	0	(3)	-	-	-	-	-
26/10/2007	Shield	Western Australia	Victoria	Melbourne	3	1	c Hodge b White	59	(147)	-	-	1	-	-
31/10/2007	Dom OD	Western Australia	Victoria	Melbourne	1	6	c Blizzard b Siddle.	12	(17)	-	-	1	-	-
08/11/2007	Tests	Australia	Sri Lanka	Brisbane	1	4	c Atapattu b Fernando	133	(249)	-	-	-	-	-
08/11/2007	Tests	Australia	Sri Lanka	Brisbane	4	5	-	-	-	-	-	-	-	-
16/11/2007	Tests	Australia	Sri Lanka	Hobart	1	4	lbw b Fernando	132	(220)	-	-	2	-	1
16/11/2007	Tests	Australia	Sri Lanka	Hobart	3	4	not out.	34*	(48)	-	-	-	-	-

Start Date	Grade	Team	Opponent	Venue	Inn	Pos	How Out	Runs	(Balls)	O	M	R	W	Ct
01/12/2007	Dom OD	Western Australia	Tasmania	Hobart	1	4	b Drew..	0	(3)	–	–	–	–	1
03/12/2007	Shield	Western Australia	Tasmania	Hobart	1	4	run out (Di Venuto).	7	(18)	3.0	0	22	0	–
03/12/2007	Shield	Western Australia	Tasmania	Hobart	3	4	not out.	59*	(116)	2.0	0	11	0	–
11/12/2007	Int T20	Australia	New Zealand	Perth	1	3	st McCullum b Patel.	22	(16)	–	–	–	–	–
14/12/2007	Int OD	Australia	New Zealand	Adelaide	2	6	–	–	–	–	–	–	–	–
16/12/2007	Int OD	Australia	New Zealand	Sydney	2	4	–	–	–	–	–	–	–	–
20/12/2007	Int OD	Australia	New Zealand	Hobart	1	4	c How b Oram..	9	(17)	–	–	–	–	1
26/12/2007	Tests	Australia	India	Melbourne	1	4	lbw b Kumble.	2	(3)	–	–	–	–	–
26/12/2007	Tests	Australia	India	Melbourne	3	4	c Tendulkar b Singh.	36	(84)	–	–	–	–	3
02/01/2008	Tests	Australia	India	Sydney	1	4	c Tendulkar b Singh.	41	(79)	–	–	–	–	2
02/01/2008	Tests	Australia	India	Sydney	3	4	not out.	145*	(259)	–	–	–	–	2
16/01/2008	Tests	Australia	India	Perth	2	4	c Dhoni b Singh	0	(8)	–	–	–	–	–
16/01/2008	Tests	Australia	India	Perth	4	4	lbw b Singh….	46	(113)	–	–	–	–	1
24/01/2008	Tests	Australia	India	Adelaide	2	4	b Pathan	22	(66)	–	–	–	–	–
24/01/2008	Tests	Australia	India	Adelaide	4	4	–	–	–	–	–	–	–	–
01/02/2008	Int T20	Australia	India	Melbourne	2	4	–	–	–	–	–	–	–	–
03/02/2008	Int OD	Australia	India	Brisbane	2	6	–	–	–	–	–	–	–	–
08/02/2008	Int OD	Australia	Sri Lanka	Sydney	1	6	c Dilshan b Amerasinghe….	10	(13)	–	–	–	–	1
10/02/2008	Int OD	Australia	India	Melbourne	1	6	not out.	65*	(88)	–	–	–	–	–
15/02/2008	Int OD	Australia	Sri Lanka	Perth	1	6	c Jayawardene b Kulasekara	25	(28)	–	–	–	–	1
17/02/2008	Int OD	Australia	India	Adelaide	1	6	c Dhoni b Pathan….	5	(21)	–	–	–	–	–
22/02/2008	Int OD	Australia	Sri Lanka	Melbourne	1	6	not out.	64*	(98)	–	–	–	–	1
24/02/2008	Int OD	Australia	India	Sydney	1	6	not out.	15*	(10)	–	–	–	–	–
29/02/2008	Int OD	Australia	Sri Lanka	Melbourne	2	6	b Kapugedera.	5	(25)	–	–	–	–	2
02/03/2008	Int OD	Australia	India	Sydney	1	6	run out (Dhoni/Pathan)….	45	(67)	–	–	–	–	1
04/03/2008	Int OD	Australia	India	Brisbane	2	6	c Dhoni b Sreesanth.	44	(42)	–	–	–	–	–
19/04/2008	Ind IPL	Chennai Super Kings	Kings XI Punjab	Mohali	1	3	not out.	116*	(54)	–	–	–	–	–

Start Date	Grade	Team	Opponent	Venue	Inn	Pos	How Out	Runs	(Balls)	O	M	R	W	C
23/04/2008	Ind IPL	Chennai Super Kings	Mumbai Indians	Chennai	1	3	b Kulkarni....	5	(7)	-	-	-	-	-
26/04/2008	Ind IPL	Chennai Super Kings	Kolkata Knight Riders	Chennai	2	4	-	-	-	-	-	-	-	-
28/04/2008	Ind IPL	Chennai Super Kings	Royal Challengers Bangalore	Bangalore	1	3	c Dravid b Zaheer Khan.....	47	(37)	-	-	-	-	2
16/05/2008	Fclass	Australians	Jamaica Select XI	Jamaica	2	4	c Ingram b Wallace..	19	-	-	-	-	-	-
16/05/2008	Fclass	Australians	Jamaica Select XI	Jamaica	4	4	-	-	-	-	-	-	-	-
22/05/2008	Tests	Australia	West Indies	Kingston	1	4	c Bravo b Jaggernauth	56	(146)	-	-	-	-	1
22/05/2008	Tests	Australia	West Indies	Kingston	3	4	b Powell	1	(15)	-	-	-	-	-
30/05/2008	Tests	Australia	West Indies	North Sound	1	4	c Chanderpaul b Sammy	10	(38)	-	-	-	-	-
30/05/2008	Tests	Australia	West Indies	North Sound	3	2	c Ramdin b Bravo.....	40	(94)	6.0	2	14	0	2
12/06/2008	Tests	Australia	West Indies	Bridgetown	1	4	c Powell b Bravo....	12	(25)	-	-	-	-	1
12/06/2008	Tests	Australia	West Indies	Bridgetown	3	4	c Bravo b Benn	18	(48)	-	-	-	-	-
20/06/2008	Int T20	Australia	West Indies	Bridgetown	1	8	-	-	-	-	-	-	-	-
24/06/2008	Int OD	Australia	West Indies	Kingstown	1	5	c Pollard b Gayle...	44	(58)	-	-	-	-	1
27/06/2008	Int OD	Australia	West Indies	St George's	1	5	c Marshall b Bravo..	62	(105)	-	-	-	-	1
29/06/2008	Int OD	Australia	West Indies	St George's	2	6	-	-	-	-	-	-	-	-
04/07/2008	Int OD	Australia	West Indies	Basseterre	1	3	c Bravo b Sammy	37	(46)	-	-	-	-	-
06/07/2008	Int OD	Australia	West Indies	Basseterre	1	5	c Findlay b Edwards.	51	(56)	-	-	-	-	1
2008-09														
30/08/2008	Int OD	Australia	Bangladesh	Darwin	1	4	b Shahadat Hossain.	85	(87)	-	-	-	-	-
03/09/2008	Int OD	Australia	Bangladesh	Darwin	2	4	not out.	8*	(20)	-	-	-	-	1
06/09/2008	Int OD	Australia	Bangladesh	Darwin	1	4	not out.	57*	(72)	-	-	-	-	1
02/10/2008	Fclass	Australians	India Board XI	Hyderabad	2	4	not out.	126*	(302)	-	-	-	-	2
02/10/2008	Fclass	Australians	India Board XI	Hyderabad	4	5	-	-	-	-	-	-	-	-
09/10/2008	Tests	Australia	India	Bangalore	1	4	b Zaheer Khan.	146	(276)	-	-	-	-	-
09/10/2008	Tests	Australia	India	Bangalore	3	4	b Harbhajan Singh...	31	(72)	-	-	-	-	1
17/10/2008	Tests	Australia	India	Mohali	2	4	c Dhoni b Sharma....	54	(119)	-	-	-	-	-
17/10/2008	Tests	Australia	India	Mohali	4	4	lbw b Harbhajan Singh	1	(4)	8.0	0	38	0	1

Start Date	Grade	Team	Opponent	Venue	Inn	Pos	How Out	Runs	(Balls)	O	M	R	W	Ct
29/10/2008	Tests	Australia	India	Delhi	2	4	b Sehwag	53	(146)	-	-	-	-	-
29/10/2008	Tests	Australia	India	Delhi	4	4	-	-	-	-	-	-	-	-
06/11/2008	Tests	Australia	India	Nagpur	2	4	run out (Vijay/Dhoni)	90	(229)	-	-	-	-	-
06/11/2008	Tests	Australia	India	Nagpur	4	5	c Dravid b Mishra...	19	(30)	4.0	2	3	0	1
20/11/2008	Tests	Australia	New Zealand	Brisbane	1	4	lbw b Martin...	35	(78)	-	-	-	-	-
20/11/2008	Tests	Australia	New Zealand	Brisbane	3	4	c McCullum b O'Brien	0	(4)	-	-	-	-	-
28/11/2008	Tests	Australia	New Zealand	Adelaide	2	4	c Redmond b Martin...	70	(183)	-	-	-	-	-
28/11/2008	Tests	Australia	New Zealand	Adelaide	4	4	-	-	-	-	-	-	-	-
17/12/2008	Tests	Australia	South Africa	Perth	1	4	c De Villiers b Steyn	0	(7)	-	-	-	-	-
17/12/2008	Tests	Australia	South Africa	Perth	3	4	b Ntini.	8	(35)	-	-	-	-	1
26/12/2008	Tests	Australia	South Africa	Melbourne	1	4	c Boucher b Steyn....	0	(9)	5.0	0	22	1	1
26/12/2008	Tests	Australia	South Africa	Melbourne	3	4	c Amla b Morkel	2	(8)	-	-	-	-	-
03/01/2009	Tests	Australia	South Africa	Sydney	1	4	c Kallis b Harris....	30	(99)	-	-	-	-	1
03/01/2009	Tests	Australia	South Africa	Sydney	3	4	not out.	45*	(92)	-	-	-	-	-
11/01/2009	Int T20	Australia	South Africa	Melbourne	1	6	run out (Gibbs)	7	(8)	-	-	-	-	1
13/01/2009	Int T20	Australia	South Africa	Brisbane	2	4	not out.	53*	(32)	1.0	0	5	0	-
16/01/2009	Int OD	Australia	South Africa	Melbourne	1	2	c Boucher b Steyn....	6	(11)	-	-	-	-	1
18/01/2009	Int OD	Australia	South Africa	Hobart	1	4	c Gibbs b Kallis....	28	(34)	-	-	-	-	2
23/01/2009	Int OD	Australia	South Africa	Sydney	1	4	run out (De Villiers/Boucher)...	12	(15)	-	-	-	-	-
26/01/2009	Int OD	Australia	South Africa	Adelaide	1	4	lbw b Botha...	28	(37)	-	-	-	-	-
30/01/2009	Int OD	Australia	South Africa	Perth	2	5	b Tsotsobe....	78	(96)	-	-	-	-	-
01/02/2009	Int OD	Australia	New Zealand	Perth	1	6	c Elliott b O'Brien.	49	(65)	-	-	-	-	1
06/02/2009	Int OD	Australia	New Zealand	Melbourne	1	5	c Vettori b O'Brien.	75	(94)	-	-	-	-	1
08/02/2009	Int OD	Australia	New Zealand	Sydney	1	6	c Taylor b Mills....	51	(32)	-	-	-	-	1
10/02/2009	Int OD	Australia	New Zealand	Adelaide	2	5	not out.	75*	(71)	-	-	-	-	-
13/02/2009	Int OD	Australia	New Zealand	Brisbane	1	5	c Diamanti b Vettori	9	(13)	-	-	-	-	2
26/02/2009	Tests	Australia	South Africa	Johannesburg	1	4	c Kallis b Morkel....	4	(21)	-	-	-	-	1

Start Date	Grade	Team	Opponent	Venue	Inn	Pos	How Out	Runs	(Balls)	O	M	R	W	Ct
26/02/2009	Tests	Australia	South Africa	Johannesburg	3	4	c Ntini b Kallis.....	0	(1)	-	-	-	-	-
06/03/2009	Tests	Australia	South Africa	Durban	1	4	b Morkel	50	(144)	-	-	-	-	-
06/03/2009	Tests	Australia	South Africa	Durban	3	4	c Kallis b Duminy....	19	(50)	-	-	-	-	-
19/03/2009	Tests	Australia	South Africa	Cape Town	1	4	b Steyn.	20	(20)	-	-	-	-	-
19/03/2009	Tests	Australia	South Africa	Cape Town	3	4	c Duminy b Steyn.....	39	(153)	-	-	-	-	-
27/03/2009	Int T20	Australia	South Africa	Johannesburg	1	5	run out (Botha)	0	(1)	-	-	-	-	-
03/04/2009	Int OD	Australia	South Africa	Durban	1	5	not out.	83*	(79)	-	-	-	-	2
05/04/2009	Int OD	Australia	South Africa	Centurion	1	5	lbw b Parnell.	3	(8)	-	-	-	-	-
09/04/2009	Int OD	Australia	South Africa	Cape Town	2	5	lbw b Van Der Merwe.	1	(4)	-	-	-	-	1
13/04/2009	Int OD	Australia	South Africa	Port Elizabeth	2	5	lbw b Van Der Merwe.	2	(9)	-	-	-	-	-
17/04/2009	Int OD	Australia	South Africa	Johannesburg	1	5	not out.	49*	(55)	-	-	-	-	-

2009

Start Date	Grade	Team	Opponent	Venue	Inn	Pos	How Out	Runs	(Balls)	O	M	R	W	Ct
06/06/2009	Int T20	Australia	West Indies	The Oval	1	7	not out.	28*	(15)	-	-	-	-	-
08/06/2009	Int T20	Australia	Sri Lanka	Nottingham	1	7	lbw b Mendis.	1	(5)	-	-	-	-	-
01/07/2009	Fclass	Australians	England Lions	Worcester	1	4	b Harmison....	150	(234)	-	-	-	-	1
01/07/2009	Fclass	Australians	England Lions	Worcester	3	6	retired hurt..	62+	(69)	-	-	-	-	-
08/07/2009	Tests	Australia	England	Cardiff	2	4	c Prior b Anderson..	3	(16)	-	-	-	-	2
08/07/2009	Tests	Australia	England	Cardiff	4	4	-	-	-	-	-	-	1	-
16/07/2009	Tests	Australia	England	Lord's	2	4	b Flintoff....	51	(91)	-	-	-	-	-
16/07/2009	Tests	Australia	England	Lord's	4	4	c Collingwood b Swann	27	(63)	-	-	-	-	1
24/07/2009	Fclass	Australians	Northamptonshire	Northampton	1	4	....	75	(123)	-	-	-	-	-
24/07/2009	Fclass	Australians	Northamptonshire	Northampton	3	5	not out.	9*	(23)	-	-	-	-	-
30/07/2009	Tests	Australia	England	Birmingham	1	4	b Onions	0	(1)	-	-	-	-	-
30/07/2009	Tests	Australia	England	Birmingham	3	4	c Prior b Broad	64	(130)	-	-	-	-	-
07/08/2009	Tests	Australia	England	Leeds	2	4	lbw b Broad...	10	(10)	-	-	-	-	1
07/08/2009	Tests	Australia	England	Leeds	4	4	-	-	-	-	-	-	-	-
20/08/2009	Tests	Australia	England	The Oval	2	4	lbw b Broad...	0	(3)	-	-	-	-	1

Start Date	Grade	Team	Opponent	Venue	Inn	Pos	How Out	Runs	(Balls)	O	M	R	W	Ct
20/08/2009	Tests	Australia	England	The Oval	4	4	c Cook b Swann	121	(263)	–	–	–	–	1
04/09/2009	Int OD	Australia	England	The Oval	1	6	b Sidebottom...	20	(15)	–	–	–	–	1
06/09/2009	Int OD	Australia	England	Lord's	1	6	b Swann.	8	(14)	–	–	–	–	–
09/09/2009	Int OD	Australia	England	Southampton	2	6	not out.	8*	(4)	–	–	–	–	1
12/09/2009	Int OD	Australia	England	Lord's	2	7	–	–	–	–	–	–	–	–
15/09/2009	Int OD	Australia	England	Nottingham	2	5	c Sidebottom b Mascarenhas	6	(9)	–	–	–	–	1
17/09/2009	Int OD	Australia	England	Nottingham	1	4	c Denly b Swann	65	(69)	–	–	–	–	1
20/09/2009	Int OD	Australia	England	Chester-le-St	1	5	c Denly b Bresnan...	49	(54)	–	–	–	–	–
2009–10														
26/09/2009	Int OD	Australia	West Indies	Johannesburg	1	4	c Fletcher b Bernard	6	(14)	–	–	–	–	1
28/09/2009	Int OD	Australia	India	Centurion	1	4	c Tendulkar b Sharma	67	(65)	–	–	–	–	–
30/09/2009	Int OD	Australia	Pakistan	Centurion	2	4	b Naved-ul-Hasan...	64	(87)	–	–	–	–	–
02/10/2009	Int OD	Australia	England	Centurion	2	4	–	–	–	–	–	–	–	–
05/10/2009	Int OD	Australia	New Zealand	Centurion	2	5	c Patel b Mills	11	(9)	–	–	–	–	1
25/10/2009	Int OD	Australia	India	Vadodara	1	5	c Kohli b Sharma.....	73	(54)	–	–	–	–	–
28/10/2009	Int OD	Australia	India	Nagpur	2	5	b Jadeja	53	(60)	–	–	–	–	–
31/10/2009	Int OD	Australia	India	Delhi	1	3	not out.	81*	(82)	–	–	–	–	–
02/11/2009	Int OD	Australia	India	Mohali	1	5	c Sharma b Yuvraj Singh....	40	(41)	–	–	–	–	1
05/11/2009	Int OD	Australia	India	Hyderabad	1	5	not out.	31*	(22)	3.0	0	26	0	–
08/11/2009	Int OD	Australia	India	Guwahati	2	5	not out.	35*	(62)	–	–	–	–	–
26/11/2009	Tests	Australia	West Indies	Brisbane	1	4	c and b Benn.	66	(132)	–	–	–	–	1
26/11/2009	Tests	Australia	West Indies	Brisbane	4	4	–	–	–	2.0	0	3	1	–
04/12/2009	Tests	Australia	West Indies	Adelaide	2	4	c Ramdin b Roach....	41	(126)	–	–	–	–	1
04/12/2009	Tests	Australia	West Indies	Adelaide	4	4	c Ramdin b Bravo....	29	(81)	–	–	–	–	–
16/12/2009	Tests	Australia	West Indies	Perth	1	4	c Ramdin b Rampaul.	82	(172)	–	–	–	–	–
16/12/2009	Tests	Australia	West Indies	Perth	3	4	c Dowlin b Benn	17	(32)	–	–	–	–	2
26/12/2009	Tests	Australia	Pakistan	Melbourne	1	4	lbw b Saeed Ajmal....	82	(113)	–	–	–	–	1

Start Date	Grade	Team	Opponent	Venue	Inn	Pos	How Out	Runs	(Balls)	O	M	R	W	C
26/12/2009	Tests	Australia	Pakistan	Melbourne	3	4	lbw b Mohammad Aamer	4	(3)	-	-	-	-	1
03/01/2010	Tests	Australia	Pakistan	Sydney	1	4	c Misbah-ul-Haq b Mohammad Asif.	28	(52)	-	-	-	-	1
03/01/2010	Tests	Australia	Pakistan	Sydney	3	4	not out.	134*	(284)	-	-	-	-	1
14/01/2010	Tests	Australia	Pakistan	Hobart	1	4	c Sarfraz Ahmed b Mohammad Aamer	6	(12)	-	-	-	-	1
14/01/2010	Tests	Australia	Pakistan	Hobart	3	4	not out.	13*	(21)	-	-	-	-	-
22/01/2010	Int OD	Australia	Pakistan	Brisbane	2	6	not out.	35*	(37)	2.0	0	12	0	1
24/01/2010	Int OD	Australia	Pakistan	Sydney	1	6	c Shoaib Malik b Mohammad Aamer.	29	(34)	-	-	-	-	-
26/01/2010	Int OD	Australia	Pakistan	Adelaide	1	6	c Younis Khan b Umar Gul..	49	(28)	-	-	-	-	-
29/01/2010	Int OD	Australia	Pakistan	Perth	1	6	c Mohammad Yousuf b Saeed Ajmal.	67	(75)	-	-	-	-	-
31/01/2010	Int OD	Australia	Pakistan	Perth	2	6	not out.	40*	(46)	-	-	-	-	-
07/02/2010	Int OD	Australia	West Indies	Melbourne	1	6	c Ramdin b Rampaul..	28	(25)	-	-	-	-	-
09/02/2010	Int OD	Australia	West Indies	Adelaide	2	5	-	-	-	-	-	1	-	-
12/02/2010	Int OD	Australia	West Indies	Sydney	1	6	b Smith.	44	(53)	-	-	-	-	-
14/02/2010	Int OD	Australia	West Indies	Brisbane	1	6	b Pollard	23	(17)	-	-	-	-	-
03/03/2010	Int OD	Australia	New Zealand	Napier	1	6	b Bond..	59	(59)	-	-	-	-	2
06/03/2010	Int OD	Australia	New Zealand	Auckland	1	6	c (S)McCullum b Bond	56	(63)	-	-	-	-	-
09/03/2010	Int OD	Australia	New Zealand	Hamilton	2	4	c Ingram b Southee..	9	(15)	-	-	-	-	-
11/03/2010	Int OD	Australia	New Zealand	Auckland	2	6	not out.	28*	(17)	-	-	-	-	1
13/03/2010	Int OD	Australia	New Zealand	Wellington	2	6	b Southee	46	(55)	-	-	-	-	-
19/03/2010	Tests	Australia	New Zealand	Wellington	1	4	c Watling b Martin..	4	(11)	-	-	-	-	1
19/03/2010	Tests	Australia	New Zealand	Wellington	4	5	-	-	-	-	-	-	-	-
27/03/2010	Tests	Australia	New Zealand	Hamilton	1	4	c McCullum b Southee	22	(48)	-	-	-	-	1
27/03/2010	Tests	Australia	New Zealand	Hamilton	3	4	c McCullum b Arnel..	67	(160)	-	-	-	-	-
06/04/2010	Ind IPL	Chennai Super Kings	Mumbai Indians	Chennai	1	5	not out.	14*	(15)	-	-	-	-	-
10/04/2010	Ind IPL	Chennai Super Kings	Deccan Chargers	Nagpur	1	5	c Sumanth b Symonds.	8	(11)	-	-	-	-	-
15/04/2010	Ind IPL	Chennai Super Kings	Delhi Daredevils	Chennai	1	5	c Dilshan b Sehwag..	15	(18)	-	-	-	-	-
02/05/2010	Int T20	Australia	Pakistan	Gros Islet	1	5	run out (Kamran Akmal).....	17	(8)	-	-	-	-	2

Start Date	Grade	Team	Opponent	Venue	Inn	Pos	How Out	Runs	(Balls)	O	M	R	W	Ct
05/05/2010	Int T20	Australia	Bangladesh	Bridgetown	1	7	not out.	47*	(29)	–	–	–	–	3
07/05/2010	Int T20	Australia	India	Bridgetown	1	6	b Nehra.	8	(10)	–	–	–	–	1
09/05/2010	Int T20	Australia	Sri Lanka	Bridgetown	1	7	not out.	39*	(26)	–	–	–	–	1
11/05/2010	Int T20	Australia	West Indies	Gros Islet	2	7	–	–	–	–	–	1	–	–
14/05/2010	Int T20	Australia	Pakistan	Gros Islet	2	7	not out.	60*	(24)	–	–	–	–	–
16/05/2010	Int T20	Australia	England	Bridgetown	1	7	not out.	17*	(10)	–	–	–	–	–

2010

Start Date	Grade	Team	Opponent	Venue	Inn	Pos	How Out	Runs	(Balls)	O	M	R	W	Ct
17/06/2010	Int OD	Australia	Ireland	Dublin	1	6	c O'Brien b O'Brien.	8	(17)	–	–	–	–	–
22/06/2010	Int OD	Australia	England	Southampton	1	6	c Kieswetter b Yardy	28	(38)	–	–	–	–	–
24/06/2010	Int OD	Australia	England	Cardiff	1	6	b Anderson....	14	(27)	–	–	–	–	–
27/06/2010	Int OD	Australia	England	Manchester	1	6	b Collingwood.	21	(21)	–	–	–	–	–
30/06/2010	Int OD	Australia	England	The Oval	1	6	run out (Anderson/Strauss)	1	(1)	–	–	–	–	–
03/07/2010	Int OD	Australia	England	Lord's	1	6	c Anderson b Broad..	79	(60)	2.0	0	22	0	1
05/07/2010	Int T20	Australia	Pakistan	Birmingham	2	6	b Umar Gul....	18	(15)	–	–	–	–	–
06/07/2010	Int T20	Australia	Pakistan	Birmingham	2	7	lbw b Umar Gul	25	(14)	–	–	–	–	–
13/07/2010	Tests	Australia	Pakistan	Lord's	1	5	not out.	56*	(100)	–	–	–	–	1
13/07/2010	Tests	Australia	Pakistan	Lord's	3	5	c Imran Farhat b Umar Gul.	0	(1)	–	–	–	–	2
21/07/2010	Tests	Australia	Pakistan	Leeds	1	5	lbw b Umar Gul	5	(13)	–	–	–	–	–
21/07/2010	Tests	Australia	Pakistan	Leeds	3	5	c Umar Akmal b Mohammad Aamer...	8	(16)	–	–	–	–	1

2010-11

Start Date	Grade	Team	Opponent	Venue	Inn	Pos	How Out	Runs	(Balls)	O	M	R	W	Ct
18/09/2010	Dom T20	Chennai Super Kings	Victoria	Port Elizabeth	1	1	c Finch b McGain....	25	(28)	–	–	–	–	–
22/09/2010	Dom T20	Chennai Super Kings	Warriors	Port Elizabeth	1	1	b Botha.	50	(39)	–	–	–	–	2
24/09/2010	Dom T20	Chennai Super Kings	Royal Challengers Bangalore	Durban	1	1	c Steyn b Vinay Kumar	6	(12)	–	–	–	–	–
26/09/2010	Dom T20	Chennai Super Kings	Warriors	Johannesburg	2	1	not out.	51*	(46)	–	–	–	–	–
01/10/2010	Tests	Australia	India	Mohali	1	5	lbw b Zaheer Khan...	17	(76)	–	–	–	–	–
01/10/2010	Tests	Australia	India	Mohali	3	5	lbw b Harbhajan Singh	28	(72)	–	–	–	–	2
09/10/2010	Tests	Australia	India	Bangalore	1	5	c Sehwag b Zaheer Khan....	34	(45)	–	–	–	–	–

Start Date	Grade	Team	Opponent	Venue	Inn	Pos	How Out	Runs	(Balls)	O	M	R	W	C
09/10/2010	Tests	Australia	India	Bangalore	3	5	lbw b Ojha.....	20	(51)	-	-	-	-	-
20/10/2010	Int OD	Australia	India	Visakhapatnam	1	4	lbw b Ashwin...	69	(77)	-	-	-	-	-
29/10/2010	Shield	Western Australia	South Australia	Adelaide	2	3	c Klinger b O'Brien.	0	(1)	-	-	-	-	1
29/10/2010	Shield	Western Australia	South Australia	Adelaide	3	3	c Smith b George....	3	(11)	-	-	-	-	-
03/11/2010	Int OD	Australia	Sri Lanka	Melbourne	1	4	not out.	71*	(91)	-	-	-	-	-
05/11/2010	Int OD	Australia	Sri Lanka	Sydney	2	6	c Mathews b Muralidaran...	15	(19)	-	-	-	-	-
07/11/2010	Int OD	Australia	Sri Lanka	Brisbane	2	4	not out.	6*	(26)	-	-	-	-	1
17/11/2010	Shield	Western Australia	Victoria	Melbourne	1	3	c Hussey b McDonald.	0	(18)	-	-	-	-	-
17/11/2010	Shield	Western Australia	Victoria	Melbourne	3	3	c Hill b Wright	118	(160)	-	-	-	-	1
25/11/2010	Tests	Australia	England	Brisbane	2	5	c Cook b Finn.	195	(330)	-	-	-	-	1
25/11/2010	Tests	Australia	England	Brisbane	4	5	-	-	-	-	-	-	-	-
03/12/2010	Tests	Australia	England	Adelaide	1	5	c Collingwood b Swann	93	(183)	-	-	-	-	1
03/12/2010	Tests	Australia	England	Adelaide	3	5	c Anderson b Finn....	52	(107)	-	-	-	-	-
16/12/2010	Tests	Australia	England	Perth	1	5	c Prior b Swann	61	(104)	-	-	-	-	1
16/12/2010	Tests	Australia	England	Perth	3	5	c Swann b Tremlett..	116	(172)	-	-	-	-	1
26/12/2010	Tests	Australia	England	Melbourne	1	5	c Prior b Anderson..	8	(41)	-	-	-	-	-
26/12/2010	Tests	Australia	England	Melbourne	3	5	c Bell b Bresnan.....	0	(7)	-	-	-	-	-
03/01/2011	Tests	Australia	England	Sydney	1	5	b Collingwood.	33	(92)	1.0	0	2	0	1
03/01/2011	Tests	Australia	England	Sydney	3	5	c Pietersen b Bresnan	12	(49)	-	-	-	-	1
16/01/2011	Int OD	Australia	England	Melbourne	2	5	c Tremlett b Bresnan	21	(15)	-	-	-	-	-
03/03/2011	Shield	Western Australia	Queensland	Perth	2	3	b Hopes.	19	(53)	-	-	-	-	-
03/03/2011	Shield	Western Australia	Queensland	Perth	4	3	c Hartley b Gannon..	11	(40)	-	-	-	-	-
13/03/2011	Int OD	Australia	Kenya	Bangalore	1	6	c Obuya b Odhiambo..	54	(43)	-	-	-	-	1
16/03/2011	Int OD	Australia	Canada	Bangalore	2	6	-	-	-	-	-	-	-	-
19/03/2011	Int OD	Australia	Pakistan	Colombo	1	6	c Misbah-ul-Haq b Abdur Rehman..	12	(22)	-	-	-	-	1
24/03/2011	Int OD	Australia	India	Ahmedabad	1	5	b Zaheer Khan.	3	(9)	-	-	-	-	-
09/04/2011	Int OD	Australia	Bangladesh	Mirpur	1	6	c Mahmudullah b Suhrawadi Shuvo.	33	(51)	-	-	-	-	-

Start Date	Grade	Team	Opponent	Venue	Inn	Pos	How Out	Runs	(Balls)	O	M	R	W	C
11/04/2011	Int OD	Australia	Bangladesh	Mirpur	2	6	-	108	(91)	-	-	-	-	-
13/04/2011	Int OD	Australia	Bangladesh	Mirpur	1	5	lbw b Shafiul Islam.	83*	(56)	-	-	-	-	-
16/04/2011	Ind IPL	Chennai Super Kings	Royal Challengers Bangalore	Chennai	1	1	not out.	8	(10)	-	-	-	-	-
18/04/2011	Ind IPL	Chennai Super Kings	Kochi Tuskers Kerala	Kochi	1	1	c Patel b Singh	8	(10)	-	-	-	-	2
22/04/2011	Ind IPL	Chennai Super Kings	Mumbai Indians	Mumbai	2	1	c Pollard b Malinga.	41	(33)	-	-	-	-	-
25/04/2011	Ind IPL	Chennai Super Kings	Pune Warriors	Chennai	1	2	c Pandey b Taylor…	61	(48)	-	-	-	-	-
27/04/2011	Ind IPL	Chennai Super Kings	Pune Warriors	Mumbai	2	1	c Pandey b Kartik…	9	(18)	-	-	-	-	-
01/05/2011	Ind IPL	Chennai Super Kings	Deccan Chargers	Chennai	1	2	c Sharma b Harmeet Singh…	46	(41)	-	-	-	-	1
04/05/2011	Ind IPL	Chennai Super Kings	Rajasthan Royals	Chennai	2	1	not out.	79*	(55)	-	-	-	-	-
07/05/2011	Ind IPL	Chennai Super Kings	Kolkata Knight Riders	Kolkata	1	1	c Morgan b Balaji…	15	(26)	-	-	-	-	-
09/05/2011	Ind IPL	Chennai Super Kings	Rajasthan Royals	Jaipur	1	1	b Botha.	46	(30)	-	-	-	-	-
12/05/2011	Ind IPL	Chennai Super Kings	Delhi Daredevils	Chennai	1	1	lbw b Pathan..	5	(4)	-	-	-	-	-
18/05/2011	Ind IPL	Chennai Super Kings	Kochi Tuskers Kerala	Chennai	1	1	c Gnaneswara Rao b Jadeja.	32	(37)	-	-	-	-	-
22/05/2011	Ind IPL	Chennai Super Kings	Royal Challengers Bangalore	Bangalore	1	1	b Zaheer Khan.	4	(7)	-	-	-	-	-
24/05/2011	Ind IPL	Chennai Super Kings	Royal Challengers Bangalore	Mumbai	2	1	lbw b Zaheer Khan…	0	(4)	-	-	-	-	-
28/05/2011	Ind IPL	Chennai Super Kings	Royal Challengers Bangalore	Chennai	1	1	c Mithun b Syed Mohammad..	63	(45)	-	-	-	-	1
2011–12														
10/08/2011	Int OD	Australia	Sri Lanka	Pallekele	2	5	not out.	2*	(11)	-	-	-	-	1
14/08/2011	Int OD	Australia	Sri Lanka	Hambantota	2	5	-	-	-	-	-	2	-	-
16/08/2011	Int OD	Australia	Sri Lanka	Hambantota	2	5	c (S)Randiv b Malinga	63	(76)	-	-	-	-	3
20/08/2011	Int OD	Australia	Sri Lanka	Colombo	2	5	c Sangakkara b Prasanna…	0	(1)	-	-	-	-	-
22/08/2011	Int OD	Australia	Sri Lanka	Colombo	1	5	c Sangakkara b Prasanna…	6	(16)	-	-	-	-	1
25/08/2011	Fclass	Australians	Sri Lanka Board XI	Colombo	2	3	st Silva b Perera…	28	(52)	-	-	-	-	-
25/08/2011	Fclass	Australians	Sri Lanka Board XI	Colombo	4	3	-	-	-	-	-	1	-	-
31/08/2011	Tests	Australia	Sri Lanka	Galle	1	5	lbw b Dilshan.	95	(177)	-	-	-	-	-
31/08/2011	Tests	Australia	Sri Lanka	Galle	3	5	c Paranavitana b Herath…	15	(37)	-	-	-	-	1
08/09/2011	Tests	Australia	Sri Lanka	Pallekele	2	5	c Sangakkara b Samaraweera	142	(244)	1.0	-	1	1	1

Start Date	Grade	Team	Opponent	Venue	Inn	Pos	How Out	Runs	(Balls)	O	M	R	W	C
08/09/2011	Tests	Australia	Sri Lanka	Pallekele	4	5	-	—	—	4.0	2	2	1	-
16/09/2011	Tests	Australia	Sri Lanka	Colombo	1	6	b Eranga	118	(178)	2.0	1	5	0	-
16/09/2011	Tests	Australia	Sri Lanka	Colombo	3	6	c Welagedara b Dilshan….	93	(138)	-	-	-	-	2
24/09/2011	Dom T20	Chennai Super Kings	Mumbai Indians	Chennai	1	1	c Blizzard b Ahmed.	81	(57)	-	-	-	-	-
28/09/2011	Dom T20	Chennai Super Kings	Cape Cobras	Chennai	2	1	st Vilas b Duminy…	29	(24)	-	-	-	-	2
02/10/2011	Dom T20	Chennai Super Kings	Trinidad & Tobago	Chennai	2	1	c Ramdin b Rampaul..	13	(12)	-	-	-	-	-
04/10/2011	Dom T20	Chennai Super Kings	New South Wales	Chennai	2	1	lbw b Clark…	37	(27)	-	-	-	-	1
19/10/2011	Int OD	Australia	South Africa	Centurion	1	4	not out.	30*	(21)	-	-	-	-	-
23/10/2011	Int OD	Australia	South Africa	Port Elizabeth	2	4	run out (Botha/Boucher)…	37	(62)	-	-	-	-	1
28/10/2011	Int OD	Australia	South Africa	Durban	2	6	not out.	45*	(64)	-	-	-	-	-
01/11/2011	Fclass	Australians	South Africa A	Potchefstroom	2	6	not out.	41*	(86)	-	-	-	-	1
01/11/2011	Fclass	Australians	South Africa A	Potchefstroom	4	6	-	—	—	2.0	0	7	0	-
09/11/2011	Tests	Australia	South Africa	Cape Town	1	6	c Boucher b Morkel..	1	(18)	-	-	-	-	-
09/11/2011	Tests	Australia	South Africa	Cape Town	3	5	c Prince b Morkel…	0	(1)	-	-	-	-	-
17/11/2011	Tests	Australia	South Africa	Johannesburg	2	6	b Steyn.	20	(27)	4.0	0	10	0	1
17/11/2011	Tests	Australia	South Africa	Johannesburg	4	6	lbw b Philander	39	(77)	5.0	0	14	0	-
01/12/2011	Tests	Australia	New Zealand	Brisbane	2	6	c Ryder b Vettori…	15	(49)	2.0	0	5	0	-
01/12/2011	Tests	Australia	New Zealand	Brisbane	4	6	-	—	—	4.0	1	7	1	-
09/12/2011	Tests	Australia	New Zealand	Hobart	2	6	c Young b Boult	8	(16)	-	-	-	-	-
09/12/2011	Tests	Australia	New Zealand	Hobart	4	6	lbw b Bracewell	0	(1)	-	-	-	-	2
18/12/2011	BigBash	Perth Scorchers	Hobart Hurricanes	Perth	2	4	c Laughlin b Lockyear	0	(6)	-	-	-	-	2
26/12/2011	Tests	Australia	India	Melbourne	1	6	c Dhoni b Zaheer Khan	0	(1)	5.0	0	15	0	1
26/12/2011	Tests	Australia	India	Melbourne	3	6	c Dhoni b Zaheer Khan	89	(151)	-	-	-	-	2
03/01/2012	Tests	Australia	India	Sydney	2	6	not out.	150*	(253)	2.0	0	8	0	-
03/01/2012	Tests	Australia	India	Sydney	4	6	-	—	—	5.0	0	5	0	-
13/01/2012	Tests	Australia	India	Perth	2	6	c Sehwag b Vinay Kumar….	14	(29)	-	-	-	-	-
13/01/2012	Tests	Australia	India	Perth	4	6	-	—	—	3.0	0	—	0	1

Start Date	Grade	Team	Opponent	Venue	Inn	Pos	How Out	Runs	(Balls)	O	M	R	W	Ct
24/01/2012	Tests	Australia	India	Adelaide	1	6	run out (Gambhir)…	25	(33)	6.0	0	18	0	1
24/01/2012	Tests	Australia	India	Adelaide	3	6	lbw b Sharma…	15	(40)	2.0	0	3	0	1
05/02/2012	Int OD	Australia	India	Melbourne	1	5	c Kohli b Vinay Kumar	45	(32)	–	–	–	–	1
10/02/2012	Int OD	Australia	Sri Lanka	Perth	1	5	c and b Kulasekara.	23	(32)	–	–	–	–	–
17/02/2012	Int OD	Australia	Sri Lanka	Sydney	1	5	c Sangakkara b Mathews….	13	(23)	–	–	–	–	–
19/02/2012	Int OD	Australia	India	Brisbane	1	5	c Raina b Pathan…..	59	(52)	–	–	–	–	–
24/02/2012	Int OD	Australia	Sri Lanka	Hobart	1	5	b Malinga	21	(14)	–	–	–	–	–
26/02/2012	Int OD	Australia	India	Sydney	1	4	run out (Ashwin/Pathan)…	10	(21)	–	–	–	–	–
02/03/2012	Int OD	Australia	Sri Lanka	Melbourne	2	5	c Sangakkara b Thirimanne.	29	(56)	–	–	–	–	1
04/03/2012	Int OD	Australia	Sri Lanka	Brisbane	1	7	not out.	19*	(10)	–	–	–	–	–
06/03/2012	Int OD	Australia	Sri Lanka	Adelaide	1	5	b Malinga	6	(5)	–	–	–	–	–
08/03/2012	Int OD	Australia	Sri Lanka	Adelaide	1	4	run out (Dilshan)…	1	(3)	–	–	–	–	–
16/03/2012	Int OD	Australia	West Indies	Kingstown	1	4	c Roach b Bravo	32	(57)	–	–	–	–	1
18/03/2012	Int OD	Australia	West Indies	Kingstown	1	4	c Baugh b Narine…	24	(52)	–	–	–	–	–
20/03/2012	Int OD	Australia	West Indies	Kingstown	1	5	st Baugh b Samuels..	67	(95)	–	–	–	–	–
23/03/2012	Int OD	Australia	West Indies	Gros Islet	2	5	c Baugh b Russell…	26	(30)	–	–	–	–	1
25/03/2012	Int OD	Australia	West Indies	Gros Islet	1	6	c Pollard b Russell.	25	(28)	–	–	–	–	–
27/03/2012	Int T20	Australia	West Indies	Gros Islet	2	3	not out.	59*	(45)	–	–	–	–	2
30/03/2012	Int T20	Australia	West Indies	Bridgetown	2	4	c and b Samuels	14	(10)	–	–	–	–	–
07/04/2012	Tests	Australia	West Indies	Bridgetown	2	6	c Baugh b Roach	48	(167)	2.0	0	6	0	2
07/04/2012	Tests	Australia	West Indies	Bridgetown	4	6	b Roach.	32	(26)	–	–	–	–	–
15/04/2012	Tests	Australia	West Indies	Port-of-Spain	1	6	c Brathwaite b Deonarine.	73	(207)	6.0	1	19	1	1
15/04/2012	Tests	Australia	West Indies	Port-of-Spain	3	6	b Roach.	24	(47)	–	–	–	–	–
23/04/2012	Tests	Australia	West Indies	Roseau	1	6	c Sammy b Shillingford….	10	(37)	–	–	–	–	–
23/04/2012	Tests	Australia	West Indies	Roseau	3	6	c Sammy b Shillingford….	32	(57)	–	–	–	–	–
30/04/2012	Ind IPL	Chennai Super Kings	Kolkata Knight Riders	Chennai	1	2	run out (Lee/McCullum)….	18	(19)	–	–	–	–	1
10/05/2012	Ind IPL	Chennai Super Kings	Rajasthan Royals	Jaipur	2	1	run out (Tait)	19	(32)	–	–	–	–	1

Start Date	Grade	Team	Opponent	Venue	Inn	Pos	How Out	Runs	(Balls)	O	M	R	W	Ct
12/05/2012	Ind IPL	Chennai Super Kings	Delhi Daredevils	Chennai	2	1	c Jayawardene b Pathan....	38	(32)	-	-	-	-	1
14/05/2012	Ind IPL	Chennai Super Kings	Kolkata Knight Riders	Kolkata	2	1	c Bhatia b Narine....	56	(39)	-	-	-	-	-
17/05/2012	Ind IPL	Chennai Super Kings	Kings XI Punjab	Dharmasala	1	2	c Gilchrist b Kumar.	7	(10)	-	-	-	-	-
23/05/2012	Ind IPL	Chennai Super Kings	Mumbai Indians	Bangalore	1	2	c Kulkarni b Franklin	49	(39)	-	-	-	-	-
25/05/2012	Ind IPL	Chennai Super Kings	Delhi Daredevils	Chennai	1	2	c Ojha b Aaron	20	(22)	-	-	-	-	1
27/05/2012	Ind IPL	Chennai Super Kings	Kolkata Knight Riders	Chennai	1	1	b Kallis	54	(43)	-	-	-	-	1
2012–13														
25/08/2012	Int OD	Australia	Afghanistan	Sharjah	1	5	b Karim Sadiq.	49	(37)	-	-	-	-	1
28/08/2012	Int OD	Australia	Pakistan	Sharjah	2	4	lbw b Saeed Ajmal....	5	(12)	-	-	-	-	-
31/08/2012	Int OD	Australia	Pakistan	Abu Dhabi	1	4	b Saeed Ajmal.	61	(72)	1.0	0	8	0	1
03/09/2012	Int OD	Australia	Pakistan	Sharjah	2	4	b Junaid Khan.	65	(72)	-	-	-	-	-
05/09/2012	Int T20	Australia	Pakistan	Dubai	1	3	c Shoaib Malik b Sohail Tanvir..	1	(3)	-	-	-	-	-
07/09/2012	Int T20	Australia	Pakistan	Dubai	2	3	c Shoaib Malik b Umar Gul.	23	(27)	-	-	-	-	-
10/09/2012	Int T20	Australia	Pakistan	Dubai	1	4	b Saeed Ajmal.	12	(14)	-	-	-	-	1
19/09/2012	Int T20	Australia	Ireland	Colombo	2	3	lbw b O'Brien.	10	(11)	-	-	-	-	1
22/09/2012	Int T20	Australia	West Indies	Colombo	2	3	not out.	28*	(19)	-	-	-	-	-
28/09/2012	Int T20	Australia	India	Colombo	2	4	–	-	-	-	-	-	-	-
30/09/2012	Int T20	Australia	South Africa	Colombo	2	3	not out.	45*	(37)	-	-	-	-	-
02/10/2012	Int T20	Australia	Pakistan	Colombo	2	3	not out.	54*	(47)	-	-	-	-	-
05/10/2012	Int T20	Australia	West Indies	Colombo	2	3	c and b Samuels	18	(12)	-	-	-	-	-
14/10/2012	Dom T20	Chennai Super Kings	Sydney Sixes	Johannesburg	2	1	c Lumb b O'Keefe....	16	(19)	-	-	-	-	-
01/11/2012	Shield	Western Australia	Victoria	Melbourne	1	3	c Hussey b Herrick..	65	(107)	-	-	-	-	-
01/11/2012	Shield	Western Australia	Victoria	Melbourne	3	3	c Wade b McKay	3	(16)	2.0	0	8	0	3
09/11/2012	Tests	Australia	South Africa	Brisbane	2	6	c (S)Du Plessis b Morkel..	100	(129)	4.0	0	21	0	1
09/11/2012	Tests	Australia	South Africa	Brisbane	4	6	–	-	-	-	-	1	-	-
22/11/2012	Tests	Australia	South Africa	Adelaide	1	6	b Steyn.	103	(137)	1.0	0	7	0	-
22/11/2012	Tests	Australia	South Africa	Adelaide	3	7	c Steyn b Morkel....	54	(95)	-	-	-	-	-

Start Date	Grade	Team	Opponent	Venue	Inn	Pos	How Out	Runs	(Balls)	O	M	R	W	Ct
30/11/2012	Tests	Australia	South Africa	Perth	2	7	c Smith b Morkel....	12	(40)	-	-	-	-	1
30/11/2012	Tests	Australia	South Africa	Perth	4	6	c De Villiers b Steyn	26	(52)	4.0	0	26	0	-
09/12/2012	BigBash	Perth Scorchers	Adelaide Strikers	Perth	1	3	c Richardson b Putland.....	4	(9)	-	-	-	-	1
14/12/2012	Tests	Australia	Sri Lanka	Hobart	1	6	not out.	115*	(184)	-	-	-	-	2
14/12/2012	Tests	Australia	Sri Lanka	Hobart	3	7	not out.	31*	(38)	1.0	0	5	0	-
26/12/2012	Tests	Australia	Sri Lanka	Melbourne	2	6	c Heath b Dilshan..	34	(68)	-	-	-	-	2
26/12/2012	Tests	Australia	Sri Lanka	Melbourne	4	6	-	-	-	-	-	-	-	-
03/01/2013	Tests	Australia	Sri Lanka	Sydney	2	5	run out (Karunaratne)	25	(51)	2.0	1	1	0	3
03/01/2013	Tests	Australia	Sri Lanka	Sydney	4	5	not out.	27*	(42)	1.0	0	6	0	1
16/01/2013	BigBash	Perth Scorchers	Melbourne Stars	Perth	2	5	not out.	21*	(12)	-	-	-	-	-
19/01/2013	BigBash	Perth Scorchers	Brisbane Heat	Perth	2	6	c Christian b McDermott...	10	(9)	-	-	-	-	-
24/01/2013	Shield	Western Australia	New South Wales	Blacktown	1	4	c Dawson b Tremain..	29	(64)	-	-	-	-	1
24/01/2013	Shield	Western Australia	New South Wales	Blacktown	3	4	lbw b Copeland	8	(28)	-	-	-	-	-
30/01/2013	Dom OD	Western Australia	New South Wales	Sydney	1	5	b Bollinger...	30	(21)	-	-	-	-	-
02/02/2013	Dom OD	Western Australia	Queensland	Brisbane	1	5	c Moller b Gale	1	(3)	-	-	-	-	-
04/02/2013	Shield	Western Australia	Queensland	Brisbane	1	3	c Hartley b Gannon..	5	(23)	-	-	-	-	-
04/02/2013	Shield	Western Australia	Queensland	Brisbane	3	3	c Boyce b Hopes	8	(24)	-	-	-	-	2
19/02/2013	Dom OD	Western Australia	Tasmania	Perth	2	3	c Dunk b Faulkner....	4	(3)	-	-	-	-	-
21/02/2013	Shield	Western Australia	Tasmania	Perth	2	5	c Bailey b Butterworth.....	3	(24)	-	-	-	-	1
21/02/2013	Shield	Western Australia	Tasmania	Perth	4	5	c Dunk b Faulkner....	44	(76)	-	-	-	-	-
07/03/2013	Shield	Western Australia	South Australia	Adelaide	2	5	not out.	99*	(154)	-	-	-	-	1
07/03/2013	Shield	Western Australia	South Australia	Adelaide	4	5	c and b Botha..	6	(22)	-	-	-	-	-
14/03/2013	Shield	Western Australia	Queensland	Perth	2	5	c Burns b Harris....	96	(190)	-	-	-	-	1
14/03/2013	Shield	Western Australia	Queensland	Perth	4	5	c Hartley b Harris..	37	(79)	-	-	-	-	1
06/04/2013	Ind IPL	Chennai Super Kings	Mumbai Indians	Chennai	2	1	b Harbhajan Singh...	20	(23)	-	-	-	-	-
10/04/2013	Ind IPL	Chennai Super Kings	Kings XI Punjab	Chandigarh	2	2	not out.	86*	(54)	-	-	-	-	2
13/04/2013	Ind IPL	Chennai Super Kings	Royal Challengers Bangalore	Chennai	2	1	c Agarwal b Vinay Kumar....	6	(16)	-	-	-	-	-

Start Date	Grade	Team	Opponent	Venue	Inn	Pos	How Out	Runs	(Balls)	O	M	R	W	C
18/04/2013	Ind IPL	Chennai Super Kings	Delhi Daredevils	Delhi	1	1	not out.	65*	(50)	-	-	-	-	1
20/04/2013	Ind IPL	Chennai Super Kings	Kolkata Knight Riders	Kolkata	2	1	c Pathan b Balaji...	40	(51)	-	-	-	-	1
22/04/2013	Ind IPL	Chennai Super Kings	Rajasthan Royals	Chennai	2	2	run out (Dravid)....	88	(51)	-	-	-	-	1
25/04/2013	Ind IPL	Chennai Super Kings	Sunrisers Hyderabad	Chennai	2	1	c De Kock b Mishra..	45	(26)	-	-	-	-	-
28/04/2013	Ind IPL	Chennai Super Kings	Kolkata Knight Riders	Chennai	1	2	c Das b Narine	95	(59)	-	-	-	-	-
30/04/2013	Ind IPL	Chennai Super Kings	Pune Warriors	Pune	1	1	b Richardson...	5	(8)	-	-	-	-	-
02/05/2013	Ind IPL	Chennai Super Kings	Kings XI Punjab	Chennai	1	2	st Gurkeerat Singh b Chawla	35	(29)	-	-	-	-	1
05/05/2013	Ind IPL	Chennai Super Kings	Mumbai Indians	Mumbai	2	1	c Smith b Ojha	22	(26)	-	-	-	-	-
08/05/2013	Ind IPL	Chennai Super Kings	Sunrisers Hyderabad	Hyderabad	1	1	b Perera	67	(42)	-	-	-	-	-
12/05/2013	Ind IPL	Chennai Super Kings	Rajasthan Royals	Jaipur	1	1	b Binny.	40	(40)	-	-	-	-	-
14/05/2013	Ind IPL	Chennai Super Kings	Delhi Daredevils	Chennai	1	1	c Sehwag b Yadav....	26	(26)	-	-	-	-	-
18/05/2013	Ind IPL	Chennai Super Kings	Royal Challengers Bangalore	Bangalore	2	1	c Rahul b Zaheer Khan	6	(5)	-	-	-	-	-
21/05/2013	Ind IPL	Chennai Super Kings	Mumbai Indians	Delhi	1	1	not out.	86*	(58)	-	-	-	-	1
26/05/2013	Ind IPL	Chennai Super Kings	Mumbai Indians	Kolkata	2	1	b Malinga	1	(2)	-	-	-	-	1